Forewor

CW00429832

John Breeding's *Necess*
is a work of genius. He has a unique
understanding of the damage that
psychiatry causes society. Foucault
would have been proud. Breeding's
argument is so well researched,
thought out and articulate that it would
be difficult for anyone not to be
convinced by him. There is no
escaping the pain that comes with
reading the text. As the survivor
realises how they are victims of
psychiatry and lights of understanding
are switched on one feels like crying
out aloud: "Me? No way! That's me. I
don't believe it."

Like any great work of literature
what Breeding says is controversial.
The publication of his book in Europe
and particularly within the UK will
inspire the mental health survivor
movement to speak up and speak out.
His brilliant philosophy gives more
venom to the social model of madness
and distress in the UK. As we struggle
to develop our own philosophy
Breeding's book can be used as a tool
to give the social model the
momentum it so desperately needs.
Widespread circulation and
consumption of this book within the
UK survivor movement would make
an underdeveloped philosophy

developed. Breeding is so lucid and enlightening that he gives us all hope. There is no need for apathy anymore. It's payback time.

Jason Pegler

Chipmunkapublishing

FOREWORD

John Breeding, Ph.D. has woven his own thoughts into a wide array of sources to expose the shadow of modern psychiatry. More importantly he provides clear information and guidance for positive perspectives that support human transformation.

The book begins with a story of a woman he helped in his role as counsellor. She begins experiencing a potentially transforming altered state, but gets pulled into the psychiatric system by the phone call of a neighbour. John experiences his own transformational crises through his attempts to spare Cindy the brain numbing effects of psychiatric medications, and legally sanctioned social control. From these experiences John was inspired to write *The Necessity of Unproductivity and Madness: Psychiatric Oppression or Human Transformation*.

Several chapters are devoted to developing an understanding of oppression. The story begins with historical roots, and John then draws a line to the psychiatric practices in Nazi Germany and the United States. There is an important chapter on language and the way it gets used with oppressive practices. He also dispels the basic assumptions that modern psychiatric thought rests upon. Psychiatry emerges as a method of social control that involves big money and the expression of power over vulnerable individuals.

My own work is as a counsellor. I was inspired to do this work from an experience of madness and psychiatric practices. The psychiatric system treated me rather mildly, compared to many I know of. When I think of how disruptive it was to be hospitalized, drugged, and diagnosed, as well as the tremendous affects it has had on my life, I feel for those that have experienced electroshock, long term medication, hospital commitments and worse. Many have been cast into the role of chronically disordered. They have lost personal freedom and cognitive power, capabilities that many, have lost awareness of even possessing. Interestingly, the depth of their human light can still shine, even with the psychiatric /mental health system as parent. I am very grateful that I was able to slowly find persons and resources that saw my experience of madness as having a wisdom that was understood in the context of a spiritual, religious, or psychic transformation. John Õs book has given me greater clarity as to how I came to be a counsellor and it also provides a framework upon which I can reflect and be guided on my journey of personal transformation. Most importantly, John confirms my own experiential truth. The more I do personally transforming work, the better I am for the people I relate with.

Inspired by this book, my current awareness is of the exhaustive treadmill of contemporary society. On the one hand I have hope this will generate a transformational crisis, but I am also aware that society as a whole is ignoring a large realm of human experience that is potentially very enriching. John's book gives hope to those of us that see the great potential in embracing the whole of human experience. Madness can be seen for what it is. There is nothing to fear or suppress. It is something to be supported and integrated. Unproductivity is just as necessary as productivity in a world seen for what it is, whole and inclusive. Nothing has been cast out of the garden in John's world view. We are full and whole spiritual beings in a potentiated and/or happening process of dynamic evolution. Naturally, peeling off the worn aspects of the Self can be a very dynamic and non-ordinary experience. It is who we are and we need to support experiences out of the narrow and seemingly getting narrower corridor of acceptability.

John offers a powerful story from the Iroquois to paint a picture of the forces involved in transforming oppressive energy. It left me with an important piece of the puzzle as I struggle with my own fears and limitations, and desire for others to experience a supportive context for their extreme state of mind. Most significantly, John uses the story to honour those that have experienced psychiatric oppression and continue to fight for change.

The final chapter offers alternatives to current practices. I resonated most with the discussion of Re-Evaluation Counselling. It is peer based and it helps me with the felt limitations of the help -expert model that I work in. Re-Evaluation is also very positive in the way it conceptualizes what we now see as human distress. John offers several other possibilities that can support individuals during a transforming experience rather than making them pawns in the dehumanizing psychiatric model. John discusses Birch House and similar places. I had occasion to call the Birch House one time and spoke with a staff member. He told me he was there to learn from the residents. Can you imagine the level of empowerment residents feel when they are treated this way? I made a personal visit to a similar place in San Diego. I recall the supervisor telling me he had gotten interested in the job when he saw an ad in the paper looking for someone with the capacity to be loving. These strike me as very different approaches and attitudes from so much of what I have seen and heard of in the mental health field.

Overall, I see *The Necessity of Madness and Unproductivity* as an important document not only for psychiatric survivors and mental health professionals, but also for those interested in the process of human oppression and transformation. Personally it will be a continual source of rediscovery on the journey.

By Jim Moore

Jim Moore is a counsellor with the Texas Department of Mental Health and Mental Retardation, who lives and works in Waco, Texas.

Necessity of Madness and Unproductivity: Psychiatric Opression or Human Transformation
First published in 2000
by Online Originals
London and Bordeaux

Copyright © John Breeding 2000

TABLE OF CONTENTS

PROLOGUE

I heard an angel speak last night,
    And she said, "Write!
Write a profession's curse for me.
And send it over the frozen sea."

I faltered, a protesting man:
    "Not me, wise woman!
If curses must be, choose another
To send your curse against my brother.

For I am bound by loyalty,
    By blood and love and money,
To brothers who dance with me on frozen waters,
Who give me finger food and share their daughters."

"Therefore," the angel said, "shall you write
    my curse tonight.
From the summits of cold loyalty a curse is driven
As a Thunderbird screams down from heaven."

"Not so," I answered, "A curse
    is woman's purse.
And I am a man who lives with my kind
On lofty peaks of chilly mind.

"A woman's curse needs flowing waters,
    warm waters, boiling waters, rushing waters.
My mountain lake is frozen ice with not a leak,
And I gaze down upon it from my majestic peak.

"It's true," said I, "My heart is sore
⠀⠀⠀⠀for what my land has bore,
For the souls of zombified child and ravaged elder,
But my waters do not flow, ever."

"Therefore," said the angel, "Build your flame.
⠀⠀⠀⠀Build a searing blaze, and roar your shame.
Shout out the glory of your mountain height
And let the fires burn bright.

And when the celebration wanes, stoke the fire.
⠀⠀⠀⠀Add more logs when you begin to tire,
And when dissension rises, pour on the gas.
You must be keeper of a flame that lasts."

"Too much," plead I, "The task you make.
⠀⠀⠀⠀No wild allowed on frozen lake.
Control of wildness is our fame.
We keep a managed flame."

"Remember, then," the angel said, "your heart so sore
⠀⠀⠀⠀And what it bore.
Make wild fire until frozen waters melt and flow like blood,
And write a curse from the depths of womanhood."

So I danced and sung and ranted and raved,
⠀⠀⠀⠀The fires roared and blazed
Until I felt my heart's blood leak
Its frozen waters down my craggy peak.

So thus I wrote, and mourned indeed,
⠀⠀⠀⠀What all may read.
And thus, as was enjoined on me
I send it over the frozen sea.

THE CURSE

1

Because you work in a nation which has gained for thee
    the privileges of liberty,
Indignantly decrying threats to your own autonomy,
Yet then coerce, bind, and thong
Others against their will — for this wrong
    This is the curse.   Write.

 Because you stand tall in honors won,
    A noble profession,
And vow no harm, but only good,
Yet keep calm footing all the time
on writhing victims of your tortures — for this crime
    This is the curse.   Write.

Because you stand as pillars of victorious position,
    scientific truth over superstition,
And take pride in the fruits of scientific progress,
Yet preach a superstitious pseudoscience using technology's
feat
To dominate your fellow humans — for this deceit
    This is the curse.   Write.

Because you are part of a nation proud of being victors
    over Nazi eugenicist murderers,
And espouse a kind benevolence,
Yet go forth practicing social control and calling it pity,
branding others as genetic defects — for this atrocity
    This is the curse.   Write.

Because you prosper in love's name,
 With a claim
To honor in the eyes of the world,
Yet do the fiend's work perfectly
In strangling martyrs — for this lie
 This is the curse.   Write.

2

You will watch while soulful men and women
Degenerate in your institutions into chronic specimens,
   Forcibly incarcerate, forcibly poison, forcibly molest
Their peace, their freedom, and their flare,
And, warm and snug in your own palace, you shall never dare
   To question or breathe even a sigh of protest.
     This is the curse.   Write.

You will watch while your colleagues violate the law,
Guidelines of professional ethics and human decency flaw;
   And only under your breath will you mutter disapproval
While you remain loyal to the blood bond of your profession
And stand in defense of your evil station.
You will remain silent. You will remain alone. No disavowal.
     This is the curse.   Write.

You will watch when souls unite, breaking the chains of tyranny
And celebrate their liberation from patriarchy's knee,
   Smugly seeing mania and waiting for the fall,
Doomed to embrace your false reality and chilly judgment,
Warmth and loving passion forever frozen like cement
   In the icy depths of your own soul.
     This is the curse.   Write.

When wounded souls reveal their anguished strain
And desperately plea for help, you will feel no empathic
pain
    Nor gratefulness at having the balm of gilead to offer
free;
You will hear only the tinny sounds of defective tools,
And bury deep within yourself the hopeless despair you
hand these souls
    By poison drugs and brain-damaging electricity.
        This is the curse.   Write.

When these same souls erupt in chaos, screaming for
redemption,
Rent by Pluto's havoc and destruction,
    You will not bend head nor knee in awe-filled wonder.
Pluto's force that may have saved you yields not a humbling
prayer
That might redeem you, but only frozen terror
    And a brutal squashing of what might have been, forever.
        This is the curse.   Write.

When families present their daughters and sons
Singing canary sounds of leaking poisons,
    You will not see the spirited souls of untamed young,
But only poor defective neuro/bio unfortunates behold,
And bury deep within yourself the hopeless despair you
have sold
    As you feed them venom of your forked tongue.
This is the curse.   Write.

When old people are cast out of their communities
    And brought before you with desperate pleas,
        You will not speak in honor of each elder,
    Nor at the disrespect we show them will your outrage flare;

You will be mute and bury deep within yourself the shame
and despair
   Of sealing their graves with poison drugs and
electroshock, silencing forever.
      This is the curse.   Write.

When brave ones question the wisdom of your solution
And courageously resist control and coercion,
   You will reject this gift in haughty indignation
And throttle them backward to death,
Deprived forever of the joy of empowering health
   And the gift of turning inward for your own salvation.
      This is the curse.   Write.

When good people are praying erect
That the Spirit may liberate her oppressed elect
   And deliver the earth,
The prayer in your ears, said low,
Shall sound like the tramp of a foe
   That's driving you forth.
      This is the curse.   Write.

When wise men give you their praise,
They shall halt in the heat of the phrase,
   As if carried too far
When you boast your own charters kept true,
You shall blush; for the thing which you do
   Derides what you are.
      This is the curse.   Write.

When fools cast taunts at your gate,
Your scorn you shall somewhat abate
   As you look over the wall;
For your conscience, tradition, and name,
Explode with a deadlier blame

Than the worst of them all.
This is the curse.   Write.

Go, wherever ill deeds shall be done,
Go, plant your flag in the sun
Beside the ill-doers!
And recoil from clenching the curse
Of God's witnessing Universe
With a curse of yours.
This is the curse.   Write.

(An adaptation of Elizabeth Barrett Browning's 1860 poem, A Curse For A Nation, directed at the United States for slavery. The poem retains Browning's structure, rhyme and meter, as well as many of her words.)

A Story Behind The Curse

I want to tell you how this anima curse you have just read came to be. I had just completed another draft of this book manuscript, and didn't know what to do next. I had begun to fret about how I would ever get the thing published, and my writer friend, Katya Walter, offered to give me a consultation about what my next step with the book should be. Katya has devised an oracle of her own creation, a set of "Kairos Cards," loosely described as a combination of Tarot, Rorschach, and Thematic Apperception tests. The cards combine the elements of psychological projection (revealed by what one sees in an undefined image) and oracular revelation (that which is revealed in the particular card one selects, apparently by chance, upon meditation on the question one has posed).

My question was "What should I do now about my book?" The card I drew was a photograph of several men who appeared exhausted, dirty, sleeping lying and sitting, crowded together in a bare concrete room, some on a sparse metal bunk with thin mattresses, some on the floor. My first thought was that it was a concentration camp. Then I thought that, though obviously exhausted and poor, they were not emaciated — a refugee camp, perhaps. Cold, stark, destitute, hopeless was how I felt about that card. Katya revealed to me that the picture was of immigrants to the New World, in New York prior to World War II. They were indeed poor and exhausted, but they had hope and were living as cheaply as possible in the face of the awesome challenge of establishing a new life in a new country. The consultation reflected to me some of the feelings I had about this project. I had known my share of exhaustion and hopelessness along the way, and was working through those feelings once again. More importantly, it was revealed to me that, just as the hard, bare conditions in which these men were living had no feminine qualities, so too my dry, intellectual book was lacking a feminine balance. Without the support of a loving inner woman, one easily falls into the destructive machinations of compulsive productivity, as ironically did in pushing myself to produce an earlier draft of this book on the value and necessity of unproductivity. So my next step was not to put on a masculine surge of energy out into the world of publishing and money, but to somehow bring more of the feminine into this work.

I sighed deeply and shook my head. In the terms of Jungian psychology, one of a man's primary tasks, and one of my own great challenges, is to establish a positive, supportive union with his inner feminine, known as the anima. I already knew that a core function of psychiatric oppression was to suppress expression, especially emotional discharge. (In this book, for the sake of brevity, I will generally refer to the mental health system as psychiatry. By this I mean institutional psychiatry, a system of beliefs and practices which I will expound upon throughout this book; will refer to the actions and effects of this system as psychiatric oppression, and most specifically define the concept in Chapter 2.) Now it is becoming clearer and clearer, at a level deep within me, that the oppression is very much about suppression of the feminine. My own experience of compulsive productivity can, on one level, be seen as a reflection of the same internalized oppression as the practitioners of psychiatry must suffer. Just as I need to bring the anima into my book and into my life, so does psychiatry need a woman's touch.

After I consulted the Kairos cards and discovered the need to bring the feminine into this book, I still didn't know what to do or how to do it. I didn't feel capable of it. So I groped inside for direction, and I thought that perhaps I could begin to look at poetry as a way into the feminine. So I pulled an old book off Katya's shelf — Victorian poetry published in 1930. I browsed around, and then I saw Elizabeth Barrett Browning's powerful poem, 'A Curse For A Nation.' Written in 1860, this poem is directed at the United States in its practice of slavery. It reflects, in Browning's words, the truth that:

> "A curse from the depths of womanhood
> Is very salt, and bitter, and good."

My inclination in turning to poetry was to seek and find suitable pieces to insert at various points in my book, and my first thought was to use Browning's curse as she wrote it. As I sat with her poem, however, it dawned on me to write an anima curse pointed more clearly and specifically at psychiatry, and so I devised an adaptation of her work, greatly altered and re-directed, but retaining much of her original wording. I thought I was done with an earlier draft which laid the curse and followed the meter, but then I realized that I had completely overlooked the rhyming pattern. It seemed very important to remain true to the rhyme as well, so I did. And I believe the potency of the curse is greater as a result. I felt some hesitation about taking her awesome work and shredding it to pieces and making a new work with inferior poetic elegance. But then I had a dream that my fingers were chapped and bleeding. In the dream, a woman, whose work was to heal such wounded hands, was tenderly holding mine in her own. My friend Katya also happens to be the author of a wonderful book on dreams, called 'Dream Mail', and a facilitator of classes in dream drama. She told me that bleeding fingers in a dream usually have something to do with the creative urge. In working on this piece, I felt a bond with Elizabeth Browning; I think of her as the woman who held my bleeding hands. I believe that "An Anima Curse For A Profession" is true to the spirit of "A Curse For A Nation," and that its potent charge is largely due to her ancestral energy. I think she'd like it.

I have a few more words to say about this business of anima curses. First off, it is important to understand that when I was failing in marriage or driving myself into exhaustion in compulsive productivity, it was not that I had no relationship with the feminine. On the contrary, I had a terrifyingly powerful relationship — victim of an anima curse, so to speak. Similarly, the oppression of psychiatry is far from no relationship. Psychiatric oppression is forced on you; it's called coercion. This kind of curse is not about "I wish something awful and terrible to befall you." Rather, it is an intense amplification of that which already is, like a horrific nightmare by which the psyche calls your attention to something which must not be denied. Psychiatry does need a woman's touch, and it needs to wake up to the reality that "Hell hath no fury like a woman scorned!" Browning's curse of slavery, and this curse of psychiatry are angry eruptions that call attention to savage misdirection. I hope its fire provides some light to help us seek a better way.

A Vision

> "You may say I'm a dreamer, but I'm not the only one. I hope some day you'll join us and the world will live as one."
> — John Lennon

Imagine no coercion. Imagine a world of complete respect for yourself and for all other people, all forms of life. Imagine a world of people guided by a knowing of themselves as spiritual beings, full of the spirit of love and truth. Imagine a wisdom which understands that the inherent nature of human beings is that we are loving, cooperative, zestful, completely connected with each other and with all of life. Imagine a world of wise humans who understand the nature of human distress, and that the effects of being physically or emotionally hurt include deviation from our inherent goodness into patterns of rigidity involving thoughtless doing of harm to self and others. Further imagine that wisdom including a clarity and respect for the natural, built-in ways we have of healing ourselves of these effects, and a knowing of ways and means to aid and encourage this natural process of healing.

Imagine a world of adults who take full responsibility not only for themselves but for the development of their children and the healing of their fellow adults who have been hurt. Imagine a world where people enjoy the visible gifts of our physical universe, but value even more highly the invisible gifts of spirit such as love, wisdom, truth and compassion.

Imagine a world of people who understand that the journey of a soul begins with the need of a child to develop mastery of the physical and social realms, and the importance of a tribe to nurture and provide stability as the energy of spirit is so fully invested in the world of form and relationship. Imagine further that these same people also understand that, once childhood mastery is developed, at the same time as the adolescent develops even greater mastery of the tribe's social conditions, he also experiences the tell-tale yearnings of the soul to master the inner life. Imagine the profound understanding of mature adults that the adolescent is going through a necessary process of questioning tribal beliefs and tribal authority as she begins the most important next step of spiritual maturity-that is, to become an independent individual who is not ruled by external authority, but by the authority of her own inner truth.

Imagine the wisdom, guidance, patience, encouragement, tolerance, good humor, and loving support that would be available for individuals on this road to spiritual maturity. Imagine a world of adults who had plumbed the depths of their own psyches, were familiar with the often overwhelming archetypal energies of the human psyche, and had come through enough of this to establish themselves in an abiding attitude of relaxed trust and confidence in the natural process of psychological and spiritual growth and maturation. Imagine the depth of compassion and support available for those who flounder or the rocky shoals of uncertainty and confusion that go with becoming an individual guided by the dictates of an invisible, largely mysterious spirit force. Imagine the patient tolerance and support that flows from an understanding of the need to withdraw from the means of tribal productivity in order to get to know and trust oneself at ever-deepening levels. Imagine all of this for yourself, your friends, your family, your community, for all of us.

Imagine what can happen as enough of us hold, express and live such a vision at the same time as we see the current reality of social alienation and psychiatric oppression. Imagine the endurance, determination, creativity and compassion that will expand our world even more into the vision I have described. I imagine this book as one effort to support this vision.

> "A popular government without popular information, or the means of acquiring it, is but a prologue to a farce, or a tragedy, or perhaps both. Knowledge will forever govern ignorance; and people who mean to be their own governors must arm themselves with the power which knowledge gives." — James Madison (1)

> "The less a person knows about the workings of the social institutions of his society, the more he must trust those who wield power in it; and the more he trusts those who wield such power, the more vulnerable he makes himself to becoming their victim. No one who has read or seen Ken Kesey's One Flew Over The Cuckoo's Nest — or similar stories about psychiatry, going back to Chekhov's classic Ward No. 6 — can claim to be ignorant of the dangers mad-doctors pose to every man, woman and child in America. How can this be? Psychiatrists are physicians, and physicians are supposed to help people. That is true. But it does not follow that the result is necessarily helpful for the so-called patient — as he, the patient, would define what constitutes help." — Thomas Szasz (2)

" 'The Shock Shop, Mr McMurphy, is jargon for the EST machine, the Electro Shock Therapy. A device that might be said to do the work of the sleeping pill, the electric chair, and the torture rack. It's a clever little procedure, simple, quick, nearly painless it happens so fast, but no one ever wants another one. Ever.'

'What's this thing do?'

'You are strapped to a table, shaped, ironically, like a cross, with a crown of electric sparks in place of the thorns. You are touched on each side of the head with wires. Zap! Five cents' worth of electricity through the brain and you are jointly administered therapy and a punishment for your hostile go-to-hell behavior, on top of being put out of everyone's way for six hours to three days, depending on the individual.' " — Ken Kesey (3)

Introduction

My purpose in writing this is to educate people on psychiatric oppression: what it is, how it works, and how it came to be. I want to reveal the harm done by the practice of biopsychiatry, and to show that psychiatry suppresses and punishes experiences which are completely natural and, in fact, necessary to achieve spiritual maturity. Experiences of temporary "madness" and unproductivity, while violating society's demand for continuous productivity, are essential if individuals are to grow and mature. Psychiatry enforces society's demand to keep working and be happy, no matter what. I suggest a clear alternative, a view of human nature and personal transformation that offers real hope to individuals in need. My intention is to provide a model which resonates with the truth of human transformation and has reverence for our spiritual nature. I also take a deep dive into the question of why "good people" (mental health professionals) can do so much harm while being so convinced they are doing good. My hope is that readers will find information to help themselves and their families, that psychiatric survivors will be helped to understand their experiences and find guidance for the process of renewal, and that professionals will be stimulated to think in new ways about their work and about the system in which they play so vital a role.

I am the oldest son from a Catholic family of eight children. I was shy and introspective, a very good boy who had every intention of becoming a priest, until I became a teenager. Then at age 20, working alone in a warehouse in Denver, I reconsidered, took a last, longing look at the possibility of entering the priesthood, and then said goodbye forever to that vocation. Returning to college, I finally settled into psychology at the University of Texas, my fourth degree plan at my fourth undergraduate university. Very uncertain about my direction in life, I chose psychology largely for two reasons: it was an easy major, and it allowed me to indulge my naturally introspective bent and desire to figure out what life was all about.

Upon graduating with my bachelor's degree in 1975, I knew that a graduate degree was necessary to work as a psychologist, but I had grave doubts about my ability to work with others. At age 12, I had made a conscious decision one day to stop talking to my family. I remember the moment: riding in the back of the car, listening to yet another quarrel, probably involving my parents and older sisters. I decided to stop sharing anything about my inner life, and to withdraw physically as much as possible. I played sports and spent a lot of time with my buddies. By 1975, though I had begun to come out over the years in college and away from home, I was still shy, still didn't talk a lot, still had difficulty being very close to people.

So I took a job at the Oaks Treatment Center of the Brown Schools, working as a "mental health worker" with "disturbed" children. I worked for 18 months at the Oaks, and another 18 months at the children's unit of the Austin State Hospital, which paid a bit more than the minimum wage I started out at with the Brown Schools. These three years were my initiation into psychiatry. I learned that psychiatrists had minimal contact with the "patients," but absolute control. In both settings, those of us who had the most contact and relationship with the children "patients" were least trained and most definitely least paid. I learned that psychiatric drug use was the norm. It was much later that I discovered just how unlearned most psychiatrists really are in the ways of human psychological distress and healing.

My initial insights about oppression in these settings had little to do with the underlying assumptions and practices of biopsychiatry which I expose in this book; they were more to do with fair labor practices, patriarchal hierarchy, the ethics of big money for little contact, and the function of the psychiatric institutions as warehouses for children whose families and communities were failing them. I did fulfill my objective of finding out whether I could work with people; at least I learned that I could relate well to children. So I began graduate school in the fall of 1978.

I did well enough in graduate school. This experience usually emphasizes abstract academics, rather than human intimacy, and I was well-trained in the arts of memorization and test-taking. And I was determined and disciplined enough to stay the course. Early on into the program, my girlfriend began to suffer from terrible insomnia, becoming extremely frightened, agitated, and suicidal. It became painfully apparent that I hadn't a clue of how to help her, and neither did the University Mental Health Center. I cried and cried when she entered the State Hospital for a few days, and I visited her there, this lively Hispanic woman heavily sedated to suppress the great pain she was experiencing.

She survived the ordeal, but our relationship ended shortly before I left to do my internship in 1982. I completed my dissertation, and graduated in 1983. I got a job with the New Moon Wilderness Program, offering outdoor challenge experiences for "at-risk" youth. Within my first year there, I experienced what I call my first breakdown, an energetic collapse with symptoms of physical and emotional distress. Floundering about, finally reaching for help out of desperation, I began to do my own inner work. The help I received was seemingly unrelated to anything I learned in graduate school — breathwork, bodywork, emotional release work, discharging birth trauma, a variety of modes that led me from the teachings of academic cognitive-behavioral theory to the foreign wonders of transpersonal psychology. I worked on myself, and gradually incorporated some of the practices which helped me in my work with others. I was working outside the scope of mainstream mental health, and I knew that the human experience involved so much greater depth than the reductionistic theories I learned in graduate school, but I didn't have much insight or understanding about psychiatric oppression.

Becoming a parent was my next initiation. I was so full of joy, then so full of stress that my back went out. I learned about the realities of what I now call parental oppression, and I learned the truth of parenting as an ordeal. I painfully discovered that my own unconscious hurts were restimulated by my children at every level of their development. The law seems to be that, as a parent, you are faced over and over again with a choice of suppressing your child or transforming your life. (1) I also discovered that most of what I had learned about parenting, similar to what I learned about human beings in graduate school, was not very helpful. Fortunately, I found Re-evaluation Counseling and was reminded about the true nature of human beings (intelligent, curious, zestful, loving, etc.), and the process of recovery from emotional hurts. In particular, I learned about the value and necessity of emotional discharge (shaking, crying, laughing, etc.), something unrevealed to me in graduate school.

When I began working as a psychologist fifteen years ago, I quickly discovered that the healing work for most of my clients required much more than conventional therapies and modalities. Family-of-origin work related to childhood hurts is the nuts-and-bolts of such counseling and I imagine will continue to be so. Adjustment to or handling of present time is, and I imagine always will be, another significant domain. Transpersonal approaches relating to birth and beyond are not so mainstream, but they have a place, as does the broad spectrum of psychospiritual technologies. My discovery was not a variation on a theme of which approach is best or to which I am personally most suited to facilitate, although I certainly have experimented, and certainly believe in and enjoy some more than others. Nor was my discovery directly related to the question of interface between psychology and spirituality, although I have intense interest in this. No, my discovery came from the simple observation that so many of my clients came to me carrying deep hurts suffered at the hands of those to whom they had previously reached for help. Some of these injuries, such as sexual violation by a therapist, were great psychological traumas. More common than most people realize, these instances are at least agreed upon and recognized as abuse and ethical violation by both the lay and professional communities.

Sexual abuse aside, the vast majority of these injuries come in ways that are not considered violations of ethics by the professional community. A very large number of these are a result of the underlying beliefs and practices of our mental health system which are accepted and supported, for the most part, by lay and professional alike. I am referring to the belief that "mental illness" is a real "disease" and that individuals "suffering from this disease" are incapable of making decisions for themselves. The practice that naturally flows from such belief is called coercion, or "involuntary treatment." Individuals are forced into "treatment " against their will. This is a violation of their civil rights; it is also a great injury. Authentic recovery for people who have undergone such coercive "treatment" cannot help but involve a tremendous amount of work around traumatic violation suffered at the hands of mental health professionals.

The greatest number of these kinds of injuries today comes from the practices, once again mostly accepted and supported by both lay people and professionals, of the dominant theory of mainstream psychiatry. These are the practices of biological psychiatry (biopsychiatry). Psychiatrists today are almost all biopsychiatrists; they believe in "mental illness," and that such "disease" is biologically or genetically based; therefore, their belief is that biological/physical treatments are both necessary and desirable. The primary and now ubiquitous "treatment" in our own culture is drugs, called psychopharmacology; the backup "treatment" is electroshock. I see over and over again, everyday in both my professional and private lives, the harmful effects both physically and psychologically of taking psychiatric drugs and accepting the identity of a biologically or genetically-flawed "mentally ill patient." In my own case, however, what really woke me up were the clients who had undergone electroshock. It continues to astound me that there are so few of my fellow "mental health" professionals who are not appalled to be part of a profession which routinely inflicts permanent brain damage on the people who come to them for help, and calls it "treatment."

All of the above and more constituted my introduction to what I now call psychiatric oppression. I have mentioned only a few of the most dramatic issues and examples to show how I came to be aware and later, an activist opposing psychiatric oppression. Electroshock survivors woke me up, and I gradually became active as an ally on their behalf and on behalf of all of us in challenging this barbaric practice. I began writing and speaking out about electroshock, became a member of the advisory board of the World Association of Electroshock Survivors, and joined forces with the contingent in my home state of Texas fighting for legislative bans on electroshock.

Every year, hundreds of thousands of Americans are coerced into psychiatric treatment. Literally millions are on psychiatric drugs. Over six million adults are on one drug alone (Prozac); over four million school-age children are on one drug alone (Ritalin). About 100,000 are given electroshock treatment each year. Virtually every American is directly or indirectly affected by psychiatry today. This particular fact never ceases to amaze me. Consider your own life and how psychiatry has affected you directly or indirectly through your friends or family. How many people do you know who are on psychiatric drugs? I guarantee there are many more in your life of whom you are unaware. I conducted a radio show on psychiatric oppression for awhile with my friend, Dr Moira Dolan. We did many interviews and one of my criteria for being a guest was that the individual tell a story of how psychiatry had affected his or her life. I learned a lot from that. One was that many psychiatric survivors are not about to share their personal experience, either because the fear is so great (understandable given the coercive trauma they have suffered at the hands of psychiatry), or because the stigma is so severe. Another realization was the extent of unawareness or denial of many people about the issue. I have a friend, formerly an electrician, now a hands-on healer trained in the Barbara Brennan school of energy work. Moira and I were telling him about our show at lunch, and I queried him about how he had been affected by psychiatry. He said he was fortunate that he had had little to do with psychiatry. Testing my theory that we have all been affected, I probed just a bit more, and he shared that his mother had been in and out of psychiatric institutions much of his life. I've seen a lot of this phenomenon.

The mental health system is dominated by those who believe in the theory and practice of biopsychiatry. More and more, problems in living are attributed to "mental disease," and cause for psychiatric "treatment," wanted or not. The world view of biopsychiatry has permeated the public consciousness. Not only are individual lives seen through this lens, but societal and even global conditions are interpreted as a function of biologically based "mental illness." Our most prestigious academic and governmental institutions are proselytizing on behalf of this biopsychiatric view of the world. Consider, for example, the fact that the Harvard School of Public Health and the World Health Organization combined to conduct a global study called 'The Global Burden of Disease and Injury Series.' Their report argues that "mental illness" is the number one cause of disability and responsible for almost 11 percent of the worldwide disease burden. These researchers say that depression is the leading cause of disease burden for women and they expect psychiatric conditions to increase their share of the total disease burden by almost half by 2020! (2)

It is incredible to witness the extent to which we are now interpreting the world's problems, through the distorted lens of biopsychiatry, as due to biological or genetic mental disease. These problems are not, holds biopsychiatry, due to poverty, malnutrition, overpopulation, pollution, or any form of social ill; it is simply that individuals are suffering from biological disease. Women are not melancholy, passive or unhappy because of oppressive lives; rather, they suffer from biologically-based "mental illness." Disability is not a factor of social dysfunction, oppression, or environmental toxicity; it can be simply explained as psychiatric illness.

Harvard University and the World Health Organization confirm that today's society has ordained psychiatry as the modern-day giver of care to individuals "in need." I put this in quotes because the mission of the ordained ministers of institutional psychiatry is not only to take care of those who see themselves as in need. Society has also granted, in fact mandated, power to the psychiatric priests to determine who is "in need" and to enforce the administration of "care."

This mission is extraordinarily effective as measured by the standard evaluative criteria of capitalism. The numbers are incredible; millions and millions of our citizens are diagnosed and labeled as "mentally ill." Revenues from psychiatry are huge; psychiatrists and other professionals, hospitals, insurance companies and public service workers are all profiting. The psychopharmaceutical industry has established a multi-billion dollar niche for itself.

It is a fact that today we live in a world of great stress and distress. We are caught in the effects of urbanization and the industrial revolution which have proven so dehumanizing and disruptive to our evolutionary bond with the natural world. Further, we find ourselves in the middle of an electronic revolution which bombards our senses with information and stimulation at extraordinary, relentless, and unprecedented rates. The words of Chellis Glenndinning that "I am in recovery from Western Civilization" ring true for all of us with any modicum of self-awareness. We all suffer to varying degrees from what might be called "traumatic stress" as a result of living today. (3)

The earth is in peril. All forms of life are in peril. Human beings are grossly suffering all over the world. In the United States, the land of plenty, home of the free, the psychospiritual toll is especially frightening. In the face of social and ecological crisis, the forces of urban-industrial civilization plow relentlessly on. A stalwart and growing contingent of planetary defenders carries on a good fight. Such individuals show their awareness of social justice issues and of our planet's ecological concerns. They are caring and courageous souls.

It is my view, however, that many, if not most, of this contingent of progressive activists have a profound blind spot. All too few see and understand what is happening with psychiatry today. The truth is lost not only among the proverbial mass of humanity, but even progressives who are generally aware and politically correct on social justice issues such as racism, sexism and economic inequality appear not to see what is happening. Fallen under the powerful illusions of biopsychiatry and the rhetoric of "mental illness," they have been duped. They do not see the harm, the coercion, the mechanisms of social control. They do not see how psychiatric oppression acts to enforce and hold in place all forms of societal oppression. They do not see how labeling and diagnosing victims of oppression as defective, or "mentally ill," acts to absolve society from responsibility to really grapple with eliminating oppression. They don't see the injustice or the pain.

Just suppose for a moment that what I am saying is true — that psychiatry does great harm and that even relatively awake and aware people tend not to see it. Imagine then how exceedingly difficult it would be for those who are thoroughly conditioned into this system to see this truth. Imagine how hard it is for someone thoroughly indoctrinated in the system, with confidence in the truth and importance of his actions to awaken to the fact that he has been so greatly hurt and deceived. We have all been hurt and deceived; it is time for compassionate healing.

Healing requires an openness to reality and a cooperation with the rhythms of our true nature. Good, reliable information is most helpful. It is my view that the mental health system, as reflected in the theory and practice of biopsychiatry, is a gross and harmful violation of human nature. It is an ongoing, progressive assault on people of all ages, all walks of life. This book is my gift to you of the information I consider most important to understand psychiatric oppression, see through the illusions of biopsychiatry, and take a strong stance in support of growth and transformation for yourself and others.

Chapter 1 tells a story of my personal experience with the painful and frustrating challenge of working with an individual in crisis when a full spectrum of humane alternatives for help is not available. Chapter 2 provides information and theory on psychiatric oppression. Chapter 3 provides a historical context. Chapter 4 focuses on the use of language, as understanding here is crucial to gaining a clear perspective.

Chapters 5 and 6 emphasize the conditioning of mental health professionals in response to the question:

"How can good people do great harm with sincere conviction that they are doing good?"

Chapter 7 provides further lessons in psychiatric oppression, elaborating on my experience with Cindy described in the first chapter, emphasizing the role of a community in determining whether a human crisis becomes labeled and suppressed as "mental illness," or supported and facilitated as a necessary process of spiritual emergence. Chapter 8 goes even further to argue for "the necessity of madness and unproductivity" in order to become an individual and achieve spiritual maturity. These two chapters are representative of my own response to and growing awareness of the fact that our "mental health system," like so many of our other "systems" (e.g., welfare and nursing homes), are pathetic substitutes for authentic community. I vow in my own life to keep working toward creation of supportive community for myself and others.

Chapter 9 zeroes in on the specific practice of electroshock. I provide basic information about this "treatment" as a paradigm of psychiatric deception and violence. Electroshock practice is a close, specific, and revealing account of medical "healers" systematically violating their Hippocratic Oath to "do no harm." This chapter also includes a summary of 'The Truth About Electroshock' for anyone who wants to help spread the word and support the effort to ban this horrible abuse. Chapter 10, called "Silence," speaks to the forces which encourage passive complicity with psychiatric oppression, and the important challenge of speaking out against the oppression. Leonard Frank, editor of 'The History of Shock Treatment', provided much of the material for this chapter.

Chapter 11 is devoted to the issue of psychiatric drugs and drug withdrawal. The emphasis is on the human decision to take (or not) these drugs in the face of the massive propaganda and pressure with which we are constantly inundated. I also offer guidance for those who wish to withdraw from the psychiatric drugs they are already taking. Chapter 12 provides information on the process of emotional recovery, important not only for successful drug withdrawal, but for all of us. Chapter 13 tells a story of my experience challenging the use of psychiatric drugs to suppress our elders in nursing homes.

Chapter 14 tells the story of the Peacemaker, a man who transformed vengeful warring tribes into the Iroquois confederacy. This rich legend has much to share with us about the ways and means to overcome oppression, in both its external and internalized forms. Chapter 15 provides a perspective on human nature which affirms life and is capable of enhancing the process of human transformation. Chapter 16 offers information about alternatives and suggests directions in facing the reality of our current situation.

Dr Moira Dolan contributed Appendix A, which backs up my assertions about electroshock.

Appendix B, 'Working Axioms For Understanding Psychiatric Oppression And Implementing A Program Of Personal and Social Transformation', is a summation of this book.

CHAPTER 1
CINDY AND ME: A STORY OF TRANSFORMATIONAL CRISIS

I share the following story to make real and present the difficulties we face, on the levels of both inner and outer resources, in a world where psychiatric oppression looms so large. It is one of my experiences as an individual struggling with the challenge of supporting myself and others through life crises.

In the fall of 1996, I met a young woman who, new to our community, was becoming a regular member of the lunch crowd at the community center I frequent. I had seen her enjoying conversations with some of my acquaintance friends; she was thirty, beautiful, intelligent, curious, and had an irreverence that was attractive. Cindy (a pseudonym) had recently moved to Austin from Colorado, and worked a a local bakery. Cindy's real passion, however, lay in her poetry and music, and in her yoga practice. Her intention was to enroll in an intensive yoga teacher training with her local instructors. She saw yoga as her path of spiritual progression and service.

One day at lunch, I was celebrating the publication of my new book, 'The Wildest Colts Make the Best Horses', with my friends. Cindy was interested and expressed appreciation for my perspective in challenging the psychiatric drugging of school-age children in this country. A short while after that, Cindy inquired as to whether I might be available as a counselor for her. I suggested that she call me; she did and we discussed her situation. It seems that Cindy had been sexually assaulted in Colorado and was receiving benefits from the Colorado Crime Victims Compensation Fund to pay for counseling. She had been working with another therapist, but felt that she needed a different kind of help now. She said that this verbal talk therapy had been helpful, but that she thought she needed to do some emotional release work (healing by release or expression of suppressed emotions associated with traumatic life experiences) which is one of my specialty areas. I considered the fact that we had met before and that we both frequented the same community center, but we were only acquaintances and I thought I could help her. So we mutually agreed to begin a counseling relationship in December of 1996.

Cindy revealed her awareness in our initial session that the sexual assault was also a repetition of abuse in her family of origin. In our second session, she told me that there was a big psychiatric history in her family, that her mother was physically abusive, her father an addict, her brother a priest and her sister a "schizophrenic." Cindy's goals were:

1/ Emotional healing by release of hurt, anger and shame.

2/ Improved self-esteem.

3/ Clarity about her life direction.

The first few sessions went very well in my opinion. We were establishing a safe relationship and she was allowing some vulnerability in the areas of emotional pain. In our fifth session, Cindy recounted a "psychotic" experience about three months earlier in which she began to feel extremely sensitive to others' thoughts and feelings and to share her perceptions. Her family had attempted to connect her with the local Mental Health and Mental Retardation program. She had actually visited a psychiatrist and been prescribed "anti-psychotic" medications, but chose not to take them and "pulled it together" enough to be left alone and continue her life. She expressed fear, however, of re-entering this state with the upcoming yoga training. Any spiritual practice which involves intensive exercises to go within and open up the energy flow in the body can bring up unresolved or suppressed emotional pain. This experience can feel overwhelming, and at times can precipitate a crisis. Cindy had been abused physically and emotionally in her childhood. She had suffered sexual assault as an adult. The memory of these traumas lay dormant in Cindy's body and psyche, exerting a continuous pressure.

We are built with an innate urge to become whole, to become aware of all that we are, including the hurts, and to heal those hurts. The hurts keep coming up some way. Sometimes it is overwhelming, even shattering when the pain is great and our ability to contain ourselves is fragile. This experience is excruciating. What psychiatry labels as "psychosis" is both the result of this great pain and, in a sense, protection from feeling the pain by "dissociation," psychologically disconnecting from it. To consciously feel, express and work through such great emotional pain is very, very difficult. It is also absolutely necessary in order to grow and to heal. The title of this book refers to this necessity.

Cindy had chosen me specifically because of my non-drug orientation and I worked to give her a context for growth that allowed intense experience without psychiatric labeling and pathologizing. I emphasized the need for excellent self-care, for gradualness and for lots of support.

The intensity of Cindy's thoughts and feelings increased, and she began to have a hard time. Many people experience such intensity and keep it to themselves. Cindy, however, revealed much of herself. She had strong spiritual beliefs which included a faith in the moment and a need to continually express her truth. She was at times scared of the intensity of emotion, but she was also highly enamored of her perceptions and thoughts, convinced that she needed to follow and express the truth of her newfound awakenings.

This young woman shared her inner life with friends; many of them became concerned as Cindy was so intense, at times frightened, at other times agitated and angry, driven more and more it seemed by an inner force that showed little respect for convention or social propriety.

Ironically, people in Cindy's life experienced her as increasingly thoughtless and insensitive, often rude or inconsiderate, interrupting, demanding attention, inappropriate; she would ask questions, share an unsolicited perception, express an opinion which another might have but would not share out of consideration. The irony is that Cindy, on the other hand, saw herself as more sensitive than ever, extremely open to others' unexpressed thoughts and feelings. She saw her uncensored expression not as rude inconsideration, but as a courageous commitment to truth and a deliberate rejection of a social nicety which deadens existence and divorces us from the living spirit.

Myself? I was riding the proverbial horns of what might be called a paradoxical dilemma. Cindy was indeed rude and inconsiderate. I watched occasionally at lunch and noticed how uncomfortable people sometimes felt around her. I experienced my own discomfort, frustration and irritation when she began to be late for or to miss appointments. She stole an audiotape of mine and then angrily walked out when I confronted her. At the same time, Cindy was writing beautiful poetry and having moments of expansive loving. She was experiencing wonderful synchronicities and even when I couldn't see the connection, it was a joy to share in her own conviction and delight at the workings of Spirit in her life. While Cindy's unsolicited sharings with friends could easily be attributed to her intensely-activated inner life, it also seemed to me that much of what she shared was at least partially true and at times right on. I experienced both her apparent distorted perceptions as well as her uncanny accuracy in pointing out my own idiosyncrasies. I had recently befriended Brad Blanton and read his book, 'Radical Honesty: How to Transform Your Life by Telling the Truth.' I was examining my own life for places of dishonesty and withholding and was challenging myself to tell the truth more. Brad is an extremely provocative model of one who disdains social nicety as a mostly fear-based deadening of life. So I could see the purity of Cindy's intentions both for spiritual awakening and social honesty. I could also see the impurity in the sense that she had not achieved a level of self-honesty that comes with acceptance and working through of the painful, suppressed traumas of our lives. She was unable to show a skepticism toward her inner experiences at this time. I will say more about this healthy function of doubt later in this book.

I began to share the concerns for Cindy expressed by many of her friends. I have seen what can happen when someone gets lost in the imperatives of an activated psyche, overwhelmed with emotion or buffeted by an intensely speeded-up thought process. I have seen individuals act impulsively and self-destructively, deliberately hurting themselves or unawarely undermining their lives through irresponsible behavior or by alienating friends and family who might lend support. I have also seen the harm that can happen when an individual voluntarily enters, or is involuntarily coerced into psychiatry.

Some of Cindy's friends began to call me. I discussed this with Cindy and we agreed that it might be helpful for me to share some information with them, not about the details of Cindy's life, but about the process of psychological upheaval as a part of emotional healing. It was an unusual position for me. Public education is part of my mission, but the fact that this was community education and counseling in relation to my client was different. I was engaging in a role largely rejected by psychologists in order to protect themselves from over-involvement and to protect the confidentiality of their clients; there are also practical concerns of time, finances and personal energy. I was trained as a school psychologist — this was an area where consultation and education with people in the extended system (teachers, parents, educational specialists, etc.) of an identified "patient" (a "problem" student) was common. I have also done family counseling and community outreach with delinquent or at-risk youth. Despite the laments of psychotherapists about the increasingly rare truly private practice (the state is almost always involved due to financial arrangements of third-party payees, health maintenance organizations [HMOs] and utilization review people), there is still a rightful homage paid to concerns of confidentiality. I considered all this and the truth for me was that avoidance of these concerned people's requests for support would have been a disservice to Cindy. So with her permission I spoke with them. My overall intent was to create the greatest possibility that Cindy would be afforded the time and support to go through this intensive unsettling period without having to enter Austin State Hospital (ASH), the local public psychiatric institution. For while many were concerned about Cindy, others were irritated and some were downright afraid. A friend called the mental health deputies, fearing she might be suicidal. Her brother, an orthodox priest who works at the state hospital, called me to express his opinion that Cindy was another "genetically mentally ill" sister who needed drugs and hospitalization. Cindy visited with the mental health deputies and with the police at the request of another friend. She even visited the hospital, but decided that she wanted to avoid it.

In our counseling, she was showing a lot of fear, but was still coherent. We worked on grounding and she expressed a desire to hold her job at the bakery which was in jeopardy because of her unreliability. Then the anger began to surface and she was really on the edge. She missed an appointment and I discovered she had stolen two of my audiotapes. We spoke that Friday on the phone and she vowed no more theft. She lost her job and was given an eviction notice by her landlord who was receiving complaints from neighbors annoyed by her rude and inconsiderate behavior. We scheduled an appointment for the next day, but I got a call instead from Austin State Hospital. It seemed Cindy was incarcerated ("involuntarily committed") after a neighbor called the police because of her intense prolonged screaming in her apartment. She was experiencing frightening visions of her brother being tortured.

I spoke with the admitting psychiatrist who said Cindy was quite lucid, and that she had no reason to hold her but wanted to make sure Cindy had an appointment with me before releasing her. I scheduled a session to meet with Cindy that same afternoon. A little later, however, Cindy called to tell me she was being held against her will on an order of protective custody. I visited her that day and she cried and was angry with her brother who was influencing the decision to keep her there against her will. It seems that he had spoken with the psychiatrist and persuaded her that there was, indeed, grounds for "involuntary commitment."

The purpose of psychiatry is not to help the inmates. Cindy's incarceration is a clear example of the truth of the following assertion by Thomas Szasz:

> "Psychiatry's aim has always been, and still is, to help a relatively more powerful person — primarily the denominated patient's parent, spouse, or other relative — by disqualifying his less powerful kin whose behavior troubles him as 'troubled', which is to say mad, and by incarcerating the victim defined as a 'patient' in a madhouse."(1)

Cindy was well-oriented when I visited. I promised to continue to be her ally one day at a time, my role being mostly a supportive caring function at this time. I was allowed to visit, but not do "therapy."

Each state has their own set of policies and procedures regarding so-called involuntary commitment. To quote my friend, Jerry Boswell, executive director of the Texas division of the Citizens Commission on Human Rights: "How does involuntary commitment occur? In two words, 'very easily'." (2) The fastest and easiest is emergency detention. In Texas, this is called an order of protective custody (OPC) which provides for a 72 hour "holding period" for observation, purportedly to determine whether a patient is dangerous to self or others (despite the well established fact of psychiatry's incapability of predicting violence). Cindy was detained on Sunday night. Her "probable cause" hearing was scheduled for Thursday morning — a judge, not a jury — would decide whether the state hospital could hold her another week before a second hearing would be held for the judge to decide whether to approve a 90-day incarceration.

I visited Cindy again the next day (Tuesday) and found her very heavily sedated (zonked); she had been forcibly injected with Atavan, a powerful tranquilizing drug, ostensibly for "non-cooperation." "Non-cooperation" is used by psychiatry to justify force. It, in fact, means force because only those who don't want the "treatment" and express it are forced to receive it. Every time you see the word "non-cooperation," force is written in imaginary big bold letters between the lines.

I felt both sad and angry, but determined to do what I could. I had been strongly challenged by this whole affair the last two weeks prior to her incarceration at ASH. I had felt rejected and attacked by Cindy, and was aware that my relationship with her was re-stimulating other similar experiences in my past. I was also facing fear about the reactions of society and the psychology profession as I put myself and my beliefs on the line with someone whom psychiatry would clearly see as in need of drugs and coercive treatment. I knew I needed friends to stand by me and did my best to reach out for support, but it was a hard time. By that Tuesday, I acutely felt my own limits and lack of power in the face of Cindy's incarceration. I had done my very best to counsel and support her to keep it together enough to avoid losing her freedom to state psychiatry. Now that she was locked up, I seriously questioned what I could do realistically and energetically. Cindy did not ask me to attend her hearing and I decided to avoid it. However, as I wrote in my personal journal on that Thursday night, "God made it possible and necessary for me to go." Here is what happened. I thought the hearing was in the morning and I went to a bodywork session for myself. The session, however, ended up with my practitioner friend challenging me to re-connect with my fighting spirit. Afterwards, I called and found out the hearing hadn't happened yet. I went and asked Cindy if she wanted me there — she did. She stayed very close to me as we waited for her turn with the judge.

Incredibly (I thought, though it is not so uncommon), Cindy had been injected again with Atavan shortly before her hearing. She was heavily sedated prior to and during the hearing. This was and is a horrible abuse of civil rights and human dignity. It is clear how little value is given to the rights of those we turn over to the hands of psychiatry. She had a court-appointed student attorney, through the Law School clinic. The state prosecution cited negligent self-care and paranoid screaming as grounds for committal. The Atavan injections were justified by a monotone reading through of the charts, something about "threats" and "redirection" and "had to shoot her up," and "not cooperative" and "mumbling about nothing." Cindy's priest brother gave testimony against her.

Cindy's own perspective, which she did articulate even with slurred speech due to the Atavan, was that she was being held against her will, that she had friends, could take care of herself and wanted out, and that I was committed to continuing work with her. In my testimony, I told the judge why I was of the opinion that she should be released — that she was working with me, that she had others who cared about her, that I had not experienced her as dangerous or suicidal. I emphasized my point of view that she must be her own authority, that no one else knows her best interest, that the best and only way to genuine recovery was to support her in her own best thinking. I also told him what I had seen: Admission, planned release, held against her will, series of assaults. I did not express my opinion that this was a brutal initiation into the role of chronic mental patient with the bottom-line of more work to do. The judge was not swayed by any of this or by outrage at the forced drugging, especially on the day of a hearing; he signed the order to hold her another week.

Did Cindy need help? Most definitely. I fervently wished that ASH was a safe, healthy place for her, but it wasn't. Had she been released that Monday morning as planned, with an open door for her to voluntarily choose to receive help there, who knows what might have happened. My own very strong belief is that if Cindy had entered a genuinely safe and supportive asylum, with caring and competent counselors to provide good attention, she would have emerged, in a fairly short period of time, having worked through part of her trauma, calm, rested, and in a position to continue her healing process out in the community. As I discuss in Chapter 16, it has been repeatedly demonstrated that, when authentic asylum is created, even those labeled with the most severe "mental illness" can and do recover without coercion and without drugs. But that was not and is not the case; psychiatry is rooted in coercion, and coercion is what happened to Cindy.

I visited Cindy and brought her food. Although I encouraged her to consider what game (compliance and the appearance of conformity) was necessary to play in order to get free, Cindy was compelled to fight. I had to admire her spirit, but I cried at the price she had to pay. I continued to work with the student lawyer and to stay in minimal contact with the psychiatrist. I showed up for the 90-day commitment proceedings and waited with the student lawyer who felt there was a good possibility of the release we hoped for. There was a delay, however, then we received word of a "situation" on the unit. I was not allowed to see Cindy, but the student lawyer did; a dispute about toothpaste had escalated to the point that Cindy received another forced injection and was not allowed to go to trial. A new OPC was issued.

It is easy to argue with great justification that Cindy's inability to hold it together and avoid conflict was evidence either of her need for "treatment" or her fear and avoidance of responsibility for her life. I thought that there was some truth in this, but I also clearly saw the persistent assault and breaking down of her strength and confidence. I saw how, in desperation, fighting back was the only real way to maintain to some degree her independent spirit. Regardless of these considerations it seemed clear to her student attorney that cancellation of the trial was a flagrant violation of the law. I encouraged the student attorney to pursue this, but she was going on spring break and her practicum was ending; she would be replaced. I contacted Advocacy, a local advocacy agency for mental patients' rights. They visited Cindy and were prepared to assert her case which they agreed was a clear violation; by that time, however, Cindy was so scared and confused she didn't trust them and refused consent. She was giving up.

On March 12, the day of the re-scheduled trial, Cindy was unexpectedly released, with absolutely no support or planning for care by the social work staff of the hospital. My best guess is that the hospital and psychiatrist knew they had broken the law and were attempting to wash their hands of the affair, an affair which I considered to be gross negligence and malpractice. Cindy found a friend to stay with and I saw her there for a session a few days later on March 16. Her friend would not keep her any longer, and Cindy was in dire straits. She had little money and I

encouraged her to stay at the Salvation Army. She was afraid
of that place, however, so she asked me for a ride to
Psychiatric Emergency Services, an outpatient drop-in
center and drug dispensary, to seek re-admission to ASH.
The ride there was tense and I cried as I let her out. They
refused her and she stayed on the street for a night. Cindy
was attempting to connect with a local homeless housing
program I had referred her to, but she was really on the
edge. There is no safe place in our community for
individuals in psychological crises to go and live. There are
only a handful in the country. Cindy had nowhere to go. I
had contacted six support people who knew her and were
available for a makeshift support program, if she could find
a place to live.

This part involved a particularly intense ordeal for me.
All through the experience, I had been testing my limits and
those of my profession, defining and redefining my role as
helper. Seeing Cindy's desperate homelessness felt
excruciatingly painful to me. I have a small two bedroom
house. Four and a half days a week it is mine alone; the rest
of the week, I share it with my two children. I agonized over
whether to offer her temporary shelter; she didn't ask and I
decided not to in the end.

Cindy showed up again the next night at Psychiatric
Emergency Services. When she was again refused
"treatment," she allegedly assaulted a nurse and the police
were called. Rather than taking her to ASH as in the initial
incident in her apartment (when she did not want to go
there) they arrested her and took her to jail (when she
wanted to go to ASH). On April 7, she called and spoke to
me from ASH where she had voluntarily transferred from
the jail to a different unit with a different psychiatrist. She
no longer wanted me as counselor; she said she was figuring

out how to turn things around. She had accepted her diagnosis as "mentally ill," was complying with "treatment," a regimen of "anti-psychotic" major tranquilizers. Cindy remained at ASH for two more months at which time (early June) the psychiatrist considered her stabilized and discharged her.

The experience with Cindy had catalyzed my desire to continue working on a manuscript I had begun on the subject of mental health system oppression. When she went to jail, I became clearer that I did not want to write an intellectual treatise, but really desired to educate the public about the dangers of psychiatry. I came up with 'The Necessity of Madness and Unproductivity' as a working title, and worked hard on this book.

On June 9, Cindy met me at my office for a session. She was humbled and on psychiatric drugs, but still thoughtful and spiritually inclined. She had a temporary job and then went for a visit to Colorado in early July where she ended up staying. A man in our community who had befriended Cindy had given her money to keep her payment current on some property she owned in Colorado. She sold this and was able to establish a home for herself, at least for awhile. Cindy's story will continue to unfold. My hope is that it will have an ending similar to the seven people who Seth Farber interviewed in his book, 'Madness, Heresy and the Rumor of Angels.' Each of these individuals was grievously harmed when they sought help from psychiatry, declared "mentally ill," locked up and given drugs. Each of them courageously learned from their experience and shed any illusions about the benevolence of psychiatry. Each ultimately rejected the authority which branded them defective, and re-engaged in the ongoing challenges of life — sans stigmatic label, sans disabling drugs. I could have chosen a story with a happier ending, or at least a happier present status as life is a journey of ongoing challenges. I chose Cindy's story because it clearly speaks to the reality of psychiatric oppression. It also reveals some of the personal struggles and frustrations that I have experienced interfacing with psychiatry.

What follows is information and experience which I hope will encourage and guide you to avoid, resist, or transform psychiatric oppression, and to more effectively support yourself and others through the challenges of personal transformation.

CHAPTER 2
A PRIMER IN PSYCHIATRIC OPPRESSION

"My doctor told me I had a biochemical imbalance that could be helped by medication."
"I didn't know what else to do."

These two statements are characteristic of the millions of individuals who are taking psychiatric drugs today. Given the misinformation and the desperation of many who reach for help, it is perfectly understandable that people accept their doctor's recommendations and turn to drugs. Given the coercive underpinnings of psychiatry, there are countless others who take psychiatric drugs because they are forced to do so.

"Nothing else works."

Although I often hear this from psychiatric consumers, it is even more a standard of psychiatry and its representatives. It is used to justify the pervasive use of drugs, the practice of iatrogenic brain damage called electroshock, and the need to force individuals into treatment and long-term care that guarantees regular income for the various constituencies of the psychiatric industry. The above three statements reflect beliefs and attitudes which are crucial for all of us to understand in order to protect ourselves and our loved ones from harm.

Too many people today are blind to the practices and

effects of asking and allowing psychiatry to be our communal response to human psychospiritual crisis. This chapter is devoted to a discussion of the theory and practice of psychiatric oppression. It is my belief that a clear understanding of how and why psychiatry is oppressive is necessary in order to make possible the creation of a community which can offer and hold a healing space for individuals like Cindy to emerge from crisis into a place of wholesome, expanded awareness.

Oppression Theory

It is important first to clearly define psychiatric oppression. By oppression, I mean the systematic mistreatment of individuals in a group simply because they are members of that group. The group in question here is, of course, "mental patients" (variously referred to by self or by others as lunatics, clients, chronics, victims, survivors, and an incredible array of disease entities). "Systematic mistreatment" is an important term: "systematic" translates to long-term and progressive; "mistreatment" is defined as doing harm. One long-standing mode of maintaining oppression is to focus on dramatic abuses and to suggest that these are outside the norm; the system is fine, abuse is an anomaly. Corporal punishment is good, a battered child is bad. Feeling sedated is good, drug abuse is bad. Slavery is good, torturing slaves is bad. Our educational system is good, certain teachers are bad. Soft porn is good, rape is bad. War is good, war crimes are bad. I will highlight some specific abuses, but it is crucial to understand that psychiatric oppression is systemic; it is inherent in the system as we know it.

Psychiatry is a deeply interlocked web of professionals (of which group psychiatrists, all of whom are MDs, are at the top of the hierarchy and including PhD psychologists, Master's level social workers and therapists, addictions counselors, psychiatric technicians, etc.), insurance companies, government agencies, hospitals and pharmaceutical companies. Given the economic structure in our country today, it is not a surprising statement to make that it is probably the pharmaceutical industry that wields the greatest influence of all these entities. The drug industry is one of the most profitable trades in the world. The evidence of who wields power in our mental health system is obvious. Take a look at the trade journals of psychiatry-mostly funded by drug companies. Conferences, workshops, trainings, and other affairs of the American Psychiatric Association are largely funded by drug companies. Even educational initiatives of our government mental health agencies are often sponsored by drug companies. Research dollars are mostly devoted to drug studies. Research on efficacy which the Food and Drug Administration(FDA) uses to evaluate and approve new drugs is typically done by the very companies who have a financial interest in the outcome. Psychiatrists make the bulk of their income from prescribing drugs; insurance companies are enforcing this trend by adhering more and more strictly to a medical model of treatment. Insurance companies today will readily pay for drugs, but fight tooth and nail to avoid payment for psychotherapy. I personally withdrew from the last managed care group for which I was a provider because of the increasingly onerous demand to justify "medical necessity" for more than a handful of counseling sessions, and the concomitant pressure to encourage use of "medication" for psychological problems. The backup treatment of biopsychiatry is electroshock (also known as electroconvulsive therapy or ECT), substantially more profitable in the short term to psychiatrists than drugs and in the long-term creating chronic "mental patients." Both private insurance and Medicare will pay for electroshock. The guiding aspect of the psychiatric worldview is not in any way unique to psychiatry; it is so pervasive that we take it for granted and tend to question it about as much as a fish questions the water in which it swims. It's sometimes called the "profit imperative" of our economic system.

I have defined oppression as the systematic mistreatment of people simply because they are members of a certain group. Most people today understand that racism is oppression; many understand the oppression in sexism and in homophobia. Too few see beyond the illusory veil of a purportedly benevolent mental health system. Behind this veil are two primary forces common to all oppressions, including psychiatry. They are money and coercion.

Money

The core of oppression is economic; oppression theory always begins and ends in economic terms. The relevant term today is classism. It was once slavery, later it was feudalism. It is now separation of people by class, the fundamental division being between those who make their living by their own work (working class) and those who make money off other peoples' work (owning class). Other divisions (poor, low, middle-class, professional, etc.) are sub-categories of working class, reflecting varying degrees of privilege or advantage in our society. It is absolutely necessary in thinking about psychiatric oppression to be very aware of economics and money. For a full and powerful exposition, I refer the reader to Thomas Szasz' book, 'Cruel Compassion', in which he shows how psychiatry serves a societal function in modern times, analogous to prisons and poorhouses of the recent past. Large numbers of people are drugged, confined and supported by the state, not because they are sick, but because they are unproductive and unwanted. "From the sixteenth to the nineteenth century adult dependents were coerced primarily on economic grounds, because they were a financial burden on the productive members of society. Since then, they have increasingly been coerced on therapeutic grounds, because they are mentally ill and hence are a danger to themselves and others. Both remedies aggravate the problem." (1)

The bottom line is that economics is the linchpin of all oppression, including psychiatry. Psychiatry serves a major societal control function by dealing with unproductive and unwanted citizens. A related point is that oppression thrives on separation, division and fear. Fear of "mental illness" is huge. Diagnosing, labeling and treating a class of "mentally ill patients" is a powerful way of maintaining separation and division among members and segments of our society. The cloak of benevolence may protect the consciences of psychiatry's agents and their supporters, but it in no way protects the bodies and psyches of its victims.

Coercion

Psychiatry is coercive. This must be acknowledged in order to have any hope of seeing clearly what's going on. In every one of our 50 states, psychiatrists use involuntary commitment and threat of commitment. State laws protect and guarantee this practice, under the guise and rationale of "public safety" and "concern for troubled individuals."

It may not be obvious to you that coercive psychiatry is necessarily a bad thing. What may be even less obvious, yet fundamental to understand, is that where there is coercive psychiatry and involuntary treatment there is no such thing as truly voluntary psychiatry and treatment. The threat is always there. Countless individuals end up in psychiatric treatment labeled as "voluntary," coerced by overt and/or covert threat of forced treatment. All of us on some level and to some degree have to struggle with fear and confusion stemming from the way this process has filtered into the ubiquitous language of our everyday lives: "you're losing your mind," "you're nuts" (loony, crazy, wacko, sick, etc.), "they're gonna lock you up," "the men in the white coats are going to come and get you." Psychiatry is, at its root, coercive and absolutely could not function as it does without being so.

The Worldview of Biological Psychiatry

The mindset of psychiatry is guided by a very specific set of assumptions which flow from the pseudomedical model of biopsychiatry. It has all the trappings of language that we associate with the scientific practice of medicine. In fact, the theory and practice of biopsychiatry, though modeled after the practice of medicine, is really about social control. The basic assumptions of biopsychiatry are as follows:

1/ Adjustment to society is good.
2/ Failure to adjust is the result of "mental illness."
3/ "Mental illness" is a medical disease.

4/ "Mental illness" is the result of biological and/or genetic defects.

5/ "Mental illness" is chronic, progressive, basically incurable.

6/ "Mental illness" can (and must) be controlled primarily by drugs; secondarily, for really serious "mental illness," by electroshock.

7/ People with "mental illness" are irrational, often unable to make responsible decisions for themselves; therefore, coercion is necessary and justified.

SOCIAL ADJUSTMENT IS GOOD

Whether you agree with it or not, this is crucial because psychiatry serves the dominant culture of mainstream society. Our education system is a principal agent of social control or conformity. We give psychiatry, by economic reward and legal power, a mandate to function on behalf of the social order where education fails to do the job, and where police action is either unwarranted or undesired. Religion often serves a similar function in our society; however, as science has usurped theology, so has involuntary psychiatry replace involuntary religion (Inquisition) as primary agent to enforce social norms (see Chapter 3). No matter how one attributes the cause or etiology, the bottom line is that people react to Cindy not because she is ill (compare a reaction to cancer, for example), but because she challenges their external and internal social order. When this challenge is insufficient to justify criminal proceedings, or when aggrieved parties feel too much guilt in pressing criminal charges, psychiatry is readily available. In a free society, involvement in psychiatry and/or religion would be voluntary.

FAILURE TO ADJUST IS THE RESULT OF "MENTAL ILLNESS"

According to biopsychiatry, failure to adjust says nothing about social issues, community issues, physical or emotional issues. The assumption is very simple. Problems are due to "mental illness," and all are absolved of responsibility to think any further. The next assumption provides the rationale.

"MENTAL ILLNESS" IS A MEDICAL DISEASE

This is based on the premise that there is this condition we call "mental illness," and that it is a disease much like cancer or diabetes or some other physical, biologically-based medical condition. This is understandable because the concept of mental illness was created by medical doctors who are steeped in the burgeoning applications of the scientific method to the practice of medicine. They created the concept of mental illness as a metaphor for physical illness. Now psychiatry says that "mental illness" is physical illness; it is not. Criteria for psychiatric diagnoses are strictly social and behavioral — no blood tests, urine tests, tissue samples, x-rays, etc. "Mental illness" is a metaphor. The diagnosis of "depression," for example, is a metaphor saying that this behavioral phenomena is a medical disease. Let me illustrate this with two metaphors:

John lies around all day on the couch, a potato lies

around all day; John is a couch potato.

John feels tired and lethargic and lies around all day on the couch, a person dying of cancer feels tired and lethargic and lies around all day; John is a medical disease (depression).

Cancer is diagnosed through physical, scientific, medical tests. The psychiatric diagnosis of depression is a metaphor. There are no medical tests; the diagnosis is made on the basis of behavioral observation and self-report of subjective experience. "Mental illness" was created as a metaphor, then it was forgotten that it is a metaphor and treated as if it were as real as that which can be proven by a lab test.

"MENTAL ILLNESS" IS THE RESULT OF BIOLOGICAL AND/OR GENETIC DEFECTS

Biopsychiatry assumes that the basis of this observed behavior and subjective experience is biological or genetic. Psychiatry continuously offers up the promise that in five or ten years, it will be proven. In the meantime, the assumptions are presented falsely as if they were fact, and the media dutifully conveys this lie to the public. Ty Colbert's book, 'Broken Brains or Wounded Hearts', is a particularly clear exposition of the falsity of this assumption. Dr Colbert points out that fictitious mental diseases are created and substantiated through systematic and repetitious assertions of untruth. A brief description of what Dr Colbert calls 'The Four False Pillars of Biopsychiatry', follows here.

False Pillar #1 — The Inheritance Pillar

The main premise of this pillar is that since "mental illness" runs in families it must be inherited. Most of us have heard this claim. The media keeps us so constantly inundated with assertion of this belief that most people today seem to believe it, especially about so-called schizophrenia and manic-depression. Psychiatry textbooks report concordance rates (the probability that if one twin is diagnosed with "mental illness," the other will be also). Dr Colbert takes a close look at the data and demonstrates the truth that, in the most accurate studies, the concordance rate is only 23 percent. At least 77 percent must be related to the environment and much of the 23 percent could be due to identical environments that twins share. Twin studies simply don't hold up as evidence for a genetic cause of schizophrenia or any other "mental illness."

False Pillar #2 — The Chemical Imbalance Pillar

This pillar relies on the assertion that psychiatric drugs work by correcting a chemical imbalance. A drug is given, it has an effect, the interpretation is made that the effect is due to correction of chemical imbalance which causes "mental illness." Colbert reviews several "medications" and disputes each of them; he shows how these chemical imbalance theories which are the pride of biopsychiatry should not be called theories at all, because they are arrived at in reverse order. Rather than making a legitimate medical diagnosis and then testing a drug for its therapeutic efficacy relative to the already established imbalance, it is argued that imbalance is responsible because the drug reduced a symptom. I am most familiar with the example of Ritalin use with so-called Attention-Deficit

Hyperactive Disorder (ADHD) children. Here's a quote from my book, 'The Wildest Colts Make the Best Horses':

"Children diagnosed as ADHD do not respond to Ritalin because it corrects a biological defect; they respond because they're taking an amphetamine. A long-demonstrated effect of amphetamines is that users experience a narrowing focus of attention and concentration on detail and are less in touch with their feelings. Any child becomes more docile, obedient and willing to concentrate on boring, repetitive tasks."

There is no evidence to support the idea of chemical imbalance as cause of "mental illness." Psychiatric drugs do not magically correct a chemical imbalance; their most common effect is to disable the brain.

False Pillar #3 — The Defective Gene Pillar

The main premise is that genetic markers have been found that will eventually lead to defective genes. The news media has led many to accept the belief that genes are responsible for certain "mental illnesses." Dr Colbert shares the scientific fact that finding a genetic marker only suggests the possibility that a specific gene exists. He then reveals the more damning evidence that even the markers haven't really been found and that the probability of doing so is exceedingly low.

False Pillar #4 — The Brain Scan Pillar

Modern technology has provided yet another opportunity for the relentless never-ending search of biopsychiatrists for evidence to validate their position. This pillar is based on the premise that evidence of a diseased brain can be seen through the use of brain imaging instruments. Researchers do two kinds of studies, looking for either structural (shape or form) or functional (e.g., how glucose is processed) defects in the brains of individuals diagnosed as "mentally ill." Colbert's review of structural studies reveals no demonstration of structural defects, but slight evidence for one difference; that is, people diagnosed as "schizophrenic" may tend to have slightly enlarged ventricles. As Colbert concludes, this may very well be due to the known brain-damaging effects of antipsychotic drugs. He also points out that research has demonstrated that stress can cause brain damage and ventricular enlargement. Quoting Colbert: "If the biopsychiatric community is going to conclude anything from structural brain scanning studies, it should be that the emotional stress that the schizophrenic must endure-from the unhealed pain from childhood, the stress of being labeled mentally ill, the stress of hospital stays, the effects of medications, and so forth-is a possible cause of brain damage." (2) Functional studies offer no more credence to the diseased brain premise. Results are inherently confounded by the fact that, under stress, our brains work harder in different areas that show up on functional brain scan tests.

The truth, remarkable as it may sound, is that no problem routinely seen by psychiatrists has been proven to be of biological or genetic origin. We are so thoroughly conditioned into the idea that human distress is the realm of medical psychiatry that it is hard to hold onto the key truth that so-called psychiatric "treatment" is really about conduct and behavior. Psychiatry is acting out of a desperate, misinformed misunderstanding of human nature largely bereft of ideas which can guide practices to soothe and encourage those in personal or inner crisis. Furthermore, many who get psychiatrized are not in any crisis. The bottom line is that the idea of "mental illness" is used to justify coercion of nonconformists or deviants. "Depressed" people, for example, are major violators of the primary imperative of our own society which is to be productive; hence the title of this book.

A Note on Biology

As obvious at it may seem, my experience is that it is necessary to explain that rejection of biopsychiatry and its superstitious belief in biologically based "mental illness" does not imply dismissal of the truth that biology and genetics are an undeniable component of our well or not-so-well-being. To date, despite decades of intensive effort, psychiatry has not identified a consistent genetic component, lesion, virus, cellular abnormality or other measurable physical anomaly. Nevertheless, physical well-being provides our very foundation on this earth, and our physical health obviously affects both mood and thinking. There are many "alternative" biological approaches to adult "mental illness," and many "alternatives" to Ritalin for so-called ADHD. Many individuals have found relief through alteration of diet or environment. I am all for exploring alternatives. Just beware of an eternal search for "the magic product," and neglect of the needs of emotional recovery, spiritual development and social justice.

"MENTAL ILLNESS" IS INCURABLE

The worldview of biopsychiatry reduces the complexities and richness of human experience and social interaction to mechanisms of biological function within the body of an individual who presumably operates as an isolated physical entity. By reducing the complexities of human life to the dictates of biology and genetics, a remarkable and tragic result occurs. I call it a magic trick. Once an individual is labeled with a biologically-based "mental illness" (whether it be a difficult interface between child and school, or an elder and her family or Cindy and her community), the result is the same. The school, the family, the community, society, are all magically absolved from the need and responsibility to keep thinking, to examine themselves, to question the nature of the community, to look at oppression at any level in the society. Instead, everyone can act as if the situation were explained and accounted for by bad genes or biology causing "mental illness" in the poor soul who is the identified patient. Just as we all are absolved from responsibility to face societal oppression, so also are we absolved from the need to do whatever it takes to care for and support recovery and healing in the individual.

"MENTAL ILLNESS" CAN (AND MUST) BE CONTROLLED

This is an inevitable assumption which justifies use of dramatic physical interventions. Today, these are primarily drugs and secondarily electroshock. Historically, these practices include any manner of barbarisms. To quote Johann Heinroth, a German physician in 1818:

"A special building must be set aside for the physical treatment of the mentally disturbed. This building should have a special bathing section, with all kinds of baths, showers, douches, and immersion vessels. It must also have a special correction and punishment room with all the necessary equipment, including a Cox swing (or better, rotating machine), Reil's flywheel, pulleys, punishment chair, Langermann's chair, etc." (3)

The mid-twentieth century included a fondness for so-called psychosurgery, or lobotomy, a most popular procedure involving insertion of an icepick through the eye socket, followed by a rapid twisting which severed connection of the frontal lobes of the brain. Psychosurgery still has advocates today, and is actually practiced under disguise, euphemistically referred to as a type of neurosurgery.

If this seems remarkable, consider that Benjamin Rush, the author of the following words, also in 1818, is still honored as founding father of American psychiatry, his face emblazoned on the official seal of the American Psychiatric Association:

"TERROR acts powerfully upon the body, through the medium of the mind, and should be employed in the cure of madness. ... FEAR, accompanied with PAIN, and a sense of SHAME, has sometimes cured this disease. Bartholin speaks in high terms of what he calls "flagellation" in certain diseases." (4)

PEOPLE WITH "MENTAL ILLNESS" ARE IRRATIONAL, OFTEN UNABLE TO MAKE RESPONSIBLE DECISIONS FOR THEMSELVES; THEREFORE, COERCION IS NECESSARY AND JUSTIFIED.

The six assumptions just reviewed provide the rationale for a coercive "final solution," a logically inevitable expression of a dangerous and distorted worldview. Psychiatry supports and defends the power structure, values, practices and appearances of the status quo; it looks at the world and selects out "defective" individuals for "treatment." Much more will be said about this process.

If it's not "mental illness", then what is it?

Psychiatric oppression is fundamentally a social and economic phenomenon, an agency of social control, an enforcement of societal status quo. While psychiatry's action has mostly to do with defense against the threat of change, we all know that humans are highly vulnerable to psychological distress, and often need help in that regard. Psychiatry, in its original meaning as a science of the soul, is an expression of caring for humans at a psychological level. Psychiatry today, however pathetic, is a modern response to humans in distress. So before continuing with this primer on psychiatric oppression, I want to share some ideas about the nature of human distress. We all see, and at times experience ourselves, the faces of such distress. Let's not pretend otherwise, and let's not deny that some of these faces are very extreme. If this is not, as I argue, "mental illness," then what is it? If biologically-based "mental illness" is not the real threat to human well-being, then what is it that causes us to have such a hard time? Let's first take a look at how we view human nature.

Human Nature

Psychiatry's basic philosophy and theory of human nature was summarized in the seven assumptions listed above. In order to see clearly, it is necessary to consider many ideas that are "opposite" to the assumptions of biopsychiatry. The first and foremost idea has to do with the nature of human beings. It is my view that the inherent nature of human beings is completely good, loving, intelligent, zestful and cooperative. Also inherent in human nature is an ethical sense; we feel righteous indignation at injustice and want to act powerfully against oppression.

A second aspect of our nature as human beings stems from our long, extended childhood involving complete dependency on others. Optimal development requires wise parenting and broad social support. The challenge is extraordinary and rarely does one of us get the optimum. I will say more later about how our treatment results in certain conditioned patterns of thought and action; just now, what I want to convey is that when we are hurt physically or emotionally, the result is distress. This distress affects us on all levels — physically, emotionally, mentally and spiritually. We are not able to think clearly or rationally when we are hurt. This effect, which I call distress, is what psychiatry calls "mental illness."

When distress, and the effects of distress, are labeled as "mental illness," coercive and suppressive treatment with drugs and electroshock logically follows the imperative to control this dread disease. A wiser perspective understands that, while human beings are indeed susceptible, we fortunately have a built-in mechanism for healing from the distressing effects of being hurt. This mechanism is a natural human behavior of resolving our emotional distress by expressing ourselves through talk, anger, fear, grief, or laughter. In a healthy situation we naturally discharge or release the effects of having been hurt. When it is not safe to do so, we inhibit this discharge process, and carry both the hurts and the effects of the hurts which manifest as a contracted physical body, a reduced or exaggerated range of emotion, and irrational thinking. It follows , then, that the suppression of emotional discharge, which is the core of psychiatric oppression, is exactly the wrong approach to helping individuals in distress. Authentic help involves acting in ways which encourage, promote and allow natural healing by emotional discharge in safe and appropriate ways.

A Note On Extreme States of Mind

You might be thinking that this sounds alright for relatively mild forms of distress, what psychiatry would call "neuroses," but what about the so-called "psychoses," what refer to as extreme states of mind. As Dr Edward Podvoll puts it:

"There is a silent despair in the modern world about the possibility of recovery from psychosis. Only occasionally is the despair publicly acknowledged, but privately, for the vast majority of psychiatrists and psychologists, recovery does not exist. They have become accustomed to seeing patients 'relapse' — make a temporary adjustment to life and then fall apart under the pressure of life into the same psychotic world as before. They have seen this so often that they have come to believe that relapse is inherent in the illness, the expectable natural history of the disease. This professional belief system has been accepted and has passed into the general culture. Most people have become acclimatized to a belief that psychosis is a terminal illness, and have thus become unconscious and numb to their own despair." (5)

Edward Podvoll is a man who knows whereof he speaks. I refer to his work at various points in this book, especially in Chapter 16, on alternatives. His Windhorse Project successfully facilitated recovery for individuals labeled "chronically mentally ill" and "psychotic" for several years. His excellent book, 'The Seduction of Madness', provides insightful teachings, from a Buddhist perspective, about the workings of the mind. While there are organic causes of extreme states of mind (see listing in Chapter 11), these are the exception. Podvoll paints a detailed picture of the truth that such states are not biopsychiatric diseases, but reflect imbalance or derangement of inherent functions of the mind. We all experience these states at times, and we are all vulnerable to getting lost in them given the necessary conditions (e.g., massive trauma and stress overload).

The professional, and public, belief system regarding "psychosis," described in Podvoll's above quotation, has little to do with the true nature of extreme distress; the "silent despair" reflects the hopelessness that comes from ignorance of human nature and absence of genuine alternatives for helping. Emotional release work is one crucial ingredient of recovery for individuals in such crisis. The fact is that emotions are often intense; eruption of suppressed emotion can be overwhelming and scary to both the experiencer and the observer. Much of what is labeled pathological is just such an intense expression; given safety and support, it becomes a necessary step on the road to recovery. An individual is seeking emotional discharge or spontaneously having lots of discharge without a counselor. As mental health liberation leader Jamie Alexander puts it, "that's what we're often looking at when we're looking at people who are institutionalized — basically an accumulation of distress and a prohibition against discharge." (6)

Janet Foner is the International Reference Person for Mental Health Liberation for the Re-evaluation Counseling Communities. She is also a psychiatric survivor, a woman subjected to a variety of coercive psychiatric "treatments" for so-called psychosis. She re-emerged, with tremendous work and a lot of help, to become an international leader. The following statement of hers is direct and to the point:

There is no such thing as "going crazy."

You can't "lose your mind."

What is "mental illness" really? It's a very long "session" seeking discharge or having lots of discharge, without a counselor. (7)

Coercion Revisited

I cannot emphasize it enough: the most important thing to know about psychiatry is that it is inherently coercive. Society has given institutional psychiatry a mandate to maintain the status quo. In Chapter 3, I will provide some perspective on how it happened that society gives psychiatry a power to violate individuals' most sacred human rights in way that no other agency, even the police, can legally do. Biopsychiatry provides a theory which justifies this coercion by declaring that "mentally ill" individuals are defective and potentially dangerous to themselves or others. Countless individuals become "voluntary patients" because of covert or overt threat of involuntary commitment. Furthermore, once a person voluntarily enters psychiatric "treatment," it is extremely difficult, often impossible, to gain release without a psychiatrist's approval. Cindy's case is not unusual in this regard.

In the eyes of our current society, it doesn't really matter that all of this biopsychiatric rhetoric is assumption on the order of a superstitious belief. Enough people say it, print it in the newspaper enough, broadcast it loudly enough, and we are allowed to rest with smug confidence in the false notion that it is true. We comfort ourselves with this false notion, and avoid facing the truth that biopsychiatry is about social control through brain disablement. (8) This is where it really gets dangerous for people like Cindy. Members of the community assumed she was "mentally ill," that it had nothing to do with any of them, that it was , in fact, a phenomenon that was not only entirely alien(not like them), but also utterly incomprehensible except by professional , medical mental health professionals. These community members, self-identified concerned friends of the troubled or troubling one, then turn to the "state" to get "help" for their friend. They do not identify this process for what it is. They call it help, assuming that psychiatry is the proper agent to respond to what they define as a "medical" emergency which they know nothing about, not being professionals and all. It is true Cindy needed help; she was acting in many ways that were self-defeating. She needed a place of refuge, protected space for her inner work. She needed more than friend/acquaintances were able to give. Members of our community are sincere, concerned, caring people — many people had bad information from having been led down the garden path by all the forces involved in modern day psychiatry. All of us are, of course, subject to and frustrated by the limits of living in our current fragmented, isolating and incredibly exploitive society. Nevertheless, people need to know that calling in the "state" is not about appropriate "treatment" for "mental illness;" rather, it is a pathetic substitute for real community and real understanding. That it appears to be the only alternative for many is nothing more than a sad indicator of how far we are at this point from a truly aware and compassionate society.

The bottom line of this action of calling the state, or otherwise intervening without permission in another's life, is that it is coercive. No matter what the justification, it is coercion; no matter how deep your concern, no matter whether it hurts you to do it, no matter how certain you are that it is for his or her own good. My suggestion is simply to call it what it is — coercion — and decide and act from that knowingness. Decide and act, also, from the knowingness that "mental illness" is a metaphor, and that the theory and practice of biopsychiatry is not based in science, but is a set of superstitious assumptions. My physician friend, Moira Dolan, provided me with a great analogy of what the practice of biopsychiatry is like. A psychiatrist prescribing extremely powerful mood-altering drugs and/or electroshock as treatment for biologically-based conditions affecting psychological well-being is like a caveman who discovers a laptop power book, figures out how to manipulate the on-off switch and thinks he understands semi-conductors. Leonard Frank doesn't like this analogy because a laptop doesn't hurt anyone. He suggests that a better analogy might be something to the effect that the caveman finds a revolver with a bullet in one chamber and starts playing Russian roulette with someone else.

Mechanisms of Psychiatric Oppression

Psychiatry acts as a stop sign on the road to liberation from other oppressions. (9) There are four primary mechanisms by which psychiatry enforces or holds other oppressions in place:

1/ Suppression of emotional expression.

2/ Distraction from social injustice by blaming the victim.

3/ Enforcement of conformity and adherence to proscribed social rules.

4/ Providing false hope and absolution.

SUPPRESSION OF EMOTIONAL EXPRESSION

This first oppressive mechanism is most important since it suppresses the natural process by which people resolve emotionally charged experiences. We heal by expressing ourselves emotionally in the presence of good attention from another warm, caring human being. There is an extremely strong trend in this society toward suppression and inhibition of discharge of emotional or physical hurts by expression of emotion(crying, shaking, sweating, storming, screaming, yawning, etc.). All of us know this from the ubiquity in our experience of statements such as "big boys don't cry," "get a grip on yourself," "you're losing it," "it's alright," "just be positive," "go to your room until you can be nice," "crybaby," "I can't stand your whining," "that's not ladylike," "they're gonna come take you away," "you are _____ "(wacko, nuts, crazy, sick, bonkers, pathetic, weak, loony, off your rocker, insane, schizophrenic, clinically depressed, ADHD, out of your mind, a sissy, a wimp, a bitch, and on and on and on). You get the picture. In our personal lives, we all have reason to experience shame and fear around intense, uninhibited emotional expression.

Psychiatry supports and enforces this basic and fundamental aspect of our conditioning, acting to enforce this practice of suppressing the very mechanism which allows us to release and heal the hurts and the effects of the hurts. The core of psychiatric oppression is suppression of emotional expression. Mainstream (meaning the agencies of the economically, politically and socially powerful in society) mental health practices center around systematic inhibition of emotional expression, thus systematically disrupting and disallowing the possibility of genuine emotional healing and recovery. The practice of locking up groups of individuals in extreme states of mind with each other and giving them disabling drugs also deprives these people of the healing and calming effects of such practices as conversation, meditation, healthy nutrition and exercise.

The heart of current psychiatric practice is psychopharmacology. Other control patterns (ways of suppressing expression) range from seemingly benevolent (psychotherapy attempts to soothe away "too much crying") to cruel and severely damaging practices such as electroshock and psychosurgery. Psychiatry's physical treatments (drugs, shock and psychosurgery) are often used coercively and almost always without genuine informed consent.

DISTRACTION FROM SOCIAL JUSTICE BY BLAMING THE VICTIM

The second mechanism by which psychiatry acts to hold oppression in place involves a trick of magic or sleight of hand. Political versions involve so-called red herrings or straw men. The mechanism is indirection and illusion.

"Now you see it, now you don't." "Before you get a glimpse of social injustice, let me show you mental illness." "Before you think about racism and economic injustice, let me show you genetic predisposition to violence in young black males." Institutional psychiatry has been so successful in its magic show that few people realize that "mental illness" is, at best, merely a metaphor. To quote Peter Breggin, foremost writer and outspoken challenger of the tenets of biopsychiatry: "It is scientifically incontrovertible that there is no convincing evidence that any condition routinely seen by psychiatrists has a genetic or biological origin." (10) Biopsychiatry is performing the greatest magic show on earth. The incredible illusion of biologically caused "mental illness" serves as a powerful enforcer of oppression, consistently distracting our attention from the reality of social injustice and its devastating results on individuals and on society. I'll give you a hint now on one way to see through this illusion. Keep your eye on where the money goes. Or as investigative journalists are advised, "Follow the money." I give two examples below in this chapter.

ENFORCEMENT OF CONFORMITY

The third way that psychiatry acts to deflect resistance against other oppressions has a much more elastic quality, adapting to specific groups and individuals. It functions similarly to law enforcement. It is hard to get hold of because the laws, though well-known, are unwritten. They are the laws of oppression, the laws of adultism, racism, sexism, heterosexism, anti-Semitism, etc. The mechanism is simple. If people step outside the bounds of the oppressive conditioning, (i.e., fail to act in the way that a child, woman,

man, person of color, etc., is supposed to act), then psychiatry's agents are available to punish them for the transgression, enforcing their prescribed role. The mass drugging of young children who don't conform to expected classroom behavior is one disgraceful example; the electroshocking of thousands of our elderly women, when they aren't sweet and pleasant, is another.

HOPE AND ABSOLUTION

Belief that human suffering is caused by biologically-based "mental illness" leads to biological treatment, which results in much more than altered brain chemistry. Individuals who are hurting and needing help almost always carry some level of desperation, guilt and shame. We often reach for help because we have tried everything we know to do and are in despair. We feel ashamed that we have problems and can't handle it on our own; we feel guilty that it is somehow our fault. Other individuals end up in "treatment" not by reaching directly for help, but because it is forced on them by others who think they need it. Since this coercion always conveys to the one coerced that s/he is defective, incompetent and irrational, it is an extremely rare individual who survives such "treatment" without taking on a heavy load of desperation and shame. Human beings have turned to religion for thousands of years to gain hope and absolution for their sins. Today, psychiatry offers hope and absolution to individuals in the form of a psychiatric diagnosis and treatment by drugs and/or electroshock. The message offered by psychiatry is that we know what's going on, this treatment will help you, and perhaps most importantly your problem is not your fault.

Bob is in despair about ever gaining relief from crippling anxiety or disabling melancholic inertia. His family feels helpless and hopeless that their loved one, who alternates between isolation in his room and angry outbursts of frustration at them, will ever have a normal life. Finally, psychiatry explains the problem as a diagnosable, biologically-based "mental illness." There is relief at having an explanation, and hope that this brain disease can be medically treated through pharmacology. That a label of mental disease offers hope is a tragic reflection of the depth of despair so many feel today. The foundations of biopsychiatry, including the core idea of biologically-based "mental illness," are superstitions rather than scientific facts. The truth is that a psychiatric diagnosis offers only despair and further suffering. In addition to whatever hurts were already present, individuals so labeled now have to deal with that stigma as well as having an even longer path to follow back to the truth of themselves as spiritual beings. Any hope experienced will usually be short-lived and ephemeral. As to the "treatments," the harm is overt and physical. Only in the world of biopsychiatry can such an act of despair (acceptance of self as biologically defective and needing to take toxic drugs or be electroshocked to function in life) be called hope.

If despair is hope, what then is absolution? Many experience relief at finding a name for their problem. I think this relief comes from a temporary lessening of feelings of guilt and shame. Guilt is the feeling that I have done something wrong; shame is the feeling that something is wrong with me, that I am inadequate, incompetent, defective, worthless, etc. Guilt feels awful, so it is understandable that we gain relief through being able to say that we have done nothing wrong, that we are the victims of a disease. So psychiatry absolves individuals from guilt by saying that it's not your fault, you are suffering from a genuine disease. Naming things is of value in handling life's challenges; the catch is that the name must bear some semblance to reality. Diagnoses of psychiatric disease are based on illusion and serve only to cloak or distort reality. The end result is that a true lessening of guilt becomes all the more difficult. Guilt usually stems from a violation of our internal ethics; it reflects a conflict between our image of how we should be, on the one hand, and our behavior, or the other. There are two true means of guilt reduction that know of; both involve an internal review whereby we compare our behavior with our image of what we believe to be the right thing to do. The first way of releasing guilt is to change our belief about what is right. We may decide that what we once were taught and accepted no longer rings true, so we change our code of ethics, and the behavior that once triggered guilt no longer does so. The second possibility is that we have violated our code of honor and truly are in conflict with a valued moral belief. In this situation, we must forgive ourselves, and where necessary make amends and/or reparation. The religious function of confession, the 12-step recovery program, and all good counseling offer support for this process of atonement. Biopsychiatric diagnosis only obscures the search for truth, and makes it all the more difficult to resolve guilt.

Absolution from shame is an ancient religious function. In the Catholic church , for example, theology teaches that we are born with original sin, inherently shameful and fallen from God. The sacrament of Baptism is meant to cleanse a soul of this condition. All parties involved (psychiatrist and "patient") often experience temporary relief from shame as a result of their actions. For "patients" in today's world, it can feel better to think they have a psychiatric disease than to sit with an unspecified general feeling that they are worthless. (See Chapter 5 for a description of the process whereby shame is taken on, internalized, split off, and finally projected onto another as a protection against feeling so awful ourselves.) For mental health professionals, and for the rest of society, stigmatizing and "treating" the "mentally ill" is an all too convenient way of avoiding the anguish of facing and working through these awful feelings inside ourselves.

The truth is that, while biopsychiatry offers no authentic support, it does offer a false absolution; it absolves us all from responsibility. "Patients" are not responsible because they suffer from a physical "disease" that renders them irrational and incompetent; psychiatrists are completely justified in coercion, purveyance of toxic drugs, and administration of brain-damaging electroshock. The public is justified in leaving it all to the professionals. And, most importantly, everyone is absolved from responsibility to keep thinking about what is really going on, and to keep working to find ways to create a compassionate society and to respond to individual human needs .

Examples

I want to briefly highlight just a few examples. One of the core oppressions is called adultism, the systematic mistreatment of children and young people simply because they are young. The pattern is one of massive disrespect and each of us as adults needs to critically examine our own tendencies. One key to knowing whether you are acting as an agent of such oppression is to ask yourself whether you would treat an adult the same way you have treated or are about to treat a child or young person. The overall conditioning against emotional expression is initially laid down through adultism.

A specific, and especially shameful oppression that demonstrates both the "magic" misdirection of biopsychiatry and specifically targets young people, especially boys, is the ubiquitous prescription of Ritalin for so-called Attention Deficit-Hyperactivity Disorder (ADHD). As many as five million school-age children are on this one seriously addictive drug. (11) Voila! Stop our thinking about the failures of society and schools to meet the needs of our developing young people, and send money instead in massive amounts to the unholy alliance of medicine, insurance and drug companies. A bit of investigative journalism, "following the money" by John Merrow, revealed that Ritalin's manufacturers, Ciba-Geigy contributed nearly $1,000,000 in 1994 plus a similar amount of in-kind donations to a family organization called CHADD (Children with Attention Deficit Disorders) which is actively lobbying Congress and the Drug Enforcement Administration to relax restrictions on Ritalin (12) In my book, 'The Wildest Colt Make the Best Horses', I expose abuses related to Ritalin, ADHD and other "disruptive behavior disorders."

In 1993, it was estimated that 10,000,000 people worldwide (6,000,000 in the U.S.) took Prozac. Prozac revenues for Eli Lilly are now about $2.5 billion a year. Greg Critzer's article, 'Pills, Prozac and Paradise', shows how the drug companies are now bypassing the medical profession and marketing directly to consumers. (13) The exponential growth in profits of the psychopharmaceutical industry further demonstrates how effectively the public is swayed by psychiatric propaganda. The public is literally inundated with misinformation propagated by the media, the government, the schools, and all that can be bought in our modern advertising industry.

Another example demonstrates how psychiatry enforces the parameters of sexism and ageism. One of the most offensive events in modern day psychiatry is the persistence, even resurgence, of the hideous practice of electrically shocking the brains of "mentally ill" patients. Electroshock involves the attachment of electrodes to one or both temples, and the administration of approximately 70 to 600 volts of electricity to the frontal lobes of the brain. Chapter 9 goes into detail about electroshock:

approximately 100,000 people each year are subjected to electroshock's brain damaging effects. Statistics show that women, and particularly elderly women, receive the brunt of these "treatments." In 1994, an 80-year-old nursing home resident named Lucille Austwick sparked a national grassroots protest campaign on her behalf. It all began when she said "No!" to psychiatrists' requests to give her electric shock. The precise quote of Ms. Austwick's was "Bull! Ridiculous! If they want to do that let them go shock themselves!" The psychiatrists then took Ms. Austwick to court for a hearing to see if they could forcibly electroshock her. The court ruled in her favor and she was not shocked. Data collected by the Texas Department of Mental Health and Mental Retardation reveals that by far the largest single age receiving electroshock is 65, which just happens to be the age when individuals become eligible for Medicare.

Even a brief exposition of psychiatric oppression must make mention of the so-called Federal Violence Initiative. This incredible program, more aptly known as the "Racist Violence Initiative," was put forth by Frederick Goodwin, top-ranking psychiatrist in the Bush administration and director of the National Institute of Mental Health (NIMH). This initiative includes ongoing "research" into the supposed biological basis of inner-city violence and includes proposals for biomedical social control. The U.S. government asks "Are Black People Genetically Violent?" and plans a psychiatric screening program which would lead to mass drugging of innocent inner-city children, the vast majority of whom are young people of color. The National Science Foundation, the Centers for Disease Control, and the Justice Department are all involved. Elaborate pseudoscientific language, and much of the federal government's effort, goes into obfuscating and/or directly denying this initiative's plain racist intent. Meanwhile, "research" has begun in Chicago. (14)

The Federal Violence Initiative is a clearly racist practice, just one legacy of a distorted biopsychiatric theory frighteningly analogous to the practices of Nazi Germany. As Dottie Curry, a social activist from Austin, Texas, and an international leader in the Re-evaluation Counseling Community put it, "The 'violence gene theory' is now added to the 'stupid gene theory' to further convince society that the African will not fit in the USA, and is dangerous to the world."

I close this chapter with a quote from Frederick Goodwin, then director of NIMH, to demonstrate that the proponents of biopsychiatry represent the same awful lineage as the Nazi eugenicists. The following excerpt is from a speech he delivered on February 11, 1992, to the National Health Advisory Council, on the unveiling of the Federal Violence Initiative. Goodwin's quote is not an abusive anomaly; it is a faith-full expression of the thoroughly flawed, morally bereft, and dangerous biopsychiatric worldview underlying psychiatric oppression. It graphically reveals the same distorted view of social Darwinism that guided the Nazis:

> "If you look, for example, at male monkeys, especially in the wild, roughly half of them survive to adulthood. The other half die by violence. That is the natural way of it for males, to knock each other off and, in fact, there are some interesting evolutionary implications of that because the same hyperaggressive monkeys who kill each other are also hypersexual, so they copulate more and therefore they reproduce more to offset the fact that half of them are dying.
>
> Now, one could say that if some of the loss of social structure in this society, and particularly within the high impact inner cities have removed some of the civilizing evolutionary things that we have built up and that maybe it isn't just the careless use of the word when people call certain areas of certain cities jungles, that we may have gone back to what might be more natural, without all of the social controls that we have imposed upon ourselves as a civilization over thousands of years in our own evolution." (15)

CHAPTER 3
LOOKING BACK

"Well then, maybe it would be worth mentioning the three periods of history. When man believed that happiness was dependent upon God, he killed for religious reasons. When he believed that happiness was dependent upon the form of government, he killed for political reasons ... After dreams that were too long, true nightmares ... we arrived at the present period of history. Man woke up, discovered that which we always knew, that happiness is dependent upon health, and began to kill for therapeutic reasons ... It is medicine that has come to replace both religion and politics in our time." — Adolfo Bioy Casares (1)

Psychiatric oppression wreaks enormous harm on humankind.

Assume with me for the moment that the above sentence is true and that the practices of biopsychiatry are as damaging as I have argued. If biopsychiatry is so awful, how does it have so much legitimacy in a society which prides itself on enlightened democracy and humanitarian treatment of its troubled citizens? One perspective is to survey history as a never-ending story of war, of violence perpetrated by humans upon humans, over and over again, with every manner of justification. Add the wide variety of other social injustices such as inequality of wealth, poverty and neglect of our children, and a burgeoning prison industry, and it is easy to view psychiatric oppression as more the norm than anything else. My experience, however, is that even those who see hypocrisy in the great distance between political rhetoric and social reality on most issues of social justice tend not to see or be aware of psychiatric oppression. Why is this? Why don't people see it?

Most of us rarely see anything objectively. We see what we expect to see, what we are conditioned to see. If this sounds far-fetched, consider the intriguing little research study which had a masked intruder barge unexpectedly through a university classroom; there were as many differing descriptions and interpretations of the event as there were witnesses. As another example, think about times when you react to someone's words in a very different way than they intended, or vice versa when a friend misinterprets your communication. We see what we already believe inside of ourselves, and our actions are guided by the beliefs we hold on a very deep level.

Looking back at history yields as many different interpretations as there are individuals who do the looking back. A question inevitably leads to more questions than answers. So my purpose is a humble one. It involves going back only as far as the 16th century to help illuminate the question of how and why we see in such a way that biopsychiatric practices somehow make sense to us, or at least fit with the way we experience and understand reality.

Our Philosophical Soil

Western culture as we know it today grew from a base of Judeo-Christian theology in which human beings were seen as shameful, fallen sinners. In 16th century Europe, the Inquisition and the horrific torture and killing of women as witches was underway. Human beings saw themselves as a special creation of God, made in His image, and placed in the center of the universe. Being at the center and bearing the stamp of divinity, however, presented an ideal of perfection which was exceedingly difficult to live up to. Theodore Roszak, in his book on ecopsychology, 'The Voice of the Earth', describes the official cosmology or world view:

> "And in the Judaeo-Christian tradition, the teaching is that mankind failed in that assignment. In the old geocentric astronomy, after all, the center of the universe was the bottom of the universe, a vale of tears, a den of iniquity. Christian theology interpreted this to be the proper home of a flawed and fallen creature, one that had many sins to work off, many failures to make good. In the Christianized Ptolemaic world-system, heaven and the angels in their perfection were at the distant perimeter; the Earth was the cesspool of creation; it was regarded, in the words of one sixteenth-century theologian, as 'so depraved and broken in all kinds of vices and abominations that it seemeth to be a place that hath received all the filthiness and purgings of all other worlds and ages.' The lowest level of creation lay at the core of the Earth itself; it was called Hell, the point most hopelessly distant from God. In his 'Divine Comedy', Dante was even more explicit. The exact dead center of the universe was Satan's anus frozen forever into the icy foundations of perdition. Centrality was hardly a laudatory status." (2)

Our inherited theology set body and nature apart from soul, and attacked women (who remembered the ways of "natural" medicine and midwifery, who gave birth and nursed babies) as embodiments of sinful nature. Human beings were shameful, fallen sinners living in the cesspool of creation; clearly the only hope for salvation was "wholly other" from nature and our own natural bodies.

It is essential to recognize the core beliefs that we are shameful beings and that we deserve punishment; the emotions which go with these beliefs are called fear and shame. Shame is an awful feeling, associated with the belief that one is inherently flawed and defective. Both shame and fear are desperate inner states, leading to desperate outer actions striving to assert control over the world and over people, to avoid constantly perceived threats of punishment or exposure as a shameful being. The Inquisition was not only a natural result of Christian theology, it was also a natural action of a people living with intense levels of shame and fear.

From Religion to Science

The nineteenth and twentieth centuries witnessed a coming forth of scientific reason, the age of enlightenment. Mankind prided itself in the development of a growing knowledge of the world and gradually turned to science as source of hope and optimism in the quest to assert dominion in a dangerous existence. It is important to understand that this dramatic shift from "superstitious" religious beliefs to "rational" scientific beliefs did little or nothing to affect the foundational conditioning of humans as unworthy and inadequate creatures; it only transferred this core state of shame and fear from theological rhetoric to a denatured objectivity. The Industrial Revolution provided incredible means to amplify the situation by a rapid shift from rural to urban life. Roszak calls these very recent blips in our planet's history "City Pox," declaring that these urban concentrations are "declarations of a wishful biological independence from the natural environment ... the modern city ... the ancient dream of a totally encapsulated existence free of disease, dependency, the dirt and discomfort of organic life, perhaps even finally of death". (3) It is no wonder that the result is increasing social isolation and urban decay when we are driven by a vision that we are fallen sinners or mere accidents in a random mechanistic universe, "strangers and afraid in a world we never made."

Neither Christian theology nor scientific rationalism and their psychological correlates can, of course, be separated from the surrounding social and institutional structures of Church and State. History could simply be seen as a progression from slave to feudal to capitalist class-based societies, different forms but all upholding the reality of a small privileged few living at a much higher standard, a the expense of the rest. In the sixteenth and seventeenth century, the Inquisitors not only punished sinners to save their souls, but in so doing asserted and defended the powe of the ruling class. The Church was an extremely powerful agent of social control.

However, the power of the Church was gradually eroded as theology was challenged by developing science. Nonetheless, science did not significantly alter humankind' underlying feelings of shame and fear. The compulsion to control a dangerous and unpredictable world remained strong, as did the economic and political desires of the ruling class. Thomas Szasz provides a brilliant analysis of the way that psychiatry replaced religion as the primary institutional agency of social control in his masterpiece, 'The Manufacture of Madness: A Comparative Study of the

Inquisition and the Mental Health Movement.' (4) Szasz takes the Inquisition as a starting point, clearly documenting the torturing and killing of hundreds of thousands, probably millions of individual "heretics," mostly women accused of witchcraft, and Jews. He then traces the shift in worldview as science replaced theology as guiding principle; focus on religious salvation of sinners was replaced by concern with eradication of "mental illness" in patients. Psychiatry became a secular priesthood, and inherited from the Roman Catholic Church the social control function of punishing deviance. Szasz offered a brief summation by way of metaphor: The Inquisition is to heresy as Psychiatry is to mental illness.

On Selection

The history of psychiatric oppression consists of a pseudo-scientific, medical justification for perpetuating the Inquisitional practices of selecting out deviant (now "sick," formerly "sinful") individuals for coercive treatment. Fearful, distrusting and insecure in their existence, the Inquisitors were driven to emphasize the absolute truth and necessity of their one and only true faith by eradicating heresy. They desperately needed heretics to validate the goodness and authenticity of the Church they represented. They needed scapegoats, and they found them or created them in large numbers. Szasz points out that the Inquisitors saw two ways to handle heretics selected out for persecution (attempted salvation); the heretical soul was either converted to believe and profess the proper faith, or killed to purge the devil from the earth and protect the faithful who remained.

The key word is selection. Once selected, the treatment is a given, diagnosis merely a justification. The Inquisitors, like other generations before and after, feared the Other and tried to destroy it; paradoxically, they also desperately needed the Other, and would create it if necessary, so that by exterminating evil, they felt themselves as good. The first step is to identify the Other; the need was to select individual scapegoats, called heretics. For the Inquisitors, it was the Jews, and then the witches. The 'Malleus Maleficarum (The Hammer of Witches)', 1486, affirmed that "the belief that there are such things as witches is so essential a part of the Catholic faith that obstinately to maintain the opposite opinion manifestly savors of heresy." (5) Sixteen German editions, eleven French, two Italian and several English attest to the importance of this manual; hundreds of thousands of deaths attest to its effectiveness. Identifying the Other was accomplished by eliciting confessions through means which have been faithfully copied by the secret police of modern totalitarian states. Representatives of coercive psychiatry improve upon it by acting as if and believing that they are friends and allies of "patients;" refusal to "cooperate" is interpreted as a sign of "mental illness" and coercion for the patient's own good is completely justified.

The second principal method for identifying witches was to find witch's marks on the body of the accused. These marks presumably indicated a spot on which the possessor was branded by the Devil. Given that we all have marks, this search was almost always fruitful; nevertheless, a backup assured the task. Physicians, known as witch-prickers, searched for invisible marks made by the devil which were revealed when a pin prick resulted in neither blood nor pain. The diagnostic machinations of modern psychiatry (see next chapter) allow as much leeway and ambiguity as any system possibly could; there is no human alive who could not be diagnosed, probably with several unique disorders, as "mentally ill."

Test by "swimming" was a popular seventeenth century method in England. The accused witch was restrained and thrown into the water. If she floated, she was guilty; if she sank, she was innocent. That the latter usually resulted in drowning was not a problem since her soul went to heaven. Szasz argues that the results of modern diagnostics closely resemble the swimming ordeal. He states that "In more than twenty years of psychiatric work, I have never known a clinical psychologist to report, on the basis of a projective test, that the subject is a 'normal, mentally healthy person.' While some witches may have survived dunking, no 'madman' survives psychological testing." (6) My own experience has taught me the related truth that it is the rare child selected out for testing of so-called Attention Deficit Disorder who is not labeled as "mentally ill." Research clearly validates that there is a presumption of "mental illness" by mental health officials, and that it is rare for judges to not go along with a psychiatrist's opinion that an individual needs "treatment." (7)

The Inquisitors presumed guilt; psychiatry presumes "mental illness." What makes Inquisitors and psychiatrists so dangerous is that in both cases the government authenticates and justifies their actions. These discretionary powers are granted largely due to the fact that Inquisitors and psychiatrists, each in their time, were seen not as punishing persecutors but as healing helpers. Szasz points out that the pious Inquisitor would have been outraged at the suggestion that he was the heretic's foe, not his potential savior. In our modern days, there is no more surefire way to elicit a psychiatrist's rage than to suggest he is the adversary of his involuntary patient.

Just as the Church had state support to perpetrate the horrors of the Inquisition, psychiatry was granted the power to perpetrate all the horrors which collectively constitute the history of psychiatry. In so doing, Western society's need for social control and censure of deviancy has been served, as has been the need to avoid examination of oppressive and exploitive practices. As Szasz reveals, psychiatry re-interpreted the Inquisition not as an act of oppression against individuals who did not pay homage and conform to institutional power; rather, it was simply a case of misdiagnosis. Consider the following quotation by Jan Ehrenwald, an American psychiatrist:

"Far from recognizing their plight for what it was, the witch hunters and exorcists fought the witches' delusions on the level of the deluded, and whenever the patient failed to respond to exorcism by persuasion, prayer or the sacraments, they saw no choice but to resort to their own brand of shock treatment: burning at the stake." (8)

Psychiatry agreed that torture and killing were wrong but the real problem was the diagnosis. The selected women weren't witches, but they were "mentally ill" and in need of "treatment."

Society is continually absolved from the responsibility of looking at oppressive practices; people who are hurt are viewed not as victims of oppression but of "mental illness." History has shown that the agents of oppression, mental health professionals, are absolved of their refusal to embark on the great and painful challenge of realizing their dilemma. Psychiatric oppression, like all oppression, involves a mutual hurt. "Patients" are hurt by "treatment" psychiatrists inflict; psychiatrists not only remain unaware of how they have been hurt to be cast in such a role, but also suffer an ongoing moral hurt they impose on themselves as agents of a doctrine which offers so few options for humane care. Inquisitors were passionately convinced of the need, indeed moral imperative, of coercively saving the possessed souls of heretics. Psychiatrists and other professionals are often just as passionately convinced of the dire need, indeed moral imperative, of coercively treating their "mentally ill" patients.

Biopsychiatry and Nazi Germany

Perhaps the most impassioned moral imperative, one of very recent history, was that of Adolf Hitler and his Third Reich when the Nazi regime mandated the creation of a pure race. Hitler's philosophic dogma of eliminating defective individuals (those who were not healthy and productive Aryans) evolved into the infamous 'Final Solution', a horrific holocaust which tortured and destroyed millions. The Third Reich perfected the use of propaganda, and Hitler was a master of virulent rhetoric which resonated with Germany's residue of fear and shame from a long history of war, migration and suffering. The Holocaust is one of our most vivid and dramatic examples of fear and shame-based efforts of social control. Due to the ceaseless efforts of a small group of determined people such as Nazi hunter Simon Weisenthal, humankind has been required to face and remember the Holocaust. We have had to fashion some sort of explanation for the monstrous evil. While most still evade a full accounting by laying blame at the feet of Adolf Hitler, many of us grapple with the larger question of how so many ordinary human citizens could participate in or turn their backs on such unspeakable cruelty.

Virtually every corner of Hitler's life has, in fact, been thoroughly investigated. The philosophy on which the Nazi ideology was based has remained obscure, however. Hitler came to power in 1933; six years later, he openly announced his plan for the "extermination of the Jewish race in Europe." These were the times of scientific progress and expansion of the Industrial Revolution. Remember that psychiatry, under the guise of scientific medical rhetoric, was the successor to religion as enforcer of social norms. I present here the fact that psychiatry provided the philosophical and theoretical rationale for the "racial hygiene" practices of Nazi Germany. Fredric Wertham wrote a powerful expose in 1966, but it is largely in the last decade that this information has surfaced, primarily through the efforts of a few dauntless researchers such as Lenny Lapon and Benno Muller-Hill. (9) The men behind Hitler were psychiatrists who not only provided a pseudoscientific theory to justify the hideous Nazi practices, but also actively encouraged and participated in the tortuous activities. A recent book, 'Psychiatry: The Men Behind Hitler' by Röder, Kubillus, and Burwell, provides a most clear and thorough documentation of the role of psychiatry in Nazi Germany, and convincingly demonstrates that the Holocaust was not an anomaly but a logical conclusion of a theory and perspective which still guides psychiatry today.

It is important also to acknowledge the history of racial hygiene in the United States. The theories of Thomas Malthus and James Darwin shaped the direction of biological science. These theories of population growth and natural selection appealed to influential philosophers who espoused seminal theories of racial inequality and "social Darwinism" or "survival of the fittest" applied to human beings. The turn of the century in the United States witnessed a significant eugenics movement, organized by Charles Davenport. As director of the Carnegie Institution's Station for Experimental Evaluation and acting with seed money from a wealthy widow of a railroad tycoon, he founded the Eugenics Record Office (ERO). Harry Laughlin was ERO's superintendent from 1910 to 1940, and helped promote the two main objectives of the American eugenics movement:

a. an immigration policy restricting non-Nordic immigration;

b. enactment of laws for compulsory sterilization of the "socially inadequate."

Laughlin defined "socially inadequate" as "one who ... fails chronically ... to maintain himself or herself as a useful member of the organized social life of the state ... " He categorized ten classes of the "socially inadequate," including feeble-minded, insane, criminalistic, epileptic, inebriate, diseased, deaf, deformed and dependent.10 The developing "science" of genetics and racial hygiene was insufficient, however, to convince people with unfavorable genetic traits to undergo voluntary sterilizations.

Laughlin was an ardent activist; he assisted sympathizers in getting legislation passed in various states by drafting a model Eugenical Sterilization Law. The law was designed for all persons who because of defective genetics were seen as potential parents of socially inadequate offspring. In 1905, Pennsylvania passed the first law, "an act for the prevention of idiocy." Eighteen states had passed compulsory sterilization measures by 1912; by 1940, 30 states had such laws on their books, and over 100,000 sterilizations had been forcibly performed on American citizens by our own government.

Concurrently in Germany, psychiatry became obsessed with genetics as the key to improving the human race, and played a major role in marrying eugenics to the racist ideology of the Third Reich. Ernst Rüdin was an especially prominent German psychiatrist who worked hard to make racial hygiene as acceptable as possible. In 1911, he co-authored a study on population called 'Procreation, Transmission, Racial Hygiene' which stated:

"All nations have to haul around with them an extraordinary large number of inferiors, weaklings, sickly and cripples ... The demand for the organization of systematic data is the next item that racial hygiene has to put on the state administration ... It is not enough to have a moral awakening ... of a truly national sentiment and lifestyle. Hopefully the time is not far away when lawmakers will realize that the people(are rewarded) ... for this service by the procreation of a strong next generation. Through a wise legislation along this line ... we would also be able to pursue rationally the best avenues for breeding. Voluntary sterility of physical and moral inferiors would then go without saying!" (11)

In 1920, two German scholars — psychiatrist Alfred Hoche, and doctor of law and philosophy Karl Binding — published a sensational paper on euthanasia entitled 'The Permission to Destroy Life Unworthy of Living', in which they stated:

1/ The suffering of a sick or wounded person who is about to die can be shortened through the use of a medical drug.

2/ This acceleration of the death process is not an act of murder but "in truth a pure act of healing." (This justification was later used specifically by the Nazis in defense of their extermination programs).

3/ A doctor should be able to employ euthanasia on any unconscious person without legal consequences.

4/ There are people who are worthless to society. Primary among these are the inmates of the 'idiot institutes', who are 'not only worthless, but of absolutely negative value.'

5/ The incurably dumb who can neither agree to survive or to be killed should be killed. Their death will not be missed in the least except maybe in the hearts of their mother or guardian ... When we become more advanced, we will probably be saving those poor humans from themselves.' This was intended to be the scientific justification for the murders being advocated. Ethical matters were to be figured out later. (12)

In May, 1930, Ernst Rüdin gave a lecture at the First International Congress of Mental Hygiene in Washington, D.C. on 'The Importance of Eugenics and Genetics in Mental Hygiene.' Here is a sample of Rüdin's 1930 writing:

> "We have to do something about the positive and negative eugenics before it is too late. For the negative, the sterilization of the genetically sick has to be closely looked at ... It would be a blessing to know that genetically incompetent, unhappy people would not be produced anymore. Much more national expansion would be created through positive eugenics than we can imagine.
>
> The fertility rate of the genetically undesirables is so great today that we have every reason in the interest of humanity to address ourselves to the prevention of the genetically weak. The increase of the hereditarily healthy that is so necessary to us as a nation today will cause us less of a headache in the future." (13)

On January 20, 1933, Adolf Hitler was elected

Chancellor of the Reich. The first concentration camp at Dachau was established on March 22, 1933. Less than four months later, on July 14, 1933, the Law for the Prevention of Genetically Diseased Children was passed. Rüdin was one of three scientists who composed the legal argument for this act and its main proponent. This law, which cleared the path for wholesale euthanasia, was taken almost verbatim from Laughlin's Model Eugenical Sterilization Law. German decisions about "life unworthy of living" followed almost the exact same guidelines. Another psychiatrist, Werner Heyde, was one of the chief organizers of the euthanasia program and became psychiatric head of all of the concentration camps in 1936.

Psychiatry provided the scientific theory and the moral imperative for the Holocaust. Psychiatrists led the way in philosophy and in action. An estimated 100,000 psychiatric patients were murdered before Hitler came to power; according to Wertham, the most reliable, conservative estimates of the total numbers of psychiatric patients killed are at least 275,000. (14) Compulsory sterilization of between 100,000 and 350,000 in 1934 and 1935 gave way to the first systematic transfers of the "mentally ill" to concentration camps by 1936, the beginning of Heyde's tenure as psychiatric head of the camps. A psychiatric facility called the Working Association of Sanitariums and Caretaking Facilities of the Republic (known by the infamous code name of T4) served as euthanasia headquarters. T4 was not only the forerunner of ensuing mass extermination of beings deemed unfit, but was actually the ongoing nerve center of the extermination campaign. Heyde was the director, supervising a consulting staff of 30 mostly psychiatric physicians. These psychiatric euthanasia consultants marked those who were to be killed, and were well-paid for their efforts, their income directly proportional to the number of death sentences issued. By 1941, eminent physicians and psychiatrists began to visit the concentration camps (KZs) where, according to one psychiatrist, "the killing in the KZs went along the exact same lines and with the same registration forms as in the insane asylums." Roder et al conclude that "it ran like a well-oiled machine because the sick and the infirm of the asylums had served as a ghoulish dress rehearsal." (15) Psychiatric hospitals acted as training ground and preparation for the Holocaust. Academic psychiatry institutes sought and received "material" for research; for example, the prominent Kaiser Wilhelm Institute for Brain Research in Berlin received nearly 700 brains of murdered victims.

So there you have the well-kept, yet well-documented secret of psychiatry's prominent role in the Holocaust, directly attributable to the pseudoscientific theory of biopsychiatry and to its evangelical believers and practitioners. Beyond these events, however, there is a related secret regarding the psychiatric perpetrators of these horrors. Röder et al show that the majority of these men not only escaped punishment, but actually resumed or assumed prominent positions of leadership in the psychiatric community. These authors make this point chillingly clear by reviewing a host of the past presidents of the Society of German Neurologists and Psychiatrists. These include Ernst Rüdin, the aforementioned "father" of Racial Hygiene, president from 1935 to 1945, and T4 consultants Werner Villinger, president from 1952 to 1954, and Friedrich Mauz, president from 1957 to 1958. The basic thrust of biopsychiatric theory (eugenics) and practice (selection and coercion) was maintained intact and dominant in German psychiatry through post-war times and up to this very day.

The career of Ernst Rüdin, whose resume could be seen as an indictment for crimes against mankind, serves to highlight this phenomenon. On his 65th birthday in 1939, Rüdin was awarded the Goethe Medal for Art and Science by Adolf Hitler. Five years later, the Fuhrer personally honored Rüdin with a bronze Swastika medal and the honorary title of 'Pioneer of Racial Hygiene'.'In February 1992, the prestigious Max Planck Institute for Molecular Genetics, the modern successor to the Kaiser Wilhelm Institute mentioned above, praised Rüdin for "following his own convictions in racial hygienic measures, cooperating with the Nazis as a psychiatrist and helping them legitimize their aims through pertinent legislation." (16)

An American organization, the National Alliance for Research on Schizophrenia and Depression (NARSAD) celebrated the growth of "psychiatric genetics" in a 1990 newsletter, honoring Ernst Rüdin as the founder. Major forces shaping American social sciences can be traced through educational lineage to Germany. Psychiatric, psychological and educational leaders around the turn of the century looked to advanced and prestigious German institutes for training and brought their theories and practices to the United States. German psychiatrist émigrés to the United States in the 1920s and 1930s included Franz Kallmann, whose 1939 study, 'The Genetics of Schizophrenia', was simultaneously published in Germany and the United States. Kallmann was obsessed with the sterilization of anyone even remotely associated with schizophrenia, demanding the sterilization of the schizophrenic's children and siblings, and even marriage partner and children. Benno Muller-Hill quotes Dr

Kallman's last speech in Germany, at the International Congress of Population Problems, in 1935: "It is desirable to extend prevention of reproduction to relatives of schizophrenics who stand out because of minor anomalies, and above all, to define each of them as being undesirable from the eugenic point of view at the beginning of their reproductive years." (17) This man became the most influential geneticist in the world, and later became president of the American Society for Human Genetics.

American eugenics and biopsychiatry resonate as well with American racism and elitism and economic considerations as they do with German. Roder et al list a few of the other émigrés to America:

Lothar Kalinowsky, pioneer of electroshock

Franz Alexander, a leading German psychiatrist

Erich Lindemann, a military psychiatrist who experimented with truth drugs

Heinz Lehmann, a strong proponent of drug therapy

Sandor Rado, Professor of Psychiatry at the Berlin Psychoanalytic Institute

Zigmund Lebensohn, who would train military psychiatrists

Paul Hoch, who worked with Kallmann and Kalinowsky at the New York Psychiatric Institute and later in CIA mind control programs

The authors give detailed information about many of these individuals. Of particular interest is the fact that another German-trained psychiatrist who emigrated before the war, Leo Alexander (unrelated to Franz) became an American military psychiatrist who investigated Nazi war crimes at Nuremberg. According to Roder et al, Alexander wrote about his investigations without once mentioning the role psychiatrists played in the instigation of and participation in the Holocaust murders. At the same time, he published papers promoting the use of data gathered by experimentation on prisoners in concentration camps. Historian Muller-Hill noted in 1988:

> "Almost no one stopped to think that something could be wrong with psychiatry, with anthropology, or with behavioral science. The international scientific establishment reassured their German colleagues that it had indeed been the unpardonable misconduct of a few individuals, but that it lay outside the scope of science. The pattern of German anthropology, psychiatry and behavioral science continued essentially unchanged, and it will continue so, unless a substantial number of scientists begin to have doubts and ask questions." (18)

The American Asylum

Ernst Rüdin and the other apostles of racial hygiene in Germany and in the United States, like the Inquisitors, sincerely believed that their philosophy and practices were for the betterment of humankind. While the biological theories of Malthus and Darwin provided fodder for scientific justification of racist oppression, the age of enlightenment and reason also led to another dramatic trend in the United States. The founders of American psychiatry supported eugenics, on the one hand, believing in "mental illness" as a neurological or biological, genetically-based disease. At the same time, however, there blossomed forth a fervent reform movement, ironically guided by another German influence, the teachings of Wilhelm Wundt, which formed the cornerstone of psychology taught in American universities. The prevailing psychological theory was that the mind operated by association, rather than inherited ideas. So, while genetics was a factor, determinants of mental status had to do with what were called "exciting causes." "Mental illness" still meant a diseased brain, but the effect was largely due to noxious, disabling effects of too much or the wrong kind of stimulation.

An impassioned post-Civil War reform movement was convinced that vice was the cause of crime and stress the source of insanity. David Rothman's book, 'The Discovery of the Asylum', brilliantly reveals the tremendous fear citizens felt in these days of a rapidly-burgeoning Industrial Revolution. Theirs was a sincere desire to upgrade the treatment of the "mentally ill." Inspired by images like Philippe Pinel freeing the insane from their chains at Salpetriere in France, Americans could relate to freedom from bondage and desired to bring freedom to others. The reformers sincerely believed in the idea of gentler, more humane treatment of the "mentally ill;" their thinking, however, was heavily tinged with fear. Against the norms of Puritan colonialism, the Jacksonian times appeared chaotic. Medical authorities, carrying the same anxiety as the rest and representing the upper classes in the social order, "were certain that their society lacked all elements of fixity and cohesion because they judged it by a nostalgic image of the eighteenth century. Frightened by an awareness that the old order was passing and with little notion of what would replace it, they defined the realities about them as corrupting, provoking madness. The root of their difficulty was that they still adhered to the precepts of traditional social theory, to the ideas that they had inherited from the colonial period. By these standards, men were to take their rank in the hierarchy, know their place in society, and not to change positions." (19) The prescription for a well-ordered society, one that would not generate insanity, flowed from this.

As is the pattern with great movements, including the Inquisition and the Third Reich, the ideological rhetoric intensified as reformers lamented the chaotic decline of a moral order in society. Fear was played upon with persistent warnings of an epidemic of "mental illness;" an almost hysterical sense of peril was conveyed, the very safety of the republic and its citizens was at stake. And there was absolutely no room for the shadow of a doubt that the medical authorities knew an infallible cure. The cure was to draw on the proverbial "good old days;" in this case, obedience, precision, neatness, orderliness, regularity and discipline were the necessary antidotes to a social disorganization which bred madness. As the reformers were not able to reverse the trends of a society so wildly out of control, they logically opted for the creation of alternative models of social order. They concluded that since the society around the "mentally ill" individual was hopelessly disorganized, the best and only hope was to remove the affected individual from the over excitement of excess freedom, stimulation and responsibility. Thus, the asylum was born on an immense scale. I hope this playing on fear of "mental illness" to justify coercive "treatment" has a familiar feel to the reader. It is ubiquitous in our language and in the media today.

These institutions were built with great attention given to the enunciation of elaborate detail in how to create a facility affording the ideal well-ordered environment necessary to convey the curative effects of "moral treatment." Some of the initial efforts, though not in keeping with the consistent boasts of a virtually 100 percent cure rate by medical superintendents, were actually at least partly successful in offering gentler, more humane care. By 1870, however, even the best of facilities designed in the 1830s had suffered dramatic decline. The reality was all too often more like a dungeon than a well-ordered retreat, patients systematically subjected to every imaginable form of deprivation and suffering.

Failed expectations in no way obviated the usefulness of the insane asylum to public policy. A caretaker operation was quite satisfactory to legislators and to the public as a way of dealing with the "insane," particularly since the demise of almshouses; the significant numbers of lower class and foreign-born patients is also indicative. The practice of eugenics, promoted by the likes of Charles Davenport and Harry Laughlin, resulted in the involuntary sterilization of 45,127 "insane" or "feebleminded" persons in the United States by 1949; 467 institutionalized persons were sterilized involuntarily as late as 1963. The scientific prevention of social ills is a powerful motivation, regardless of the cost. At the same time as these forced sterilizations were occurring, the population of state mental hospitals dramatically expanded, from 150,000 to 445,000 between 1903 and 1940; its peak was 550,000 in 1955. (20) The United States, through the practice of psychiatry, was engaging in compulsory sterilization of tens of thousands and dungeon-like torture of hundreds of thousands of its own citizens during the same years as the Third Reich was developing and enacting the horrors of the Holocaust. Insulin coma treatment was common practice in the 1940s. Routine use of electroshock to manage "patients," even electroshocking entire wards, continued well after the war. (21)

Lest the reader think my use of the expression

"dungeon-like torture" is exaggerated, I quote Albert Deutsch from his 1948 book, 'The Shame of the States', which, together with Mary Jane Ward's 'The Snakepit' played a large part in exposing the horrors of our state mental hospitals:

> "Most of them were located in or near great centers of culture in our wealthier states such as New York, Michigan, Ohio, California and Pennsylvania. In some of the wards there were scenes that rivaled the horrors of the Nazi concentration camps — hundreds of naked mental patients herded into huge, barn-like, filth-infested wards, in all degrees of deterioration, untended and untreated, stripped of every vestige of human decency, many in stages of semi-starvation.
>
> "The writer heard state hospital doctors frankly admit that the animals of nearby piggeries were better fed, housed and treated than many of the patients in their wards. He saw hundreds of sick people shackled, strapped, straitjacketed and bound to their beds; he saw mental patients ... crawl into beds jammed close together, in dormitories filled to twice or three times their normal capacity."

Asylum

While I have just provided a brief description of the American asylum, French social historian Michel Foucault analyzed in depth the rise of the asylum during the so-called Age of Reason in Europe. Particularly during the late eighteenth and early nineteenth century, madhouses began to proliferate. (22) These perverse institutions were created under a rhetoric of human enlightenment, understanding and caring. It is a mistake to consider them no more than a historical anomaly. While changes have occurred, a close look at our wards, at heavily drugged patients, at the practitioners and victims of electroshock, at involuntary commitment proceedings, at all of psychiatry, reveals that not very much has improved. The fact is that psychiatry continues to create asylums and to inflict great harm masked in a posture and rhetoric of benevolence.

To explore how this can be, we need to clearly define the hallmark characteristics of an "asylum." These are not the specific practices because they vary; these characteristics refer instead to the structure inherent in the space and in the relationships within the space. Regarding space, the defining characteristic of an asylum, based on results such as I just revealed regarding the rapid filling and overcrowding of American asylums, is that it must be filled. Regarding the philosophy/science underlying the whole affair, as I attempt to reveal throughout this book, the treatment theory is based on ignorance. Finally, the most important defining characteristic of the asylum is coercion, the same most defining characteristic of psychiatry. The result is techniques of relating to people that are harmful and punishing.

So how is it really that we continue to produce the environment of a "lunatic asylum?" Dr Edward Podvoll says, and I agree, that "It is because creating an asylum stems from a particular state of mind, an asylum mentality, which can resurface anytime and anywhere and recapitulate the history of the asylum." (23) The asylum mentality is essentially about power, about exerting "therapeutic" power over others. Podvoll provides a brilliant analysis of the manifestations of asylum mentality, which I quote below:

1/ Asylum preserves what is called "nonreciprocal observation." One is observed without being able to observe properly. One's state of mind — mistakes, awkwardness, and transgressions — is catalogued, diagnosed, and studied; whereas one's own observations are held in suspicion and doubt and are called unsound, resistance, arrogance, transference, and the like. An examination by the insane of their conditions, including the state of mind and therapeutic intentions of all their caretakers, is more or less prohibited. It is a situation bound to evoke paranoia.

2/ Asylum mind treats illness as childhood. It relegates the asylum confinees to the status of minors — intellectually, morally, judicially. This prejudice stems from what is known as the "damage theory" of psychosis, that people in psychosis are undeveloped, arrested, deficient, or defective. It lays the foundation for a wide variety of treatment theories and beliefs as to what can be expected from "recovery." Most of all, it excuses insufficient care.

3/ Asylum embodies the idea that madness must first be subjugated for recovery to take place. In the words of Samuel Tuke — a reformer who tried valiantly to break out of the asylum tradition, only to create a more subtle asylum called "moral treatment" — insane people need to be "dominated." The mind of insanity must learn to bow before the superior power of reason and logic.

4/ Asylum manifests in an organization of people whose hierarchy is based on a conviction of its moral sovereignty over the insane. This involves a further notion of the subjugation of insanity. One is to be cured within a moral social order based on the principle of the bourgeois patriarchal family. The asylums that practice "moral treatment" emulate that structure and try to refine it into a perfected family institution. It was meant to be a new, ideal asylum, but it carried with it many of the restrictions of old asylums.

5/ Asylum is a moral domain where recovery is measured against many differing notions of "mental health." Wherever there is insanity, issues of "spirituality" arise. In the Victorian asylums, the principles of the established church were the measures of sanity. Perceval (see Chapter 12 on the natural function of doubt) observed that the spirituality professed by doctors was so uninformed and narrow-minded that they hardly recognized that most people in psychosis were involved in a variety of life-threatening spiritual crises. When the medical view of sanity and psychosis came to ascendance, a seemingly ageless understanding of insanity as a spiritual crisis was lost. Asylum mind sees spirituality as "religiosity" and as dangerous to the welfare of the patient. Yet it does not hesitate to promote and enforce its own ideologies about sanity, in therapeutic environments whose various social designs incorporate the whole spectrum of religious and political beliefs.

6/ Asylum is a place of refuge. It rescues people from degraded, animal-like environments and brings them into social conditions of a higher order. This principle arose from a growing understanding that madness springs from a diseased or problematic environment of some kind. Asylum mind poses itself as the rescuer, to which one should be grateful and obedient. It has to distinguish itself from a patient's previous life by ignoring and belittling the richness, energy, and seduction of insane worlds.

7/ Asylum, with or without walls, views madness in all its expressions as a primitive arrogance, an insufferable presumption, which sporadically arises in the human condition. And it must be punished. Michel Foucault traces this therapeutic belief to the Inquisition: "His torment is his glory, his deliverance must humiliate him." Such a theory justifies brutal and constraining treatment of all kinds, as a necessity.

The most subtle form of asylum mind has been called the "silence that humiliates," a studied interpersonal rift between doctor and patient. The professional separation between them creates a loneliness and silence for the patient in which to reflect on madness — to intensify it, so that it might mock itself. Asylum mind demands a confession to the error of arrogance and to the ancient crime of spiritual self-exaggeration; its goal is for the patient himself to come to believe that his suffering harsh treatment is deserved and necessary for recovery. A residue of guilt is meant to last far into the future, to be an armor and reminder against any excessive self-presumption in the future.

Many early asylum directors worked diligently with their staff to design ways and means of mockery, to humiliate and thus bring a patient to his senses. From this has come some treatment plans that prescribe the outright terrorizing of patients, in order to inspire a fear that might shock them to their senses. The asylum belief is that recovery cannot take place without sufficient inner self-mortification and an attitude of apology. But that does not occur; instead, outrage and defiance in an asylum culture was, and is, rampant.

8/ Finally, asylum is fundamentally a medical space. Somewhere at the turn of the eighteenth century, medical specialists took complete responsibility for the care of the insane. This new territory was even royally sanctioned when the lunatic doctors were given full authority to treat George III. Their status was assured. From that point on, the lunatic doctor assumed the privilege of deciding who was insane and could commit someone to an asylum merely by his signature. (24)

Asylum reality flows from asylum mentality. Given that none of us appear to be entirely immune from at least subtle appearance of asylum mentality, especially when faced with situations of dealing with the intense energy and emotions of someone in an extreme state of mind, what are we to do? Dr Podvoll has some very good advice. He suggests that one can engage in a practice based on an awareness of the subtle workings of asylum mentality described above. The practice is to train oneself to recognize it at an early moment and avoid slipping further into this dangerous and outmoded belief system. One can then cultivate a "healthy doubt" about how to treat an individual in severe distress.

Deinstitutionalization

A discussion of asylums would be incomplete without at least a brief consideration of the latter twentieth century phenomenon known as deinstitutionalization. Many Conscientious Objectors (COs) to World War II were sent to hospitals to perform their alternative to military services. The COs formed the National Mental Health Foundation to publicize the fact of inhumane care in mental hospitals. Such overt exposure of cruelty understandably led to a postwar sentiment that was pro-patient. Even though Menninger and others were having some success in arguing the case for preventive psychiatry, another term for mental hygiene, the profession was in trouble.

The die was cast for deinstitutionalization when the

states concurrently realized that hospital costs had to be contained. Meanwhile, rather than curb psychiatry's power after the "snake-pits" were publicly exposed, Congress created the National Institute of Mental Health (NIMH) in 1946 and continually boosted its appropriations by huge increments beginning in 1948. The remedy for deplorable hospital conditions was a much increased role for psychiatrists. Ironically, Albert Deutsch, in the very expose quoted above, lent his endorsement which, together with very effective lobbying by William Menninger and other military psychiatrists, helped the psychiatric profession to persuade Congress. Deutsch stated that: "It is because modern psychiatry is a stranger to so many hospital wards that many more patients don't return to their communities as cured." (25) Nazi and American psychiatrists, purveyors of unspeakable cruelties, were both not only absolved of responsibility for their crimes, but promoted to positions of power and privilege in their respective societies.

Ann Braden-Johnson, in her revealing book about deinstitutionalization, 'Out of Bedlam', writes that during a National Governor's conference in 1954, "representatives of all 48 states agreed that their states would almost certainly go bankrupt unless they did something with the chronically mentally ill other than continue to support them for life in state hospitals. But then medical science stepped forth, ready to revolutionize care for the 'mentally ill' with a wonderful new drug. The cure for mental illness had arrived just in time, and best of all, it took the form of a pill — small, easily administered, and inexpensive. It was what doctors call a 'clean' method — uncontroversial and unlikely to upset relatives and journalists, unlike lobotomy or shock treatment. In the general euphoria, no one cared to remember that only fifteen years earlier, lobotomy and shock treatment, too, had been touted as almost certain cures for mental illness." (26)

History reveals that lobotomy and electroshock would be touted again. And the magic pill was Thorazine, the first neuroleptic. The true miracle was not of medicine, but of modern marketing technique. The real result is horrendous. The evidence of Tardive Dyskinesia alone justifies Peter Breggin's statement that "Psychiatry has unleashed an epidemic of neurologic disease on the world." (27)

Much of deinstitutionalization involved turning over the burden of care that state hospitals had assumed for our nation's elderly. Beginning in 1965, nursing homes became able to collect Medicaid payments; large numbers of elderly patients left the state mental hospitals between 1965 and 1975, and by far the bulk of them wound up in nursing homes. Johnson cites a 1973 report by Grafton State Hospital (Massachusetts), revealing that deinstitutionalization really means re-institutionalization: "Of a total of 641, some 497 patients — some 78 percent — wound up in institutional settings. If we leave out those patients who died (8 percent), we find that only the remaining 14 percent can conceivably be said to have been deinstitutionalized." (28) A large portion of these discharges were to nursing or rest homes. See Chapter 13 for an example of how psychiatry continues to "treat" the elderly in nursing homes. However much asylum treatment was discredited, asylum mentality retains its power, and people keep getting unnecessarily hurt as a result.

Any honest effort to expose psychiatric oppression requires a cold hard look at the facts and a ruthless determination to pierce the illusory veil of biopsychiatry. The theory of biopsychiatry is that of mental hygiene and eugenics. It is a soulless reduction of human beings to "material" to be manipulated and shaped according to someone's judgments and economics. The realities are psychiatric leadership and collaboration in Nazi Germany, its subsequent denial and cover-up, and its unchecked progression after the war up to the present day. The realities are psychiatric leadership and collaboration in the degrading horrors of American asylums, subsequent whitewashing of responsibility, and unchecked progression of harmful biopsychiatric methods to the present day. Biopsychiatry is a misguided and heartless pseudoscience with horrific results, then and now, in Germany and in the United States. Rüdin and other Nazi psychiatrists were honored after perpetrating horrific cruelties. Psychiatry in the United States (the American Psychiatric Association) has the image of Benjamin Rush (the "father" of American psychiatry) on its official seal, thereby glorifying a man whose practices can most appropriately be described as cruel and barbaric. Psychiatry thus far has been completely unable and unwilling to look at itself responsibly and humanely. The Inquisitors were not stopped by other clergy. Slavery was not stopped by slave owners. The Holocaust was not stopped by Nazis. It is unlikely that psychiatric oppression will be stopped by psychiatrists. But like witch hunting, slavery and the Holocaust, it will be stopped. And the first step is to see it for what it is.

CHAPTER 4
ON LANGUAGE

> Once the whole is divided, the parts need names.
> There are already enough names.
> One must know when to stop.
> Knowing when to stop averts trouble.
> Tao in the world is like a river flowing home to the sea.
> — Lao Tsu (1)

The language of psychiatry incredibly obfuscates reality and acts as a powerful deterrent to clear vision and thinking. Any honest attempt at thinking about psychiatric oppression involves freeing oneself of unconscious conditioned behaviors. A first step in this process requires the use of more accurate language. Language allows us to operate in the world of abstract relations, while providing opportunities and great advantage in fluidity and flexibility of communication. Language also allows us to confuse reality. Removing us from immediate, concrete interaction with our physical universe, language can create unbelievably powerful illusions and delusions. Linguistic conceptions can be fabricated. They can be deliberate lies which are enforced as real. They can be mistakes which are enforced as real. They can be metaphors which are enforced as real. All too often, a concept is either deliberately suppressed or it is forgotten that it began as a lie, or an inaccuracy or a metaphor. It is the nature of oppression, in fact, that requires us to forget.

Psychiatric oppression is based on this dynamic; it thrives on fundamental epistemological errors. Psychiatry operates on the assumption that "mental illness" is a real thing, that it is something tangible like a cancer cell or a virus. It forgets that the concept of mental illness was created as a metaphor. To say that someone is "mentally ill" is a metaphor; it is a concept created to parallel physical illness. It has become a concept that carries incredible extra weight, weight that shows the power of language to obscure reality. Such mystification serves only one useful function; that of social control. An illustration:

An individual is "diagnosed" as having a "mental illness." The diagnosis is presented as if it were objective information, simply describing reality. The tendency of most people is to accept this "reality" without question. School indoctrination and media propaganda has been so effective that a 1990 federal law, the Americans with Disabilities Act, was enacted in order "to diminish the stigma of mental illness and reduce discrimination involving ... at least 60 million Americans between the ages of 18 and 64, [who] will experience a mental disorder during their lifetimes." (2) Given our cultural background, how can one possibly challenge this belief? And I do maintain that it is a belief, not a fact of science. The fact that the Inquisitors "knew" there were witches does not in fact prove the existence of witches; that we today "know" that "mental illness" is an epidemic "disease" does not prove the actual existence of this "disease." Of course, people show signs of psychological distress; the psychiatric translation of this int biological and/or genetic disease is on the order of a superstitious belief, merely an attempt to imitate the practice of physical medicine.

Psychologist Ty Colbert thoroughly and intelligently

details the failures of biopsychiatry in his 1996 work,
'Broken Brains or Wounded Hearts'. The following quote
sums up his data:

> "The truth is that researchers have never discovered a
> single defective gene or accurately identified any chemical
> imbalance that has caused an emotional disorder; nor have
> they ever proven that brain abnormalities are responsible
> for even one emotional disorder." (3)

In 'The Lexicon of Lunacy', Thomas Szasz lists a full 32
pages of synonyms for mental illness. An alphabetical
sampler includes addled, batty, crackers, daffy, empty
headed, freaky, ga-ga, haywire, idiot, jambled, kooky, loco,
muddled, noodle, odd, palooka, queer, rattlebrain,
screwball, troubled, unbalanced, vacant, wacko, yarmouth,
and zany. More dangerous are the official, clinical
psychiatric labels. The 'Diagnostic and Statistical Manual'
(DSM) is the official manual of the American Psychiatric
Association. I call it the Psychiatric Bible. It holds the keys
to the psychiatric treasure chest of third-party financial
reimbursement. It has all the trappings of official sanction
and credibility. And it has grown enormously in the past
four decades with five editions, three since 1980, each time
including more and more diagnostic categories. Despite the
truth of Colbert's conclusion above, the DSM authors
pointedly state in introduction that "A common
misconception is that a classification of mental disorders
classifies individuals, when actually what are being classified
are disorders that individuals have." Dr Szasz clearly reveals
just the opposite:

> "In short, no psychiatric diagnosis is, or can be,

pathology-driven; instead, all such diagnoses are driven by nonmedical (economic, personal, legal, political, and social factors or incentives. Accordingly, psychiatric diagnoses do not point to pathoanatomic or pathophysiological lesions and do not identify causative agents — but rather refer to human behaviors. Moreover, the psychiatric terms used to refer to such behaviors allude to the plight of the denominated patient, hint at the dilemmas with which patient and psychiatrist alike try to cope as well as exploit, and mirror the beliefs and values of the society that both inhabit.

"Despite their misleading — indeed, mendacious, title — the various versions of the APA's Diagnostic and Statistical Manual of Mental Disorders are not classifications of mental disorders (or disease or conditions of any kind) that 'patients have'. Instead they are rosters of psychiatric diagnoses officially accredited as mental disease by the APA. This is why in psychiatry, unlike in the rest of medicine, the members of 'consensus groups' and 'task forces', appointed by officers of the association, make and unmake psychiatric diagnoses; and sometimes the entire membership votes on whether a controversial diagnosis is or is not a disease. For more than a century, psychiatrists created diagnoses and pretended they were diseases — and no one in authority challenged their deception. It is not surprising, then, that few people now realize that diagnose are not diseases." (4)

It is oppressive and harmful to categorize and label ou fellow human beings with fictitious diseases that tag them a defective and give no useful information about what is real going on. In fact, this action prevents and deters any possibility of really being of help. Next, an example of wha really goes on behind the veil of psychiatric linguistics.

An Exposition of Psychiatric Truth

"She suffers from endogenous depression.
Her diagnosis is DSM-IVR ... "

These two sentences stand alone, presented as a scientific, clinical description of objective reality. It is, in fact, a statement of power, bursting with knowledge, declaring and upholding the domain of psychiatric "truth." My purpose here is to expose and clarify some of this "truth."

I agree wholeheartedly with Thomas Szasz' opinion that psychiatric statements such as the one above are not, in fact, descriptive statements at all. Rather, they are prescriptive. This is very important to understand. Endogenous depression is one example of many words that comprise a general class making up the domain of "mental illness." "Mental illness" is a concept created in recent history, as science/medicine replaced religion/theology. "Mental illness" is seen as an analog of physical illness. Created as a metaphor (e.g., a woman runs swift and elegant; she is a deer), it has been suppressed and forgotten that "mental illness" is a metaphor. The concept does not describe any consistently identifiable abnormality, lesion, abnormal cell, organism, etc., as in physical illness; the search to do so, however persistent and unflagging, has been and is a bust, and likely will forever be a bust. This is not so much because of the limits of scientific inquiry, but because of our nature as human beings. Despite the protestations of those who believe only in the "objective" data of hard science, the perennial wisdom of the ages is that we are first and foremost spiritual beings. The realm of spirit and thought is invisible — not because we have yet to discover the finer nuances of physical seeing, but because there is truth in the ancient teachings that form is created out of spirit. Spirit and thought are formless, not dependent on but preceding form. In Christian parlance, it is that first there was the Word and the Word was made flesh. The flesh cannot see the Word. We cannot discern the spirit by our physical senses.

"Mental illness" is a simple metaphor for physical illness. It does not describe the highly individual, unique thoughts or feelings or physical manifestations of those who carry the tag. It does not inform as to the process of human nature, development or healing.

The concept of "mental illness," as used in the opening quotation about endogenous depression, is used as the decisive move in a discourse, a communication defining relationship, of psychiatric power. It does not describe, but prescribes a complex dynamic of power relations with enormous, often devastating consequences. (5) The prescription on the psychiatrist's pad might say "12 sessions of ECT(electroshock)" to treat endogenous depression. A fuller exposition looks something like this:

> She suffers from Endogenous Depression.
> Her Diagnosis is DSM-IVR _____ .
> She is mentally ill, chronic.
> She needs my help.
> Something must be done.
> It is my job to help her.
> Her illness is biological and genetic.
> Her response to various drugs has not been good.
> She is an ideal candidate for electroconvulsive therapy (ECT).

ECT is safe and effective.
I prescribe this treatment for her.
It is for her own good.
I am a good, caring doctor.

This is a short version of psychiatric truth, the Gospel according to the American Psychiatric Association.

Mainstream psychiatry holds these assumptions to be obvious truths. Psychiatry, in fact, creates these truths by presenting and enforcing a language defining specific knowledge and power relationships. "Mental illness exists and must be treated. You are mentally ill and we will treat you." Left out of this version of creating truth is the fact that "mental illness" is a metaphor. Just because a concept is believed and acted upon doesn't mean it is real; the fact that countless people were persecuted for witchcraft doesn't mean that they were witches. That ECT is inflicted upon thousands and thousands doesn't mean they're "mentally ill."

Admitting a crisis, problem, stress — wanting and/or needing help does not in any way constitute illness. Wanting and needing to help does not in any way bestow the right or prerogative to help. The desire to help does not correlate with harmlessness or helpfulness; it does not correlate with effectiveness. After all, the Inquisitors sincerely desired to save souls and the Nazis sincerely desired to create a purer human race. In order to help another in a good way requires much more than desire to help. Often our desire to help is far from a free and joyful outpouring of compassion. The truth is human beings are inherently good. Often, however, we have been hurt in such a way that we are compelled to be "helpful" as compensation for underlying feelings of fear and inadequacy. Similarly, we may be driven to help in order to avoid feeling guilty or unworthy; we are a "good" person only if and as long as we keep demonstrating it. At a minimum, helpful service requires a fairly clear view of reality, and genuine respect for the other.

American philosopher John Stuart Mill stated it this way:

> "The sole end for which mankind are warranted, individually or collectively, in interfering with the liberty of action of any of their number, is self-protection. That the only purpose for which power can be rightfully exercised over any member of a civilized community, against his will, is to prevent harm to others. His own good, either physical or moral, is not a sufficient warrant." (6)

Mental and emotional distress do exist. The ongoing attempt to locate their source as biogenetic illness is a failure and the present tendency to declare this as fact is a fraud.

Two portions of unrevealed knowledge: first, the underlying dynamic of interrelations we call psychiatry is really about power. Our society has designated psychiatry as a social police force and bestowed enormous power. The paradox is that psychiatry has no choice about whether to use this power. Society gives and insists that it be used. The coercers are coerced, but so thoroughly conditioned they think they are free. Any of you who have resisted psychiatry's benevolent kindness know how flimsy is the gilded facade which covers the harsh iron curtain.

The second portion of unrevealed knowledge is, in modern society, inseparable from the experience of power. It is very concrete. The fact that it was not in the above exposition of the psychiatric Bible must not in any way diminish its significance. Other than resistance to the benevolent prescriptions of psychiatry, nothing pierces the veil of altruistic selflessness faster than a failure to come up with the cash. As the song goes, "If you got the money, honey, I've got the time!" On an individual level, this is felt over and over again as termination of treatment due to insufficiency of insurance funds. On a systemic scale, an example is the unplanned turning out of so many institutionalized "chronic mental patients" through psychiatric deinstitutionalization.

Bankruptcy

A big attraction of biopsychiatry is that it responds to our desperate need to find hope, to gain relief from seemingly unbearable feelings of guilt and shame, and to escape from a burdensome sense of pressure and responsibility. The other justification for biopsychiatric "treatments" which I posted at the beginning of Chapter 2 is reflected in the statement that "Nothing else works." It is vitally important to know that this is a statement of pure despair; the individual who says this has given up, and is now justifying an action which is immoral and harmful. "Nothing else works" is a reflection of the truth that biopsychiatrists have nothing of real help to offer. Their regrettable bankruptcy in understanding human nature, distress, growth and recovery lends itself to perpetuation and justification of the unethical and damaging practices which I decry in this book. Similar to the two earlier sentences diagnosing a woman suffering from depression, the sentence "Nothing else works" also carries a wealth of meaning, partially revealed in the following expanded version:

> "I'm a doctor."
> "I am trained in the scientific practice of biological psychiatry."
> "They told me mental illness is a disease to be treated by drugs and/or ECT."
> "Society has sanctioned me to treat the mentally ill."
> "You are mentally ill."
> "Drugs are the answer."
> "Drugs aren't working."
> "You need ECT."
> "I've tried everything else."
> "Nothing else works."

What does it mean when someone says that ECT or psychiatric drugs "work." The belief of someone who accepts the premises of biopsychiatry is that it works to control or treat a brain disease. The truth is that there really is no biologically-based disease to treat. Leonard Frank, editor of 'The History of Shock Treatment' (7), came up with the aphorism that medicine has identified many diseases for which they have no cures, while psychiatry has identified many cures for which there are no diseases! My position is simple. Biopsychiatry is not about curing or "treating" illness; it is a means of social control for deviants who break no laws. Psychiatric procedures work in at least five important ways:

1/ Psychiatric procedures punish and control deviance.

2/ Psychiatric procedures absolve us all from social responsibility by identifying those who are having a hard time, or give others a hard time, not as individuals hurt by oppression and in need of recovery, but as biological or genetically inferior victims of "mental illness."

3/ Psychiatric procedures allow us to avoid facing our own hurts, our own shame, and our own responsibility to challenge injustice by labeling and coercively "treating" those who "act out" in protest of oppression.

4/ Psychiatric procedures are, at root, suppressive. Psychiatric drugs and electroshock act to suppress consciousness and emotion, to destroy memory, reduce energy, in short to abort and inhibit the process of working through and re-evaluating past hurts and current injustices. The subject is so busy dealing with the ill effects of the "treatment" that there is no time or energy left for dealing with the real problems that need to be addressed.

5/ Psychiatric procedures act to systematically quash and inhibit flexibility and creativity, and to discourage motivation for finding and developing genuine ways of supporting individuals to recover from harm, and to grow and develop as spiritual beings.

Mystification and the Manufacture of Madness

The purpose of psychiatric jargon is to mystify. The purpose of mystification is to control. Why else use unnecessary, ill-defined Greek, Latin, or other "five dollar" words if not to disempower those with whom you speak? Psychiatrists also use such mumbo-jumbo to protect themselves from being found out.

Psychiatry, through the obliging arms of corporate media, is continually spreading propaganda to the effect that we are a nation and a world in the throes of an ever-growing epidemic of "mental illness." Academic and governmental organizations eagerly fuel the hysteria. In the introduction,

I referred to research conducted by the Harvard School of Public Health and the World Health Organization. They published ten volumes of study in 1990 which purport to provide a comprehensive picture of the current and projected health in eight regions of the world. According to Dr John Docherty, Executive Director and Chief Medical Officer of Merit Behavioral Care Corporation, the following are key results of the study:

1/ Psychiatric conditions account for little more than one percent of deaths, but they are responsible for almost 11 percent of the worldwide disease burden.

2/ In both developing and developed regions, depression is the leading cause of disease burden for women.

3/ Researchers expect psychiatric conditions to increase their share of the total disease burden by almost half by 2020.

4/ In 1990 unipolar depression was responsible for the fourth highest disease burden worldwide. By 2020 it is expected to be second only to ischaemic heart disease.

Excluding death and looking at disability alone, the following results were reported:

1/ Unipolar depression was the number one cause of disability in the world in 1990.

2/ Of the ten leading causes of disability worldwide in 1990, five were psychiatric conditions. (8)

I can only imagine two reasons that you might not be astounded at these bald-faced assertions that "mental illness" is one of the leading causes of disease and disability in the world. You are either already savvy about the success of psychiatric propaganda, or you are still severely blinded by its illusion. According to psychiatry, a constantly growing percentage of the human race is "mentally ill." Psychiatry interprets everything through its distorted lens. Psychiatric "conditions" are not only "diseases" burdening our health care system, but are themselves the number one cause of disability in the world. As the epidemic of such "diseases" is ever-growing, the only "alternative" is a war on "mental illness," waged by our mental health system. At an individual level, experiences of abuse and neglect are irrelevant. At a societal level, poverty, malnutrition, unemployment, overpopulation, dislocation, environmental degradation, and any other reflections of injustice and oppression are irrelevant. When problems are reduced to individual manifestations of defective biology or genetics, there is only one solution, and biopsychiatry offers it in the way of drugs and electroshock.

Psychiatry says, then, that the problem is that so many go "untreated" — the solution, more "treatment." The vast majority of individuals "suffering from mental illness" do, in fact, go "untreated." Furthermore, they often recover from even the most serious "mental illness," "schizophrenia," without any "treatment" whatsoever, or with non-biopsychiatric treatment. (9) The work of Loren Mosher thoroughly documents the effectiveness of Soteria House, a community-led, home-like, residential center for young people diagnosed as schizophrenic in the early 1970s. (10) The truth is that countless individuals are constantly moving through inner and outer experiences which, if viewed through the lens of biopsychiatry, would be labeled and treated as "mental illness." A common result of a biopsychiatric intervention is to create a much greater likelihood that an individual will not move through such experience, but will instead assume an identity and concomitant role as "chronic mental patient". And, says psychiatry, we all know that there is nothing to do for "chronic mentally ill" people except to control their symptoms by drugs or ECT: no alternative.

The Spirit of Psychiatric Language

I have shared much of my thinking with Leonard Frank, whom I mentioned above. Leonard is a long-time activist, a philosopher, a good friend and a man who has devoted much of his life to mastery of language. Leonard loves my work; at the same time, he has found me a willing but difficult student in the discipline of proper use of language. Specifically, he has been tremendously helpful in pushing me to challenge the extent of my own conditioned use of psychiatric language and to continually become more clear and forthright. As much as I have made an effort to become more aware and thoughtful of the ways we use language to define and obfuscate reality, Leonard has consistently challenged me to go further in breaking free from the insidious and pervasive clutches of psychiatric jargon. I had been skeptical of words like "mental illness" and "treatment," although I still required an even greater discipline to consistently put such euphemisms in quotes. I would still tend to use the terms "psychosis" or "delusion" without quotes; Leonard helped me to realize that the use of these terms in everyday language supports a biopsychiatric interpretation, and obscures reality. "Psychosis" usually means strange or socially unacceptable conduct; extreme state of mind is a more useful reference to the inner experience. I carelessly referred to Cindy's "delusions;" false beliefs, while still an opinion, does not carry the heavy load of psychiatric jargon. As I said above, the language of psychiatry is prescriptive, not descriptive. It is not helpful in describing and understanding reality; rather, it prescribes a set of actions for intervention and control of someone's life. Leonard Frank calls it brainwashing.

Other examples of language use are more subtle. Leonard challenged my use of the word "appropriate" in reference to a mental health system response to someone in crisis. Similar to his challenge of the word "rational," Leonard's point was that these perfectly good words carry tremendous weight as they have been used again and again to label, shame , control and punish individuals in the context of "treatment" for "mental illness." The words "pain" and "healing" demonstrate a related concern. Leonard's argument is that because these words, when applied to the emotional and mental life, are metaphors for physical illness and recovery, their use validates and supports the very medical model that I am challenging. Is it helpful for me to challenge the metaphor in one place and then turn around and use it out of convenience where it is appealing to me and I judge it as more benign? This discipline of challenging and being as aware as I can about the use of words has been extremely valuable to me. I consider it to be an essential aspect of human liberation in general, and to "mental health" liberation from psychiatry in specific. There are now some words like "mental illness," "disease" and "treatment" that require clear, consistent and strong challenge to uncover their euphemistic veiling of coercive harm and the violation of civil rights, as well as to recreate a space for individuals to grow and develop as spiritual beings. It is not clear to me where to alter language that has been co-opted, but might best be reclaimed for literal (e.g., "rational," "appropriate") or poetic (e.g., "healing emotional pain") use. The intention is important and the effort is worthwhile.

Right Use of Language

As stated, psychiatric jargon obscures reality and lends itself to abuse of power. Plain English reveals the truth and lends itself to human empowerment. I share with you here a list which Leonard Frank put together for the 1995 conference of the National Association of Rights Protection and Advocacy (NARPA). It is a potent illustration of the scope of psychiatric misuse of language and one man's thinking about a restoration of right use of language.

Reality/Plain English	Myth/Psychiatric Jargon
Acting Bravely	Acting-Out
Angry	Upset
Assertiveness	Aggressiveness
Bio-violent Psychiatry	Biological Psychiatry
Blasphemy	Delusion
Brain Damage	Cognitive Deficit
Brainwasher	Institutional Psychiatrist
Character Assassination	Clinical Diagnosis
Confession	Catharsis
Conscience	Superego
Contemplative	Catatonic
Control	Cure
Defiance	Negativism
Denial of Mental Illness	Lack of Insight
Different	Difficult/Disturbed/Dangerous
Disrespectful	Hostile
Drug Effect	Drug Side Effect
Drug	Medication
Electroconvulsive Brainwashing ECB	
Electroconvulsive Treatment ECT	

Electroshock	Electroconvulsive Treatment
Energetic	Manic
Fasting	Anorexia
Fear	Phobia
Fidgety and Bored	Hyperactive-ADD
Forced Labor	Occupational Therapy
Habit	Compulsion
Hang-up	Complex
Happy Pill, Soma	Prozac, Zoloft, Paxil
Heresy, Nonconformity	Schizophrenia
Human Problem	Psychiatric Symptom/Disease
Human Rights Issue (Politics)	Medical Issue (Medicine)
Human Warehousing	Custodial Care
Imaginative	Irrational
Incarceration	Involuntary Hospitalization
Inquisition	Institutional Psychiatry
Inquisitor	Institutional Psychiatrist
Inspired	Grandiose
Joy	Euphoria
Maddening	Mad
Memory Loss	Memory Disturbance
Mystical Experience	Psychotic Experience
Mind-Control Drug	Neuroleptic Drug
Nonconformity	Deviance
Non-cooperation	Passive-aggression
Oppressed	Depressed
Patient Manipulation	Patient Management
Permanent Memory Loss	Temporary Memory Loss
Person	Patient
Preventive Detention	Civil Commitment
Privativeness	Secretiveness
Prudence	Cooperation
Psychiatric Inmate	Hospitalized Mental Patient

Psychiatric Survivor	Former Mental Patient
Psychiatric Prison	Mental Hospital
Punishment	Treatment
Resigned	Adjusted
Self-helping Profession	Helping Profession
Silence (Refusal to Talk)	Mutism
Single-mindedness	Obsession (Monomania)
Socially Acceptable Belief	Insight
Socially Acceptable Conduct	Appropriate Behavior
Socially Unacceptable Belief	Delusion
Socially Unacceptable Conduct	Inappropriate Behavior
Solitariness	Withdrawal
Spiritual Breakthrough	Psychotic Breakdown
Spiritual Commitment	Religious Preoccupation
Spirituality	Religiosity
Spontaneity	Impulsiveness
Stream of Consciousness	Flight of Ideas
Stupifiers (Drugs)	Tranquilizers (Drugs)
Produce stupor/stupidity	Produce tranquility
Submission	Remission
Suggestible	Amenable to Psychotherapy
Survival Conduct	Deviant Behavior
Thought Crime (George Orwell)	Delusion
Torture	Involuntary Treatment
Torture Chamber	Treatment Room
Transitional Period	Psychotic Episode
Troublesome	Troubled
Uncommunicative	Evasive
Uncooperative, Disobedient	Resistive
Unhappy/Sad	Depressed
Unsociable	Anti-social
Vision/Religious Experience	Hallucination
Watchful/Vigilant	Paranoid

Summary

Right use of language is essential to ethical action and harmonious relationships. In Buddhism, correct use of language is one arm of the noble eight-fold path to liberation. "Right speech is traditionally explained as no slander, no gossip, no backbiting, not setting one person against another, not using harsh or abusive speech." (11) Psychiatric jargon, and the process of diagnosis and labeling, is slanderous, lends itself to malicious gossip, consistently sets people against each other, and is inherently harsh and abusive. I conclude with the words of Thomas Szasz:

> "The point is not that psychiatric diagnoses are meaningless, but that they may be, and often are, swung as semantic blackjacks: cracking the subject's respectability and dignity destroys him just as effectively, and often more so, as cracking his skull. The difference is that the man who wields a blackjack is recognized by everyone as a public menace, but one who wields a psychiatric diagnosis is not." (12)

CHAPTER 5
CONDITIONING: THE BASICS

What is it that allows highly intelligent, successful professionals to create, promote or allow such a monstrosity as institutional psychiatry to determine the practices of our mental health system? Why do good people do so much harm? And how can they sincerely believe in the goodness and necessity of that harm? One of the most difficult tasks of growing up today is to suffer the profound disillusionment that comes with the discovery that the authorities and experts whom we are naturally inclined to trust and rely on are often not deserving of our trust. It is hard to believe that professionals can be so wrong, to accept that they do harm.

Why are mental health professionals so willing to go along with the program? Why do they not express outrage, speak out, resist and challenge the oppressive practices of our mental health system? Were I to respond from the worldview of biopsychiatry, I would look for biological or genetic mental diseases residing somehow in the brains and bodies of mental health professionals. Instead, I will respond to the question by painting with as broad a brush as possible. Whereas biopsychiatry views people as isolated entities functioning as independent machines, I will consider people as fully embedded in a multi-leveled, multi-faceted system.

Extremely Shaky Ground

To achieve a meaningful understanding of human behavior, in this case to speculate on the conditioning of mental health professionals, I believe it is absolutely necessary to reclaim a forgotten, fundamental aspect of our nature as human beings; that is, we are and always have been completely connected with the natural world. I have already briefly highlighted the historical, philosophical ground of Judeo-Christian theology and urban-industrial development which has violated our experience of interconnectedness with all of life. This violation causes us, at a deep level, to live with a core feeling of fear, and to act again and again out of desperation, attempting to right ourselves and dominate perceived danger in the natural world.

Perhaps a little perspective will help. Life on this planet has evolved over millions of years. Our instincts for physical and emotional survival evolved over a great deal of time. Agriculture is very recent, as is the development of our neo-cortex and its higher brain cognitive-intellectual function. Civilization as we know it is a very new experiment. I share with you here a passage from Arundhati Roy's novel of love and madness in the unraveling of modern day India, 'The God of Small Things':

Then, to give Estha and Rahel a sense of Historical Perspective (though Perspective was something which, in the weeks to follow, Chacko himself would sorely lack), he told them about the Earth Woman. He made them imagine that the earth — four thousand six hundred million years old — was a forty-six-year-old woman, as old, say as Aleyamma Teacher, who gave them Malayam lessons. It had taken the whole of the Earth Woman's life for the earth to

become what it was. For the oceans to part. For the
mountains to rise. The Earth Woman was 11 years old,
Chacko said, when the first single-celled organisms
appeared. The first animals, creatures like worms and
jellyfish, appeared only when she was forty. She was over
forty-five — just eight months ago — when dinosaurs
roamed the earth.

> "The whole of human civilization as we know it,"
> Chacko told the twins, "began only two hours ago in the
> Earth Woman's life. As long as it takes us to drive from
> Ayemenem to Cochin."
> It was an awe-inspiring and humbling thought, Chacko
> said (Humbling was a nice word, Rahel thought. Humbling
> along without a care in the world.), that the whole of
> contemporary history, the World Wars, the War of
> Dreams, the Man on the Moon, science, literature,
> philosophy, the pursuit of knowledge — was no more than
> a blink of the Earth Woman's eye." (1)

A second massive trauma results from our fear-based
love affair with technological means to control the
"dangerous" natural processes of our bodies. We now know
from psychological research and experience that our birth
experience is probably the single most powerful experience
which affects the development of human personality. Birth
is a difficult and challenging initiation into the world even
in the best of circumstances. Twentieth-century birthing
experiences have been severely traumatic. Most of us were
treated violently at birth — drugs, harsh lights, cold steel,
disruption of bonding, and a host of other unnatural and
distressing experiences were the norm.
　In this century, birth was removed from its forever

place in the home as traditional midwifery was usurped by
modern medicine's technology and doctors. The typical
twentieth century birth has involved drugs which affect
mother and baby. Many, perhaps most of us, were born
drugged. The developmental norms I was taught in
graduate school, that for two or three days babies didn't
smile or focus their eyes clearly, had nothing to do with the
development of a healthy baby. They were the norms for
children under the influence of drugs at birth. As I
experienced with my own boy and girl, children born
without drugs are usually aware and focusing immediately
upon birth.

Most of us were born into a sterile room of bright
lights, cold steel and loud sounds. We had painful drops put
in our eyes. We were held upside down and slapped. We had
forcep wounds. We were separated from our mothers and
missed important bonding times. We underwent horribly
painful circumcisions at two or three days old. Many of us
were not breast fed, missing the psychological and
physiological benefits of breast feeding. Fortunately, there
has been a dawning awareness of the need to reclaim birth
from technological medicine and medical doctors, but
countless mothers and babies still have far from an ideal
experience. For example, a much higher percentage of us
than necessary are born Caesarean, deprived of the health
benefits of vaginal birth.

The effects of all this on our psyches are extremely
potent. It seems that our birth, like all of our life experience,
is fully recorded at some level of our body/mind. The works
of both scientific researchers such as Stan Grof and
rebirthers such as Jim Leonard and Phil Laut describe what
many of us have discovered-that in non-ordinary states of
consciousness, induced by any of a variety of means (e.g.,

breathing techniques, music, drugs, fasting, hypnosis or sleep deprivation), we can re-experience our births and/or prenatal experience. (2) We can also work through and heal any related trauma by energetically and emotionally expressing the harmful effects in a safe context.

Related to twentieth century birth is twentieth century handling of infants and babies. Fortunately, an infant's crucial initial hours, days and weeks are getting better for many. Nonetheless, the vast majority of our parents had little understanding of the fact that we had evolved in nature with a basic need to be held continuously during our first six months of life. Jean Liedloff movingly describes this as the "continuum" experience of life and suggests that most of us now suffer from "in-arms deprivation" as a result of insufficient holding. (3) This deprivation results in a frozen need and a chronic feeling of anxiety, uncertainty and desperation. Without awareness and healing, these frozen needs and chronic anxieties continue to act as powerful determinants of the way we perceive the world.

These three violent ruptures — from the natural world, from our natural bodies, from a natural experience of birth and mothering, yield traumatic results. They are nearly universal and affect us all deeply, including mental health professionals. They create, promote and allow belief and acceptance of a most tragic mistake in how we identify ourselves as human beings. They make us blind and susceptible to this modern religion called physical materialism, that we are how we look and what we have. We live with what Einstein called "a kind of optical delusion of consciousness," whereby although we are part of the whole, we see ourselves as apart from the rest of creation. He expressed it very well:

"This delusion is a kind of prison for us, restricting us to our personal desires and to affection for a few persons nearest to us. Our task must be to free ourselves from this prison by widening our circle of compassion to embrace all living creatures and the whole of creation in its beauty." (4)

The heart of the matter involves a case of mistaken identity. Constantly pulled by the effects of hurt, fear and unmet needs, we think we are our bodies and that we can gain happiness by reinforcing our separateness and desperately seeking to fulfill our selfish desires. Comfort becomes more important than truth, and we cast around for someone outside ourselves on which to cast blame. Most all the forces of modern civilization, including psychiatry, work overtime to reinforce this idea. It is a huge challenge to find our way back along the path of reawakening our true nature as spiritual beings.

This point of lost contact with our spiritual nature is difficult to see for those of us raised in modern Western Civilization. Having a clear perspective on the culture in which you are immersed has been compared to a fish being able to see the nature of the ocean; it is exceedingly difficult to get outside of our containers, and view them with any sort of dispassion. Perhaps it is easier for an outsider who was raised in a very different milieu. I used birth above as one example of "violent rupture" common to our modern existence; the experience of death is also profoundly important. A very wise outsider, Sogyal Rinpoche, spiritual teacher and author of 'The Tibetan Book of Living and Dying', wrote the following:

"I first came to the West at the beginning of the 1970s, and what disturbed me deeply, and has continued to disturb me, is the almost complete lack of spiritual help for the dying that exists in modern culture. In Tibet, as I have shown, everyone had some knowledge of the higher truths of Buddhism and some relationship with a master. No one died without being cared for, in both superficial and profound ways, by the community. I have been told many stories of people dying alone and in great distress and disillusion in the West without any spiritual help, and one of my main motivations in writing this book is to extend the healing wisdom of the world I was brought up in to all men and women." (5)

Please remember that all the details which follow regarding the the mechanisms and effects of our conditioning are presented as signposts for getting back on the path to the heart of your true nature.

Some Dynamics of Conditioning

Conditioning refers to the shaping of our attitudes, tendencies and behaviors so that we become willing to go along with the program. It is malevolent when it reflects a profound distrust of human nature, systematically disconnecting us from our natural knowing and from the ability to think and act independently. A conditioned individual is incapable of thinking for themselves, of questioning authority, of following his or her own heart. Accurate information is crucial to conscious living, and I hope that this information will help shake up and loosen ignorance related to our mental health system.

"The Dawning of all great truths on the consciousness of humanity has usually to pass — says Tolstoy — through three characteristic stages. The first is: "This is so foolish that it is not worth thinking about." The second: "This is immoral and contrary to religion." The third: "Oh! This is so well known that it is not worth talking about." (6)

I am not sure about the dawning of great untruths, but the tenets of biopsychiatry are all too solidified into Tolstoy's third phase. Challenges and critiques tend to be met with the first and second reactions, condemned as foolish or immoral. I envision a time when our society will say things like, "It is well accepted that caring for our children is not primarily a medical problem, and so obviously wrong to give them toxic drugs to control their behavior."

Poor information and confused thinking due to emotional distress may be seen as the key linchpins of oppressive conditioning. It is necessary to heal the hurts which have resulted in carrying deep feelings of fear and shame which impede our ability to think and act consciously.

On Fear

A Neanderthal man confronts a saber-tooth tiger and is afraid. Fear is a basic, fundamental aspect of our evolutionary heritage, an essential warning and motivator for survival in dangerous situations.

Consider, however, the following examples. The telephone rings and we feel anxious. We face an upcoming public speaking engagement and we feel fear. We need to talk with the neighbor about his dog, and we are afraid. I want to speak with the Austin State Hospital psychiatrist about Cindy, and I am afraid. It happens over and over and over again in all of our lives. We feel as if we are facing death at the hands of a saber-tooth tiger when, in reality, we are not in any physical danger whatsoever.

This is a big one; fear is the great immobilizer. Conditioning is such that:

DISOBEYING AUTHORITY -> TERROR.

An act against conditioned patterning evokes a feeling memory that "something bad is going to happen." As a child, your survival quite literally depended on the goodwill of your parents. On an emotional level, the feeling remains that your life (job, money, status, worth) depends on obedience to authority. A key tenet of mental health liberation is that psychiatric oppression is about suppression of individual differences, that uniqueness is punished, sacrificed on the altar of conformity. While it is true that differences are not tolerated, there is a deeper dynamic. What really cannot be tolerated is anxiety, the feeling associated with memory of terror.

On the Psychodynamics of Abuse

As described in Chapter 1, a psychiatrist played the major role in wielding the power required to coerce Cindy into treatment, against her will, "for her own good." This disregard of an individual's stated desire is paternalistic; it is authoritarian parenting. Many things are necessary on many levels of community and society for this to happen. Despite all the rhetoric about benevolent "treatment," on a psychological level this action says more about the psychiatrist than the patient. I will use the teachings of Alice Miller to illustrate as she presents one of the clearest explanations of the psychology of child abuse. (7) A child victim of abuse does not have the information or power to avoid some version of these dynamics. Children experience the world with themselves as the center; whatever happens, they feel responsible that they are the cause. Parents are seen as omnipotent and all-knowing, thus assuring the feeling that anything wrong must be the child's fault. Here is how it works.

A child is hurt by a parent. The child unavoidably internalizes both sides of the experience, as victim and as powerful adult perpetrator. Naturally, the primary identification is that of victim, afraid and ashamed. When a child is not supported and allowed to express and work through the effects of hurt, he will protect himself intrapsychically by the mechanism of "splitting." In order to function without continued feelings of fear and shame, the child will "split off" the internalized experience of being a powerless, terrified victim and banish this knowledge as deeply as possible into the unconscious mind. Just as it is natural for a child to initially identify himself as terrified victim, it is equally natural that, given a later opportunity, that same child will choose to identify with a powerful perpetrator in a relational world in which abusive inequities of power are the norm. The final part of this process is that the split-off internalized victim self is projected from the unconscious depths of the psyche onto the others within interactions. The individual denies (represses and forgets) the hurt and its associated feelings of shame and fear. Her perception, however, is determined by these unconscious feelings, so she is drawn to see others as shameful and deserving of the treatment she once received. Her identification as a powerful perpetrator leads inexorably to a well-justified punishment (aka "treatment") of the deserving other.

Four stages describe the process: An act of abuse, internalization of both sides of that abusive interaction, splitting and unconscious denial of victimization, projection of the denied powerless and shame-filled victim self. Now the stage is set for recapitulation, re-enactment and perpetuation of the abusive pattern. To the individual who unconsciously projects his own experience of terror and shame onto another, that other is bad and powerless, fully deserving and in need of correction. The original victim acts on such a conviction, and is fully justified in whatever act is perpetrated. A father who was hit as a child for whining now hits his own child for whining, justifying it as necessary to teach the child a lesson. The father has identified with his own parent and projected his own split-off hurt child self onto his child. The cycle of abuse is complete. It is my opinion that oppressive psychiatric treatment can only happen when the oppressors have been deeply hurt and conditioned. On a psychological level, the female psychiatrist who locked Cindy up against her will and repeatedly ordered forced injections of toxic drugs was re-enacting her own past traumas. By the processes of identification, denial and projection described above, together with the sanctions of society and her profession, the psychiatrist is able to abuse without remorse or shame. The shame is carried by the victim.

We are able to transform the moral language of "bad, wicked, sinful" child to that of "needy, dependent, sick" mental patient which acts as a thickly concealing veil to the reality of abuse. It is crucial to understand that the core emotional states of fear and shame are unaltered in this translation. Terror resides in the experience of powerlessness and helplessness, and remains intact in the patient-professional interactional dynamics of coercive psychiatry.

Most psychiatrists, as do all properly conditioned adults, operate from an unrelenting fear of perceived danger. The unconscious or semi-conscious process is that the dangerous others must necessarily be controlled and suppressed. Furthermore, they deserve to be punished; revenge for those early traumas is an added benefit.

On Shame

Alice Miller's psychodynamic interpretation of abuse describes shame as a potent factor in human relations. Shame is the awful feeling that says "I am bad, wicked, defective, incompetent;" it says that "I am fundamentally flawed," not that "I did something wrong," but that "there is something really wrong with me." Viewing the world from a responsible center, a child naturally accepts and believes a parent's assertion by word and action that the child is deserving of whatever abuse the parents commit. The abused child inevitably carries a big load of shame. And the linguistic shift from theology to medicine, described in Chapter 4, easily holds shame in place. Biopsychiatric language of biological/genetic disease is most ideal for enforcing the dictates of shame that says, "I am a flawed, defective, unworthy being."

Psychiatry makes it all the more easy to perpetuate the legacy of shame by providing convenient, self-fulfilling protection against the inevitable tinges of discomfort that surface in the midst of unethical activity. Power inequities, labeling and paternalism are just perfectly fine when the recipients of these actions are so obviously mentally ill, irrational, completely dependent and unable to care for themselves. From this base, practices such as involuntary commitment, routine use of toxic drugs, and electroshock are all perfectly justified; to question this is, indeed, irresponsible and/or immoral.

Theodore Roszak argues that this quality of shame, manifested as a guilty conscience and fundamental distrust of self is absolutely necessary to inculcate in humans so that they will cooperate as cogs in a system which is inherently anti-human in so many ways. According to Roszak:

> "The Politics of domination begins when some people teach other people that the body, the psyche, the community, and nature-at-large are unreliable, incompetent, hostile, therefore in need of top-down supervision. Authoritarian politics roots itself as the guilty conscience. It begins by convincing people they cannot trust one another, that they cannot trust themselves." (8)

One more thing needs to be revealed about shame, and revelation is the perfect concept here. John Bradshaw helped to make it clear that a defining characteristic of shame is that it feels unbearable to be exposed or revealed; shame thrives as a hidden secret and compels the bearer to isolate and to avoid confrontive situations that threaten exposure of the unbearable feeling and conviction of fundamental worthlessness. (9) Biopsychiatry puts forth a medical diagnosis as sufficient cause of individual distress. The effect of such an action is to absolve us all from responsibility to look any further at shame-filled causative factors such as child abuse, economic oppression and all its nasty derivatives including racism, sexism, and homophobia. Once a child is diagnosed as "Attention Deficit Disorder," the problem with school is explained. It's simply a biological defect, says psychiatry, and the solution is a drug. This is how millions of our school-age children end up on drugs today. The message is that no one is responsible. It's not the child's fault — he's sick. The parents aren't responsible, they're off the hook, as is the school and everyone else. The same process holds true for adults diagnosed with "mental illness." It's explained as a medical problem and drugs are the answer. The family's not responsible. The community is not challenged to really question itself and try to understand its individuals. What's important to see is that biopsychiatry serves as "the cloak that hides a thing." Shame-filled individuals cannot bear the burden of responsible self-examination; so much safer and easier to be enchanted by the illusion that individuals suffer, not in direct proportion to societal oppression and irrationality, but because they have a disease.

Psychiatry cannot bear exposure; the public cannot bear exposure of psychiatry. Fear and shame are so pervasive that society is unbearably reluctant to face the truth about psychiatry. Nuremberg overlooked Nazi psychiatry; the legacy of the horrific Nazi psychiatric practices has been to suppress and forget. Consider the following words of a German professor of psychiatry in 1997 as representative of the push to deny and hide the truth:

> "Regarding euthanasia ... today it is no longer of any interest who had participated, under what circumstances and to what extent, in the basically condemnable Nazi extermination measures." (10)

Silence and denial are prized and necessary virtues of those who act as agents of psychiatry.

Psychologist, author and psychiatric survivor Al Siebert asks the significant question "Why has no American psychiatrist ever had to pay damages for harm resulting from a person being mistakenly diagnosed as mentally ill?" (11) He points out that thousands of patients were wrongfully confined against their will to mental institutions and badly harmed — with never a single malpractice judgment. Hundreds of thousands have suffered permanent brain damage from electroshock; a number have died. Literally millions have suffered permanent disability from psychiatric drugs; some have died. Given the pervasive acceptance of the flawed beliefs of biopsychiatry, the reality of psychiatric oppression, and the legislative support of our coercive mental health system, perhaps it should not be surprising that judgments against the practitioners are most exceedingly rare. That they are rare does not mean they are not deserved. It is time to reveal these events and to hold the psychiatric profession accountable.

CHAPTER 6
CONDITIONING: ADVANCED CLASS

All of the conditioning factors discussed thus far have a similar effect. They encourage and promote a core experience which involves distrust of self and reliance on outer authority. There is a major societal institution that thoroughly reinforces this state of alienation from self and dependency on others. Nearly everyone goes through a developmental lifetime of system indoctrination through participation in our compulsory educational system.

Our Education System

The nature of oppression requires that we forget. Have you ever wondered how and why it is that we educate the way we do? The essential components of compulsory attendance, rigidly-defined curricula, age segregation, single adult authority, and brief class periods with rigid, frequent transitions define the vast majority of public, private and even alternative schooling. Have you thought much about the developmental goals the designers of such a system had in mind? John Taylor Gatto has. New York City Teacher of the Year for two years running, he unearthed and made public the history and philosophical underpinnings of our system of education.

Much was written in the late 1960s and early 1970s decrying the deleterious effects of our compulsory education system. Writers such as John Holt, Paul Goodman and Jonathan Kozol detailed the damage our system does to young people, and saw how this system was based on a factory model. Efficiency and productivity are primary values; the system was needed to engineer a massive psychic shift from independent, land-based people, to dependent town people reliant on jobs offered by the captains of industry. Gatto's research shows how we adopted a Prussian model that was developed and proved effective for the primary intention of creating obedient soldiers and loyalists for the state. Leading thinkers who developed the philosophy of the United States system of compulsory education were, for the most part, trained in Germany. They were very clear that the function of education was to instill primary values of obedience and acquiescence to authority. In order to do so, the system was designed to enforce utter dependency and discourage original independent thought; in short, the idea was to foster "alienation from the individual's own soul." (1)

In retrospect and in the light of rhetoric praising independence and creativity, the words of these men seem appalling. The fact is, however, that our system continues to operate on these principles and the results continue to be devastating. Gatto's book, 'Dumbing Us Down', describes primary effects of this type of education. He refers to schools as inherently psychopathic: rigidly, systematically and constantly interrupting young people's work at 45-minute intervals shows no conscience, sensitivity, awareness or respect for the natural desires, inclinations and tendencies of students as the highly unique individuals they are.

The subtitle of Gatto's book is 'The Hidden Curriculum of Compulsory Schooling'. He writes of the seven lessons that are universally taught from Harlem to Hollywood Hills. They are worth recounting.

1/ Confusion - Everything is out of context with "constant violations of natural order and sequence." While it is the nature of human beings to seek meaning and relatedness, what students get is disconnected facts and the unrelatedness of everything.

2/ Class Position - Students stay in the class where they belong, in good order, with their own kind.

3/ Indifference - "The lesson of bells is that no work is worth finishing, so why care too deeply about anything."

4/ Emotional Dependency - A comprehensive system of rewards and punishments enforces dependency and teaches children to surrender their will.

5/ Intellectual Dependency - "Good students wait for a teacher to tell them what to do." This says it all and happens early on in our system. Success means doing assigned thinking, limiting ideas to received thought, sacrificing original and independent thinking.

6/ Provisional Self-Esteem - Students are constantly evaluated and judged. Value and worth is not inherent, but clearly and constantly contingent on the evaluations of certified professionals.

7/ One Can't Hide - No private spaces, no private time; constant surveillance extended by homework right into private homes.

No one who attends school is unaffected by this process. It is important to understand that it is not the content that is really the problem; alterations of content don't make a lot of difference. It is the method that is inexorable. As Gatto concludes, "School is a 12-year jail sentence where bad habits are the only curriculum truly learned." (2) It is no wonder that most of us carry massive self-doubt and have difficulty thinking independently and challenging authority.

Psychiatry and the Schools

There is another aspect of our modern school system that is just beginning to be addressed by educational critics. Psychiatry has thoroughly pervaded our modern public schools, especially since World War II. A major force for dissemination of psychiatric thought in the United States was the Mental Hygiene movement, founded in 1909 by ex-patient Clifford Beers with much help from prominent psychologist William James who served as one of the twelve founding members. James forwarded a copy of Beers' book to John D. Rockefeller who contributed millions. The National Committee for Mental Hygiene had as a primary objective the prevention of mental illness in the schools. The hygienists believed that children are very susceptible to "personality disorders," that schools were the ideal point for detecting and preventing these disorders, and that such prevention must take precedence over any other educational objective. Notice that these beliefs are totally compatible with the assumptions of biopsychiatry outlined in Chapter 2. We need only add an explicit statement that biological or genetic factors are a primary determinant of susceptibility; "personality disorder" is an obvious synonym for "mental illness."

Bruce Wiseman, in his book 'Psychiatry: The Ultimate Betrayal', shares a quote from Sol Cohen's 1982 presidential speech to the History of Education Society:

"Few intellectual and social movements of this century

have had so deep and pervasive an influence on the theory and practice of American education as the mental hygiene movement" (3)

The effectiveness of the purveyors of these beliefs is awesome and frightening to behold. Critics such as Wiseman attribute the decline of our schools to the influence of psychiatry. The mental health thrust in education has two very deleterious effects. First, a psychiatric perspective shifts the focus from academic achievement to preventing "mental illness," attempting to enforce social adjustment or conformity to social norms. The second major effect stems from the basic theory that "mental illness" is a disease residing in individuals that needs prevention and treatment. Translated, this means children are selected as disturbed, or at-risk, and schools become places of mental health intervention.

The key concept for parents to understand is SELECTION. Education and psychiatry have in common their emphasis on selection. (4) Diagnosis and treatment are no more than after-the-fact justifications; the real issue is that children are being selected out on the basis of social behavior. We used to hit them or expel them from school. It may be argued that drugging our children is more effective and efficient, but I don't consider it progress. The issue ultimately remains one of enforcement of conformity and upholding an oppressive system. A result of this philosophy is that children are seen and treated as victims. Rather than being encouraged toward personal authority and responsibility, a sense of irresponsibility and dependence on others is promoted. A great irony is that we are told that we are responsible, conditioned to believe it, yet rarely given any real responsibility aside from all the mandated activities.

Despite the rhetoric, we get a deeper message that "We are not really responsible for what we do." We teach irresponsibility to our children by telling them they have an illness and prescribing drugs to help them act right. This fosters irresponsibility in all involved adults by providing an excuse not to consider and respond to the true needs of our children. No one is responsible.

The rhetoric of humanistic (child-centered, focused on the whole child, including values, and social and personality development) education and psychiatry in the schools is most beguiling and appeals to our basic loving and caring nature. Don't let the rhetoric fool you. Watch what is done, not what is said. The reality is that psychiatry has pervaded our schools. Federal legislation of 1963 and 1965 brought forward a booming industry of educational psychiatry. Funding for special education reached $1 billion in 1977; by 1994 this system was a $30 billion per year activity, and still climbing. Also in 1994, 26 percent of U.S public school students were in special education classes, whereas in other countries the figure was one to three percent. (5)

The appealing rhetoric of humanistic education has become the tragic practice of putting millions of our school age children on dangerous psychoactive drugs. Based on the tripling of annual prescriptions during the period 1990-1994 from 3,144,000 to 9,399,000, as many as five million or more children are on Ritalin, to name just one of these drugs. (6) Ritalin is a psychostimulant which is classified by the Drug Enforcement Agency in the same category as cocaine, barbiturates, morphine and other dangerous substances. The profits are as enormous as the severe harm done to our children.

Biopsychiatry has become a potent force in the lives c

our children and the schools have become the primary institution through which this force is manifested. Rather than promoting the development of personal authority and integrity, biopsychiatry promotes dependency and irresponsibility. The mass drugging of our children is a national shame and disgrace. It is for nobody's good except the short-term profitability of pharmaceutical companies, certain psychiatrists, and other members of the mental health industry. It is a clear reflection of the muddy philosophical reduction of humans from soulful spiritual beings to biological, mechanical animals needing to be shaped, controlled, treated and prevented from further degeneration. It is an enormous tragedy that so many adults see children only as products that need fixing. If parents and teachers were able to really see the challenges their children face and to trust in their inherent nature, there is no way they would allow anyone to abuse their children by telling them they are defective and forcing them to take toxic psychiatric drugs.

Professional Education

I hope it is clear by now that for all of us growing up in Western Civilization, we carry much distress and are highly programmed and conditioned to create, promote and allow oppressive patterns to persist. It is no wonder that we have difficulty thinking clearly and acting effectively to challenge authority. With this reality as our point of entry, professional training may be seen as the "finishing school" of a lifelong curriculum preparing us to believe, accept, defend and go along with the "System."

I was at a gathering in Southern California on

Valentine's Day of 1998 of about thirty people, mostly professionals, who shared a common work in challenging the theory and practices of biopsychiatry. One person in attendance was Loren Mosher, then clinical director of San Diego County Mental Health. Dr Mosher is a psychiatrist, perhaps best known for his work as director of a National Institute of Mental Health research project called Soteria House. This project demonstrated great success, over a period of several years beginning in 1971, in treating young adults diagnosed as "schizophrenic" in a residential house, with non-professional staff, with very infrequent use of drugs. (7) Dr Mosher has witnessed the overwhelming domination of the Mental Health System in the past three decades by the forces of biopsychiatry. He stated at our gathering that by far the number one factor in this occurrence was the overwhelming economic power of the pharmaceutical companies. He said it was common practice for his colleagues to receive a $1,000 to $1,500 fee plus travel expenses for a one hour presentation paid for by a drug company. Through media and "detail men," drug companies spend an estimated ten thousand dollars per physician per year in education. The second most important factor, according to Dr Mosher, was the pathetic nature of professional training. He said that when he was trained, though far from ideal, clinical training included basic listening skills. He and his classmates of the early 1960s approached his mentor, Elvin Semrad at Harvard's Massachusetts Mental Health Center, and asked "Tell us, Dr Semrad, what should we do to learn to relate to persons with schizophrenia as you can?" Dr Semrad's response to his eager audience, after a period of silence, was: "Go and sit in a room with your patients and talk with them about their lives-if one or the other of you feels better about it-consider it useful." In contrast, Dr Mosher's observation was that psychiatrists today are taught to reduce human beings to DNA strands and neurotransmitters.

Seymour Sarason writes on the massive problem of lack of caring and compassion in clinical practice. (8) There exists a serious problem in how graduate psychology and medical students are selected; he points out that selection is guided primarily by performance on abstract academic intellectual test criteria and that, generally speaking, selected students have a very narrow range of experience. I agree and believe that this reinforces earlier educational conditioning. Many who enter doctoral degree programs have a hard time being close and affectionate. Academic success is a necessary prerequisite; social affiliation and relatedness is not. The graduate school experience only reinforces and strengthens any tendency to emphasize mental aloneness rather than physical and emotional closeness. Human relatedness necessarily takes a back seat as PhD candidates spend hours upon hours alone in the library with books, journals and ideas. The students' intellectually brilliant professors, most successful in the academic world, often have great difficulty being warm, close and affectionate. I remember one of my own professors who was a wonderful teacher — very knowledgeable, well organized and highly entertaining in the classroom. I was shocked to find out that, in a one-on-one situation, outside of his classroom persona, he couldn't even look me in the eye. I think what really needs to be clearly seen is that virtually anyone selected for graduate training is in great need of a healing experience. Professional education should include good physical, emotional and mental support. My own reference point is a doctoral psychology program; Andrew Weil describes the reality of medical school:

"Medical education is frozen in a disease-oriented mode. The clinical training of doctors remains a brutal initiation that makes it very difficult for students to maintain healthy lifestyles and develop the mental and spiritual qualifies of healers." (9)

PROFESSIONAL LOYALTY

Through training and hospital experience psychiatrists develop an intense loyalty to each other. They become a tightly-knit band of brothers, much like soldiers in a combat unit; an "us against them" attitude becomes commonplace. Breaking the bond of comradeship becomes an arch-crime. Those who do become outsiders suffer personal and professional isolation, and face loss of prestige and loss of income, the latter through fewer referrals. Not many psychiatrists, or any other human beings for that matter, have the fortitude and moral courage to endure these kinds of sanctions for long.

SHARED GUILT

Psychiatrists are very reluctant to criticize their colleagues, because virtually all of them are, to a greater or lesser degree, guilty of the same kinds of offenses. Lobotomy, electroshock, forced drugging, seclusion, restraints, and involuntary commitment are points along the same continuum. Furthermore, to complete their residencies, psychiatrists are almost always required to engage in dehumanizing, harmful practices. Residents in psychiatry, for example, who will not administer, or assist in administering, electroshock, are usually not allowed to complete their training programs. By participating with fellow residents in inhuman acts, such as ECT and forced drugging, psychiatrists become bonded in a way reminiscent of the Nazi practice of sending young SS officers to concentration camps where they would collaborate in torturing prisoners. The Nazis called this bonding "blutkitt," literally "blood cement." Afterwards, the SS officers would be assigned to local police stations where they'd brutalize other prisoners without compunction and with the encouragement of officers with similar backgrounds. Dostoevsky put it this way in 'The Possessed' (1871): "All that business of titles and sentimentalism is a very good cement, but there is something better; persuade four members of the circle to do [in] a fifth on the pretense that he is a traitor, and you'll tie them all together with the blood they've shed as though it were a knot. They'll be your slaves, they won't dare to rebel or call you to account." (10)

Consider electroshock specialists. As psychiatrists, they believe themselves to be helpers. Challengers to this belief are a threat. Countless psychiatric survivors will attest to the fact that psychiatrists are apt to feel resentful toward those patients who can't or are unwilling to be helped by them. Administering ECT to such patients, or referring them to someone who will, is a quick, easy, and often profitable way for psychiatrists to vent their anger on them. At the same time, punishing (with ECT) those patients who do not see them as helpers strengthens the psychiatrists' conviction that they are.

Benedict and Saks examined the regulation of professional behavior concerning use of ECT in Massachusetts. Their results showed that 90 percent of ECT patients received treatment inappropriately.

Concerning this phenomenon of "blood cement," the authors found that while 41 percent of the statewide sample of psychiatrists reported knowing a colleague who, they believed, prescribed or administered ECT inappropriately, only 2 percent reported their concerns to an appropriate official or body for corrective action. Furthermore, "the more familiar a psychiatrist was with threatened or instituted lawsuits involving ECT, and the more likely a lawsuit was thought to be, the greater was his or her departure from the guidelines." (11) These doctors need to be stopped.

REINFORCEMENT OF THE MEDICAL MODEL

Biopsychiatrists think of themselves as working in the trenches. Cream-puff psychiatry, as they sometimes refer to psychotherapy or talk therapy, is not for them. Psychotherapy just doesn't work with people who are "suffering from real mental illness," or so it has been drummed into them. The use of drugs and ECT confirms the biological approach to "mental illness." Biopsychiatrists see real and rapid changes in patients who are electroshocked and drugged, unlike the patients in psychotherapy where change is likely to be gradual and subtle. The changes brought about by psychiatry's physical treatments always entail a diminution of personality and a loss of brain power, temporary or permanent, minor or major (depending upon the magnitude of the insult/assault factors seldom recognized by biopsychiatrists. In fact, by an astounding twist of logic, they regard certain symptoms of the psychiatrogenic injury as signs of improvement. For example, psychiatrists perceive the temporary euphoria sometimes brought on by ECT as a lifting of the patient's "depression." A neurologist would immediately recognize this condition, when combined with other ECT effects including confusion, amnesia, and dependency, as symptomatic of trauma-induced brain damage.

ON CARING AND COMPASSION

"Medical schools effectively cure students of the tendency to give overt expression to caring and compassionate feelings. Undue competitiveness, acquisition of facts that strain memory, being made to feel ignorant and incompetent, being socialized to worship at the shrines of science and technology, being influenced by mentors who are verbally caring and compassionate but in action are otherwise, being warned against getting "overinvolved" with patients ... " Seymour Sarason (12)

My struggle in finding clarity and making decisions about my level of involvement with Cindy, described earlier, is a personally anguishing example of professional confusion on this issue. Professional boundaries are a great protection to the professional, and they can, no doubt, protect the "patient" from distressed professionals as well. These same boundaries are, however, all too often a refuge from deeper caring, and a guardian of the status quo. The individual who challenges traditional roles defined by the profession will be forced to grapple, like I was, with profoundly difficult questions and emotions. The point here is that it is rare to receive clear and meaningful guidance, with real depth, in professional training.

Graduate school in psychology places much greater emphasis than medical school on theories of human behavior, but its students get a clear message which acts to reinforce the selection criteria of intellectual academic test performance. The student who has a flair for theory and research is viewed as better or more worthy, or more respected than the student who does not. The teachers are models of academic success. While perhaps not so "brutal" as medical school, the doctoral psychology experience is anything but healing; rather, it is incredibly stressful. All forces are geared toward intellectual isolation.

A BETTER WAY

What does make sense in terms of the education and training of mental health professionals? First and foremost, professional education should convey and be guided by a profound wisdom about the nature of human beings and the human condition (both individually and in groups). The content should provide a deeply understood theory of human development, the causes and mechanisms of distress and of healing.

It is of paramount importance that the structure of training as mental health professionals be based on an awareness of one's condition upon entering training. Chellis Glendinning, psychologist and pioneer in the field of ecopsychology, describes our modern-day human condition in a beautiful book titled 'My Name is Chellis and I Am In Recovery from Western Civilization'. She argues convincingly that, simply by virtue of growing up in modern Western civilization, we may all be seen as needing to recover from chronic post-traumatic stress. (13) My own description of some aspects of our conditioning also shows some of the ways we are hurt by modern technological childbirth, by our educational system, and in other ways. That we are hurting is obvious. The fact that psychiatry's response to all this hurting is to cry in alarm at the incredible incidence of "mental illness" and place millions upon millions of adults and children on drugs should be an obvious indicator of how far off course we are as a society and as a profession. One thing that this means is that the education and training of mental health professionals needs to be a healing experience. We are hurt. Healing is required to avoid perpetual, ongoing hurt we inflict on those with whom we have relationships. It is the responsibility of all of us, but particularly those who present themselves as members of the helping professions.

There are three specific ideas which could be guiding lights in thinking about preparing mental health professionals to do more help than harm. The ideas are equally relevant for all jobs of authority or leadership:

1/ Exquisite Self-Care. This should be modeled, demonstrated, discussed, encouraged and facilitated. Any theme which violates this criteria needs to be reconsidered. Clinical practice is incredibly demanding; all of us know the challenge of self-care in the context of caring for others. We can only teach and facilitate that which we know and do. It is clear that the "brutal" initiation of graduate education massively violates this principle.

2/ Connectedness. Theory and practice of professional training needs to be guided by an experience and understanding that we are, by our very nature, completely connected with all of life. It is especially crucial that mental health professionals know and experience this fact and relate to others, particularly our clients, from this base. Unfortunately, rather than mediating this wisdom, graduate education is the finishing school for an ongoing experience of separateness and isolation in a competitive, demanding, and dangerous world.

3/ Body Pilot. This term came from Jacquelyn Small, one of my teachers, author of several books and a leader in the fields of addiction recovery and transpersonal psychology. The real and true way to help others in the path of personal growth and consciousness evolution is not by abstract intellectual operations. Overemphasis on these results is arrogance, isolation, and disconnectedness. To be a body pilot means that you do your own work, that you plumb the depths of your own body/psyche, that you seriously honor the perennial maxim "Physician, Heal Thyself."

We can only teach and model that which we embody. Change and healing comes not so much from abstract intellect as from embodied experience. The meaning of this for graduate training is that a program should be highly experiential. Theory needs to be grounded in human experience; specifically, the teachers need to have done their own personal healing work so that they can guide or facilitate the work of their students. "Talking heads" are not to be trusted; individuals who speak from a place completely connected to body and psyche have much to offer us.

Clinical practice may be seen as the struggle to really understand another in order to be of help. The more profound our self-understanding, the greater our ability to understand another. The alternative is to see the other as alien. The current practice of mental health professional education does not facilitate profound understanding; over-emphasis on abstract intellectual pursuit is a serious problem. Even more serious is the tragic, distorted view of biopsychiatry which guarantees that the other's experience is seen not only as alien, but as dangerously pathological. Iatrogenic suppression by coercive control, drugs, or electric shock, rather than being seen for its true nature of cruel and damaging oppression, becomes justified as a necessary benevolence. Mental health professionals who create, promote or allow these practices have not been afforded a healing experience; they have been badly hurt, and hurting others is one way of evening the score.

Psychiatry vehemently asserts its "truths" and coercively inflicts itself on others. Loren Mosher shared one other piece of wisdom with us at the Valentine's Day gathering, which he said was his most important guideline as a clinician. Until you really, really understand what is going on, don't do anything other than be present and reside in your loving. Do nothing but explore, investigate, get to know the person and the situation. If you still don't understand, don't do anything. Good advice. I simply add the caveat to beware of false assumptions masquerading as understanding.

In sum, the graduate training of mental health professionals tends to bring forth the worst of all the above oppressive conditioning. It is all too much an inhumane ordeal involving fear, shame, isolation, and dependence on authority. The overwhelming academic and scientist/ practitioner emphasis all too often translates into mental isolation and separation. Rather than an empathy which comes from being a "body pilot," patients are labeled and treated as objects. The medical model of "mental illness" and its biopsychiatric worldview inevitably leads to a ubiquitous proliferation of harmful acts committed on "sick" patients, for their own good, by perpetrators who live in a state of "willed ignorance."

The end result is that doctors (aka clinicians and counselors) are not only trained in certain skills and knowledge, but are also immersed in an attitude that thoroughly cloaks reality — the attitude that "we are the experts," that "we know more," that "we are responsible for our patients who depend on us to make decisions for them." Mental health professionals are thoroughly conditioned to be emotionally invested in playing a role that effectively separates them from their humanness and from the human beings who are their "patients." The effect of training and credentialling is wonderfully illustrated by Ram Dass and Paul Gorman in their book, 'How Can I Help?' The following diploma is offered:

> [Your name] has finally proved himself adequate in the eyes of the undersigned responsible parties, if not in his own. [Your name] has mastered certain rules for helping and promises to abide by them. [Your name] knows something others don't know. [Your name] has been trained in the use of a number of skills and had them licensed by the State. [Your name] will use them to make others whole. [Your name] is entitled henceforth to call himself a DCP (Doctor of Certain Powers). [Your name] may not immediately appreciate the predicament this will put him in or the constraints it may impose upon all. Best not divulge too much, too soon. Which is why all this has been written in Latin. (14)

Speculation on Two Types

Two specific personality patterns are important to recognize in mental health professionals. The counseling profession draws an unusual number of people from one or both of two backgrounds; adult children of alcoholics (ACOA) and what we call "failed clergy." The ACOA literature has been very clear about describing the good "hero" child whose adaptive pattern is to help/save/rescue a troubled family; counseling is a great way to continue enacting this dynamic. In a similar vein, the profession of counseling is about as close to clergydom as you can get in a secular mode.

It is useful to distinguish between inherent human qualities and conditioned qualities. While heroism and helpfulness are inherent aspects of our human nature, they appear as conditioned rather than free when a rigidity is involved. When one "has to be" heroic or helpful in order to protect oneself against underlying anxiety, for example, these benevolent qualities are conditioned. In order to reclaim their inherent nature, we must heal the underlying distress. Both ACOA and "failed clergy" patterns show "good," "nice," "helpful" faces and tend to have significant problems with anger. It is as if psychiatric professionals have to be good, nice, and helpful in order to prove their worth and justify their existence. From the point of view of a professional, we desperately need our sick patients; to deny this and pretend that it is only they who desperately need us is a dangerous situation and a key to holding the forces of psychiatric oppression in place.

The second pattern I want to mention here is less common, but extremely powerful and important to understanding our predicament. L. Ron Hubbard calls it the Suppressive Personality. (15) The notion is that when we are developing as children, we naturally make decisions and interpretations of reality based on our experience. There is one particular adaptation to severe abuse that is especially dangerous. It involves a decision that, in order to survive, I must actively suppress (punish, negate, put down) any

expression of another that is positive or life-enhancing —
that I survive by holding power over others. Politics and
psychiatry seem to be two of the best places to continue
enacting this childhood adaptation as a functioning adult.
The results are disastrous.

Summary of Conditioning

We are thoroughly conditioned into a cosmology of
separateness. Dante described a theology which translates
into shame-based child-rearing. Descartes described a
science of objectivity which translates into isolation and
consensual madness. Our political and theological leaders
have engineered an educational system which translates into
student passivity and unquestioning respect for authority.

Professional training as an inhuman ordeal completes
the job of training service providers to be social engineers.
Disembodied, stress-filled, non-relational academia turns
out educators and trainers who are mentally isolated. The
famous Scientist/Practitioner model results in more
separation, labeling and treating patients as objects. The
modern day marriage of medicine and psychology has
produced the model called biopsychiatry which reduces
soulful human beings to biochemical machines; human
distress is translated into "mental illness" — diseased
patients treated by expert professionals with toxic drugs and
brain-damaging electroshock. The intrapsychic and
interpersonal personality patterns that influence mental
health professionals to create, promote and allow oppressive
practices to flourish are potent, driven by deep core feelings
of terror, shame and self-alienation.

How To Get Out

Getting out of the conditioned trap, liberating one's mind to think and one's will to act in a rational and powerful way is possible. Four fundamental ideas suggest a way out.

In order to be rational and in harmony with reality, we need good information. I have described above some of the mass of false and distorted information with which we always have been and still are regularly saturated. Theology, science and education all conspire to systematically instill a sense of ourselves as separate and alienated, fundamentally flawed and in danger. The industrial revolution, advancement in warfare, today's media and urban lifestyle all serve to reinforce and exacerbate this experience. Our only havens from the terror of separation and alienation appear to be either that we either choose the deity of an organized religion, or do what we're told and "get with the program" of our cultural standards. The necessity of madness is that we must violate these beliefs in order to become free; however, it feels so scary, and others judge us as crazy-especially when we reject the "obvious" necessity and importance of constant productivity. In order to become spiritually mature individuals, following the dictates of our own truth, we must challenge the group beliefs into which we were inevitably conditioned. (See Chapter 8.)

This book is intended to provide good information. Another key involves turning to "psychiatric survivors" for help. It is a remarkable current development that large numbers of people hurt by psychiatry are now organizing themselves and speaking out. I have stood in awe at the public hearings of the Texas Legislature as scores of electroshock survivors courageously walked through their fear and gave testimony about the injuries they had suffered at the hands of psychiatry. I have the utmost respect and admiration for the psychiatric survivors around the world who are speaking out. It is a remarkable phenomenon that thousands of individuals have and are coming forward to denounce the medical procedures which were purported to be for their own good as "treatments" for their alleged "illnesses." The mental health liberation movement has a wealth of good information to offer. In order to free ourselves from conditioned collaboration with oppression in the mental health system or any other system for that matter, it is necessary to search and reach for information and perspective outside the sanctioned sources of the system. In so doing, it becomes possible to begin softening the anxious experience of feeling like "strangers in a world we never made."

The second and unavoidably significant key to liberation is to heal our own wounds by accessing and releasing (or discharging) pent-up emotional pain and re-evaluating beliefs, conclusions and ways of relating to the world based on past hurts. This requires getting good help for ourselves. As an example of turning to psychiatric survivors, consider these teachings of Janet Foner, survivor, co-founder of Support Coalition International (see Resources), and International Reference Person for Mental Health System Survivors in Re-evaluation Counseling. Jane offers a five-point program for emotional healing which she teaches in a workshop called "Take Charge of Your Mind." The program involves focusing attention away from stressful activities and thoughts, and onto empowering, fulfilling ones. The five parts are: 1) Building your personal support network; 2) Creating space in your life for fun; 3) Restructuring your life to fulfill your dreams, 4) Self-healing as a daily practice; and 5) Making a commitment to focus o now, not on the past. (16)

We mental health professionals must free ourselves from the trap of "non-sick expert." We must allow ourselves to be fully human with dependency needs, open to and receiving a lot of support. We must work through our fear and shame, reclaiming our power in the best sense of the word — not power over another, but power to be, and express, and live the truth of who we are.

One of our premier tasks as human beings is to handle and positively resolve an experience of separateness. It is absolutely crucial that we challenge the isolation, and act on the truth that we are fundamentally and absolutely interdependent. This complete interconnectedness is the core experience referred to by all the great religious traditions. It is a spiritual connection, reflected on all levels: connected internally with our bodies and our emotions, connected externally with the natural world of earth, air, fire and water, of the tree people and the two-leggeds and four-leggeds, and all forms of life, with our families, a full range of friends and humankind. For mental health professionals, this connectedness must include clients and other professionals. While our shame will deter us in going to people we admire and want to learn from, it is nonetheless important to find and connect with models who are doing things better than us so that we can learn and grow. So thirdly, while good information and personal healing are absolutely necessary, they are not enough. Reclaiming power and freedom means living in a way that knows, to borrow a Native American phrase, "All My Relations." This knowledge is grounded in the awareness that the nature of reality truly is "All for one and one for all."

Finally, my experience and growing awareness is that to stand in this truth requires action. We must act for upliftment as well as against oppression. In order to break free and remain free as individuals, it is necessary to stand up and speak out. I invite all to take action against psychiatric oppression; I believe it is a key to liberation from all oppression. Holding a focus and building good alternatives are blessed actions. Taking a stand against oppression is equally blessed. In so doing, it is possible to experience Alice Walker's teaching that "The Secret of Joy is Resistance." (17) Knowing the experience of connectedness allows this work to flow from the truth of Leonard Frank's corollary that "The Secret of Resistance is Joy."

CHAPTER 7
SPIRITUAL EMERGENCE OR SUPPRESSION OF PSYCHOSIS: LESSONS IN PSYCHIATRIC OPPRESSION

I hope you are now better able to see how the psychiatric mind views and interprets the world in general, and human behavior in particular. I especially hope you have gained insight into ways that you may have adopted the beliefs of the psychiatric worldview and been influenced by it in relating to yourself and others. My purpose in this chapter is to share some lessons that may be learned from my experience with Cindy described in Chapter 1.

Cindy frequently had lunch at the community center I frequented myself, and her crisis emerged in that setting. She had that community up in arms, so to speak — she had people reacting all over the place at the community center and elsewhere here in Austin, Texas. Cindy was, in fact, demanding a reaction, or at least a response. She was loud and disruptive at our community center. She stole my audiotapes. She missed work. She kept saying whatever came into her head, and much of it was stuff that we socialized beings prefer to keep to ourselves, revealing only in our dreams, in our private anxieties and depressions, in our entertainment sources, in our attraction to outrageous characters safely distant on the video screen or written page. Often we reveal these disturbing thoughts and feelings only in the awful hostilities, resentments , and disappointments of our most intimate personal relationships—the painful stuck places of our marriages or the awful places we reject and punish our beloved children. Some of us are fortunate enough to establish personal counseling relationships where we can reveal and work through these shame-filled aspects of our being. Whether we have this outlet or not, we all certainly know better than to "let it all hang out" at lunch with our acquaintances and/or especially at work where not only our reputations but also our livelihoods are at stake.

Cindy was violating the dictates of our social order, and she had much to lose in doing so. The results hinged not only on her actions, but on the above-mentioned reactions of our community. Cindy demanded attention; she got in your face, she pushed, she ignored social niceties. She acted out of the urgent dictates of her own flood of thought and feeling. She was very sensitive to others' energy, but not out of consideration for them — only with concern of what dangers they may have held for her. She demanded attention; refuse it and she was even more demanding; give it and she took more and more of what she so desperately needed just then. People reacted; we became afraid and irritated, we worried, we went away, we looked for help. Many of us leapt to what was available in the way of authoritative opinion. This was where it became dangerous for Cindy, because the readily-available mindset and attendant institutions of mental health authority are dangerous.

The terms "spiritual emergence" and "suppression of psychosis" emphasize very different alternatives. "Spiritual emergence" is borrowed from the Spiritual Emergence Network, founded in California in 1985 to give voice to the challenging process of personal awakening and provide a base of referral sources for people wanting help in going through such an experience, especially when it feels and seems like an emergency or crisis. Brother David Steindl-Rast, a Catholic contemplative monk and author, defines Spiritual Emergence in Emma Bragdon's sourcebook on the subject:

> "Spiritual emergence is a kind of birth pang in which you yourself go through to a fuller life, a deeper life, in which some areas in your life that were not yet encompassed by this fullness of life are now integrated or called to be integrated or challenged to be integrated. ... Breakthroughs are often very painful, often acute and dramatic breakthroughs (happen) on all levels: what we call material, spiritual, bodily-all levels." (1)

I like the term because it honors humans as spiritual beings and holds out a possibility for moving through crisis into greater fullness of life.

To me, Spirit is the mysterious energetic source which sustains our being. It is the invisible life force. It is that which animates our bodies in life and that which is missing in a corpse. Spirit is always moving. Inherent qualities of spirit include a loving which reflects the oneness or interconnectedness of existence, and a truth which does not hide from or impede the energetic flow of life. One knows the spirit also by a joy which goes with living in truth and love, and experiencing the unending source of life which resides in us. To me, the term spirit or spirituality has nothing necessarily to do with organized religion, although the spirit can be present there. Rather, to be spiritual means to live life from the inside out, guided by and expressing the invisible forces of love and truth, resting in joy that these forces are unendingly present and available. I keep a framed quotation by the Vietnamese monk and teacher, Thich Nhat

Hanh, in the entry hall of my home which says, "The energy of love is abundant, waiting to be called upon."

Spirituality also refers to an experience of deep meaning and purpose in life. There is a quality of reverence for life, and devotion to loving or compassion, and to truth or wisdom. There is meaning and purpose in a life devoted to experience of love and truth inwardly, and manifestation or expression of these same qualities in the world.

The expression "suppression of psychosis" is borrowed from the language of biological psychiatry. "Psychosis" is seen as a form of "mental illness," classified in various ways in the 'Diagnostic and Statistical Manual' of the American Psychiatric Association. There is generally no hope in this model for a satisfying resolution of the experience. When it comes to "serious mental illnesses," psychiatry clearly states that there is no cure; control or suppression of the progression of this chronic and possibly fatal "disease" is the best possible result.

Cindy is no anomaly. She is one of hundreds of thousands of people in communities all over the nation and the world in crisis. The guiding worldview of our culture and of psychiatry wields powerful influence, and this worldview is flawed, inaccurate and dangerous to the well-being of people in psychospiritual crisis. I use the term "psychospiritual" as a melding of psychological and spiritual components. This term reflects my view that we are spiritual beings having a human experience, and that psychological experience always reflects our spiritual well-being.

On Communication

As I emphasized in Chapter 4, a key in human relatedness and in our desire to optimize the likelihood of positive human transformation lies in the language we use to interpret, describe and communicate. A corollary of the ubiquitous presence of oppressive language about emotional expression is the idea that we can stop listening to a distressed friend because he is "not making any sense." What we are really saying is that we don't understand; we have wandered into an explosion of inner turmoil, unique and idiosyncratic to the individual. "Not making any sense" is code for crazy. If we had wandered into an advanced symposium of computerized astrophysics, "not making any sense" would mean because of the limits of our knowledge and understanding. My advice is do not let yourself off the hook so easily; pay attention and you will be surprised at how much you will begin to understand. Relax and you might even enjoy much of the conversation; you might also recognize certain thoughts that you have sometimes had or should have had, but chosen to inhibit. At a minimum, I guarantee that you will get to know your friend and yourself in new, challenging and even exciting ways.

Freedom of speech is guaranteed by our Constitution. Leonard Frank recommends consideration of two other fundamental freedoms as positive antidotes to psychiatric suppression of emotion and thought; these are freedom of emotion or emotional expression, and freedom of thought.

What can a Community Do: Suggestions

RESPOND RATHER THAN REACT

People react to those who are flaunting the mores of our social order. The violator, in fact, demands some sort of a reaction or response. The difference between a response and a reaction is that a response is guided by an awareness which operates creatively and intelligently. A reaction, on the other hand, is just that. It is an action guided by the dictates of our own distress with the imperative to do something to ease our discomfort and get us out of danger. In modern parlance, we have had a button pushed; we are actually reacting more to our own internal distress than we are to the objective needs of the situation, however logical and intellectual our argument and justification may sound.

People who are violating the rights of others and feeling like they cannot help it do need a response. To collude with them is escapism; to punish them arbitrarily is totalitarianism. To punish them under the false pretenses of biopsychiatry is dishonest, immoral and an abdication of responsibility. Usually, such individuals are unconsciously searching for someone to give them good attention, confident and loving support, to heal the effects of their hurts. What typically happens is that this unaware and "out-of-control" expression, often intense and challenging, triggers our own distress. Our stuff gets activated and we react. The first step to being capable of providing good support, then, is to examine ourselves. We must face our fears and our embarrassments, and get support for ourselves when we are stimulated in such a way. Once we have cleared our own distress, we will be able to think and respond well to the situation. In the meantime, it is a good idea to take a deep breath and refrain from acting on any emotional sense of urgency, be it from restimulation of past hurts or from empathy with the other. The idea is not that we are unafraid, but that we act in the true meaning of courage: that we not deny our fears, but overcome them. Similarly, the question is not whether we have problems; we all do. Rather, the question is how to resolve them. A good rule of thumb is to face them head on. Walk through any isolation and talk to friends about what's hard for you.

BE A SUPPORTIVE WITNESS

The most important thing we can do for our friends who are going through a psychospiritual emergency is to be a witness. With good information and support for ourselves, we can rest in relaxed confidence and make ourselves receptive to the inner flow, with supreme confidence in the natural healing ability of the human body-mind. Probably 90 percent of the work takes place in its own natural order and time. If we can refrain from harmful intervention, most difficulties run their own course and balance is eventually restored. The gift of aware attention offered by a caring person makes it possible for an individual to pass through the most awful thoughts and feelings. Know the significance of this gift you have to offer; realize that it truly is a part of what your troubled friend needs.

ON ASKING FOR HELP

I am not suggesting that you and your friend in need should be able to go through this alone, or that you shouldn't ask for help. We all need all the help we can get, especially in times of crisis. If you are yourself in trouble, it is important

that you find someone brave enough to listen and offer
support. If you are not fortunate enough to have such
people in your life, my advice is that finding and getting
such support has to become your first priority. An analogy is
the airline flight attendant who always instructs adult
passengers, in the event of an emergency, to get oxygen first
for themselves before assisting a child or other dependent.
The principle is called "Take care of yourself, so you can
help take care of others." If it is not safe to reach for help
from friends and family, or others in your community, you
might try calling the National Empowerment Center, the
Spiritual Emergence Network, Support Coalition
International, or other resources listed in the back of this
book. Further guidance about self-care is provided in
Chapters 11, 12, and 15.

Very few communities in these United States offer
anything in the way of a truly safe place of refuge for people
who are going through psychospiritual crises. Handling
these crises without such support is extremely challenging a
best. Perhaps in the short run, I am making life more
difficult by pointing out that much of what is presented as
help by our society in situations of personal crisis is harmful
and punitive. But I am thinking well beyond the short run. I
implore you to continue seeing your friends as fully human
and to resist in every way the pull to label them as "mentally
ill" and alien to yourself.

Barb Lundgren, home schooling activist and
conference organizer, commenting on this section of asking
for help, wrote:

> "This sounds easy as you describe it and maybe that's
> your intent. As one who provides this support for many
> friends and relatives, I'd like you to suggest the level of

commitment, effort and reflection that is required but be clear also that the return is extremely positive.

Do ask for help, not for them but for yourself. We need to acknowledge our own incompleteness and better fortune in handling life just now. It is helpful to view life as a journey to be shared, both of you on the road to higher ground."

Always ask permission before you call somebody to "help" a friend. If you do decide that you need to call in external authorities to protect yourself from harm or from liability, I recommend that you know two things about yourself. First, know that you have spoken with your friend with as much compassion and forthrightness as you can muster. Second, know that you are calling these authorities not because your friend is defective and qualitatively different, but because you and your community do not have enough resources to offer at this time, or strong enough commitments to each other. You need to know that you have done your very best and are in a good position to continue being your friend's ally and to continue standing for a community which allows people to be unique and to grow, and supports its members through crisis. It also means that you can now allow yourself to fully grieve with loving support and a clear conscience.

BE REAL

In order to be a supportive witness, you have to be honest with yourself. You can't be supportive when you're terrified, angry or exhausted; those are all times to first take care of yourself. I say this not just for you, the reader. Remember that a friend in crisis is extremely sensitive; your energy is conveyed much more potently in other ways than the words that come out of your mouth. So give attention when you can; take care of yourself when you need to.

Maintaining social order is not inherently bad or evil; it has a necessary, practical aspect. Knowing one's limits and practicing self-care is necessary and practical. It is also necessary to challenge any idea that "mental illness" absolves one from social responsibility. As Thomas Szasz puts it, "The claims and practices of modern psychiatry dehumanize man by denying — on the basis of spurious scientific reasoning-the existence, or even the possibility of personal responsibility." (2) This is a very confusing area for most people; witness the confusion in our own country's interface with psychiatry and the law. Please consider that it may be a more compassionate action to call the police than to call psychiatry; the civil rights of the offending individual are better protected as a criminal than as a mental patient. The asylum mentality described in Chapter 3 outlines the beliefs which result in our society's complete willingness to deny civil liberties to the so-called mentally ill. (3) I'm not recommending that the police be called, only that you not collude in absolving friends from responsibility for their actions. The key is to be real, to be sincere and honest. If your friend offends you, tell her. If he scares you, tell him; just be sure and take a good look at yourself first; most of the fear we feel tells more about our own past than it does about the actual danger present in the current situation. Sometimes the most loving action is a truthfulness which means telling your friend that she is living a lie. Give your friend the same respect and consideration you would like to see extended to you; talk to him directly before you resort to disappearing, on the one hand, or calling the authorities on the other.

It is not my intention either to minimize the great pain and anguish suffered by those in personal crises; nor is it to suggest that all such experiences can be resolved through the attention of friends who are supportive witnesses. Some people are hurt more than others; some people need more than we have to give. It is vital, however, that we not underestimate the creative power of love and the natural tendency of human beings toward well-being and balance. Most of the time, that is enough. When it's not, I implore you to reject the idea that it is because this individual has a biologically-based "mental illness" that somehow makes him qualitatively different from you. Of course it is true that the biochemistry of our body affects our thoughts and feelings; many have helped themselves enormously by alterations in diet or by taking supplements which correct for deficiencies in systemic functioning. As an example, the reader may be interested in Robert Sealey's 'Unipolar Depression Survival Kit' (4) in which he reviews much of the related research and offers concrete advice. Mr Sealy had a very negative experience with psychiatric drug treatment for depression. He then found that eating the right foods supplemented with vitamins, minerals, and amino acids dramatically improved his health and mood. In contrast, diagnosis and biopsychiatric treatment by powerful mood-altering toxic drugs and/or electroshock are damaging. It only worsens the condition of our body-mind, and reduces the possibility of a beneficial intervention at a physical level.

A GLIMPSE OF COMMUNITY ORGANIZING

It has become standard in our society not to know your neighbor. A basic level of community is minimal engagement, a hello and nod of the head. The continuum goes on and on, from occasional loan of a tool or pantry item to sharing of meals to heartfelt sharing and interaction. Every level involves a greater investment of energy and greater appreciation of each person as an individual. Such investment and knowingness necessarily evoke deeper feelings of concern and responsibility, and make it more and more difficult to accept an undetailed, non-textured definition of a difficult human experience as a genetic, biologically based "mental illness." The more we know of an individual's story, the less we tend to judge on the one hand, or to dismiss on the other.

It can be anguishing as we get to know someone and see their struggles and their hurts, knowing they need help, but not knowing how to help or having the energy or resource to help. This tends to be particularly true when someone we love is in an extreme state of mind. Many of us have no reference points for understanding or for confidence in moving through or resolving such an experience. Others of us are uncomfortable or even alarmed at facing our own agitation in the presence of someone in a extreme state. As Dr Edward Podvoll said, "If you have a mind, it can go mad ... "On some level, we all know and fear the consequences of extreme states of mind — cataclysmic life situations in work and relationships, incarceration, drugging and/or electroshock. We see the "chronic mental ill" and the homeless every day on our streets.

The truth is that people can and do resolve extreme states of mind, often with little support in harsh conditions. I agree with Dr Podvoll that anyone can recover with sufficient time, and proper support and understanding. I recommend his book, 'The Seduction of Madness', for those who want to read about one realized vision of how to create a therapeutic community for people in psychological crisis. (5) It involves the creation of intensively supported homes for individuals to rest, be safe, establish loving relationships, gradually work through the hurts, and balance the mind and body. Podvoll makes the wonderful point that it is much more helpful to focus on an individual's history of well-being than on his history of "insanity." It is crucial to challenge the notion that extreme states of mind are a priori evidence of unresolvable genetic defect. Instead, hold the image of well-being and assume that as genetic nature. Podvoll also emphasizes that even the most extreme "psychotic" has islands of clarity. These are moments or periods of lucidity which show up, often frequently, throughout extreme states of mind. The work is to honor and appeal to these states, patiently and gradually building on this natural tendency of the mind. What we call "madness" is a process, not a condition. How we respond to an individual in crisis can make all the difference in transforming a stumbling block into a stepping stone to positive growth and transformation.

In a simpler vein, and congruent with the level of community most of us currently have, I am thinking of two ways that we can make a difference. As is so often the case in a culture with a monetary system such as ours, many of our problems and possible solutions are inseparably bound to economics-paying the rent, buying food, paying for counseling, etc. One thing a community can do is establish a money fund to help its members in emergencies. A related idea is to establish a fund comprised of people's time. The core of Podvoll's therapeutic homes is the "basic attention" of a committed group of support people who form a therapeutic team. A "team leader" organizes individuals who volunteer a shift or two a week (three hours is

recommended) to give attention and support to someone ir
need. While some education and training is necessary to
provide this for someone in an extreme state of mind, the
principle is fairly simple. The person being helped wants
the help, of course, and is fully involved in the process.
Voluntariness must always be a necessary condition in
offering genuine help. As volunteers must always be sincere
so too must recipients always desire and ask for the help.

ENTRY INTO PSYCHIATRY (AND EXIT FROM THE COMMUNITY AT-LARGE)

Recall the story of Cindy and me. Prior to her eviction from
her apartment, Cindy was "involuntarily
committed"(incarcerated) to the State Hospital for extende
screaming in her apartment which alarmed the neighbors.
At the State Hospital, she was forcibly injected with drugs a
least three times in the first week, including the morning of
her first judicial hearing. She was released unexpectedly
after two weeks, had already alienated her friends, and bein
afraid of the Salvation Army for overnight stay, was on the
street and frequently visiting Psychiatric Emergency
Services. Four days after her release, she was arrested and
charged with assaulting someone at Psychiatric Emergency
Services. After a week in jail, she was back at the State
Hospital, on a different unit with a different doctor. Cindy
was going through a hellish nightmare.

It would be all too easy to adopt one of two stances at
this point. One is that this was all Cindy's fault and
responsibility, thereby avoiding issues of personal and socia
responsibility by blaming the victim. The beliefs of
biopsychiatry are readily available to do this with minimal
pangs of guilt, resting in the assurances of scientific
medicine that the poor woman suffers from an unfortunate

biological or genetically based "mental illness." I did my best to challenge this notion in our community, but it is deep-seated. The second stance is to resign oneself to a feeling of chronic hopelessness about our society. The work of discharging chronic hopelessness (through supported emotional release), and reclaiming power, is so important for all of us.

Those who barely knew Cindy either scarcely noticed or breathed a mild sigh of relief that lunches were less frequently bothered by social tension. Those who were most intimately involved with her, including myself and two other men who had befriended her, most definitely breathed a huge sigh of relief and were grateful for a respite from the increasingly agitated demands she was making. It appears that everyone who was close to Cindy was intensely shaken by the ordeal. One of the other two men at our community center who most cared for Cindy is the owner/manager of the center. He shared with me the anguish he was experiencing as Cindy escalated the disruptive behavior which led to her hospitalization.

It is painful to admit that even I and my friends benefit, on one level, from psychiatric oppression. My community center is more tolerant than most. Members really stretched themselves to make space for our friend who was having such a hard time. We leaned on each other for support and refrained from urges to "call the state" to intervene. We did our best to be both compassionate and real. At the same time, this community is not a family nor is it a committed intentional community of people living together and sharing the various levels of this earthly existence. It is, in fact, a group of relatively progressive individuals from various walks of life who share a common interest in health, food, and conversation. We care about each other, but mostly we live our lives quite separately and enjoy seeing each other at meals. None of us was willing to take this woman into our home to live when she faced eviction from her apartment on the grounds of being a disruptive influence there (she was).

Because we allowed psychiatry to fulfill its social mandate, the rest of us at the community center were on one level relieved, once again able to enjoy our serene lunches since the State was "handling" our disruptive frien We could enjoy our pleasant community without the disruption, stress and inconvenience of having to alter our independent lifestyles. This is a graphic example of the reality that psychiatric oppression serves to keep the status quo in place. Real change requires clear intention and effo to strengthen the level of community we share. We are discussing a plan for an ecovillage south of Austin where w would live and work together, and be in a much better position to shelter and care for each other when we need it most.

Given proper support, Cindy and others like her can get through crises successfully without coercion and witho toxic drugs. Our community, like most others, has a long way to go to become a safe and supportive place for this promise to be regularly fulfilled. Our task is awesome, ultimately a reordering of every level of our lives. I believe that each of us must begin by making a deep commitment truth and self-discovery, to responding with as much support as we can to those around us, and to lending our energies where we can to changing the world around us. W must give ourselves permission to care very deeply, and commit to express this deep caring to others. No settling f less; let us begin a gradual process of transforming self and society, one step at a time.

CHAPTER 8
THE NECESSITY OF MADNESS AND UNPRODUCTIVITY

Four centuries ago, Western civilization was involved in a horrific experience known as the Inquisition. Hundreds of thousands, probably millions of people, mostly women and Jews, were tortured and killed in the name of God. Two centuries later, during the dawning of the industrial revolution, large numbers of people were sent to poorhouses and prisons in the name of productivity; they were locked up for their debts and poverty. As I write this, it is 1998, and organized religion, while still a major force in war and brutality around the world, has moved beyond the superstitions associated with witchcraft and the attendant tortures and killings of the Inquisition. Western governments have passed laws forbidding imprisonment of citizens for debt and poverty. Nevertheless, in the twentieth century, hundreds of thousands of "mentally ill" individuals and millions of Jews were "exterminated" in the "final solution" of Nazi Germany. And today in the United States, two of the fastest growing and most profitable industries are prisons and the practice of biopsychiatry. The global market for antidepressants alone is estimated to hit six billion dollars by 1998; (1) Electroshock is estimated to be a two to three billion dollars a year industry. (2) We are constantly bombarded with the information that "mental illness" is a societal epidemic affecting up to a third of our population. The numbers of homeless individuals, adults and children, are also increasing at an astounding rate; many of these people carry psychiatric labels.

Why am I linking all of the following: witchcraft, "mental illness," poverty, productivity, prisons, homelessness, pharmaceuticals, and electroshock? For the same reason that I link madness and unproductivity in the title of this book. During the Inquisition, the Catholic Church killed and tortured vast numbers of human beings in order to save their souls. European countries placed debtors in prisons and poorhouses to teach them a lesson, and to defend and protect the values of a burgeoning industrial capitalism. The Nazis killed millions judged as unfit in order to preserve the purity of a race. These three events all have in common an active, aggressive effort to defend and preserve belief systems perceived as more valuable than the lives of those who were viewed as a threat to that system. Disbelief or failure to adhere to the guiding beliefs served as a priori evidence of the unworthy, unproductive or unfit nature of the unfortunate victims. Our modern mental health system, guided by the theory and practices of biopsychiatry, is heir apparent to these previous, horrific examples as a primary mechanism of soci control. I argue now for the value, indeed the necessity, of the very qualities which psychiatry so zealously suppresses — "madness" and unproductivity.

Re-interpretation of Once Righteous Acts

Most of us look back at the Inquisition as an unfortunate, perhaps tragic consequence of superstitious beliefs which society has since outgrown, largely as a result of the age of enlightenment and the scientific revolution. In retrospect, the guiding beliefs of the Inquisitors seem clear: belief in only one path to salvation, the human body a shameful, unclean vessel, any and all actions justified in the name of a soul's salvation. The mandate to eradicate and triumph over all vestiges of pagan heresy was completely justified and sanctioned.

We tend to view the early injustices of the industrial revolution — the cruel and severe working hours and conditions, sweat shops, child labor — as an unfortunate, perhaps tragic result of societal upheaval and transition. The belief system of those who led society in the times of poorhouses and debtors' prisons also seems clear. It was a belief in industrial progress and the advancement of civilization, bolstered by a Calvinist theology which linked material success with spiritual advancement, and lent great justification to the punishment of those who failed to succeed in the brutal realities of the marketplace.

Nazi genocide tends to be viewed merely as an aberration, the result of a madman in power or the forces of evil at work in the world. Nazi ideology, consisting of a fanatical belief in the biological superiority of the Aryan race, justified a messianic effort to exterminate the unfit in order to purify and advance the quality of humankind.

A Modern Rendition

What does the modern United States boom in prisons, homelessness and biopsychiatric practices have to do with torture, murder and debtors prison? We do not aggressively seek and destroy those seen as unworthy, surely not. We are, thankfully, more tolerant today, aren't we? We take pride in our democratic government, and justify the fact that we have by far the largest per capita prison population of the entire world as an unfortunate but necessary protection of liberty and freedom. Our economic belief in free enterprise, together with the theological belief in free will, allows us to absolve ourselves from shame and remorse at the incarceration of such a high percentage of our fellow citizens, especially young men of color from poor or working class families. We tend to view homelessness in a similar light: their responsibility, their choice.

Is it possible that the guiding beliefs of today's society are, somehow, as superstitious as those of the Inquisitors, as self-serving as the early industrialists, as inhuman and justifying of cruelty as the Nazis? Free enterprise and free will do seem a long way from imprisonment for debt and murder in the name of salvation or racial purification; certainly these are worthy values. However, I believe that most of us are grossly confused about the nature of both free enterprise and free will.

The truth is exceedingly clear, first of all, that we are far from a free enterprise economy. The interface of big government and multinational corporations is most obvious so many of our citizens and political leaders decry welfare for the poor, while providing massive subsidies for large-scale industries such as military contractors, oil and gas, and nuclear power. The astronomical amount of money involved in the recent savings and loan bailout is just one example. The gap between a very wealthy few and a growing percentage at or below the poverty line is dramatically increasing. To justify this as an artifact of free enterprise really is a superstition on the order of the Inquisition and an uncaring coldness on the order of those who justified debtors' prison; we are not a free enterprise system and our citizens do not deserve poverty and homelessness.

But what about free will? I think that any attempt to justify homelessness and imprisonment with a belief in the concept of free will is a gross misunderstanding of free will. First of all, we really don't have free will at the physical level. Rhetoric that you can do anything, be anything, is simply untrue. If you don't believe me, take a moment just now and fly on your own without an airplane. See if you can stop breathing without artificial aid; you will soon pass out and find yourself breathing. Furthermore, the quality of the air you have no choice but to breathe is a great reminder of the fact that rugged individualism is a false belief and of the truth that we are utterly interdependent, whether we choose to believe it or not. The truth is that not every child can be President. In the spirit, there may be free will; in the flesh, there is free choice. For many of us the choices are difficult and limited.

One result of our simplistic and misguided belief system is rigidity and lack of creativity in thinking about alternatives. If crime can be completely explained as weak character and a choice for evil, there is no need to think anymore about transforming society and renewing genuine opportunity and motivation for the disenfranchised. If teachers are having a hard time managing their classrooms, and we explain it simply as biological defects in the children, then there is no need to think and respond creatively to the real needs of our children. Thinking and action are quite literally constrained by the assumptions of what we believe. An unfortunate effect of false beliefs in free will and free enterprise, and the attendant philosophy of rugged individualism, is this epic political division between the "cold-hearted conservatives," on the one hand, and the "bleeding-heart liberals," on the other. People stuck in both of these camps misunderstand this dimension of free choice.

One camp tends to "blame the victim;" the other thinks the "victim" needs to be rescued. The conservatives blame the liberals and the liberals blame the conservatives, so ultimately everybody gets to be a victim. A mature conception of free choice and interdependence demands a host of other responses to our current societal challenges besides punishing the unsuccessful or grudgingly providing a welfare system which reinforces a dependent condition unsuited to human development.

Biological Psychiatry

Let us briefly review the guiding beliefs of biopsychiatry and how they relate to the Inquisition, to prisons and to Nazi genocide. Inquisitors believed that failures in social adjustment were due to the Devil; they called it heresy. Industrialists believed that failures to succeed in life were a result of moral weakness; they called it laziness and crimina negligence. Nazis believed that bad genes doomed people t weakness and inferiority. These three powerful groups had key role in common in their respective cultures; all were agents of social control, ruthlessly enforcing the norms of their societies. In the modern Western world, psychiatry continues this legacy of cruelty and suffering: it has become the major agent to enforce social norms and values, backed up by military force in the form of police, National Guard, and actual tanks and troops (kent State, Guatemala, Waco, etc.). Remember Thomas Szasz' analogy about religion anc psychiatry: "The Inquisition is to Heresy as Psychiatry is to Mental Illness." (3)

Szasz also described the link between debtors' prison and psychiatry. (4) Psychiatry plays an incredibly powerful role in supporting and enforcing the inexorable dictates of capitalism and its relentless drive for continuous productivity. The astounding increase in consumption of psychiatric stimulant drugs (the so-called anti-depressants) is one example of this force. It is more acceptable to push one's body and psyche to perform on toxic stimulant drugs than to go through a period of unproductivity. Euphemistically calling anti-depressants "medical treatment" allows for an ongoing denial of the desperation people feel at the lack of a safety net of support in our communities; one paycheck away from the street is the reality for more and more individuals in our society.

The link between Nazi Germany and biopsychiatry is the clearest and most direct of all. As I described in Chapter 3, psychiatry provided the philosophy which guided the eugenic practices of the Nazis; psychiatrists also did the dirty work. The very men who did this work were, for the most part, allowed to resume positions of leadership and prestige after the war; their students and followers carried their beliefs forward in Germany and into the United States. Today, the intellectual heirs of Nazi biopsychiatric theory and practice teach that biologically-based "mental illness" is the cause of failures in social adjustment; drugs and/or electroshock are the current biological "treatments" designed to control this genetic menace of epidemic proportion in our society. The search for genetic defects is as ardent as ever.

A final, most important commonality of psychiatry with these three horrible examples of human cruelty is that it is, at its root, coercive and violent. It is important to remember that as long as the threat of involuntary "treatment" exists, the offering of "voluntary" care is, at best, severely compromised. "Voluntary patient" is very often a euphemism for a resigned or politically smart psychiatric inmate. Psychiatry is sanctioned by our government, not only to serve those who want help, but also to impose "help" on those who do not want it. Heretics needed to have their souls saved because they were under the sway of the devil. Unpunished paupers were a threat to the beliefs and interests of Calvinist capitalism. The Jews deserved eradication for the higher good of Aryan racial purity. Likewise, the "mentally ill" are a threat to our social order, and must be controlled. The rhetoric justifying coercive treatment has always sounded good enough to relevant oppressors. The rhetoric of biopsychiatry is particularly beguiling, and most of us accept the assertion not only that "mental illness" is a genetic or biologically based disease, but that those "suffering" from this "disease" need to be forcibly incarcerated and "treated" — "for their own good," of course. Never mind the truth that the concept of "mental illness" was created as and still is a metaphor for physical illness, or that the fervent search for scientific evidence of a consistent biological or genetic cause of any problem routinely seen by psychiatrists has yet to bear fruit. Most of us unquestioningly accept the word of authority, and if the media repeats it over and over again and calls it fact, we believe it. The hard truth is that psychiatry is based in coercion; the civil rights of those with psychiatric labels are violated more easily even than those charged with criminal offenses.

False Gods: Productivity and Health

Two of the most potent and revered qualities of our present society are productivity and health. Productivity holds the status of a god, to be respected, revered, sought after, rewarded, and unquestioned. Productivity is a means and an end. It is given credit for that which is perceived as good; it is said that the solution for that which is perceived as bad can be found by appealing to this god of productivity. Money is, of course, the spiritual energy transmitted by this god, manifested as reward for proper obeisance at the physical level. Certainly, we believe, bad results in life are due to failures to worship and abide by the laws of this deity. We may not call our detention facilities by the name of debtor's prison, but we fill them with the unfortunate souls who have not reaped favor with this supreme god.

Health may be seen as a just-ever-so-slightly less powerful god, although evidence suggests a mighty jockeying for position in the spiritual hierarchy. We strive for, read about and spend massive amounts of money in the quest for "perfect health." That we spend especially incredible amounts as we get close to death is strong evidence for our desperate need to deny death, revealing the flimsiness of any true belief in or experience of our spiritual nature. It also shows the reason I see a great challenge of the supreme god by this god of health. Productivity's co-optation of health to feed his power (reflected at the physical level by inclusion of health spending in the Gross National Product) has gotten out of control. Many of us have become so completely self-absorbed with the health god that we are badly neglecting to pay proper homage to the supreme god, Productivity. It has gotten so bad that many of us are now appealing to an arm of the supreme god (the federal government) to actually take care of us in the name of this lesser god of health (witness the tremendous backlog of applications for disability at the Social Security Administration).

Generally speaking, work conditions are designed such that health is a necessary condition for productivity; not perfect health, by any means, but some modicum of health, whatever that may be. What could be the purpose of the concept of perfect health which, by all indications, does not now nor ever has actually existed? What is "perfect"? Is there such a thing at the physical level? What are the criteria? And are they the same for me as for you as for anyone else? If, indeed, there really is no such quality, what then is the value of all our desperate striving? And what is the value of the inevitable feelings of shame or inadequacy that we all feel at various times for our failures to attain the unattainable? Does it sound at all like the concept of "original sin" to any of you? "Lord, I am not worthy, but only say the Word and my body shall be healed."

Shame has a particularly significant function in this cult of productivity worship; an intense core of self-doubt and feelings of inadequacy are necessary and essential to ensure that human beings continue to willingly participate in a system which is inherently anti-human in so many ways. Without these unworthiness worms crawling in our psyches, it is highly unlikely that a classist division of humankind would be tolerated at all. That a few are able to live not on their own labor, but on the work of others is inherently exploitive; the huge and growing gap between rich and poor is far from any kind of a rational society. Placing the false god of productivity over essential human needs and the excellent care of our young is ludicrous and absolutely unacceptable. An essential maintaining factor of a class-based society is to keep the workers divided and squabbling; racism, sexism, ageism, adultism, and all other forms of oppression serve this function and keep us from seeing clearly. It makes it difficult to unite and challenge the real problems and come up with real solutions involving radical change in society. The function of shame is also to guarantee workers who are willing to participate as cogs in a system which values profit over human life; who are willing to be wage slaves, working at uncreative, unsatisfying, unfulfilling jobs, sacrificing our bodies, our families, our children, everything for the sake of a job and a paycheck.

Thou shalt not have false gods before me. Our modern version of this biblical injunction is constantly reinforced for the average American who watches five hours of television per day, and sees approximately 21,000 commercials per year. Our main religious representative, the TV, gives us 21,000 identical messages, all aggressively saying, "Buy something! Do it now!" Productivity is our supreme god; consumption is our divinely-anointed duty as children of god.

MENTAL HEALTH

So health ranks a close second in today's spiritual hierarchy. We devote enormous amounts of time, energy and money to the pursuit of optimal, preferably perfect health. "Mental health" is a sibling of the god of physical health. School children's self-esteem classes and corporate workers' wellness programs both sound appealing, and in a positive vein, reflect a growing level of self-awareness in our society. My concern is with the use of "mental health" as a criterion of social acceptability and as a flip-side reinforcer of the purported value of identifying and treating "mental illness." Modern civilization has developed an increasingly important place for the concept of "mental health" in our spheres of concern, perhaps even more spiritually significant to us than physical health. After all, an adult citizen still retains an unquestioned right to be physically ill; rarely is an individual forced to receive a treatment for physical illness against his will—the right to die is generally respected. In contrast, we routinely coerce citizens with psychiatric labels into "treatment" against their will. The fact that a "mentally ill" citizen is denied the right to refuse "treatment" is a stark indicator of the value we place on "mental health." Does this not appear similar to the Inquisitors, the poorhouse wardens and the Nazis — all placing such great value on their beliefs as to warrant complete violation of life and liberty, and all completely self-justified in the goodness of their actions?

"Mental health" is of such potent significance to us today that heresy ("mental illness") justifies incarceration and forced ingestion of powerful, toxic, brain-disabling drugs and/or brain-damaging electroshock. The particular favor given to biopsychiatry in the media is, perhaps, the clearest indicator of the high status conferred on "mental health" today. That we so easily accept the misinformation of this pseudoscience shows both the effectiveness of psychiatry and the media, and the extent of our conditioning which allows shame to hold sway as we unquestioningly defer to authorities outside of ourselves, and neglect the work of becoming our own authorities.

We are also afraid. Fear of god has always been a prime religious motivator; alongside shame, it continues to be a major factor in obeisance to the coercive and harmful practices of psychiatry. Coercion means punishment, clearly a fear-based practice. Fear of damnation, fear of psychiatric incarceration — both extremely powerful and effective motivators. What's interesting and important to understand is that not only the apparent victims hold fear. The Inquisitors lived in a world of tremendous psychic fear: of god, of the devil, of retaliation by those they tortured. Guardians of productivity tend to be most obsessive and fearful of losing their money. The Nazis lived in a nightmare world of threat and intimidation. What about mental health professionals, particularly those who operate under the beliefs of biopsychiatry? Biopsychiatry appeals to us, at least in part, because it encourages an illusion that allows us to separate from those "afflicted" with "mental illness." They are "ill" due to genetic or biological defects; we are healthy, not ill. There is a qualitative difference between us and them. Whether you call people mad, as in antiquity, or "mentally ill," as in modern times, such selection and labeling is a dangerous proposition in a society whose mental health system is based on the coercive practices of biopsychiatry.

Consider that one characteristic of our inherent nature as human beings is a constant organismic push toward wholeness and awareness, that repressed hurts are continually pushing to be brought into awareness so that they may be given attention, expressed and resolved. Consider, furthermore, that this push feels most uncomfortable, usually experienced as what we call anxiety or, at times, panic. Let's call it the edge of madness, and let's assume that all of us have and are, to varying degrees, experiencing this existential fact that we can go mad. Consider the tendencies of individuals who secretly carry an intense core feeling of inadequacy and unworthiness, along with great unconscious feelings of terror. There is every reason to assume that mental health professionals are as human as everyone else, and therefore as much on the edge of madness as anyone. There is even evidence, such as the relatively high rate of suicide, that the internal pressures of psychiatrists are even greater than average. Coercive, harmful treatment of our fellow human beings, however beguiling the rhetoric, is always a reflection of great hurt and distress in those who are inflicting the harm. This is as equally true of the agents of psychiatry as it was of the inquisitors and the Nazis.

We suppress others to avoid facing something that we cannot face inside of ourselves; adults see "bad" children who deserve punishment only when they themselves have unhealed memories of being punished for their "badness." We oppress those with psychiatric labels because they touch our own fear and shame, and remind us that we can go mad; we push "depressed" people to take stimulant drugs because we fear our own decline into grief and unproductivity. We incarcerate these people to get them out of sight and out of mind. We give them brain-damaging "treatments" to drug or shock them out of their "mental illness" which is so discomforting to us. We are also afraid of madness because mad individual may violate our most sacred beliefs and values, tends not to be nice, and can be altogether unpredictable. Rather than relishing the surprise and challenge of the unexpected, we feel anxious and afraid in the face of uncertainty. We are afraid of mad people because of our own insecurity. We don't trust our own creativity and intelligence, and we are already carrying so much guilt and shame that we cringe at the prospect of being responsible for someone in an extreme state of mind. These inner truths, together with the outer realities of an inordinately stressful, disjointed and alienated society, make it seem altogether unbearable to face madness. The pseudo-scientific and seemingly benevolent language of psychiatric care offers a welcomed and convenient escape from the anguish of our fellow humans on the outside, and our own on the inside.

The Necessity of Madness and Unproductivity

One response to an informed awareness of the danger and harm done by the practices of biopsychiatry is to work for reform, to challenge the most dangerous "treatments." Our legislative campaign to ban electroshock in the state of Texas is one example; advocacy for "patient" rights, and the search for more humane "treatment" is also in this vein. It is easy to do this while wholeheartedly continuing to embrace the core guiding values of our biopsychiatrically-based mental health system — namely, productivity and mental health. It is also exceedingly possible, and in fact common, to consider yourself an advocate and ally to the "mentally ill" while being in favor of the principle of coercive "treatment" or "involuntary commitment."

Drug use is a dramatic illustration of the assertion that productivity is the supreme god and the supreme virtue of our current society. As Jamie Alexander, a psychiatric survivor and mental health liberation leader points out, "Caffeine is the most popular drug in the world, and it is the perfect drug for the modern worker doing tedious, boring or mindless, repetitive work." (5) Alexander quoted an 1891 observer of this phenomenon: "The worker of the Nineteenth Century works beyond his strength, and in order to keep it up he resorts to stimulants — coffee, tea, spices, alcohol, tobacco." (6) Today, we add psychiatric drugs by the ton to ensure that no one gets a rest. The Leveys, in their book, 'Living in Balance', point out that 25 percent of the U.S population has difficulty sleeping and that as many as 80 percent are sleep-deprived. Twenty percent of doctor visits are related to exhaustion. Half of the burnout cases are people suffering from sleep deprivation, and the majority aren't even aware of it. (7) There is no time to ask why people are so fatigued or bored or isolated — or why they need a "pick-me-up" to increase production speed or reduce their feelings of pain and exhaustion. Prozac and other stimulant "anti-depressants" have become a multi-billion dollar industry, and the effects profile is virtually identical to amphetamines. Nobody is allowed to dwell on the question of the source of all the pain and exhaustion.

We may have instituted child labor laws, but look at the modern alternative. Ritalin, a drug known to produce repetitive, stereotypical behavior in animals, is being foisted on millions of our school-age children with the hope of enforcing classroom docility, compliance and productivity. (8)

An overwhelming value placed on productivity stems from a reduction of human nature to a soulless, mechanistic materialistic existence. The activities which appeal to our deepest nature and which inspire and enrich us are, for the most part, unproductive in a capitalist or industrialist sense. They have to do with physical closeness and affection, with emotional energy, with unmarketable creative expression, with relationships, with curiosity, with play and with inner and outer rituals by way of which we approach the numinous and the divine.

One major effect of compulsive productivity is to powerfully inhibit our ability to live in the spiritual truth of our complete interconnectedness with all of life, and particularly with our fellow human beings. Forgiveness is taught in all of our great spiritual traditions as a key to spiritual well-being. In the Christian tradition, for example the esoteric Christ is virtually synonymous with forgiveness It seems that a focus on productivity, however, is a direct impediment to the quality of forgiveness. I think it is because productivity, especially as defined within the

parameters of our competitive, capitalist, pseudo-free
enterprise system, is based on endless striving for
perfection. Perfection is based in judgment. Our
productivity system requires constant comparison:
judgment, judgment, judgment. It is absolutely necessary to
step out of perfectionism and productivity to let go of
judgment and to forgive. Forgiveness is for giving. It is a
letting go. It is entirely unproductive. Love is a gift of the
spirit. No judgment or effort required. Freely given. No
production necessary.

Unproductivity is necessary to step out of the rules of
productivity and move into forgiveness. This reflects a more
general principle about the nature of beliefs and human
development. Carolyn Myss, medical intuitive and best-
selling author, begins her tape series, 'Energy Anatomy',
with the provocative assertion that madness is an absolutely
essential stage in the attainment of spiritual maturity. (9)
The reason for this has to do with the fact that we are all
necessarily, inevitably and thoroughly initiated into the
beliefs of our tribe, or culture, from the time of our
conception onwards. These beliefs thoroughly impregnate
our body and our psyche, largely at a non-verbal level. We
are all tribal members, loyal to tribal law, way before we
even begin to approach the idea, much less the experience,
of becoming an individual.

Forgiveness is a violation of our current tribal rules of
productivity and legal contracts. "Mental illness" is the label
we give to a citizen who is disloyal to these laws. It is the
modern heresy, the mark of a defective, inferior human
being. Such heresy implies tremendous, outright disloyalty
to our tribe, in particular to the zealous tribal worship of the
great god of materialistic productivity. Forgiveness is a
perspective which allows for mystery, which places

relationship above profit, a rich inner life above material possessions, the search for meaning and purpose above the search for money. Above all, it involves placing your own truth above the truth of the tribe, and this is the greatest and most unacceptable heresy of all. Jesus was crucified because of it; today, we incarcerate these heretical souls, drug and electroshock their brains and bodies.

The teaching is essentially this. First, we are members of a tribe; later, we are presented with the opportunity and the challenge to become individuals. Somehow, some way we betray and we are betrayed. A man does everything he was ever taught that a good man should do. He is loyal to his country and fights in a war. He gets married and has children, works hard and succeeds financially. He feels empty and melancholy. He feels betrayed by all the promises of fulfillment that would come with righteous discharge of his duties. The tribe is let down by his irrational dissatisfaction and unproductivity in the face of his picture book life. He is diagnosed with depression and goes on Prozac. A woman finds a good man, has children, is financially supported by her husband, and still isn't happy. Or she has fulfilled her role and her husband leaves her. Either way, she feels melancholy about the felt betrayal. Either way, she is a candidate for psychiatric treatment.

Betrayal can happen in many ways, often by way of health or finances. But it will happen. We are betrayed by the failures of our childish adherence to tribal beliefs to fulfill the needs of our next stage of spiritual development. Being loyal to family rules of politeness, for example, may interfere with your responding to spirit's demand that you tell the truth. We betray when we take up the challenge to become individuals, begin to question tribal authority and to look inwardly for guidance. Members of your tribe may consider you disloyal when you tell the truth. One result of this decision to embrace yourself as a spiritual being and to reorder the placing of your loyalties is that you require not only significant amounts of unproductive time, but you inevitably undergo some form of madness. By definition, tribal politics consider such betrayal as madness. By experience, the anxiety and discomfort of uncertain personal transformation is at times confusing, disorienting, depressing, and frightening — call it madness. The psychiatric tribe calls it a breakdown and a malignant condition. It is infinitely more helpful to embrace the truth that madness is a dynamic process which can result in breakthroughs to deeper levels of spiritual maturity and a richer, fuller life. The spiritual journey requires tremendous courage and honesty. A result which I am honored to facilitate is liberation from slavish devotion to our wrathful deity of (mental) health which enforces the supreme tribal value of productivity through our cultural system of psychiatry.

Simply put, it becomes easier to let go of the pressure to measure up to an ideal standard, and to love and accept our bodies and ourselves as we are. We find the strength and courage to resist the incessant demands of economic productivity, to follow our own hearts and the dictates of our souls.

CHAPTER 9 /
ELECTROSHOCK

"This is a crime against the spirit. This is a rape against the soul."
> — Diann'a Loper, electroshock survivor and activist
> for a ban on ECT

Electroshock ALWAYS damages the brain.
Electroshock ALWAYS causes memory loss.
Electroshock sometimes KILLS.
Electroshock is NEVER necessary.

TERROR acts powerfully upon the body, through the medium of the mind, and should be employed in the cure of madness. FEAR accompanied with PAIN and a sense of SHAME, has sometimes cured this disease. Bartholin speaks in high terms of what he calls "flagellation" in certain diseases. (Benjamin Rush, the "father" of modern psychiatry, whose image today emblazons the official seal of the American Psychiatric Association) (1)

I open my mouth and the scream surrounds me. My body a lurch and a scream of pain. A firecracker, pain and lights, burning, searing, my bones and my flesh. I am on fire. Shorter than a second. The fragments of a bomb sear my body. Blue-white lights, fiercer than God, going through me ... I wondered when they would be over, these ritual burnings. The pain. I would never survive the searing pain. "Paranoid delusions", they wrote on my chart. "'She thinks there is a conspiracy to kill her by electrocution." (Janet Gotkin) (2)

Introduction

I deliberately keep this chapter brief because, in my mind, it is a simple issue. Our brains are exquisitely sensitive, and complex — billions of cells, trillions of connections, more vast and intricate than we can imagine. The most brilliant of our scientists, those who understand more about the brain than any of us, are most humbled and forthcoming about how little they really know about the brain. The most ardent proponents of ECT don't really have a clue as to how it might work. My own point-of-view, like psychiatrist Peter Breggin, neurologist John Friedberg, and others, is that ECT "works" to the extent that it disables the brain.

Psychiatrists call this technique electroconvulsive therapy or ECT. Given that the average ECT procedure induces a level of electricity that is approximately two and one-half times greater than that required to induce a convulsion, the term ECT is really a euphemistic misnomer. It is not a "convulsive therapy." Rather, it is systematic brain damage, and the damage is the effect; the more current, the more brain damage. Also known as shock treatment, critics often refer to the procedure as electroshock. Texas, as a result of ardent activism by a coalition of electroshock survivors and concerned allies, is one of the few states to have a systematic reporting system. Official reports on the use of ECT in Texas during fiscal year 1994 included a total of 1,644 patients. (3) The current national estimates are about 100,000 individuals electroshocked each year. After its heyday in the 1940s and 1950s as a means of intimidating and controlling "patients" in state mental hospitals, electroshock lost favor, partly due to the advent of neuroleptic drugs, partly because of the exposure of the horror of it all, as in the popular movie, 'One Flew Over

The Cuckoo's Nest'. Most citizens today think that ECT is a relic of bygone days; they tend to be surprised to hear that the practice of ECT is making a resurgence. The American Psychiatric Association is, in fact, working overtime to create an illusion that ECT is no longer even controversial.

The Need for a Backup Treatment

In most psychiatric settings today, the biological model is a given. With this model, for all intents and purposes, there are only two treatment approaches — drugs and ECT: drugs for starters and ECT for "treatment-failures" or "treatment-resisters." Thus ECT is the only available back-up treatment when the drugs fail to "work." Psychiatrists would find themselves greatly limited were ECT abandoned or abolished — they'd have nothing else to offer. Society expects psychiatrists to have the answers, and they readily admit to having them. Nothing would more quickly lower their prestige in the public's eyes, and in their own as well, than to acknowledge not having the answers. The British radical psychiatrist, R D Laing, pointed out the irony that while society gives great social police power to psychiatrists it is equally true that psychiatrists have no choice about whether to exercise that power. In granting the power, society insists that it be used. The coercers are coerced, but so thoroughly conditioned they think they are free.

Doctors are trained to be action-oriented. As a doctor you just don't stand by and do nothing. There is a reason for the absence of alternatives. Successful outcome of non-medical alternatives would threaten their place in the system; why try something new when the old is paying off so handsomely? Belief that only medical methods are effective is thoroughly ingrained in psychiatrists (that's where their identity is coming from); non-medical alternative approaches are considered inadequate, ineffective and impractical.

The Procedure

Electroshock involves the production of a grand mal convulsion, similar to an epileptic seizure, by passing from 70 to 600 volts of electric current through the brain for one-half to four seconds. Before application, ECT subjects are typically given anesthetic, tranquilizing and muscle-paralyzing drugs to reduce fear, pain, and the risk (from violent muscle spasms) of fractured bones (particularly of the spine, a common occurrence in the earlier history of ECT before the introduction of muscle paralyzers). The ECT convulsion usually lasts from thirty to sixty seconds and may produce life-threatening complications, such as apnea and cardiac arrest. The convulsion is followed by a period of unconsciousness of several minutes' duration. Electroshock is usually administered in hospitals because they are equipped to handle emergency situations which often develop during or after an ECT session.

Electroshock Modifications

Contrary to claims by ECT defenders, newer technique modifications have made electroshock more harmful than ever. For example, because the drugs accompanying ECT to reduce certain risks raise the seizure threshold, more electrical current is required to induce the convulsion, which in turn increases brain damage. Moreover, whereas formerly ECT specialists tried to induce seizures with minimal current, suprathreshold amounts of electricity are commonly administered today in the belief that they are more effective. (4) Again, the more current, the more brain damage.

Electroshock and Elders

The use of ECT is increasing, and seventy percent of the "treatments" are insurance-covered. The bottom line is that more than 100,000 Americans are being electroshocked each year; half are 65 years of age and older, and two-thirds are women. Psychiatry defends the use of electroshock with our elderly women, arguing they need it because of the intractability of geriatric depression. I call it shameful abandonment and mistreatment of our elders, clear evidence of psychiatry as agent of institutionalized ageism and sexism in our society. It is also interesting that here in Texas, our reporting system revealed a 360 percent increase in the use of ECT between ages 64 and 65.5. The only logical interpretation is to see it as a dramatic example of how much economics is really the determining factor in the practice; when patients turn 65, doctors can receive Medicare reimbursement for ECT.

Psychological Effects

The truth is that electroshock is one of the most dramatic examples ever of iatrogenic (medically-induced) disease. Brain damage, memory loss and mental disability are routine distinguishing results. In addition to obvious physical and mental damage, there are a number of other negative effects of ECT. These include:

1/ Suppression of emerging distress material;

2/ Suppression of ability to heal by emotional release;

3/ Creation of emotional distress, including deep feelings of terror and powerlessness;

4/ Promotion of human beings in the roles of victims and passive dependents of medical professionals;

5/ Confirmation of patients' belief that there is something really wrong with them (shame).

When I hear of an individual for whom electroshock is being considered, I always ask, "What is important that he or she not remember and tell about?" Or "What is it that the others do not want to hear or look at?" Often it is abuse, always it is difficult, disruptive, threatening, uncomfortable, painful. Emotional discharge is essential to healing. The distress needs to emerge, the truth needs to be told. Electroshock is an awful, violent assault on individuals, and on the possibility of healing by expressing the truth.

Individuals who have undergone ECT report horrific emotional distress resulting from this procedure. Physical and cognitive debilitation, together with intense fear, shame and hopelessness make life and recovery a tremendous challenge for many people who undergo this procedure. My own clients have reported years of fearful avoidance of medical doctors after undergoing electroshock. The fear is so great that they neglect their physical medical needs, rather than go to a doctor. Electroshock survivors often have recurrent nightmares about the electroshock or about symbolic forms of torture and death. One client recently shared with me that the reading of testimonials from Holocaust survivors was a key to her recovery; she finally found people whose depth of emotional pain and anguish was similar to her own. This helped her to overcome some of the shame and stigmatization, and to begin walking through the isolation that so many psychiatric survivors experience after their "treatment."

The whole effect of ECT is a waking horror.

Electroshock and Informed Consent

Genuine informed consent for electroshock is nonexistent because electroshock psychiatrists deny or minimize its harmful effects. For example, the American Psychiatric Association officially states, "In light of the available evidence, brain damage need not be included [in the consent form] as a potential risk." (6) In addition, in all but one state, ECT may be legally forced upon nonconsenting individuals who are said to be or are adjudicated mentally unqualified to give their consent.

There are many ways in which informed consent is violated. First, there is denial and minimization of harmful effects. The official APA literature and the typical hospital brochure are both travesties of truth. The consent form example, provided in 1990 by the APA in 'The Practice of Electroconvulsive Therapy', states that the death rate for ECT is "approximately one per 10,000 patients treated." (7) Publicly available statistics collected between 1993 and 199 by the Texas Mental Health Department show that the rate is 50 times higher. As noted above, the American Psychiatric Association recommends that patients need not be advised of ECT's potential risk. The APA gives no credence to the numerous human autopsies, brainwave studies, animal studies, clinical observations, and reports from ECT subjects clearly demonstrating ECT's brain-damaging effects. St. David's Hospital in Austin, Texas in 1994 was giving an information sheet to ECT candidates which stated that ECT was safe for pregnant women.

The second reason I argue that informed consent exists only in name is that even minimal and inadequate guidelines for the administration of ECT are routinely and systematically violated. For example, a 1995 report by the Wisconsin Coalition for Advocacy thoroughly documents pervasive and systematic violations of that state's informed consent guidelines on ECT. (8) A 1987 study by Benedict and Saks of the regulation of professional behavior regarding ECT in Massachusetts showed that "approximately 90 percent of ECT patients received treatment inappropriately, suggesting that the regulation of ECT administration is ineffective." (9) Interestingly, the authors also reported that "the more familiar a psychiatrist was with threatened or instituted lawsuits involving ECT, and the more likely a lawsuit was thought to be, the greater was his or her departure from the guidelines."

A third point is rarely mentioned by anyone except the likes of Dr Fred Baughman, a retired neurologist who has charged, in a 1998 letter to United States Attorney General Janet Reno, that "Attention Deficit Hyperactivity Disorder"(ADHD) and Ritalin is the biggest health care fraud in U.S. history. What Baughman has to say about ADHD and Ritalin is equally true for "Depression" and ECT. He points out that the legal obligation under informed consent is to provide the patient with all the information relevant to their decision-making — not just about the treatment in question, but also about their condition. Psychiatric patients are never told that their alleged disease is theoretical or metaphorical. To quote Dr

Baughman, "To say or even imply that what the patient has is biologic and a disease when there is no such proof (as in all psychiatric 'diseases') is conscious deception and abrogates informed consent. That this has become the 'standard of practice' in psychiatry does not excuse it. The abrogation of informed consent is de facto medical malpractice." (10)

Fourth, and pragmatically crucial, is that people become victims of this so-called "treatment" at a time in life when they are extremely vulnerable. At vulnerable times, people desperately need to trust and rely on others for help. Reaching out, they need complete safety and support. Their only hope, in this desperate state, is to trust the wisdom and guidance of the professionals to whom they turn for help. Informed consent is a superlative principle; it is not a protection in these conditions. So, rather than an informed consent document, I provide below what I consider to be authentic information addressed to a potential candidate for "treatment," for educational purposes, about electroshock. I encourage you to copy and share this information with others. Moira Dolan, MD, an internal medicine doctor and electroshock researcher, provides an annotated review of the research to back up each of my assertions about medical effects and lack of efficacy, which can be seen in Appendix A.

Authentic Information About Electroshock

You are being asked to consider undergoing the psychiatric procedure of electroshock, commonly referred to as electroconvulsive therapy, or ECT. It is your right, according to Texas state law, to be fully informed about the nature and effects of this procedure. Of course, you have a right to refuse the procedure.

Prerequisites to Clear Thinking About Electroshock

STATE OF MIND

A fundamental requisite of good decision making is mental competency. This means that prospective patients are able to understand this information and make a decision. At minimum:

1/ Patient is free from the influence of any and all mood-altering substances, including legally prescribed psychotropic medications.

2/ Patient is evaluated by a non-psychiatric physician, preferably a neurologist. A mental status examination is required to reveal a well-oriented mind and adequate functioning of higher level decision-making processes.

3/ Patient is functionally literate, able to read and comprehend this written material. Alternatively, he or she is able to clearly understand the communication of this material to him or her by audiotape.

STATE OF BODY

A complete physical examination by a non-psychiatric physician, preferably an internist, is recommended. The internist should evaluate for and inform the patient and psychiatrist of the potential for the individual to sustain physical complications of ECT treatment. This is analogous to what internists do in a pre-operative evaluation for surgery.

YOUR CONDITION

You are labeled as "mentally ill," diagnosed with a particular "disease" for which ECT is being recommended as "treatment." ECT is being justified as a "treatment" based on the assertion that your "disease" (probably called Depression, but possibly some other "disease" such as Bipolar Disorder or Schizophrenia) is a biologically or genetically based illness.

Your label as "mentally ill" and diagnosis as "Major Depression" or other "mental illness" is entirely hypothetical, based on subjective reports and observations of mood and behavior. There is no evidence of disease, chemical imbalance, or anything physically or chemically abnormal to validate your diagnosis as a medical illness.

What It Is

THE PROCEDURE

Electroshock involves the attachment of electrodes to the temples outside one (unilateral) or both (bilateral) frontal lobes, and the administration of electricity to the frontal lobes of the brain. Intensity of voltage may vary from approximately 70 volts to 600 volts. Duration of the electrical current may vary from one-half second to four seconds.

Administration of ECT also varies enormously in number of treatments, from one to literally hundreds over time. A typical course of treatment involves six to 12 sessions. Multiple Monitored ECT is one variation which consists of 3 treatments in one session, spaced about five minutes apart, with three sessions in one week; thus, nine treatments in one week.

Two pieces of information to know are that:

1/ The natural electrical activity of the brain is measured in millivolts, or thousandths of a volt. Thus, the power of ECT is literally hundreds of thousands of times greater than natural brain electrical activity.

2/ The average ECT procedure involves a level of electricity that can range from the minimum level required to induce a convulsion up to 40 times greater than that. (11) The official APA recommendation ranges from one and one-half to three times greater than that required to induce a convulsion. (12)

DRUGS ADMINISTERED

Electroshock is a procedure which involves administration of the following general classes of medication:

1/ general anesthesia

2/ tranquilizers

3/ muscle relaxants.

Each of these drugs has a wide range of effects on your body, mind and emotions. Listed below is a sample of possible adverse reactions as listed in the 'Physicians Desk Reference': (13)

Anesthesia [i.e., propofol]: circulatory depression, hypotension, hypertension, peripheral vascular collapse, tachycardia, arrythmia, respiratory depression, cardiorespiratory arrest, skeletal muscle hyperactivity, injury to nerves adjacent to injection site, seizures, hysteria, insomnia, moaning, restlessness, anxiety, nausea, abdominal pain, pain at injection site, salivation, and headache. (p. 3416)

Tranquilizer [i.e., valium]: drowsiness, fatigue, ataxia, confusion, constipation, depression, diplopia, dysarthria, headache, hypotension, incontinence, jaundice, changes in libido, nausea, changes in salivation, skin rash, slurred speech, tremor, urinary retention, vertigo, blurred vision, hyperexcited states, anxiety, hallucinations, muscle spasticity, insomnia, rage, sleep disturbance. (p. 2736)

Muscle Relaxant [i.e., succinylcholine chloride]: skeletal muscle weakness, profound and prolonged skeletal muscle paralysis resulting in respiratory insufficiency and apnea which require manual or mechanical ventilation unti● recovery , low blood pressure, flushing, heart attack, bronchospasm, wheezing, injection site reaction, fever. (p. 1091)

You should obtain a list of drugs recommended for ECT, including a complete listing of effects described in th PDR.

FDA Classification

The Federal Food and Drug Administration (FDA) classifies ECT machines as a Type III device. This means that ECT is an experimental procedure, classified in the highest risk category by the FDA. Class III means that the machine has not gone through the rigorous FDA testing required of medical devices, including safety testing and efficacy assessments.

Possible Medical Effects of ECT

1/ Death
2/ Brain Damage
3/ Cardiovascular Complications
4/ Extra Risks for the Elderly
5/ Seizures and Epilepsy
6/ Memory Loss

Note

Because ECT is a high-risk experimental procedure and because of the possibility of permanent brain damage, you may want to consider magnetic resonant imagery (MRI) brain scans before and after this procedure. Pre- and post-MRIs are one way to measure the possible physical effects of ECT on your brain.

Emotional Effects

1/ Terror
2/ Shame
3/ Helplessness
4/ Hopelessness

Many individuals who have undergone ECT report horrific emotional distress resulting from this procedure. Physical and mental debilitation, together with intense fear, shame and hopelessness often make life and recovery a tremendous challenge for people who undergo this procedure.

Lack of Efficacy

Research indicates the following:

1/ No lasting beneficial effects of ECT. (14)

2/ Sham-ECT (where an individual is anesthetized and told they will receive ECT, but actually do not) has the same short-term outcomes as actual ECT. (15)

3/ Research clearly shows that ECT does not prevent suicide. Suicide rates for those receiving ECT are no lower than non-ECT patients with similar diagnostic profiles.

Financial Disclosure

The cost of ECT varies significantly. Cost of the procedure itself may vary from $100 to $300 per treatment for the psychiatrist's bill. "Hidden" costs include fees for the anesthesiologist and the surgery suite (up to $800 combined per session), room and board at the hospital (usually $800 to $1,300 per day at a private psychiatric hospital), psychotherapy charges by the psychiatrist (average $100 to $150 per hour), consultant fees, and charges for whatever drugs you will be administered. Depending on the setting and whether you are in-patient or out-patient, there will be variable fees for the "operating room" and the hospital. You should obtain a full financial disclosure of all costs in writing, prior to decisions about any procedure.

CHAPTER 10
SILENCE

If what I am saying holds any truth whatsoever, and I obviously think it does, then why is there so little public outcry? My perspective is that a conspiracy of silence is always part and parcel of oppression. Electroshock can be seen as an example of the silence of involved and affected parties.

Professional Silence

Psychiatrists are reluctant to criticize one another. Few will risk the scorn and hostility of their colleagues for openly expressing their views when such views run counter to conventional psychiatric standards. A noteworthy example of this is the almost total exclusion in the professional literature of articles criticizing electroshock.

Recall the 1987 finding by Benedict and Saks that 90 percent of ECT patients in their Massachusetts study received treatment inappropriately; while 41 percent of sampled psychiatrists reported knowing a colleague who prescribed or administered ECT inappropriately, only two percent reported their concerns to an appropriate official for corrective action. Remember their striking finding that "the more familiar a psychiatrist was with threatened or instituted lawsuits involving ECT, and the more likely a lawsuit was thought to be, the greater was his or her departure from the guidelines." (1) In addition to the absence of professional criticism, ECT specialists receive active support and encouragement from their colleagues within both psychiatry and medicine. The American Psychiatric Association has long championed the practice of ECT, and the American Medical Association endorsed the use of ECT "as an effective treatment modality in selected patients, as outlined by the American Psychiatric Association." (2)

Silence of the Judicial System

The use of outright force in the administration of ECT is not as widespread as it once was. Still, ECT-resistant people are being drugged into submission (prior to scheduled sessions) or dragged off to "treatment rooms" in some facilities. The use of coercion (i.e., pressure from psychiatrists, staff, and families) is fairly commonplace. Especially in a hospital environment, the pressure can be unrelenting. Subtle and not so subtle threats can be highly effective in obtaining consent from isolated individuals. ECT candidates can be "informed" that failure to cooperate might result in their being transferred to a facility with tighter security (i.e., a state hospital), or that they will be locked up for a prolonged period, or indefinitely. By increasing the dosages of powerful psychoactive drugs (e.g. Haldol, Prolixin, Thorazine), psychiatrists can confuse and weaken uncooperative candidates, and thereby reduce their resistance to signing consent forms. Aside from the use of outright force and coercion in the imposition of ECT, there is the universal practice of uninformed or misinformed consent. Candidates are lied to, plain and simple.

All of this, of course, makes a mockery of the concept of informed consent. And none of this could be taking place without the sanction of the judicial system. Since the beginnings of institutional psychiatry more than 300 years ago, the courts have served to legitimize virtually every form of abuse meted out to so-called mental patients. From incarceration in "lunatic asylums" (now called mental hospitals) to the use of such "treatments" as bleeding, leeching, "surprise baths," hysterectomies, forced drugging, insulin shock, and lobotomy, judges have authorized pretty near every technique psychiatrists have come up with to humiliate and torment people in their charge. Electroshock is no exception to the rule. Judges act as they do because they buy into the psychiatric belief system which is based on the notion that people who won't or can't fit into the social and economic mainstream are "mentally ill," and that psychiatrists are best suited to "treat" and control them. Today, ECT is a favored "treatment" for these "difficult people." Judges accept the claim by psychiatrists that the procedure is safe, effective, and no more discomforting than a visit to the dentist's office, and reject the complaints, when heard, of electroshock survivors as further evidence of their disordered mental state.

In spite of patients' rights advocacy agencies mandated by the federal government in recent years and operating in every state, judges generally rubber-stamp requests for a wide variety of psychiatric interventions. In many states, the ruse used to disguise the practice of forcibly electroshocking individuals is called "substitute consent." Those who won't cooperate are held to be incapable of giving their consent, and consent is then obtained from a family member or a state-appointed guardian or conservator. For those psychiatrists who go this route, the process, however unethical, is entirely legal. But not all psychiatrists go the legal route, as evidenced by the record of one Wisconsin hospital. Wisconsin is one of a minority of states where "substitute consent" for ECT is not permitted: ECT candidates must personally give their consent. Responding to nine complainants, eight of whom were women ranging in age from 63 to 82, The Wisconsin Coalition for Advocacy (WCA) investigated St. Mary's for its handling of consent for ECT procedures. WCA found that there were "significant irregularities associated with the process of informed consent" in all nine cases. In 1991, the hospital staff used "coercive methods" in administering ECT to "Samantha," an 81-year-old woman, and ignored her repeated attempts to refuse ECT. Eyewitnesses reported that "restraints were applied to Samantha to ensure her cooperation with treatment." After she had received four ECTs, further sessions were canceled "apparently due to Samantha's extraordinary confusion." WCA made a number of recommendations to eliminate the "deficiencies" in the hospital's ECT policies and procedures and their implementation, but no one has brought charges against the hospital or its staff members for these and other clear instances of criminal assault contained in the report. (3) That the perpetrators of these violations were psychiatric personnel and their victims "mental patients" helps explain why the responsible parties were not held accountable for their actions. The judicial system's favoritism towards psychiatry and prejudice against the "mentally ill" runs deep.

Victims' Silence

Considering the huge numbers of people who have been

electroshocked during the last half-century (by Leonard Frank's estimate, more than 15 million worldwide), it is surprising that there has not been a greater protest against the procedure by the survivors themselves. There are several factors that help account for their relative silence.

BRAIN DAMAGE

Brain damage caused by ECT makes it difficult for survivors to recognize their disability. Those who do recognize their disability are inclined to attribute it to their "mental illness" and are reinforced in this by psychiatrists and families alike.

LACK OF SOCIAL SUPPORT: WELFARE AND DISABILITY

Alienation is a defining characteristic of our present society; genuine community and social support are hard to come by. There is little available in the way of a "safety net" for most of our citizens. In place of, or in the wake of, genuine community support, our society offers a pitiful caricature in the form of our welfare system. Of relevance here is the part of our welfare system called social security disability. There is a huge place in this system for those with "mental illness." Thomas Szasz points out that media propaganda about mental illness has been incredible. Recent federal law, the Americans with Disabilities Act, was enacted in 1990 "to diminish the stigma of mental illness and reduce discrimination involving ... at least 60 million Americans between the ages of 18 and 64, [who] will experience a mental disorder during their lifetimes." (4) With such numbers presented as fact, it is exceedingly difficult to challenge this psychiatric belief. With brain damage added to further shaming and tragic strengthening of an individual's self-image as a defective, "mentally ill" patient, it is no wonder that relatively few speak out. Given the real danger posed to individuals by psychiatry, what is actually astounding is that some do. There is a growing (both in numbers and in outspokenness) mental health liberation movement, composed mostly of psychiatric survivors. Support Coalition International now includes 60 grassroots groups in eight countries. The World Association of Electroshock Survivors (WAES) and the Committee for Truth in Psychiatry are two legs of this broader coalition which focus specifically on the elimination of electroshock.

Given the injury, given the disability, given the dire lack of alternative support, given the growing number of United States citizens in poverty or prison, homeless and destitute, what can be expected? Many shock survivors end up on Social Security Disability Income. It is understandable; it is about survival. A tragedy is that it can effectively lock up an individual forever in an identity labeled defective, ill, and dependent. An irony is that psychiatry justifies imposed "treatment," so often paid for by the state through Medicare, which results in creating permanent welfare dependents.

FEAR

Many survivors experience electroshock as torture. The procedure has actually been used as such for interrogation purposes. Frantz Fanon, the well-known author and critic of imperialism, himself a psychiatrist, has written:

> "Attention must be called to the habit formed by certain psychiatrists [during the Algerian War] of flying to the aid of the police. There are, for instance, psychiatrists

in Algiers, known to numerous prisoners, who have given electric shock treatments to the accused and have questioned them during the waking phase, which is characterized by a certain confusion, a relaxation of resistance, a disappearance of the person's defenses. When by chance these are liberated because the doctor, despite this barbarous treatment, was able to obtain no information, what is brought to us is a personality in shreds." (5)

Rarely recognized, let alone acknowledged, by anyone other than its victims, are the torturous aspects of electroshock as it is customarily administered. Ken Kesey, author of 'One Flew Over The Cuckoo's Nest', has described ECT as "a device that might be said to do the work of the sleeping pill, the electric chair, and the torture rack ... [N]o one ever wants another one. Ever." (6) Keeping silent about the truth of ECT is for many a small price to pay to reduce the danger of being reinstitutionalized and shocked again.

For individuals actually undergoing electroshock, complaints of torture, memory loss, etc., are usually futile and likely to be regarded as "delusional." Electroshock specialists are trained to think a certain way about complaints from ECT subjects. One leading psychiatric textbook supplied the all-purpose answer to ECT-caused amnesia: "All patients who remain unimproved after ECT are inclined to complain bitterly of their memory difficulties." (7) The implication is clear: if ECT subjects complain, they're still sick and therefore in need of more treatment. ECT specialists as a rule will continue treating the patient as long as the complaints persist. As a matter of fact, the cessation of complaints is regarded as a hallmark of ECT's effectiveness.

MEMORY LOSS

Patients often forget the period of time when they received the shock treatment. What they were told about the treatment during this time and their possible resistance to being treated is forgotten. Survivors tend to blame themselves and are encouraged to do so. There is no looking beyond the immediate personal situation; family, vocational, political factors are given short shrift.

THE ELDERLY

As reported in the previous chapter, a breakdown by age of ECT victims in FY 1994 in Texas showed that the most frequent age victim by far was age 65! Stigma and disability prevents victims from speaking out effectively. Elderly survivors are even less inclined to speak out against ECT. They are especially vulnerable to electroshock's devastating effects. Often friendless, politically isolated (e.g., in nursing homes), age-weakened and suffering from medical ailments, ECT rarely leaves the elderly in any condition to protest what has happened to them and what is more likely to happen to them again if they complain. Could it be that so many elderly people are now being electroshocked because they are "malpractice proof?" Rarely are the elderly in any condition to testify in court about their ECT-related injury especially memory loss. And even when they are, the courts usually believe opposing psychiatric expert witnesses who are quick to attribute the memory difficulties of the elderly to senility and not ECT.

Family Silence

Psychiatrists seldom administer ECT without the

cooperation of the subject's family, or at least its key member or members. When family relationships break down and the breakup of the family itself is threatened, certain family members are likely to turn to psychiatry for help. If talk and drug therapy prove ineffective, electroshock, in our present "mental health" climate, often becomes an option. Psychiatrists may use family members to help persuade or pressure the "problem" member to accept ECT. This failing, a family member may agree to sign a substitute consent form. Following ECT, the family is brought in as a support system during the subject's recovery period. The family's role can be a major factor in the outcome of an ECT case. If the procedure does not produce the intended results, family members, having committed themselves to and having participated in the process, are not likely to criticize any of the responsible parties, themselves included. More likely, family members will adopt the psychiatric position, that the "patient" or the "disease" is to be blamed. In accusing the other, family members thereby excuse themselves and the psychiatrists. It is not only the passivity and silence of families that helps perpetuate the myth that ECT is a beneficial method. Some family members have become active proponents of ECT at public meetings, in lobbying efforts, and in media appearances.

This is why most consumer groups are not to be trusted. The National Alliance for the Mentally Ill (NAMI), for example, is notorious as a bedfellow propagandist and apologist for biopsychiatry and the APA. It is composed of family members of the "mentally ill." There is a huge payoff in avoidance of responsibility for self-examination when a loved one's distress can be explained away as a biological or genetic defect inside of them; nothing to do with me!

Public Silence and Support

To justify and legitimize psychiatric interventions, a belief system has been formulated. The psychiatric credo has gotten such a hold on the collective psyche that its basic tenets are no longer even being questioned. The notion that "mental illness is a brain disease" is accepted as a given in the same way that "2 plus 2 equals 4" is. The public's acquiescence to psychiatric authority has resulted in indifference and silence. Rarely is any connection drawn between institutional psychiatry and institutional religion, both of which since their beginnings have always served to reinforce the existing social order. In our own time, the collapse of religious authority has led the way to the emergence of psychiatric authority as a mighty social force. In fact, psychiatry has become a secular religion replacing traditional religion as "the opium of the people."

Enforcement of Silence: Control

FAMILY CONTROL

The presence of one nonconformist, defiant family member can and often does have a divisive effect on other family members. Threatened with disruption and perhaps dissolution, many families see psychiatry as a practical option. As parents, the choice, over and over again, is to transform our lives or suppress our children. We used to do it by physical punishment, now we use psychiatric drugs. Similarly, more and more families are turning to psychiatry to explain the disruption and distress they feel. Labeling a family member with a biological or genetic mental disease a seductive explanation, providing relief from the struggle understand, and absolution from guilt or shame. It's a socially approved, medically sanctioned, modern day version of creating a scapegoat.

INSTITUTIONAL CONTROL
In the early days of electroshock, the procedure was used on a wholesale basis to exercise overt control of the inmate population. Entire wards were shocked almost as typically as they are drugged today. Patients undergoing shock were not likely to cause any management problems. Nowadays in those places where ECT is being used, most patients are controlled indirectly. They see that those patients who don't cooperate or who don't "get better" quickly enough find themselves on the shock roster. Out of fear they shape up fast. Thus ECT "works" directly by bludgeoning patients into adopting the "right" attitude and cooperating, or indirectly by intimidating them into doing so.

SOCIAL CONTROL
It is to the state that psychiatry owes its power. Without backing from the police and the courts, psychiatry could hardly function. But in this world you get nothing for nothing, and what psychiatry gives back to the state is its unquestioning support of the status quo. In return for their privileged place in society, psychiatrists act as social regulators, or enforcers. With moral, social, political, economic, and environmental decay accelerating and staring everyone in the face, the social system is doing what it must to hold on. More and more, the state relies on the police and psychiatry to maintain itself. The police are a visible force; psychiatry is mostly an invisible force, because its

function is disguised. Beneath its benevolent mask, psychiatry serves the interests of the state against the interests of the individual. Were the mask ripped off, the public would not stand for it. Hence the large propaganda machine that has been built up to keep the public enthralled — "psychiatrists are like other doctors," "mental diseases are like any other diseases," "psychiatric treatments are like any other treatments," and on and on, ad infinitum. It's not enough that growing numbers of people become marginalized because of the social system's shortcomings. The marginalized must also be stigmatized (so that the marginalizers will not be plagued by guilty consciences) and controlled (so that they do not disrupt mainstream operations). In all this, the police and psychiatry play their separate roles. The police enforce written law, except where social code takes precedence. Psychiatry enforces social code where written law is unavailable or seen as too harsh. In either case, when persuasive means fail, physical force, or the threat of force, is invoked. And so the lid is kept on what is essentially an increasingly volatile social/political situation.

Brainwashing

Electroshock is a brainwashing technique par excellence. Throughout history, tyrants have usually preferred to enslave their enemies rather than kill them. Slaves can be useful; the dead cannot. When, for example, the Roman legions conquered a territory, segments of the population were killed off as an object lesson to the survivors: accept enslavement, or else. In the twentieth century, the process of making slaves of captive individuals or groups has been refined and systematized; it's called "brainwashing."

This technique came to the public's awareness during the early 1950s when Edward Hunter, an American journalist, began writing about its use in Communist China. (The method was also practiced around the same time, and somewhat earlier, in the Soviet Union.) The term "brainwashing" (Hunter's coinage) derives from a Chinese colloquialism which literally means "wash brain." Individuals who refused to cooperate with the new regime were placed in camps where they were subjected to intense psychological and physical pressure until they changed their minds — actually, until their minds were changed for them. The specifics are today fairly well-known: subjects are isolated, put on short rations, deprived of sleep, threatened, beaten, endlessly interrogated, and harangued (during the "softening-up" period) to the point of nervous and physical exhaustion when they confess their supposed "thought crimes"/sins and give up their beliefs (in Communist China, their "reactionary" ideas). Being now in a highly suggestible state of mind, the victims are ready for "re-education" (by way of personal instruction, classes, study groups, etc.). The insertion of a new belief system converts brainwashees to the brainwashers' ideology, whatever that happens to be. When the process works, victims not only "willingly" work for the system but may also become active supporters of and proselytizers for the system.

Rarely recognized is the fact that the brainwashing techniques used in Communist countries have their roots in institutional psychiatry. For more than 300 years psychiatrists, until the twentieth century called "mad doctors" or "alienists," have been using fear, pain, and exhaustion to force troublesome or troubled citizens/ "difficult patients" to confess their delusions (admit to being "mentally ill"), accept the psychiatric worldview, and return to society as happy, or at least silent, cooperative members of the work force. The older exhaustive methods, sometimes called "depleting treatments," were direct attacks on the body and included "hydrotherapy" (submersion in hot or cold water for prolonged periods), and the "rotating swing" (tying an individual to a chair and revolving it hundreds of times a minute to terrorize and induce vomiting).

Psychiatry's newer techniques, those introduced in the twentieth century, differ from the older ones in being direct assaults on the brain. Electroshock is one of three such assaultive methods; the other two are psychoactive drugs and psychosurgery. Electroshock is a classic example of brainwashing in the most meaningful sense of the term.

To point out the similarities between brainwashing and psychiatry, I offer here a diagrammatic comparison compiled by Leonard Frank. (8)

BRAINWASHING	PSYCHIATRY
Thought Reform Center	Mental hospital (Psychiatric Center)
Interrogator/Brainwasher	Psychiatrist
Prisoner	Patient
Political Model	Medical Model
Crimes	Symptoms
"Thought-Crimes"	Delusions
Denial of Guilt	Lack of Insight
Imprisonment	Involuntary Commitment
Punishment	Treatment
Interrogation	Psychotherapy
Humiliation	Stigmatization (Diagnosis

Isolation	Seclusion and Restraints
Softening-Up Process	Somatic, or Physical, Treatment
Sleep/Food Deprivation	Psychiatric Drugs
Sensory Deprivation	Electroshock (ECT)
Confusion and Helplessness	Disorientation and Dependency
Suggestibility	Amenability to Psychotherapy
Confession of Guilt	Admission of Mental Illness (Insight)
Conversion	Cure
Obedience	Cooperation
Work Occupational	Therapy
Study Groups	Group Therapy
Re-education	Rehabilitation

Conclusion

Psychiatry doesn't operate in a vacuum; society sanctions psychiatric fear and force. Without the support, or at least the acquiescence, of virtually the entire society, it could not persecute individuals labeled "mentally ill." The same could be said of the Inquisitorial and Nazi persecutions, respectively, or heretics and Jews. What American Catholic theologian Mary Jo Leddy has written concerning the Holocaust applies as well to the psychiatric holocaust: "The evil of the Holocaust was realized through the exercise of a certain kind of power — coercive power. It was a power that sought to dominate and control. It was a power legitimated through law, buttressed by propaganda, augmented by terror, and affected through all the institutions of society." (9) As with the Nazi Holocaust, the psychiatric holocaust involves millions of people. The essential difference between the two is that Nazi victims were utterly destroyed whereas only the humanity of psychiatry's victims is destroyed.

Electroshock is perhaps the nastiest aspect of the nasty business of psychiatry. That the public's perception veers so significantly from the reality poses an enormous danger for everyone. The words of CS Lewis, the English scholar and writer, are worth re-considering here:

> "Of all tyrannies, a tyranny sincerely exercised for the good of its victims may be the most oppressive. It may be better to live under robber barons than under omnipotent moral busybodies. The robber baron's cruelty may sometimes sleep, his cupidity may at some point be satiate but those who torment us for our own good will torment us without end for they do so with the approval of their own conscience ... Their very kindness stings with intolerable insult. To be "cured" against one's will and cured of states which we may not regard as disease is to be put on a level with those who have not yet reached the age of reason." (10)

Breaking the Silence

"This is darned scary, to come out and tell you that, as a forty-year-old, I can't put the alphabet in order, that when was tested by Texas Rehab so that I could get back into the work community, I tested out with a comprehension level above 68 percent of the nation, and a one percentile in reading, writing and arithmetic. ... We're through being victimized. We're not going to go away. This treatment's going to be banned one day. Texas is a good place to start."

— Amie Rankin, Shock Survivor, testifying at the 1995
Texas hearings on the bill to ban ECT.

Silence is the rule that allows oppression to thrive.
Amie Rankin and thousands of other psychiatric survivors
are speaking out. Breaking the silence requires tremendous
courage, but is necessary to fully re-emerge as individuals,
and to stop the external oppression. Here is a sample of
what this looks like in Texas. Our state has been the scene of
a terrific effort to expose and put a halt to the practice of
electroshock. Diann'a Loper's electroshock treatments
caused her to have a permanent epileptic condition, and
affected her memory so greatly that she could not retain her
position as a well-known and effective political lobbyist. It
did not dampen her fighting spirit, however, and she has
been a major force in the Texas effort to ban electroshock.
Here is an excerpt from her testimony at the 1995
legislative attempt to ban electroshock in Texas:

> "Issues such as slavery, witch burning, crucifixion,
> widow burning, lobotomy and clitorectomy are not choice
> issues. We do not dignify them with the legitimacy of
> choice. Once recognized for what they are, we ban them.
> We disallow them. We abolish them. ECT belongs in the
> category of those devices which society has come to
> disallow because they were finally recognized as devices of
> inhumanity and torture — devices to control, to maim, to
> cause fear and terror — devices to blunt the emotions, to
> robotize — devices designed to make persons and groups
> more amenable to conformity and authority; identical to
> the goals of castration, lobotomy and brainwashing." —
> Diann'a Loper, Electroshock Survivor, professional lobbyist
> ,and co-founder of the World Association of Electroshock
> Survivors.

Another great freedom fighter, Jerry Boswell, executive director of the Citizens' Commission for Human Rights, has spearheaded an enduring effort to ban shock. Many others have contributed, but it is these two leaders who provided the heart and soul of the Texas 1990s initiative to ban electroshock.

Here is one unusual example of public disclosure by a psychiatrist. The Texas Department of Health (TDH) investigated Amarillo's Pavilion Hospital in 1997, and discovered a nefarious example of psychiatric elder abuse, thanks in part to a formal complaint filed by Amarillo psychiatrist Allan J. McCorkle, who told me that he was angry that his own patients were being transferred to the Pavilion without his knowledge. According to the Amarillo Daily News, TDH cited the Pavilion for sending its staff into local nursing homes to offer services without patient consent or physician orders. (11) It appears that these psychiatrists would go through the records of nursing home residents, evaluating insurance and other factors making for good ECT candidates. Certain of these nursing homes had arrangements for transferring residents to in-patient ECT treatment at the Pavilion. The Health Department uncovered this phenomena, including examples of obvious invalid consents for both hospital admission and electroshock treatment, due to mental incompetence of the patients (a violation of state law). The TDH report also cited the Pavilion for keeping patients in restraints without appropriate monitoring. The Dallas Morning News revealed that the TDH report also described the investigation of the case of a 79-year-old woman who died within 24 hours after receiving electroshock at the Pavilion. Medical records revealed that she had been suffering from diabetes and unstable blood sugar, incontinence, bedsores and swollen hands and feet: "She was able to ambulate only three to four steps with maximum assistance, choking easily on food and fluids, needing total assistance with personal care." (12) TDH reported that she was also disoriented and confused. Still, she was allowed to sign herself into the psychiatric unit, and to sign their "informed" consent for electroshock. In May of 1997, the hospital closed down its ECT program because Medicare threatened to repeal certification to receive Medicare funds. The Dallas Morning News quoted Richard Falls, The Pavilion's top administrator: "It is a corporate business decision. There has been a lot of (anti-ECT) propaganda over the last 18 months. And harassment of hospitals that do it." The Pavilion became the eighteenth hospital statewide to shut down its shock program in the last two years, mostly due to our efforts to expose and challenge this practice. We can and are making a difference.

Besides the 18 and counting hospitals to stop doing electroshock, there have been other accomplishments, including the following:

1993 - Texas passes the toughest informed consent law in the nation and bans electroshock for citizens under 16 years of age.

1995 - Two days of dramatic public hearing, with testimony from scores of shock survivors and other activists fails to convince the Public Health Committee of the Texas House of Representatives to send a comprehensive banshock bill to the floor of the House for a vote by the full Congress.

1997 - Texas passes a bill providing for greater controls and safeguards on the use of electroshock on elder citizens age 65 and older.

1999 - The fight continues!

CHAPTER 11
ON PSYCHIATRIC DRUGS AND
DRUG WITHDRAWAL

A woman reaches out for help because she is hurting. The helper assures her that it's not her fault, that there is really nothing she can do about it since the cause is in her genes and biology. The best she can do is to accept her condition and keep it under control with "medication." She is a victin of this disease. She is dependent on the expert's opinion an on the drug. She has the privilege to attribute her problen to her disease and to resent anyone who expects too much of her. She will also resent her helpers who offer the allure of a cure, because the reality always falls short. Opportuni for genuine healing and authentic empowerment is aborte Telling the truth about her life, how she was hurt and oppressed, and expressing the emotional pain from these hurts is not supported; it is, in fact, suppressed by the interpretation and by the drugs.

Reclaiming power by becoming her own authority is sacrificed for the sake of dependence on professional authority. This negation of one's authentic power as a spiritual being and resignation to the status of helpless victim is probably the most harmful result of the practice c biopsychiatry. It is living a lie. There is always a heavy pric to pay for living an illusion; the incessant call to truth will continually be a goad to move out of victimization into authentic power. For those who know it is a lie, the toll is doubly great. We are responsible for what we know.

America now more than ever has embraced drugs as

way of life, as a way of work, as a way of leisure, as a way of child, adolescent and young adult development, as a way of mourning, as a way of celebration, as a way of dying. The fact is that most Americans are born to mothers using drugs at birth, and most Americans are on drugs in death. In between, the array of licit and illicit, prescription and non-prescription drug use in this country is astounding. Consider the people with whom you live and work; how many of them can you truly say are not regularly taking drugs (caffeine, nicotine, alcohol, Tylenol, Midol, anti-inflammatory, anti-anxiety, anti-depressant, thyroid, blood pressure, marijuana, cocaine, etc.)? Pharmaceuticals are now one of our country's most profitable industries.

This chapter addresses this fact of ubiquitous psychiatric drug use in our society, and challenges the ethics of biopsychiatry and the hopelessness of so many who take these drugs. It also discusses both the decision to take (or not) psychiatric drugs, the decision to withdraw from these drugs once addiction is present, and practical issues around the process of withdrawal. The following chapter emphasizes the importance of emotional recovery, as it pertains to drug withdrawal and to all of us.

A Question of Ethics

We are a nation of people on drugs. The primary treatment modality of our "health care system" (more aptly titled "disease care system") is drugs. Psychiatry operates and avidly promotes a practice which adds force and power to this sad state of affairs, a practice which consists almost totally of prescribing powerful, brain-disabling drugs. Although the majority of psychiatric drugs are prescribed by non-psychiatric physicians, it is the profession of psychiatry as a legitimized branch of medicine that provides the theory and rationale to sustain the phenomenon, powerfully reinforcing the dictates of our drug culture. Conventional wisdom is that those who are experiencing distress often turn to, or are pushed into psychiatry. Less conventional, but true beyond a doubt, is that those who experience distress often push others whom they blame for their distress into psychiatry. A tragic irony is that when those who are resisting drugs and attempting to consciously struggle with the massive stresses and oppressions of societ reach for help to, or are forced to seek helping professionals, these professionals give them drugs — powerful, toxic, addictive, brain-disabling drugs.

Most of my psychotherapy clients do not take any psychiatric drugs, and I don't recommend it. I have supported a client's decision to take a sleeping pill to break relentless period of sleep deprivation, when unable to recruit enough support to counsel at home on whatever all the distresses were around bedtime or sleeping. For most c my clients, drugs are not an issue. Quite often, however, during hard times, a client will consider drugs, usually at tl behest of a friend or family member who offers hope of some relief for my client's anguish. Typically, the suggestio comes with a personal testimonial of how much they or someone they know have been helped by "medication." There is always ample support from magazines or newspapers declaring the "truth" of biopsychiatry and the efficacy of these new "miracle" drugs. There is a boundles supply of mental health professionals who, if not enthusiastically singing the praises of drug "therapy," see the need and desirability of "medication" in dealing with psychological turmoil.

Above all else, I consider this drug issue to be a question of ethics. Individuals in psychological distress are reaching for help from a place of tremendous vulnerability. Much of their effort is to undo and recover from the effects of unresolved trauma suffered during the years of childhood when we really were dependent on the care and treatment of others. Connecting with a friend or counselor brings forward this experience of wounded dependency, and therefore it is a great responsibility of the friend/counselor to provide a safe space which allows full expression and does no further harm. The sufferer has got to trust someone in order to recover and move on with life. Drugs offer neither safety nor hope to a person in need. Instead, the message is that you are biologically defective, that your anguished and chaotic expressions of hurt offer no promise of redemption, but are, in fact, symptomatic evidence of your disease. Perhaps most significant, and representative of the breakdown of community in Western societies, is the related message that your disease has nothing to do with our community — it is your defect! Furthermore, the unfortunate "side effects" of these toxic "medicines" are a necessary evil, well worth it to control the progression of your "disease" and allow you to function appropriately in society.

The language is usually more subtle, couched a bit less harshly, but the message is the same. People are even writing books now about the desirability of cosmetic pharmacology, arguing that refusing a mood enhancer reflects only a Puritan belief that suffering is necessary for growth. We are constantly inundated with advertising messages singing the glory and availability of comfort, pleasure and immediate gratification. An important part of this message is that discomfort, pain and delayed gratification are unnecessary and easily avoided with the use of such and such drug product. The fact is we are all thoroughly conditioned to believe in the desirability and possibility of perfect health (including mental health, of course), and that something is wrong with us if we are not consistently "mentally healthy" (happy), as defined by whomever.

Don't get me wrong. Psychiatric drugs have an enormous effect on people, whether or not they are labeled with a psychiatric diagnosis. They most definitely do work! They work by disruption of normal brain function. The therapeutic effect is due to the fact that the drugs impair higher human functions. In fact, as Peter Breggin states, "All biopsychiatric treatments have a common mode of action — the disruption of normal brain function." (1)

Given the level of chronic hopelessness many people carry, the results of impaired brain function often appear desirable. The drugs usually suppress emotional sensitivity and responsiveness, dulling the pain, lessening "difficult" reactivity. They can impede self-awareness and insight, making patients more acquiescent and compliant with authority. Consistent with the necessity of productivity, amphetamine stimulated arousal is often encouraged as a welcome relief from the struggle involved in working through grief, loss, uncertainty or disillusionment. Effects like apathy and indifference are often considered acceptable even desirable, alternatives to anger and agitation.

While my clients generally don't use these drugs, I have elected to work with a few people who are already taking psychiatric drugs when they come to see me. I can't recall anyone who actually liked it that they were taking a psychiatric drug; often they came to me because of my reputation for eschewing "medication." One new client —

31-year-old woman, call her Vicky — had been on "antidepressants" and or Lithium since age 15 with two brief intervals where she took herself off the drugs. The latest interval was the previous three months. Prior to seeing me at her boyfriend's request, she had become discouraged and unmotivated, was even feeling suicidal. A week before she came to see me for our first appointment, Vicky's boyfriend made an appointment at the University Student Health Center for himself , spent a few minutes telling a psychiatrist about symptoms he had made up for the purpose of obtaining drugs, and came out with a month's supply of Lithium and Wellbutrin for his girlfriend! Vicky wants to be off the drugs, but she is afraid, and she knows they work. She has been told for 16 years that they work to control her "bipolar disorder," the label for a "mental disease" said to cause mood swings from high or excitable (mania) to low or melancholic (depression) affect. Whenever Vicky started to feel worse after discontinuing the drugs, the readily available explanation was always that her "symptoms" were evidence of her "disease" and the need to resume "medication." No one had ever given her any information about or considered the possibility that there might be other explanations for her symptoms. At the end of our third session, after considerable introductory exposure to some new information, my client asked me very directly, "Is it really possible (for me) to make it without drugs?" My answer was "Yes." The first step is always to rekindle hope where chronic hopelessness has reigned. She did not continue psychotherapy with me so I don't know what happened to her.

I worked with another client, Harold, off and on over a three year period during completion of his doctorate degree in music theory and an arduous, but ultimately successful hunt for a University professorship. Harold had been taking an "antidepressant" for some time before he came to see me, and continued on one drug or another throughout all of our counseling, except for a two month period between his acceptance of a university position and his relocation to that area. When he first came to see me, his "depression" was an entirely foreign "black box" which was the source of great anguish and suffering in his adult life. In psychotherapy, he did tremendous work in recognizing and letting go of much of the content of this black box. Harold had been tormented as a boy by his critical, abusive father and as a youth by the agonizing ordeal of constant shame, guilt and atonement for his sinful homosexual nature. He was a devout Catholic and, as a youth, he would lock himself in his room and pray on his knees for hours every day. His first counseling experiences as a young adult involved intense effort to overcome his "sinful and distorted" homosexuality; a second best alternative was to learn to live as an ascetic who could deny his sexual desire as an offering to God. During this prior counseling period, he was prescribed and began taking psychiatric drugs for his "biologically-based mental illness," "depression." Harold continued to see me and, periodically, we would address the question of "medication" or drugs. H was exceedingly clear that I did not think he needed drugs, and I honored my initial commitment to support his (now more fully informed) decision to take a psychiatric drug. The hardest part for me was allowing him to complain about the not infrequent undesired effects of this or that drug, as he would change "medication" in his search for the right one. I was happy for him when he finally was able to experience life for awhile without mood-altering drugs, even if only for two months. I don't believe, however, that he had enough time to complete withdrawal, usually a four to six month period. In any event, his fear of sinking again into depression outweighed other considerations as he started taking another antidepressant before moving to his new job (productivity reigns).

These two cases offer a brief picture of the pushes and pulls in the human interface with mood-altering psychiatric drugs. My experience with Vicky had only just begun. Harold is in an exciting stage of beginning a new career. For now, he is resigned to using a toxic drug to ward off a fall into deep depression. Harold's situation is increasingly common. Over the last half of this twentieth century, we have become inured to the presence of large numbers of "chronic mental patients" maintained for life on "medication." People labeled "schizophrenic" or some other "psychosis" are "able to function" on Thorazine or some other neuroleptic drug. Also called major tranquilizers, these drugs are extremely powerful, disabling the central nervous system, and causing permanent neurological damage in a significant percentage of people who use them. Research reveals a cumulative four to seven percent per year rate for relatively healthy young adults of Tardive Dyskinesia, a movement disorder involving permanent neurological damage. Another even more damaging disorder, called neuroleptic malignant syndrome, results in at least one out of 100 cases. (2)

We have accepted brain damage, central nervous system impairment and a host of other damaging effects as unfortunate but necessary consequences of the benefits of these drugs which allow "disabled" people to function. All too few of us consider books such as John Modrow's 'How to Become a Schizophrenic'. (3) Modrow describes his experience of all the classic symptoms of "schizophrenia," including bizarre delusions and vivid visual hallucinations, assuring us that he should clearly qualify for the label. He reveals in detail the cumulative traumas that led to these "symptoms," and shows how these "symptoms" were, in fact, meaningful and purposeful attempts to cope with his emotional pain. He strongly challenges the pervading fatalistic belief in the genetic inferiority of these individuals and presents a thoughtful, non-medical model of psychological crisis and recovery. Despite the available truth, in these last two decades we are witnessing another level of acceptance of biopsychiatric despair. Millions are resigning themselves to the ingestion of toxic so-called antidepressants (stimulant drugs) to help cope with life. For more and more, it is becoming a way of life. The question and possibility of ever coming off these drugs is being deferred again and again; for many, it is no longer even seriously considered. The message from the doctors is: "you have a treatable illness that will never go away."

Hopelessness and Despair

Two excellent writers recently brought home to me in a powerful way that, while information is necessary and helpful, it is not enough to counter the hopelessness and despair that go along with depression and especially with a acceptance of the biopsychiatric premise that you are genetically defective. Greg Critser, in an essay titled 'Oh, How Happy We Will Be' provides a thorough and revealing expose of what he calls "on-the-run-pharmo-capitalism." He details the immense growth and profits of psychiatric drug sales, various "egregious violations" of false advertising, and at best questionable ethics of drug promotion. Members of the American Medical Association and the American Psychiatric Association "suck up" free promotional money and research dollars from the drug companies. The current marketing trend is to bypass the doctors and go straight to potential consumers via mass media. More than ten billion dollars spent every year on marketing "buys a lot of understanding" for the drug industry. The fraud, greed and all-around bad ethics of the drug manufacturers are highly effective in reaping hundreds of billions of dollars each year in sales. Psychiatric drugs are a particularly rewarding growth industry. According to Critser, "The global market for antidepressants is expected to reach more than $6 billion by 1998 — having doubled in four years." (4)

Critser's article is outstanding not only because of the valuable research data he reports, but also because he weaves in his personal experience with psychiatry. After eight years of "talk therapy," he was referred to Dr R, reportedly "conservative with drugs." Critser describes Dr R as a "wise, learned man with a Talmudic sense of irony." The two "spent much of our time talking about medication," hardly surprising since "For five years, [Dr] R cycled me through a blizzard of drugs and drug combinations." Despite all his information and his frustration and disappointment with drugs, Critser ends his story with a resigned statement that "this spring my suffering has somewhat dulled ... I was on a straight regimen of Prozac, 40 mg. There are side effects; they show ... At this point I'm inclined to believe that, depression-wise, this may be my state of the art." He has internalized the "Talmudic irony" of Dr R, who lectured him patiently on how "no one really knows why" some depressed people are "long-term chronic."

Even more remarkable is that Critser had, a few years ago, discovered a monograph entitled "Metaphysical anguish in the poetry of Domenico Stromei," an analysis of his great-great-great-granduncle's life and poetry which the author had given to Critser's grandmother. Domenico Stromei supported himself and his family by working as a cobbler; he called his poetry la poesia del dolore which means the poetry of grief. The monograph's author, Sandro Sticca, describes this poetry: "Stromei's philosophy takes its root in the direct observation of reality ... the poet comes directly in contact with that reality and he develops a philosophical mode, stoic in essence, which helps him deal with it and bear it. Within this mode is expressed la poesia del dolore, a poetry which, transfigured by phantasy and feeling, conquers his pessimism and even the dolore itself ... Even in the most vehement revolt, the poet returns to a tranquil sense of submission to an inexorable destiny, in a virile and dignified manner." Critser also learned from Sticca's monograph that his ancestor Domenico suffered, on the night of March 14, 1854, "a terrible fall" after having been ill for an entire year. Sticca wrote that this accident precipitated a marked change in Stromei's poetry, and that from then on, he showed a "growing realization of the mysterious nobility and rationality of life within the Christian context." In contrast, Greg Critser, the great-great-great-grandnephew of this man who lived his late life in spiritual serenity, describes himself this way: "I am someone who takes a pill for my sorrows. I wonder if my depression is 'unbearable' without medication only because I know that this medication exists. I also wonder if the drugs are preventing me from finding the solace that Domenico did. Who am I now without medication? Will I ever know?

David Karp is another dramatic example of the

profound resignation and despair reflected in Critser's description of himself. One of our country's leading academic sociologists, Karp wrote a book called 'Speaking of Sadness', an in-depth analysis of extensive interviews with individuals who have taken or are currently taking psychiatric drugs for depression. (5) Karp's work reveals an incisive understanding of the power of the medical model of biopsychiatry to define "appropriate" responses to emotional problems. He discusses the social construction of reality, borrowing the term "Universe Maintenance Specialists" (6) to illustrate the function of the beliefs of biopsychiatry to define and control another's reality. Karp states that "a necessary condition for widespread depressive illness is a culturally induced readiness to view emotional pain as a disease requiring medical intervention." He is equally clear and congruent with what I am saying when he states, "The so-called medical model is based on two apparently unassailable premises:

1/ Normalcy is preferable to abnormalcy.

2/ Normalcy is a synonym for health and abnormalcy a synonym for pathology."

Health, like beauty and thinness, is equal to conformity. Presumably objective scientific research avoids accusations that psychiatry is about sociocultural control patterns. Karp really gets the idea about psychiatric oppression and how, by allowing the "Universe Maintenance Specialists" to define life problems as individual biopathology, it blinds us to social justice issues.

Karp makes a great contribution when he delivers the powerful insight that, for the people he interviewed, the process of becoming a psychiatric patient on "medication" bore all the trappings of a religious conversion. He describes a well-established sociological observation that people to whom psychiatric drugs are recommended for depression tend to go through four discernible stages that are very similar to those of religious conversion. These four stages are:

1/ Resistance,
2/ Trial Commitment,
3/ Conversion,
4/ Disenchantment.

At first, just as most people initially resist evangelical efforts, the vast majority of individuals are highly resistant to the idea of taking drugs for depression. Eventually, many agree to experiment on a trial basis, reluctantly considering the possibility that they may in fact have some sort of genetic, biochemical defect requiring "medication" to control. A potent seduction of this disease model is the temporary relief from toxic guilt and shame that many people feel (similar to the disease model of alcoholism) when they are encouraged to attribute their problems to a disease, rather than something in the domain of moral or personal responsibility. Family members are often very attracted to and at times vehemently attached to biopsychiatry for the same reason; groups like The National Alliance for the Mentally Ill (NAMI) and Children with Attention Deficit Disorders (CHADD) are ardent defenders and promoters of the biopsychiatry agenda.

The third stage is referred to as the actual Conversion whether to a new religious dogma or to a belief in the tenets of biopsychiatry. There are various sociological and psychological theories to account for the fact that it is extremely difficult and stressful to last for long in the phase of trial commitment. The pressure and dissonance are great and the next step is to assume a full-fledged identity as a religious seeker of God or mentally ill seeker of the right drug, as the case may be.

The fourth stage is called Disenchantment. I consider this to be a most appropriate term since belief in the superstitions of biopsychiatry is like the fairy tales when an enchantment is cast over the land. The distorted perception of both the biopsychiatric world view and the view of someone on potent mood-altering psychiatric drugs act like an enchantment on those who fall prey to such a "spell." "Falling prey" is actually an excellent description of what happens because it supports what is perhaps the most powerful enchantment of this entire travesty; that is, acceptance of the false belief that we, as spiritual beings, are helpless victims of material force and circumstance. In any event, people become disenchanted with the drugs because not only do they fail to provide nirvana, but virtually always do provide a host of undesirable and unpleasant "side effects."

Disenchantment may or may not lead to deconversion, depending on many factors. A genuine deconversion involves disavowal of the "false god" and a reclaiming of authentic power. Increasingly common are those who live in a place of resigned dissatisfaction and frustrated ambivalence, often on a never-ending search for the "right" drug as the current one wears thin, the negative effects become too great, and/or tolerance results in diminishment of the so-called therapeutic effect. Like Greg Critser, David Karp has done some great research and incisive thinking about drugs and biopsychiatric treatment for depression. Like Critser, Karp shares not only his research, but also his personal experience of drug treatment for depression. Like Critser, Karp ends his story in a place of profound resignation. He states that "Through the years my attitude toward drugs has remained steady — a mixture of hostility and dependence." The consistent effect of conversion to an identity such as defective biopsychiatric mental patient is an attitude of childlike victimization. This role inevitably fosters a victim's dependency. It also fosters resentment, a victim's privilege to blame another for the dependency.

To Be Or Not To Be A Psychiatric Drug User

It is exceedingly possible, even in today's world, to be deeply hurt and recover completely without psychiatric drugs. With good support and understanding, virtually any psychologically based distress can be alleviated and resolved. Most of the time, extreme states of mind and behavior are peoples' ways of showing us the nature of the hurts they have suffered. Persistent irrational feelings and behavior are usually precise reflections of specific distress recordings from traumatic events. When understanding and adequate support are not available, it is understandable that someone would choose to suppress the pain with drugs, prescription or otherwise. That is an individual's choice in a free society; it is an individual's right to make that choice, but only from a place of fully informed consent. This means not only having access to all the information about a drug's effects, but also knowing the truth that the decision is not about "medicine to treat a disease;" rather, it is whether to use a toxic brain-disabling drug to suppress thought or feeling.

A recent counseling session with a 34-year-old man illustrates this. I had worked with David off and on for about a year. David had done some excellent emotional release work, and reported being less tense and volatile in his work and relationships. He unloaded a lot of the feeling

of shame that he brought into counseling, was more
confident and had moved from working as a security guard
and part-time junior college teacher to a full-time teaching
position at a University. He took a break from counseling,
although he was still faced with a chronic pattern of pushing
himself , not unusual for males. I did not see David again for
about three months. When he did call and come in for an
appointment, he was overextended and stressed from
overwork. Tired and discouraged, he had been feeling
"depressed." His sister was taking Prozac and suggested that
my client try it. He did and he liked it; he was more able to
"get with it" and keep up with the workload. He had
obtained his own prescription, had been taking the drug for
less than two weeks, and he wanted to talk with me about it.
I listened to his story and to his ambivalence about Prozac. I
answered his questions regarding what I knew about Prozac,
including the well-established fact that the effects profile of
Prozac is virtually identical to amphetamines. We also
talked about the difficulty of seriously challenging a chronic
pattern of pressured overwork and negligent self-care.
Spring break was coming up, and I encouraged him to rest
and to take sweet care of himself.

   During our next appointment two weeks later, David
reported being off the drug for a wonderful spring break,
during which he had indeed taken good care of himself,
restored some balance to his life, and "still gotten a lot
done." Monday morning, though, he had resumed taking
Prozac, referring to it as "medicine." I simply let him talk;
he kept going and went through it again, this time referring
to the Prozac as "speed," and expressing frustration with
himself at needing a drug to keep going. By the end of the
session, he sounded quite clear about the choices he was
faced with, whether to take a stimulant drug to cope with

life, or, ultimately, whether to take full responsibility for his lifestyle and for the inner work he still needed to do. In our next appointment two weeks later, the last prior to this writing, David reported that he had not taken Prozac since our last session. He told me that he is keeping the bottle on his bedside table by the alarm clock (how appropriate), choosing one day at a time not to use drugs. He said that was working for him just now.

The very first thing to remember when addressing the question of whether to take psychiatric drugs is that they are called psychiatric drugs because they are recommended by psychiatrists, all of whom are medical doctors. These doctors call the drugs medicine, and this label becomes part of our programming, or conditioning, about illness and medicine and health care. Once we succumb to this belief system, it is as though we've fallen under an enchantment and can no longer see or remember what is real. What's vital to remember is that these "medicines" are labeled "medicines" because they are prescribed. The very same substances are illicit drugs when sold and consumed on the streets for recreation, escape, sedation, getting high or whatever the case may be. You are in a much better position to make an informed decision when you call a spade a spade. The truth is that you are not making a decision about medication; after all, your "mental illness" is only a metaphor. You have no medically verifiable "mental illness" which should be medically treated. The decision you are making is whether to attempt to control your behavior or alter your mood with chemicals. The decision of a psychiatric "patient" to take psychiatric drugs is essentially no different than any individual's decision to use mood-altering substances, legal or not. The major exception is when an individual is incarcerated, or threatened with incarceration by psychiatry. In this common scenario, the decision to take drugs is a legal and political decision with serious consequences regarding survival and liberty.

There are most potent forces pushing individuals to take psychiatric drugs. Internal pressure comes from all the misinformation and propaganda with which we are saturated. Accurate information is most helpful in resisting the tendency to go along with the cultural program and the falsehoods of biopsychiatry. We also feel internal pressure which arises from fear and shame we carry from past experiences. I think fear and shame are the very biggest forces behind this whole phenomenon of culturally-sanctioned oblivion. When an individual carries heavy loads of fear and shame, he feels a relentless pull to be a victim, to passively accept the dictates of authority, and to willingly settle for less than complete respect and good attention to oneself. After all, fear says "Avoid conflict or you'll be hurt worse." And shame says, "You know the doctor's right. You are defective." Again, conversion to the role of a psychiatric patient on drugs is perfectly suited to an attitude of childlike victimization. It is an utter negation of your authentic power as a spiritual being. It is a denial of your right and privilege to develop and mature through the hardships and challenges of life. There is a huge payoff to the illusion that you are a defective being who needs drugs to cope with life; the payoff is that you are no longer responsible for your thoughts and your actions. You can live in dependency, in blame and in shame. These attitudes have nothing to do with our true nature; they are useful only as indicators of where we have been hurt and need healing attention. The pressures to take drugs are enormous. Given our failures in providing authentic community to support individual healing and growth, it is all too understandable that so many of us succumb to the pressures to take drugs. No blame. Nevertheless, taking psychiatric drugs can be a great hindrance to emotional healing and re-emergence as a courageous, worthy individual who is completely in love with him or herself. To call it medicine for a disease is a lie.

A Note on Organic Wounds

There is a tremendous variety of physical illnesses or traumas which can interfere with brain functioning, and may result in major disturbances of consciousness. When that happens, the inner experience may be indistinguishable from psychologically induced distress, from hallucinogenic drug intoxication, and from that which psychiatry calls "psychosis." One major problem with a ready psychiatric diagnosis of "mental illness" and immediate prescription of "antipsychotic" drugs is that any real contributing medical condition is masked and obscured. Therefore, it is crucial to rule out these conditions when someone presents with "bizarre" symptomatology. Here is a list of brain-body insults that also cause a mental wound, provided by Dr Edward Podvoll in 'The Seduction of Madness': (7)

1/ Allergic viral encephalitis (which may follow infections of measles, German measles, or chicken pox)

2/ Allergic reactions to wheat or rye or dairy

3/ Toxic brain pathology in reaction to local anesthetics, penicillin, and other drugs

4/ Endocrine imbalances, such as hypothyroid or hyperthyroid crises, adrenal diseases, and steroid replacement

5/ Central nervous system involvement from autoimmune illnesses such as multiple sclerosis, systemic lupus erythematosus, and AIDS

6/ Central nervous system involvement from the steroid medications used to treat the preceding diseases

7/ Introduction of, or withdrawal from, a host of psychoactive ("neuroleptic") medications that affect the many known and unknown neuro transmitters

8/ Overdosage of stimulant drugs such as amphetamine, cocaine, etc., even caffeine intoxication

9/ Reactions to antimalarial drugs and antiasthmatic drugs

10/ Postoperative complications, e.g., following coronary artery bypass surgery

11/ Chronic epileptic disorders of all kinds, most notably with temporal lobe seizures

12/ The consequence of childbirth, e.g., postpartum psychosis

13/ Head traumas of all kinds (more commonly from right-sided injury)

14/ Assorted brain abnormalities, such as basal ganglia calcification, frontal arterial-venous malformation, brain-stem tumors, thalamic infarction, and the effects of aging or senility

15/ End-stage kidney or liver failure

16/ Vitamin B-12 deficiency

17/ Chronic dialysis brain inflammation

18/ Acute alcohol poisoning

19/ Prolonged sleep deprivation, from whatever cause

20/ A variety of sensory isolation phenomena

It is also not uncommon to see "symptoms of psychosis" which are very specific effects of a psychiatric drug. I have seen this with elders in nursing homes and with children in my private practice.

The Decision to Withdraw from Psychiatric Drugs

The decision to withdraw from psychiatric drugs involves all considerations already mentioned, and more. Accurate information about the nature of human beings (essentially good, intelligent, zestful, and quite capable of recovering from the effects of psychological hurts without drugs) is vital. Of particular importance is knowing that the fundamental mechanism of psychological healing is emotional expression (crying, shaking with fear, storming in anger, laughing at embarrassments, etc.). In order to withdraw from psychiatric drugs, you must understand that the practices of biopsychiatry, in this case drugs, are intended specifically to suppress emotional discharge, to put a stop to the very expression that is necessary for healing. Biopsychiatric theory interprets your spontaneous efforts to show and bring attention to your distress, not as promise of a possible recovery, but as symptoms of a dread disease — a disease which is chronic and incurable, manageable with "medication." Shaking, trembling, and being overwhelmed by fear is labeled "panic disorder" and suppressed with drugs-it is more helpfully seen as spontaneous discharge of terror held in the body. Shutting down and sinking into melancholy is labeled "depression" and "treated" with drug — a necessary period of withdrawal to deeply grieve or to find the courage to face great fear is denied. Biopsychiatric theory is unfounded in scientific fact; it is a superstitious belief.

To effectively withdraw from drugs, you will also need another related piece of information. I have seen many people attempt to withdraw from psychiatric drugs, only to experience a worsening of "symptoms," interpreted as evidence that they still need the drugs. Amazingly enough it appears that the majority of psychiatrists are either not well-versed in the process of drug withdrawal, or else so steeped in the superstitious convictions of biologically-based mental illness that everything is interpreted as evidence of psychiatric disease. In any event, what typically happens is that the "exacerbation of symptoms" is immediately interpreted as evidence that you are still ill and in need of medication. To withdraw from drugs, it is essential to know and name the simple truth that you are withdrawing from drugs. You are addicted to one or more mood-altering chemicals, physically and psychologically dependent. Therefore, you must go through drug withdrawal. Biopsychiatry ignores drug withdrawal and interprets withdrawal symptoms as evidence of "mental illness." The truth is that it often takes several months to get through the experiences of drug withdrawal, and you will have great difficulty knowing the condition of your mental status until withdrawal is complete. David Cohen, one of the top researchers in the world on psychiatric drug use and withdrawal, points out that withdrawal symptoms are generally similar to the drug effects. So a good way to get a general idea of what you might experience in withdrawal is to remember how the drug affected you when you took it. To get a general picture, simply review the list of effects in the Physician's Desk Reference. Cohen also points out that symptoms which were controlled or suppressed by drugs will tend to return on withdrawal, and may be even more intense for awhile due to a rebound effect. He has observed that withdrawal symptoms tend to unfold in reverse order of drug effects upon administration. For example, if upon ingestion of a particular drug, one experienced nausea, followed by cessation of shakiness, followed by cessation of insomnia, then withdrawal effects would tend to be sleep disruption, shakiness and nausea, in that order. (8)

Accurate information is essential, and information is power. One key to getting off drugs, then, is to name the reality of withdrawal, learn the specific withdrawal symptoms associated with the drug(s) you are taking, and proactively develop a plan that will lend the best possible support as you go through withdrawal. On a practical level, 'Dr Caligari`s Psychiatric Drugs' by David Richman, though somewhat dated, is the best I've seen for solid information and common sense advice about psychiatric drugs and how to get off of them. (9) What this is really about is compassionate self-care. It is crucial to feel and understand the profound necessity of compassionate self-care in our journeys of healing and recovery. We must relinquish the harshness and the judgments, and move over and over again to a place of acceptance, gentleness and compassion toward ourselves. The following common sense basics of self-care on a physical level form the necessary foundation for the intense and challenging emotional and mental work we are called to do for ourselves.

Practical Suggestions

Dr Caligari places great emphasis on scheduling your withdrawal; problems are minimized by reducing intake gradually. As a rule of thumb, the 10 percent formula is a useful guideline. Drug withdrawal is accomplished by slowly reducing the drug dose in sequential steps, by 10 percent of the current dose in each step. Gradualness is a real key, and I strongly recommend it, even though I am aware that many, if not the majority of people who get off psychiatric drugs do so all at once or "cold turkey." Please do avail yourself of Richman's guide; he provides a wealth of information. I include here a long excerpt of his practical suggestions regarding the process of drug withdrawal:

DIET

One of the purposes of withdrawing form psychiatric drugs is to cleanse the body, to rid it of accumulated poisons. Nausea, vomiting, and other stomach problems can be anticipated. What you eat during this period will influence your experience of the withdrawal and its outcome. Therefore, it is important to eat well, regularly, but not to excess. Some people report good results by concentrating on grains, beans, fresh vegetables, fresh or dried fruit, and uncooked, unsalted nuts, and avoiding junk food, sugar (candy, cakes, ice cream, and soft drinks), processed foods (canned and frozen), fried foods, animal products (meat and dairy), caffeine (coffee, most commercial teas, and some soft drinks), alcohol, and drugs like marijuana, cocaine, and speed. (Richman also advises that it is not wise to stop smoking at the same time you are withdrawing from psychiatric drugs. Each can lead to increase in tension; together, this can be overwhelming. The recommendation is to get off the drugs first, then deal with the smoking.)

SLEEP AND RELAXATION

Insomnia (difficulty getting to sleep or staying asleep) is a common withdrawal problem. Adequate sleep and rest during the withdrawal period is extremely important. If sleep does not come easily, it is better to rest in bed than to pursue some activity. Some people have found it helpful to drink an herbal tea (valerian and chamomile are good ones) to relax. Others have benefited from yoga and breathing exercises, warm baths, and massages before sleep.

PHYSICAL EXERCISE

As your body becomes free of drugs, in time you will almost surely have more energy than you had while taking the drugs. This energy can be used to further the withdrawal process if it is channeled into an exercise program. Some sort of regular activity will assist your body in eliminating the drugs. You might start swimming, walking, dancing, or doing yoga or aerobics. Moderation is a key principle: as you increase your activities, do so gradually.

MENTAL EXERCISE

Your mind is likely to become more active during withdrawal. For some people this has proven to be a good time for learning new survival and social skills, as well as for study, reflection, and meditation.

MENTAL ATTITUDE

Withdrawal from psychiatric drugs can be a very trying experience. You should know that withdrawal can cause moderate to severe discomfort and outright misery at times. Being mentally prepared for this decreases the chance that you will become scared or discouraged. Patience and determination are needed.

ENVIRONMENTAL FACTORS

Having a stable life situation during the drug withdrawal period is very important. Count yourself lucky if you are among people who understand the nature of drug withdrawal and support your efforts to go through it. If you must be among people who disapprove of your decision to go off drugs, you should insist upon their respecting your right to do so. Of course, during withdrawal you are better off being by yourself than with unsympathetic or hostile people. Many individuals have withdrawn from drugs on their own. As you come down from the drugs, you are likely to feel better physically and have more energy for improving your relationships and developing new ones, getting involved in the community, and tying in with your support system or creating your own. (10)

CHAPTER 12
ON THE PROCESS OF
EMOTIONAL RECOVERY

The basics of drug withdrawal discussed previously are vitally important. Part of the big lie of biopsychiatry, and o our pill culture in general, is that you can avoid the basics c self-care by taking a drug. It is so tempting to embrace the illusion that you can escape responsibility for altering your lifestyle, that you can avoid the ruthless discipline that is necessary to live a decent life in a society which is so alienated and distressed. You have to sacrifice the fantasy that someone, or some doctor, or some drug is going to make anything all better for you. The truth is that life is, ir many ways, an arduous journey. And coming off psychiatri drugs can be a particularly intense part of that journey. My own experience leads me to conclude that, as vital as accurate information and common sense are, emotional factors are what really hold people back from this crucial step toward self-empowerment. Three particular qualities attitude are necessary to challenge and overcome forms of emotional distress that interfere with successful withdrawa from drugs and reclaiming of power. These qualities are hope, courage, and complete self-appreciation; they are specific antidotes to hopelessness, fear and shame. As I discuss this process of what might be most aptly called emotional recovery, I will be referring to and recommending that you receive the good attention of another safe, caring human being as you do this work. I wi use the terms counseling and counselor, but please know that I mean this in a generic sense. A counselor is someone who sacrifices his or her own concerns for a time to pay attention and listen to you. It can be a professional; it can also be a friend. I personally recommend the grassroots peer counseling organization called Re-evaluation Counseling as one great source of theory and counseling support. (1) Please know, however, that RC sometimes will not accept people who are on psychiatric drugs. Psychiatric survivor groups are another great resource. The important point here is that you don't have to go through this alone; you need and deserve good counseling support.

Hopelessness Into Hope

We begin by facing our feelings of hopelessness. Disillusionment is absolutely necessary for recovery and well-being. Disillusionment of our fantasies about a magic rescuer or a magic pill hits us hard. Chronic hopelessness is pervasive in our society; it is a root cause of our full scale abdication to biopsychiatry, and the despair which leads millions upon millions of us to turn to drugs for ourselves and for our children as a solution to life. Those of us who hurt enough to turn to psychiatry for help, and who were then hurt further by being labeled as biologically and/or genetically defective, and "treated" with toxic drugs, understandably feel hopeless much of the time. Within the framework of biopsychiatry, hopelessness is a rational response; after all, your condition is seen as essentially incurable and you are said to need drugs to manage any decent kind of life at all. The good news, once again, is that it is simply a lie that you are defective, and it is simply a lie that you need drugs to treat your defect. Your condition is not hopeless.

It can get better. This simple sentence forms the basis of your recovery, any recovery in fact. Hope is the building block, and a necessary contradiction for times when we are overwhelmed with feelings of chronic hopelessness. It really can get better. We really do have natural, built-in ways of psychological healing. With good attention and adequate resource, anyone can reemerge from even the greatest distress and most extreme states of mind. On a practical level, due to lack of understanding, there are times when we cannot gather enough resource to adequately help individuals in crisis in our society. Our current inability to help people in extreme states of mind is not because they have a psychiatric disease; it is simply because of the unavailability of sufficient resource. It's helpful to know that, although in times of distress, it almost always feels like you can't get enough, the truth is most of the time you can. The feeling is called a "frozen need;" it is a memory from childhood when we really did not get what we needed to thrive and develop as well as possible, when our survival truly was at stake. So even though it may feel like it's never enough, you usually can get what you need. On a practical level, a key is to find support people who are relaxed and confident about your ability to recover, who trust in the goodness and wholeness of your inherent nature, and who see through the lies and illusions of biopsychiatry. It can get better, and you can get off the drugs.

Fear Into Courage

Earlier I discussed fear and shame as emotional qualities which pull us into a victim-like attitude. These two emotions are, I think, the most loyal forces of the opposition, acting as obstacles to liberation from the role of psychiatric patient in general, and freedom from psychiatric drug addiction in specific. Let's take a look at fear. For many of us, certainly for those who have experienced the effects of coercive treatment or incarceration by psychiatry, terror is a more appropriate word. In any event, fear acts as a most potent force in decision-making for most of us. It takes great courage to face any trauma,and psychiatric abuse is doubly scary. The word courage means big heart, and that's what it takes. As you discharge the fear, it gradually gets a little easier, but it still always requires courage to face our own hurts and to challenge oppression in our society.

I would venture to say that fear is the one greatest obstacle to successful withdrawal from psychiatric drugs. There is the fear of losing control, of going mad, that they might be right about you, that you'll lose your job, that you won't be able to function, that you'll end up back in the hospital, etc. This list goes on and on; the fear is enormous. If at all possible, you counsel extensively on your fear as a first step in making and acting on the decision to withdraw from psychiatric drugs. The next few paragraphs will help clarify why I so strongly advise you to do this.

Once again, accurate information is a good place to start. First of all, it is important to validate the reality that many of these fears are not "paranoiac delusions;" many of you do know that interface with psychiatry can be dangerous. You have been incarcerated, forcibly drugged, electroshocked, and god only knows what else. A good place to start in counseling on fear about coming off drugs is to tell your story to a relaxed, confident and sympathetic listener. Tell your story many times, and really emphasize the details of your experiences with psychiatry and with drugs. Make a point of noticing the attention you are receiving from your counselor or friend; it is important to know you are safe and that you are not alone in your courageous decision to work on this.

Secondly, just as with other types of emotional expression, release of fear is usually interpreted by psychiatry not as a healing process but as a disease symptom, evidence of the need for intervention and treatment with drugs. Once again, you've been given some bad information. Most people think of fear as a mental phenomenon having to do with irrational or unrealistic expectations about the future. When psychiatry is not entirely biological in emphasis, the cognitive (mental) domain is often emphasized. Undoubtedly, how we think is fundamental, and cognitive behavior modification (i.e., working with your self-talk) can be helpful. When it is not enough, however, I encourage you not to jump to the biopsychiatric conclusion that your enduring problem is due to a genetic defect. What I've learned about fear is that it is less about our thoughts than our emotions, and less about anticipation of the future than memory of the past. Fear is tension held in the body, a memory of past situations when we felt that our survival was in danger, and we were not allowed to release the fear in the way that is natural to us. When we are in danger, we become tense and we feel fear. This tension and this emotion stay with us until we are safe enough to let down our guard; then we release the fear. Fear is released in a specific way. Light fear is often released by laughing and shaking. Heavy fear is discharged by shaking, trembling, cold sweat, and sometimes screaming. Many so-called psychiatric symptoms (anxiety, insomnia, night terrors, panic attacks, etc.) may be more helpfully viewed as spontaneous efforts of an overloaded body/mind to do what it is naturally designed to do: restore calm and equanimity by discharging fear from traumatic experiences. Some fear can be discharged alone, but experience shows that we often need a supportive ally to help us work through fear. After all, our instinctual survival nature is geared to protect us from being overwhelmed with scary feelings; a warm, confident, relaxed friend or counselor can make all the difference.

Spend as much time as you need telling your story. When you're ready, it's a good idea to spend time talking about your decision to get off the drugs. Specifically, you will want to fully deal with your fear of getting off the drugs. It's helpful to run through all your worries and concerns about what might happen to you, both internally in your state of mind and emotions, and externally through work, family, friends, etc. Be sure and really go into fears about what psychiatry might do to you. This may sound like counterproductive dwelling on negativity, but I assure you that, with a safe ally close by, this is very useful in releasing fear. After all, the thoughts and emotion are already inside of you; this is about getting it out in a safe way. Some of your concerns will be valid, others not. For the purposes of working through fear, it doesn't matter. The end result is that you will be able to look at all of the possibilities with greater clarity as a result of discharging some of the enormous fear you've been carrying.

Another really useful direction is to talk about the upside of what your life will be like without drugs. Talk about how your body will feel, how clear your thinking will be, how you won't have a dry mouth anymore, how great sex will be, whatever. Allow yourself to imagine and share with your counselor all the wonderful benefits of being drug-free. At some point, you will want to go beyond this and imagine and dream out loud about the very highest goals and visions you have for yourself.

As you talk about and remember your experiences of fear in the presence of a safe counselor, you will at some point find your body responding with its own natural ways of discharging the physical and emotional tensions of fear. As I described above, you may laugh, sweat, shake, or tremble. This means that you now know that you are safe enough to come out of numbing terror and release fear from your system. It is useful during this time to have your counselor frequently remind you that you are, indeed, completely safe, that you made it out to a safe place. Focusing on the benign reality of your present situation is most helpful direction: "now I'm safe," "they can't touch m now," etc. One of the greatest contradictions to fear is closeness with another safe, warm human being; a direction such as "You and me, counselor (friend, partner, etc.), completely close!" said with delight and enthusiasm can sometimes really help discharge the fear.

Shame Into Complete Self-Appreciation

Alongside fear, our greatest emotional obstacle to spiritual maturity and authentic power is this feeling we call shame. discussed shame in Chapter 5 as a root cause of psychiatric oppression; now we will consider it in light of emotional recovery. Shame is a word for the emotional experience th goes with thoughts that "I'm no good," inadequate, incompetent, not enough, stupid, unworthy, inferior, defective, etc. Distinct from guilt, it does not express that did something bad," but that "I am bad." Shame feels just awful, and we are often most eager and willing to go to great lengths to avoid feeling shame; we prop ourselves up however we can, often by projecting the contempt we'd rather not feel for ourselves onto some other person we can judge, scorn, criticize, or somehow deem inferior. (The so-called "mentally ill" fill this scapegoat role to a great extent in our society.) Another characteristic of shame is that it feels unbearable to be exposed. When we carry shame, we want to hide, and again will go to great lengths to keep hidden those parts of ourselves which we reject and despise.

In working with feelings of shame, a necessary first step is to give it a name. Shame feels just awful, and it feels like who we are. When experiencing intense shame, we don't usually think, "I'm having this awful feeling of shame that I'm re-experiencing as a result of having been shamefully abused by an adult caretaker when I was a dependent child." It's generally more like "I'm a worthless piece of shit" — not a feeling I'm having, but the felt truth of who I really am. So it is very important to give this awful feeling a name, and thereby give yourself a buffer against taking this lie in so deeply. Then you can say, "Oh, I'm having a shame attack;" that it's not who you are, but a toxic feeling that you're carrying. It still feels lousy, but now you're in a position to work with it.

The next step is to challenge the pull to avoid exposure. Shame thrives in secrecy, and cannot sustain itself when exposed to safe people who listen with respect and compassion, and are delighted that you are getting free. The voice of shame, similar to the voice of biopsychiatry, will tell you that you are inherently defective in some way; the truth is that your feelings of shame are strictly an add-on. Shame is a feeling that you carry from having been treated shamefully; the feelings have nothing to do with the goodness of your inherent nature; they have everything to do with having been treated badly by someone who was projecting their own denied feelings onto you. When an adult says "You are a bad child, you deserve to be punished," what is actually happening is the end stage of the following process:

1/ A child is called bad and punished by a parent, grandparent, teacher, person of authority.

2/ The child internalizes both victim and perpetrator sides in this abuse of power; the feeling message that "I am bad" and the energetic communication that "You are bad."

3/ The child "splits off" and denies the experience and the feelings in the interests of self-preservation. The memory is banished into the unconscious mind as protection against feeling the hurt and the shame.

4/ The child grows up to be an adult.

5/ The repressed energies of shame and abuse are restimulated around a child.

6/ The unconscious feelings of shame are projected onto the child. Again in the interests of self-preservation, the adult will, given the choice, unconsciously identify with the powerful perpetrator of abuse rather than the powerless victim.

7/ The child is then punished, "for her own good." (

So, in order to recover and get free, you make a decision to expose your shame, to reveal the parts of yourself that you judge as despicable and unworthy. And as you do this with people who are supportive, understanding and without judgment, the shame will gradually melt away.

As you do this work of exposing your shame and healing from its effects, the concept of shame reduction wi be very useful. Shame is not a part of your essence; it is a toxic add-on, and as with all toxins, the human organism always strives to discharge them from the system. This is as true of psychological toxins as it is for physical poisons. Shame is not a part of who we really are; it is something we carry as a result of having been treated badly. Shame reduction refers to the process of unloading this carried shame. Practically speaking, it means:

1/ naming the feeling as shame,
2/ identifying the source of the feeling, including the specific individual(s),
3/ holding that individual(s) accountable, and
4/ returning the carried shame to the individual(s). (3)

I do want to mention that "holding the perpetrator accountable" does not necessarily mean that you have to confront the individual in the flesh. Often that individual is very different, perhaps 30 or more years older, from the individual who hurt you as a child. It is that "ghost" figure inside of you, the one who hurt you at the time of the incident(s) that it is necessary to confront. So most of that work can be done inwardly or through role play. If you do decide that a physical confrontation is necessary, lots of counseling on it first is a good idea. Intense feelings of hurt, fear and anger usually surface at some point. Releasing these emotions can make a big difference. For another perspective on confrontation, check out Brad Blanton's provocative book, 'Radical Honesty: How To Transform Your Life By Telling The Truth'. (4) Brad is a strong advocate of the notion that we can become free only to the extent that we are willing to tell the truth. The bottom line is to do whatever it takes to reclaim your energy and your power, so that you can release these people from your psyche and not continue draining your energy into thoughts and feelings of victimization and revenge.

ON ANGER

Shame reduction work generally involves intense feelings of hurt and anger, which are inevitably bound up with shame. My friend and teacher, Dan Jones, taught me that two of the greatest allies against shame are laughter and anger. Having a sense of humor and laughing about our predicaments helps tremendously because shame feels very heavy and serious, and because we discharge embarrassment or humiliation by laughter. Our other great ally, anger, requires some discussion. Most all of us have a hard time with anger, and with tense conflict. The anger we grew up with was either denied or outright dangerous. On the one hand, many of our families and other teachers often pretended that there was no anger as in "We never fight," and punished us for showing anger as in "Go to your room and don't come out until you can be nice." Others of us experienced irresponsible, out-of-control anger in the form of overt verbal, emotional, and physical or sexual abuse. When anger is repressed, there is a backlog which tends to come out as rage, usually dumped on the less powerful, often the children. And when children are abused by powerful adults, they learn to be silent and to suppress and repress their anger.

As psychiatric survivor and therapist Laurie Prescott points out in her powerful audiotape, 'The Truth About Women, Sexual Abuse and Revictimization', (5) such abuse is not an aberration; it is, in fact, normal in the sense that it is still very common in our society. Revictimization refers to the fact that trauma survivors are often hurt by psychiatry when they either reach for help or are coerced into "treatment" by friends, family, or others in the society. Prescott's voice of experience reveals the truth that much psychiatric trauma has to do with anger, the repressed anger of the "helpers," and the suppression of anger in the "patients." Psychiatry tends to have little tolerance for anger in its "patients," interpreting it as "acting out," "resistance," "non-cooperation with treatment," or other clinical/pathological concept. There is very little understanding that the faces of anger in psychiatry's "patients" are natural responses to a history of abuse and oppression, and/or a present-time experience of coercion, misunderstanding, and disrespect.

Expression of anger, even the intense, bottled-up rage of a lifetime of abuse, is absolutely essential for emotional healing and recovery. While it is a tremendous challenge to facilitate the release of rage in safe and appropriate way, it can be done, but only by those who have sat in the fire of their own anger, and are not in denial. Simply viewing the expression of anger, even in distorted forms such as self-mutilation, not as prima facie evidence of "mental illness," but as cries for help and unaware efforts to heal by expressing the truth of how one feels, can make a big difference. True violence is most often the result of suppressed feeling, rather than verbal and emotional expression, however intense it may be. Arny and Amy Mindell's (6) worldwork facilitating dialogue in hotspots around the world is great evidence of this truth. These teachers have facilitated hundreds of meetings of intensely polarized groups around the world (e.g., U.S. inner city race issues, religious or ethnic conflicts in Beirut, South Africa, or Northern Ireland). It is often extremely intense with expressions of deep-seated rage; thus far, they've never had an incident of overt physical violence. This does not mean that physical restraint is never necessary. I do strongly agree with Laura Prescott, however, that with genuine support and counseling for anger work, and respectful listening throughout, the use of restraint in psychiatry would be reduced enormously. My book, 'The Wildest Colts Make The Best Horses', has a section on working with anger that is useful for all ages. John Lee's book, 'Facing The Fire', (7 is a very good resource for theory and techniques for counseling on anger.

The last and most important direction for healing an recovery from shame is called complete self-appreciation. This is all about self-love, and it truly is the way out. Shame absolutely cannot abide residence in the presence of self-love. Singing 'A Song of Myself', to borrow the title of Wa Whitman's epic poem, is the first, best, and last way to overcome shame. Everything from the simplest and most halting baby steps of loving kindness toward yourself (e.g., taking time for a walk, a bath or a nap, asking for touch, forgiving yourself for being hard on yourself) to the most exalted and shameless (8) boasting is great for this work. I cannot encourage you enough to keep challenging the lim: that hinder your progress toward self-love. Spend lots of counseling time and time alone appreciating yourself. Forgive yourself again and again and again for any and all judgments you place on yourself, and keep moving in the direction of loving kindness and compassionate self-care. Jamie Alexander shares one excellent way to work on this. Her suggestion is to take pride in how well you function o the drugs and on how well you function off the drugs.

> "People who feel they need drugs to function at all w discharge very well if asked to take pride in how well the function off drugs, if they are first given space to be prou of how well they function on the drugs. It is important to

focus on how well they function in either case and not
make them feel that we are putting pressure on them or
that we have a 'moral' stance. People who have decided to
continue to take drugs usually feel (and fear) that they
cannot function at all without them. The contradiction
here is to have them describe times they functioned well
while not on drugs." (9)

You were born wonderful, always have been
wonderful, and still are completely wonderful. Allow
yourself time to fully discover this important reality.

The Natural Function of Doubt

I want to include here a few observations about the role of
doubt in human nature and human distress. Part One of
Edward Podvoll's book, 'The Seduction of Madness' (see
Chapter 2), is called Parables of Madness. Each of the first
four chapters is a remarkable portrait of a historic
individual's journey into madness; each experience provides
critical insights into the ordinarily hidden dimensions of the
"psychotic" experience. Of particular interest here is the
story of John Thomas Perceval (1803-1876), a Victorian
English gentleman, son of a beloved prime minister of
England. Perceval was confined to an asylum against his will
at age 29. There he experienced the full panorama of the
"psychotic" experience. Totally alone and against all odds,
he largely recovered during the first year of hospitalization
but was not released until two years later. He then devoted
his whole life to telling the truth about what happened. He
detailed his inner experience and his outer experience. He
showed how his mind worked, that recovery is possible, and
how it is possible. He told the truth about, and actively

campaigned for the rest of his life against the horrors of
psychiatric oppression. As Podvoll points out, the anti-
psychiatry movement did not begin in the 1960s; it began as
soon as psychiatry began.

Psychiatry has tried in vain to identify the biological
or genetic defect which causes "mental illness," in this case
"psychosis." Perhaps the most significant of Perceval's
discoveries, which, according to Podvoll, he announced on
almost every page of his writings, was that the root cause of
his mental aberration was "a disturbance of the normal and
intelligent function of doubt." (10) Perceval, like so many o
us, like myself, like Cindy, was a spiritual seeker. He was
striving to find God, to align his will with God's will, to hea
and follow the dictates of the highest truth he could
perceive and comprehend. Like anyone who seeks after
truth, he was struggling to discern which of the myriad
conflicting thoughts, beliefs, ideas, voices, visions was really
true. All thoughtful people work to sharpen and refine their
faculties of discernment. So did Perceval. What began as an
exciting and inspiring journey, however, somehow resulted
in a descent into a hell of inner torment and outer brutality

How did this happen? One part of the picture, then a
now, had to do with the misunderstanding and mistreatmer
of those who purported to care for him; psychiatric
oppression was as real then as it is now. But the inner
mechanism which to Perceval was the key to his
vulnerability and desolation was about doubt. Perceval was
greedy for spiritual power, and desperate to be a special,
chosen emissary of the Spirit. He saw doubt as willful
procrastination, reasoning that, in order to maintain his
inspired connection to divine guidance, he must never
hesitate, but must submit to an immediate, unquestioned
execution of the letter of the commands of his inner voices

So he declared open warfare on doubt, and compensated by turning doubt into its opposite: wild hope and blind faith.

It appears to me that the three key emotional obstacles I described above — hopelessness, fear, and shame — were all intensely present in Perceval's experience. His desperation reveals hopelessness and fear, emotional distress compelling self-destructive behavior. Desperation, particularly as reflected in the need to be so special, and the pain of believing himself unworthy, is also about shame. Our shame makes it very difficult to tolerate doubt and uncertainty, because uncertainty implies inadequacy, incompetence, and unworthiness. We often attempt to compensate for and avoid feeling shame by proving and justifying how we really are superior to others; spiritual arrogance is one of the faces of shame. Perceval overrode the natural function of doubt in his search for the truth. The intensity of his torment was in no small part a reflection of the emotional distress — the fear and shame — he carried inside, and activated when he chose to search so deeply within. Cindy's experience was similar in many ways. She, too, was a spiritual seeker, and took great pride in her special connection to divine guidance. She, too, overrrode her natural doubt function, speaking and acting unquestionably on the dictates of her inner experience. Like Perceval, Cindy was incarcerated and subdued by psychiatry. She, too, paid a price. Psychiatric drugs were not on the scene in Perceval's day. Though treated horrifically, his mind was not poisoned with toxic drugs. For whatever reason, largely a tribute to his indomitable will and strength of spirit, he found his way and emerged as a teacher and activist for reform.

According to Perceval himself, the key was in his coming to terms with doubt. He caught glimpses, even in the midst of his most intense and constant "hallucinations," of clarity, wherein he had reason to doubt the absolute truth of his inner experience. Gradually and painstakingly, he learned to embrace and work with doubt, to question things, to check things out, to bring his mental experiences in for a "reality" check on the physical plane. And he eventually emerged, becoming a forceful, articulate and tireless champion in the fight against psychiatric oppression.

When we carry a lot of fear and shame, the direct results of having been treated in frightening and humiliating ways, we have a very difficult time exercising any of the natural functions of our mind, in particular the crucial one of doubt. On the one hand, we labor under a cloud of self-criticism and constantly doubt ourselves. Or we compensate, as Perceval attempted, by forcibly overriding doubt, and clinging to wild hope and blind faith. The first alternative is sad, forlorn, discouraging and depressing. The second can be wild and exciting for awhile, but it inevitably leads to disaster. These are flip sides of the same tarnished coin of natural doubt. Direct work on fear and shame is a key to creating a level of calm and self-acceptance which allows for self-examination without force, despair, and desperation.

Buddhist teacher Sogyal Rinpoche, author of 'The Tibetan Book of Living and Dying' (11), points out that all of us must deal with minds riddled and confused with doubt. He thinks that contemporary education, in fact, glorifies doubt, leading us to conclude that to be intelligent we have to doubt everything, always point to what's wrong, to denigrate inherited spiritual ideals and philosophies, or simple innocence and goodwill. No wonder, then, that the inward journey is treacherous; it means uncovering, directly facing and working through this fear and shame-based compulsion to use a perverted, cynical form of doubt on ourselves and others. No wonder the attraction of forcibly doing battle with and overriding such a painful compulsion. Rinpoche's answer is to replace our modern cynical form of doubt with what he calls "noble doubt." He presents this noble doubt as an integral part of the spiritual path, just as Perceval presented healthy doubt as integral to his own recovery and journey through life. Mean-spirited doubt is very serious, morally judgmental, black-and-white, even fanatical. Noble doubt is "open-souled and generous," "free, humorous, and compassionate." Noble doubt has to come from a place of at least relative freedom from shame and fear, a place of relaxed self-appreciation, a place where it really is okay to be wrong, make mistakes, and laugh at ourselves. Rinpoche shares the advice of a Hindu master which is very similar to how Perceval emerged from terrifying submission to his own relentless inner voices and visions. The master's advice is to "turn the dogs of doubt on doubt itself, to unmask cynicism and to uncover what fear, despair, hopelessness, and tired conditioning it springs from." Then doubt is not an obstacle, but a pathway to liberation. Remember that this process is exactly not about force; it is about patience and gradualness. Fear and shame are woven deep into our bodies, and recovery is gradual. Doubts do not resolve themselves immediately, but with patience and persistence we can slowly uncover and embrace more and more of the truth. No force. No hurry. Gentleness.

Guidelines

There really is no formula for working through issues

related to your decision of whether or not to use psychiatric drugs. Please understand that the actual process of recovery is totally unique, organic, and most definitely not a linear experience. Here are some guidelines to support you in your decision to withdraw from psychiatric drugs:

1/ Take exquisite care of yourself on every level — physical, emotional, mental, spiritual. Be practical.

2/ See yourself through the eyes of compassion.

3/ Get the best information you can on the nature of life, human beings and personal transformation. There is a wealth of written material and an array of support groups and activities. Always check the information out inside yourself. Take what rings true and is useful. Discard the rest.

4/ Establish the very best support for yourself that you can.

5/ Find a safe person to talk to. At first this may feel scary. Ask yourself if this person is safe to talk to. Ask them if they are willing to listen. As you get stronger, this gets easier because you grow in confidence that you can protect yourself.

6/ Counsel on chronic hopelessness. Work on the possibility that it can get better.

7/ Tell your story in detail.

8/ Counsel on fear of getting off drugs; be dramatic about what could happen.

9/ Talk about what will be good about life without drugs.

10/ Reach for closeness with your counselor, friend, mentor, partner.

11/ Focus on how safe you are now.

12/ Allow yourself to discharge the fear by laughing, shaking, trembling, and sweating.

13/ Take as long as you need. Allow patience and gradualness, but keep your eyes on the prize of a drug-free life.

14/ Establish some sort of regular practice of going inside to be with yourself through meditation or prayer. Besides the known physical and emotional benefits of meditation, it is essential to go within to discover yourself and become your own authority.

15/ Keep a journal.

16/ Always remember that it is your decision whether or not to use drugs!

No one else is in your body, no one else has had your experience, no one else knows better than you what is the best decision for you. My purpose is not to say that you should get off drugs. It is to say that most people are on psychiatric drugs under false pretenses, and it is to say that there are inevitable consequences to drug use. My intention is to lend support to the possibility of your making a fully informed consent regarding any decision to use psychiatric drugs. This means that you know and understand that it is not a "medicine" for a biologically-based "mental illness." It is a decision about using mood-altering drugs, usually to slow down or speed up what is happening in your body/ mind. You have every right, knowing the issues involved and the full range of drug effects, to decide that it is in your best interests to take a drug, or to continue taking a drug or drugs you are now using, and to which you are likely addicted. Regardless of your decision, the good news about working on these issues is that emotional release often frees up your intelligence to make clearer decisions that are not based in fear or shame.

Speaking Out

My final thoughts to share with you on this issue are based on a discovery I have made in my own life, and in my observations of the inspiring individuals I have come to know in the mental health liberation movement. I have had the privilege to watch and work with many people who identify themselves as psychiatric survivors, individuals who feel grievously harmed by psychiatry, who call themselves survivors, and who have become active in challenging the oppression they see in psychiatry. Withdrawal from drugs is one very specific and important example of personal recovery. It is also very much a political decision and action overtly challenging and rejecting an ideology and a system of power. Tremendous courage is required.

Freedom from psychiatric drugs stands alone as an outstanding accomplishment for anyone who has become addicted to these drugs for whatever reason. Life appears to be set up, however, such that we can never rest on our laurels for long. There is always a next step, another level of recovery or personal growth. My own experience is that a huge part of reclaiming my power is about my willingness to speak the truth, to take a stand and speak out against oppression. I do not recommend that anyone go straight from drug withdrawal into political activism; learning and building a foundation of personal healing and compassionate self-care needs to be top priority. Speaking to safe people and discharging should come before going public. Liberation from the effects of psychiatric abuse can be so frightening; it is vitally important to have good support and strong allies such as organizations like Support Coalition International and The National Empowerment Center. (12) Nevertheless, what I have observed is that speaking out publicly and lending a hand and a voice against oppression is a necessary step to a full-bodied recovery. The activist survivors that I know are living examples of this truth. Each of us does this in our own unique way. Just know that speaking out at some point will greatly facilitate your own personal growth. Besides, we really need your help.

CHAPTER 13
NURSING HOME BLUES: ONE MAN'S CHALLENGE OF THE PSYCHIATRIC DRUGGING OF OUR ELDERS

Chapters 9 and 10 pointed out the shameful use of electroshock to suppress elders in our society. The last two chapters addressed issues around psychiatric drugs. This chapter provides an example of psychiatric oppression from my own experience in the form of the large-scale use of psychiatric drugs to control elders in nursing homes. The chapter also shows some of the difficulties we are up against in challenging this oppression.

When my private practice recently hit a slow spell, I responded to a nursing home service agency seeking psychologists to assist elders. Elders were much on my mind as I'd just testified before the Texas legislature against the use of electroshock. When the agency, Senior Psychology Services (SPS), asked for my services full time, I had serious reservations. Taking the job would mean giving up some of the private practice I'd developed, and confronting biopsychiatry head-on. It would mean doing battle in personal terms over the practice of electroshock, a brain-damaging form of psychiatric abuse — I consider its use predominantly with elders in this country a national shame. I am also deeply concerned with the routine prescription of psychiatric drugs to chemically restrain older people. I discussed these issues at length with my interviewers at

'Mountain Valley', a pseudonym for the 'home' at which I'd be employed. I insisted that electroshock be forbidden wherever I worked, and I spoke vigorously against over-reliance on psychiatric drugs. From my standpoint, spiritual law holds that if you participate in an unethical situation, you must change it, or become unethical yourself. The administration at Mountain Valley assured me that they, too, were concerned about the overuse of psychiatric drugs, and saw their alliance with SPS as an opportunity to reduce the amount of psychiatric drug use in their facility.

Because the facility was clean, the staff seemed sincere, and the administration appeared to agree with my concerns, I accepted a part-time contract, anticipating becoming a full-time SPS employee as my caseload developed.

The Situation

Mountain Valley is a pleasant and well-respected skilled nursing facility in Austin, Texas. Most of the residents have significant medical difficulties. Many have heart conditions or have had strokes; some are on dialysis; many have conditions requiring therapy from the in-house rehabilitation staff. Wound and skin care are issues for a high percentage of residents; many are bedridden from surgery or other disability; sores and skin tears are a constant problem. A profound trend in many nursing care institutions is the greater disability of residents because of the reimbursement requirements of our welfare system.

Mountain Valley has an average daily census of about 210, though capacity is slightly greater. Space is a major problem. Some staff members office in converted closets or bathrooms; patient roommate conflicts are a constant challenge. Outdoor space is limited to a small sitting area at the front entrance and a slightly larger concrete back patio with a few tables and chairs. The patio, surrounded by walls and a chain link fence, leads to the parking lot, which serves as the smoking area. Most residents never go outside. For those who do, the most popular activity is smoking. Indoor activities include church services, hymn-singing once a week with a volunteer piano player, an exercise group, and an occasional volunteer entertainer.

Staff, for the most part, are friendly and respectful to residents, although staff turnover and shortages are a constant problem. Mountain Valley lost one of its two social workers and the admissions director within the first month of my tenure. The other social worker, my primary contact, had been there about six months in her first job out of graduate school. She was covering the entire facility plus admissions until a new person could be hired.

Life in a nursing home often means the profound alteration of time. Many residents have significant short-term memory loss; some have Alzheimer's and are profoundly disoriented or impaired. Those who still have the mental capacity (and many do) must have a strong will to stay focused despite major boredom and incessant routine in an enclosed, never-changing interior.

For many, the loneliness and isolation are extreme; physically, it's cold air and sterile conditions. A skilled nursing facility is much like a hospital. It's better, in the sense of more community, because residents stay a longer time, and many are ambulatory and socially active, at least to a small degree. It's worse in the sense that most hospital stays are brief and patients go home sooner. Most families just can't keep up the support and visitations long-term, at least not at the level of acute hospital stay.

The most anguishing aspect of being with the residents at Mountain Valley was the fact that virtually none of them wanted to be there. Some thought that since I was a "doctor," I held the power to liberate them. They wanted out of there. Others saw the situation more clearly, but still wanted my help to get out. One delightful woman, on dialysis three times a week and having been "cut on" at least twelve times, had lived there seven years and called it "home." She was president of the resident council, and had very good support (regular weekend visits, letters, etc.) from her extended family. She was the most spirited fighter I met there, constantly angry and frustrated about food or conditions or staff negligence. She felt neglect of place or people as a violation of her home. A few others I met in passing appeared to have achieved some degree of peace; mostly, there was resignation, despair and a great deal of bitterness.

Nursing Home as Psychiatric Hospital

From my point-of-view, the biggest problem was that nursing homes today are so like psychiatric hospitals. This is not readily visible on the surface, although I worked with one woman whose combination of dementia, fear, chronic pain and throat problems resulted in a constant screeching and yelling which leads many to immediately think of madness; another called the place a "loony bin" and used these plaintive screams as evidence for her assertion. A third woman, head hung in her wheelchair, roamed the halls plaintively crying out "Help me!" Lost in time and desperately pleading for help or fighting off perceived threats, these lost souls inevitably evoked images of a madhouse.

Much of the time it was quiet, but so today are psychiatric hospitals. In the 1940s, electroshock was discovered. It became immensely popular as a mechanism restoring order and quiet in mental asylums across the country. The advent of psychiatric drugs, the so-called neuroleptics or major tranquilizers in particular, gradually replaced electroshock as a more "humane" means of controlling so-called madness.

Shortly after beginning work at Mountain Valley, I was provided a list of all residents on psychiatric drugs. Although prepared to expect a goodly number, I was taken aback when handed a 28 page computer printout. Accordi to the pharmacy consultant, roughly 20 percent of the residents were on each of the categories of anti-psychotic, sedative-hypnotic, and anti-anxiety drugs, respectively. Ov 30 percent were on anti-depressants. Including PRN (as needed) orders, over half of the residents had prescription for psychiatric drugs. My own supervisor, when I wondere out loud about it, assured me that Mountain Valley is fairl representative of the overall picture in nursing homes toda This picture, with its heavy reliance on psychiatric drugs t control mood and behavior, is a focused snapshot of the overall trend in our society at-large. Jerry Avorn, MD, was quoted in the Boston Globe ten years ago: "My concern is that people are having their minds blunted in a way that probably does diminish their capacity to appreciate life." F was commenting on a study of 850 residents in 12 Massachusetts nursing homes which found that during a one-month period "nearly two-thirds of the residents had prescriptions for one or more psychoactive medications." (

A June 1998 press release by the National Center on Addiction and Substance Abuse at Columbia University

(CASA) highlights the results of a biopsychiatric world view from a slightly different angle. CASA surveyed primary care physicians with a significant number of women patients over 59 years of age. Results showed that when presented with the classic symptoms of alcohol abuse in a mature woman, only 1 percent of primary care physicians considered substance abuse. Instead, more than 80 percent of physicians considered a diagnosis of depression, which might lead to prescriptions for sedating psychiatric drugs, a potentially deadly mix with alcohol. The report also revealed that one in four mature women (6.4 million) are using at least one psychiatric drug, and an average of five prescriptions, psychiatric and otherwise, at the same time. The study lists a host of deleterious health effects in the vulnerable population.

Former Secretary of Health, Education and Welfare, and President of CASA, Joseph A. Califano, stated that "For a large percentage of (these women), we have written off the last quarter of their lives, years that should be rewarding and fulfilling ... We leave millions of grandchildren without grandmothers and children without mothers. We saddle others with the avoidable burden of caring for an ailing parent. What's inexcusable is that these tragedies are readily preventable." (2) The biopsychiatric world view blinds physicians and others to what is really going on, in this case to substance addiction and neglect of our elders.

The fundamental argument in defense of psychiatric drug use is based on the belief of biopsychiatry in biologically-based mental illness: therefore, the value and necessity of psychopharmacology as "treatment" to hold these "diseases" at bay. A common justification is that to withhold such "medication" from the "mentally ill" is a form of cruelty. From this vantage point, it is argued that to let an elder be anxious or depressed when these drugs are available is immoral. A corollary of this is the argument that it is more humane to use these drugs and therefore allow a resident to remain at the nursing home, then to discharge the resident and send him to a psychiatric hospital. The belief is in the biological or genetic cause of "mental illness;" other causes are either minimized, ignored or regretfully considered as useless to think about.

There was another important factor, in part common to nursing homes today, and in part unique to Mountain Valley. The common factor was the active role of a consultant psychiatrist in the facility. This psychiatrist was one of a growing number of geropsychiatric specialists; his practice consisted solely of nursing home consultations. He travels with two psychiatric nurses who handle the charts and record-keeping while he consults and prescribes "medications." This particular psychiatrist is active in many local nursing homes and has interfaced a lot with SPS. The uncommon aspect was that the Mountain Valley administrator and director of nursing were not pleased with the psychiatrist's work, and told SPS prior to my own hiring that they intended to have him excluded from working at their facility. The director of nursing told me one day, when the psychiatrist showed up to make his rounds, that she thought he had been fired already. When I queried the director, he told me that he planned to talk with the psychiatrist as soon as possible.

Dealing with Doctors

In approaching the task of reducing the heavy reliance on psychiatric drugs in the facility, I had decided to follow proper etiquette as much as possible, communicating with the doctors primarily via facsimile notes mediated by the nursing staff. My first communication of this nature was regarding an 84-year-old woman referred for "failure to thrive;" eating virtually nothing and complaining of constant nausea, she had reportedly been withdrawing and declining for about six months. Her doctor had started her on ten milligrams of the antidepressant Paxil just days before I met the woman. I wrote the doctor a note suggesting she consider discontinuing the Paxil as a frequent effect of the drug is nausea and appetite suppression, and since we were just beginning a psychosocial intervention. The doctor cancelled the order immediately. The woman continued to have a hard time for awhile, though consistent (every two hours) attention by a speech therapist who gave her very small amounts of food each time began a slight positive trend. The doctor ordered a stay at the hospital for a week of intensive medical tests and tube feeding. The tests revealed no identifiable medical condition; the feeding intervention, however, appeared to help the woman begin to come out of a severe deficiency. I encouraged the family and had regular sessions with the woman. The Paxil was obviously not the major issue in this woman's situation, nor was it necessary. Getting some nutrition made her at least minimally available energetically. The relative flood of caring attention was a massive contradiction to the despair and discouragement that had contributed to this woman giving up. The positive response of this particular doctor (a young female resident) to my suggestion about the Paxil was encouraging.

My next fax went to the consultant psychiatrist who had approximately ten percent of the residents on his caseload. (Remember that most psychiatric drugs are

prescribed by non-psychiatric physicians.) I was referred an
85-year-old woman, having difficulty with "adjustment to
the facility;" staff reported incidents of combativeness and
resistance to care. When I visited her, however, she was in a
stupor; extremely lethargic, she slumped in her chair, spoke
in a mumbling whisper, and seemed to have great difficulty
pulling up her thoughts. What she did say was coherent,
though she was not well-oriented to time. Orientation to
time often seems the first to go in senility; many residents
know very well who and where they are, but live in a world
frequented by long-dead friends or family members. This
particular woman had lived independently until just a few
months ago when she reportedly had a "psychotic break"
and was admitted to a psychiatric hospital where she began
a heavy-duty regimen of psychiatric drugs. She came to
Mountain Valley from the psychiatric hospital. When I met
her, she was on the following drugs: 15mg of Remeron,
10mg of Zyprexa, and 1mg of Haldol PRN.

Haldol, one of a class of drugs known as neuroleptics
is extremely powerful , and has been very popular over the
years for use with people labeled "psychotic." Neuroleptic
are widely used in a variety of institutions including
psychiatric hospitals, institutions for the mentally retarded
children's facilities and, of course, nursing homes. Peter
Breggin declares that: "Psychiatry has unleashed an
epidemic of neurologic disease on the world. Even if tardi
dyskinesia were the only permanent disability produced by
these drugs (i.e., neuroleptics), by itself, this would be
among the worst medically-induced disasters in history." (
Tardive dyskinesia is a neurological disorder, usually
permanent, marked by rhythmical, involuntary movement
of the mouth, tongue, jaw, and/or extremities; it is often
accompanied by impaired mental functioning (i.e.,

dementia). Breggin calls the therapeutic effect of these brain-disabling drugs a chemical lobotomy. Ron Leifer, another leading critic of psychiatry, says that Haldol is "internal ropes." Social control is the therapeutic effect of Haldol and other similar drugs.

An interesting phenomenon within medicine in general, and psychiatry in particular, is the annual or biannual release of the newest and latest pharmaceuticals, touted as miracle drugs: better, more accurate, more specific, fewer "side effects," etc. Typically, these drugs are the rage for awhile, with glowing testimonials and ever more incredible marketing claims. The twentieth century is replete with examples: cocaine, amphetamines, benzodiazepines (eg., Valium), etc. After usage becomes widespread, effects begin to show, disenchantment sets in. Sometimes the drugs become illegal, as in cocaine and certain amphetamines; usually people become resigned as in Valium, and other newer, "better" substitutes come to the fore. Zyprexa happens to be another one of these "newer and better" drugs, touted to be a significant improvement over other antipsychotic "medications." It also happens that Eli Lilly and Company's ten percent gain in third-quarter earnings in 1997 was due in part to strong sales of one of its newest products, Zyprexa. In its first twelve months on the market Zyprexa sales totaled $550 million. (4)

There are a number of people in nursing homes who have come there to end a long identity as "chronic mental patient." Generally subdued and on "maintenance" drugs to keep their "schizophrenia" under control, these individuals are usually passive and compliant, resigned to die quietly in whatever facility they reside; they are generally not referred to a psychologist for counseling. The 85-year-old woman on Remeron and Zyprexa was not a "chronic mental patient," however. She had been involved with psychiatry only a few months, but she was labeled "psychotic," and in the business of psychiatry, psychosis is generally not considered a transitory phenomenon; the use of brain-disabling drugs will usually ensure, in fact, that it is not transitory. This particular woman did have some organic complications, including a syphilitic condition with neurological effects. I could not help wondering, however, to what extent her so-called psychosis was about anger and frustration with her situation and with her daughter's decision that mom needed to move from her own apartment to institutional living. Not that the daughter was necessarily inaccurate in her judgment that her mother's declining abilities of self-care precluded independent living, just that rage at daughter as conveyor of such a doomsday message might be understood as an emotional response to an awful reality, rather than as evidence of a psychopathological disease. Too rapid grasping of a biopsychiatric interpretation almost always precludes genuine consideration of the human factors involved.

I have just revealed a glimpse of the thorny issues involved in this woman's life, not unrepresentative of many nursing home residents. My immediate concern was that I perceived this woman to be in a lethargic stupor, and I suspected that it was largely drug-induced. Her referral to me was due to her anger and combativeness, energetic behavior that was a far cry from the woman I was seeing. The social worker completely agreed with my hypothesis. Interestingly, however, many of the frontline staff didn't even consider that drugs might be a factor. A wonderful occupational therapist who had worked there for six years, and was both respectful and affectionate with the residents, liked this woman; yet he was taken aback when I suggested that we didn't have a clue what her personality was really like unless we got to be with her in a drug-free state. In any event, I faxed the psychiatrist a note saying that the client appeared to be in a stupor and did he think a dose reduction might be appropriate. He didn't respond to me, but he lowered the Zyprexa dosage from 10 to 7.5mg. I detected a slight improvement, but things became complicated with the doctors before going further with this direction.

I had begun working with a blind woman whose primary physician gave consent for me to work with her. This man, call him Dr Z, had the largest number of residents at Mountain Valley under his care, next to the medical director of the facility who reportedly was a primary mentor of Dr Z. The woman was referred to me for "ineffective coping with the loss of her husband," who was also blind. They had moved to Mountain Valley several months ago from another facility because she was extremely dissatisfied with the quality of care they received at the former institution. The husband had been seriously ill for awhile and died several weeks prior to this referral. Staff were concerned that this woman, normally very active, was showing signs of withdrawal, and that she was avoiding talking about and grieving for her lost husband. They were also concerned that the woman was suspicious and distrusting, both of her daughter and of the facility; the psychiatric label is "paranoid." This woman's first reaction was to have nothing to do with me, a not uncommon response I soon found out. In her case, the primary reason was a "bad experience" with a former counselor; she changed her mind when I assured her that I would not push her to explore painful feelings that she preferred to leave alone. As I began meeting with her, however, she quickly opened up and used me as a listening resource. She talked a lot about her husband, and about her frustration and dissatisfaction with his care at both Mountain Valley and at the former facility. She was angry and I could see her fear. She had some ideas about her daughter conspiring against her. Although I never got to really check this out, it was the kind of talk that quickly gets labeled "paranoid." My definite sense in her situation was that, while she probably dramatized some of the literal facts, there was also truth, especially about her own experience of her situation. Like almost all of the residents with whom I worked, she did not want to be there. A large portion of her counseling time was spent complaining about her frustrations and the inadequate responsiveness of facility staff. Complaints about food and food delivery were by far the most frequent with all the residents I met, with medications second. My client had major complaints about both.

I had been working with this woman for about four weeks when she was admitted to the hospital for a weekend of intensive blood and gastrointestinal testing after routine blood-work had shown some anomalies. Early the next week, Dr Z had left a message indicating his concern that she was psychologically disturbed. She was refusing to take all of her medications (these were not psychiatric drugs), and told me she did not at all trust her doctor now. She had doubted the necessity of the medical tests; the negative results had convinced her there was deception going on, especially since the pills she was taking were slightly different. Being blind, she relied mostly on tactile feel of the pills to verify their consistency. The form of Tylenol she was given at the hospital was a gel-cap which she had taken previously on her own and which she liked because it did not upset her stomach, whereas she did not like the hard form at the nursing home. She was on strike, a determined non-cooperation until this was resolved.

It quickly became clear to me that the hospital visit had scared my client. The procedures were highly invasive and had hurt her; she was suspicious and felt that some negative results must have been kept secret from her; after all, why else would she have had to go through all that and why would the pills be different. I had a strong impression that honoring her request for the other form of Tylenol would have resolved the situation, but this option was refused because Medicare would pay for the hard tablets, not the gel-caps. The social worker's suggestion of taking a little petty cash and going to Walgreen's for the gel-caps was ruled out as against policy. So I found the most involved nurse and we met with this woman and began answering all her questions about the medications in detail; her questions were clear and specific. All along, despite her fears, I was impressed that the woman was one of the clearest thinkers of all the facility residents. She could be most stubborn and difficult, she became confused at times, but she was persistent and independent-minded. She was still refusing the medications, but I thought we were making progress in restoring trust and good communication.

I then learned that a psychiatric consultation had been ordered for this woman. I called Dr Z to discuss this with him, explaining my thought that his patient had been extremely frightened by the hospital experience, and that I and the facility staff were actively engaged with her in re-establishing safety and trust. I also told him that, as his patient was feeling a lot of fear and distrust of doctors just now, another consult might exacerbate the situation. I told him that her thinking, as evidenced by the questions she was asking, appeared clear and strong. I did not express my experience that psychiatric consultation virtually always

results in a prescription for psychiatric drugs. Dr Z told me
that he had already gone over in detail the medications with
his patient, that whatever I was doing apparently wasn't
helping much, and that he wanted a psychiatric
consultation. He wanted me to support this; I told him that
I would certainly do nothing to interfere, but that I did not
agree with the decision. We hung up the phone with tension
between us. I was delighted and encouraged that he called
back in a few minutes, and expressed his desire not to "get
off on the wrong foot," and that he favored the general
direction of my work. I told him that I did not want to com
across as if I had all the answers, that I greatly appreciated
his calling back, and that I really wanted us to be able to
work together. He went over again his reasons for a
psychiatric consult, that maybe this psychiatrist could help
that maybe anti-depressants would be helpful, that he
wanted more input. I listened, then reiterated my
perspective on the woman's situation, and concluded that w
disagreed. The next day, he called to cancel his order for
psychotherapy, firing me from the woman's case.

Another patient of Dr Z's with whom I worked was a
86-year-old Spanish-speaking woman who spoke very little
English, and who had a serious heart condition. She was
referred to me for "physical abuse of staff and residents,"
anger, combativeness, and verbal communication deficits.
spoke enough Spanish for limited communication, but I al
included her bilingual daughter-in-law in some of our
interactions to make sure all communications were clearly
understood. The woman was far from robust; it was hard
imagine her being physically abusive, but staff reported th
there had been incidents of angry verbal tirades and physi
striking out. She had been at the facility for less than six
months, having lived independently until that time. She

seemed resigned to being there and had good family support. Upon interviewing the staff and meeting this resident, it was clear that she had genuine difficulty adjusting to the facility, and that she became afraid and frustrated. These reactions are common due to the loss of so much in the way of family and home, typically compounded by a frightening decline in both physical and mental condition. Impairment of short-term memory, as in the case of this woman, tends to be scary in and of itself. She communicated in Spanish, and few of the nursing home staff could understand. My impression was that, besides the anguish associated with her illness and having to be separated from her community, the immediate cause of her "abusive" incidents was frustration with an inability to be heard and understood. I worked closely with her and her family and facility staff, assuring her that I would do everything I could to see that her needs and desires could be expressed and understood. I found facility staff who were bilingual and who could be called upon when anyone did not understand what she was saying. I took a strong interest and kept in touch with her, and I asked her daughter-in-law to stay closely involved and help monitor the situation.

When I got this referral, I also discovered that the woman had, just a few days prior, had a psychiatric consultation and been prescribed a small dosage of the aforementioned Zyprexa. After my initial contact, I saw absolutely no reason whatsoever that she should be on so-called anti-psychotic medication. In speaking with the family, I found out that, as is so often the case, they knew nothing about the "medication." The policy of this facility, common to nursing homes in general, is that a blanket consent to doctors' decisions regarding "medications" is required as a condition of residency. (I did not address the question of whether such a blanket consent to medical treatment, including psychiatric drugs, is a gross civil rights violation.) The family did not think she needed it; they were mostly concerned about the burden of any extra medications, given the severity of her physical condition. (I later found out that my talking about "medications" with family was a significant black mark against me in the eyes of not only the doctors, but also the administration.) With this information, I approached the administrator and director of nursing to discuss how to proceed. The administrator had already told me that he was going to speak to the psychiatrist about his desire to discontinue working with him. I had already been counseled by my supervisor to stay out of the middle of the conflict between the facility and the psychiatrist, so when he asked my advice, I simply suggested that it seemed necessary to have his medical director strongly aligned with this decision. After all, the doctors were making referrals to the psychiatrist; their cooperation was absolutely necessary. In any event, I gave my assessment of this woman's situation and expressed my opinion that it would be nice to work with her for awhile and see if positive change could happen without the Zyprexa; since she had just started the drug, it would be good to discontinue it as soon as possible. The next day, the nursing director informed me that she had called the medical director, and that he immediately discontinued the Zyprexa. I continued to work with the woman, and over the next three weeks, she showed improvement in her mood. There were no more "incidents."

As I said earlier, Dr Z had already fired me from the blind woman's case. We had had a few phone conversations by that point, but had not met in person. When he showed up in the first floor nurses' station just a few days after firing me from the one case, I took the opportunity to introduce myself, and to confirm that he still wanted me off the case. His response was that yes he not only wanted me off that case, but was canceling orders for my involvement with two others as well: the Spanish-speaking woman and the 85-year-old woman discussed earlier about whom I interacted with the psychiatrist regarding what I perceived to be a drug-induced stupor. Dr Z let me know that he would have liked to have removed me from all his patients, but there was one other whom he thought I was helping. The bottom line, he said, was that he couldn't work with anyone who didn't agree with him.

> Physicians are like kings —
> They brook no contradiction. (5)

He gave the example of a heart surgeon calling in a consultant; if the consultant didn't agree with the procedure, how could they possibly work effectively together? I was amazed. I thought the idea of a consultant was to get another opinion, but at least he was clearly defining his conditions. He brought up the Spanish-speaking woman, and when I responded that he was obviously very angry about this, he reacted and let me know in no uncertain terms that he was not angry. When I said that it sure felt like it to me, he said that feelings were my business and that he did not appreciate my speculations about his. So I said that, in any event, he strongly disapproved, and he acknowledged that. (I later learned from another source that he had been offended by this remark and by my, at some point, touching him with my hand. I also learned that he had verbally attacked at least two nurses and the social worker about the changing of this woman's medication. The social worker's subsequent frustration with and distancing from me is a good example of what often happens when someone challenges authority; it is similar to the anger and scapegoating one sees in alcoholic families when one member courageously confronts the alcoholic and gets attacked by the others for doing so.)

Dr Z took great pains to let me know that these decisions were his responsibility, that he was the doctor. My explanation that I thought I was going through proper channels, that I convey my opinions to the nursing staff, that they contact the doctors, that it remains the doctor's decision as only they can give orders regarding medication. I explained that the medical director had apparently been on call for him when this happened, and that if he had an issue with the director's decision, he should handle that with him. He acknowledged that he would do that, but he was far from satisfied. He went on to let me know that he had worked with SPS psychologists before and that they had always been "seen but not heard," and that this was how it should be. Our talk got heated at times, and at one point when he made it clear that it was really the psychiatrist's order (collegial loyalty is always a major factor in any attempt to challenge medical authority), I shot off that at that very moment the psychiatrist was in the administrator office, and my understanding was that he was being told that the facility did not want him there. He didn't say much but the social worker who was sitting with us assured him that it would be a gradual termination, that the man couldn't just be fired from his current patients, and I agreed

Restoration of Order

Later that day, Dr Z met with the administrator for a long time. I queried the administrator later, and he said that it was no big deal, that after being a nursing home administrator for awhile, his back was like leather, the anger and conflict just rolled off. He said he had discovered that the psychiatrist couldn't be dismissed, and that we needed to try to work with what were "appropriate" levels of medication. I nodded, but also pointed out that in the conflictual case of the Spanish-speaking woman, our consensus (the administrator, the head nurse, and myself) had been that no medication was appropriate. He shrugged. The psychiatrist and Dr Z had met with the administrator on Wednesday. I don't know what else happened, but when I approached the director of nursing, she was extremely distant and reticent. My own supervisor showed up on Friday saying that there was a hubbub, and wanted to know everything I could tell her about what happened as she was preparing to meet with the administrator. I filled her in with as much information as I had. The one comment that most disturbed my supervisor was that I told the doctor during our heated exchange about my understanding that the psychiatrist was being told he wasn't wanted here even as we spoke. She reminded me that she had counseled me to stay out of the middle of this; my comment was a big mistake in her eyes, a significant failure to keep my boundaries.

On Monday night, my supervisor called and informed me that the administrator wanted to replace me with a psychologist who was "more experienced in long-term care." He had presented her with a list of examples that demonstrated my inexperience. She went over the list with me. Most of it was factually accurate; I had been very upfront from the beginning about my inexperience in this setting, asking a lot of questions, etc. I learned quickly, though, and am sure that I was doing a good job. My supervisor listened to my interpretation that "more experienced in long-term care" means "passive and unquestioning of doctors," that I was being scapegoated as the administration quickly backpedaled to appease the doctors. She didn't say much in response to this. Senior Psychology Services wanted to work in that facility and in the chain of which it was a part; the bottom line, my supervisor told me, was that they needed to do whatever the administrator wanted; in this instance, replacing me. The next day I went in, saw the rest of my clients, and began vacating my office. I went back the next Monday and terminated with all of my clients, letting them and some of their families know that the facility had decided to replace me. I said a few good-byes, but never really talked about what happened with anyone there except one physical therapist who was curious about a note in the chart canceling orders for individual psychotherapy. I passed my keys to the social worker and left. The supervisor had asked me if I would talk with my replacement(s) and I said yes, but they never contacted me.

The saddest part of the whole affair is that so many of these elder residents remain unnecessarily on toxic psychiatric drugs. The doctors were more interested in asserting their authority than in listening to what I had to say and looking at what was actually happening with their patients; they put the Spanish-speaking woman right back on Zyprexa even though she clearly did not need it. It was more desirable for the administration and staff to allow and accept unnecessary drugging than to risk conflict and job loss.

Afterthoughts

It is my view that the primary role of psychiatry in nursing homes is as an agent of social control, allowing facilities to handle large numbers of individuals in need of extensive care with inadequate numbers and preparation of staff, and inhuman environment. The result is oppressive, and as usual money plays a major role in oppression. There is big profit in nursing homes. Figure Mountain Valley at 210 residents. Medicare pays about $85/day; a rough estimate of daily income would be $17,850. That translates to well over $6,000,000 per year for just one facility. The doctors bill separately, and we know that drug companies are exceedingly profitable.

My own primary concern is that so many of us are literally blinded by psychiatric beliefs and rhetoric. The psychological problems of nursing home residents can be roughly classified in two categories, each of which involves a perfectly understandable human response:

DESPAIR. Also known as loneliness, grief, sadness, helplessness, hopelessness, and giving up, despair leads to withdrawal and decline. Our elders experience these feelings in response to abandonment by friends and families, loss of a decent home, and ongoing loss of their ability to function in various ways. It is not difficult to imagine humane and helpful care for individuals feeling despair. It's called social involvement, caring friends, warm affection, colorful and engaging environment, opportunities to be of service, etc. Instead, psychiatry helps to promote and allow the obscuring of common sense by attributing human problems to a medical, biologically-based "mental illness" and "treating" it with drugs.

FRUSTRATION. Also known as irritation, anger, hostility, non-compliance, and being difficult, frustration leads to belligerence and rejection and alienation of friends and helpers. Elders who still have emotional energy and are what we call spirited individuals experience intense frustration at everything they've lost. They often feel humiliated at the loss of autonomy and at having virtually everything done for them. Common sense would address these feelings as completely understandable and work to create an environment which allowed opportunity for many varying levels of personal responsibility. I listened to elders yearn for an opportunity to prepare their own meal, for example. Blinded by irrational belief in the tenets of biopsychiatry, common sense is sacrificed to the complicated world of drugs and diagnosis. "Medication" is the very first line of defense in the war against incipient "mental illness."

Let us not turn our backs to the immoral and unethical psychiatric drugging of elders in nursing homes. is tragic and unnecessary damage and it needs to stop. To stop it we all need to grow up and become our own authorities. We must sacrifice once and for all the childlike illusion that societal authorities, in the guise of medical doctors, know more than we do and can be trusted to take good care of our elders.

CHAPTER 14
PERSPECTIVE ON HUMAN NATURE AND TRANSFORMATION

In 1934, Chicago University sociologist George Herbert Mead defined an attitude as "an organized predisposition to respond." (1) I have argued that the "attitude" of biopsychiatry constitutes an organized predisposition to respond in ways that are disrespectful, harmful and dangerous. This chapter offers a framework for an attitude which I hope will predispose readers to respond to themselves and each other with wisdom, love and compassion. What follows are further thoughts about a more accurate and useful way of viewing our human nature, and the nature of both maturation in general and recovery from specific hurt. My purpose is to speak the truth as I see it, and to stand with those who are working to create and hold a space for all of us to be ourselves, to fully express ourselves, to recover from harm, and to grow and mature as spiritual beings.

More on Human Nature

My view of human nature is that we are inherently good, intelligent, zestful, responsible, and cooperative (see Chapter 2). When we lack accurate information or are fed inaccurate information, we are more likely to make mistakes. When we are hurt, we feel distress which interferes with our inherent nature. Certain hurts can result in the perpetuation of oppressive patterns in individuals and society. Fortunately, we have a built-in mechanism for restoring our intelligent functioning; we resolve emotional distress by expressing ourselves through talk, anger, fear, grief or laughter. A big piece of helping each other is to allow, support and facilitate this natural process of emotional discharge. Throughout this book, I have pointed out how psychiatry acts to inhibit and suppress this natural healing process. Chapter 12 presented key theory on how release of emotions such as hopelessness, fear, anger, and shame is necessary to reclaim inherent human qualities of hope, courage and complete self-appreciation.

My way of viewing our inherent nature also recognizes that we are multidimensional beings; that is, we exist with varying degrees of conscious awareness, on many levels. Most commonly acknowledged are the physical, emotional and mental levels of experience; the spirit is said to enfold, energize, and sustain us on all these levels. For practical purposes, I have found it extremely useful to consider two primary modes of consciousness. Quantum physics calls them wave and particle, religion calls them human and divine. There are many ways to describe the truth of our twofold nature, that we can know and experience both oneness and separation. Most of us live in the feeling of separateness most of the time, yet most all of us when asked can call forward memories of feeling oneness. I have heard that the Buddha said, "The guardians of truth are paradox and confusion." Our double nature, which simultaneously holds the truths that "All is one" and that "Each one of us a unique individual" is an amazing paradox. It is no wonder that confusion guards the door of truth; reconciliation of our two natures is extremely challenging.

One of my teachers, Stanislav Grof, psychiatrist,

author, theorist, and practitioner of transpersonal psychology, refers in his books to two primary modes of consciousness. (2) Hylotropic, derived from the Greek hyle, "matter," and trepein, "to move toward," means matter-oriented or moving toward matter. This is the particle, the separateness; it includes not only our evolutionary animal survival nature, but also our powerful urge and determination to preserve and defend our ego. Philosopher Alan Watts, a Western authority on Zen Buddhism, aptly coined the term "skin-encapsulated ego body," a great reference point for hylotropic consciousness. For practical purposes, this is what we refer to as the ordinary, everyday experience of consensus reality. It is how and where we identify ourselves most of the time.

Holotropic, derived from the Greek holos, "whole," and trepein, "to move toward," means aiming for wholeness or totality. This term characterizes what we commonly refer to as nonordinary, or altered states of consciousness, including meditative, mystical and psychedelic experiences.

What seems to happen is that, through birth and the experience of developing over the long period of human dependency, we become intensely identified with the hard-earned identities we have created for ourselves. We experience and think of ourselves as separate particles in a particle world; Chapters 5 and 6 on conditioning constitute one description of this process. From this perspective, it is understandable when we assume that hylotropic consciousness, or matter-oriented separateness, is, if not the only way of being, certainly the dominant and causal way.

One of Stan Grof's most fundamental teachings, and one that stayed with me, is that the truth is usually upside down and backwards from conventional understanding. We all go through seemingly endless experiences of disillusionment if we keep thinking and investigating as we go through life. I myself experienced this over and over again as I learned facts about the arms race and military/government agendas, and the foundational theories of our education system. Like so many young people, I accused my elders of hypocrisy. Grof's point goes way beyond issues of hypocrisy; he is saying that the biggest misunderstanding comes from the placing of supreme value on a worldview which lies in separateness, in matter, in materialism, in consensus reality. He provides a scientist's perspective to support the ancient mystical teachings that there is another way of being which is primary and causal, which actually subsumes the separateness. Holotropic includes hylotropic matter arises out of wholeness.

A basic assumption of depth psychological theory is that we humans are built with an innate push or urge toward wholeness. Experience has revealed to many of us, over thousands of years, that we are constantly being pushed, pulled, nudged, shoved, drawn to expand and discover more of who we are. Grof's work supports the notion that as conscious human beings we are capable of identifying with anything in the universe. My experience is that, in my own life and in my clients, there is a high price paid for denial and resistance to this constant unfolding, both in physical and emotional pain.

Natural Recovery

Imagine the seashore. On one side the sand, the dunes, the cliffs, the land. On the other, the water, the waves, the ocean. Where the two meet, there is the surf, the waves pounding on the rocks — dynamic, electric, where the sharks hang out. Grof and others such as Arnold Mindell, founder of what he calls process psychology, teach that what we call symptoms are actually signposts for growth. (3) The seashore is dynamic, and it can be dangerous, even deadly. Distressing symptoms are the result of our resistance to change and expansion by holding on to a fixed identity or position of our ego/body. I have argued throughout this book that psychiatry only makes things worse by diagnosing, labeling and treating these so-called symptoms.

The force of our inherent nature inexorably pulls us in the direction of love and truth. Call this force energy, spirit, life force, chi, God, consciousness; however we refer to it, the fact is that it requires tremendous energy to resist this relentless urge to know and express the truth of who we really are. What people don't realize is that most behavior which is out of line with our inherent nature is actually an unconscious attempt to express and release feelings related to past hurts. Coercive treatment of our fellow human beings is always a sign, on one level, of unconscious reenactments of old hurts. Interpretation of unusual or apparently self-defeating behavior as symptoms of psychiatric disease is usually a reflection of the interpreter's lack of understanding. Rather than being signs of pathology, this is more usefully viewed as spontaneous healing; expressions of emotional overwhelm almost always reflect a spontaneous release of emotional or physical hurt. Given supportive attention, these expressions will result in a positive movement toward restoration of an individual's ability to function with intelligence and zest, according to inherent nature.

Withdrawal and Return

Withdrawal-Initiation-Return: this is the hero's journey. In 1949, Joseph Campbell's 'The Hero With A Thousand Faces' was published. This remarkable book documents the fact that cultures throughout our planet's geography and history tell a story of the hero, a story with universal similarities. It is what Campbell refers to as a monomyth, a story which reveals profound truths about human nature. All of us are called at times in our lives to face some great challenge, usually seen or felt in both our inner and outer worlds. The s/hero is one who answers this call and undertakes the arduous hero's journey. The truths of this journey are as relevant for each of us today as they ever wer in any ancient culture. Another writer, P W Martin, amplifies Campbell's teachings through the works of Carl Jung, T S Eliot, and Arnold Toynbee. Martin makes this transformational journey very real for anyone who cares to undertake the arduous task of self-realization today. These two works are useful to further discuss this question of our true nature, especially as it applies to the process of person transformation.

"The hero is the waker of his own soul." (4)
This teaching is about responsibility. Most of us are confused about responsibility, conditioned to feel it as a burden and a source of guilt and pressure. I believe this is because our parents and teachers were themselves conditioned to believe in a view of human nature as flawed defective, sinful, irresponsible. If we view children as naturally irresponsible, our job becomes that of teaching them to be, making them, responsible. This attitude leads inevitably to efforts to control and shape the target of our

concern, to guilt, shame, pressure. This is, in fact, one of the most frequent concerns I hear from parents. How do I teach, get my child to be, "make them," responsible?

Psychology and education tend to answer this question by supporting the basic position of this last question; various subtle or not-so-subtle versions of behavior modification (reward and punishment) are offered. This validates the underlying assumption of children as naturally irresponsible, similar to the way a yes or no answer to the question "Is my child ADD?" validates the erroneous assumption that there is such a "mental illness" as ADD (Attention Deficit Disorder). Instead, I respond first by probing the question and leading the parent to consider that there is no need to "make" their child responsible. The child, as all humans, already is responsible. It's her inherent nature.

I often demonstrate this with two arguments, both of which involve looking at young children. The first point comes from what we know about the effects of child abuse. A child who is abused inevitably carries a heavy load of guilt and shame which comes from the certainty that "If I am abused, I must be bad. It is my fault (responsibility) and I deserve it." Children naturally conceive of themselves as responsible centers of the universe, when abused, they take responsibility for it. This point is well understood by anyone who has worked on healing early traumas and explored the depths of their own conditioning; those who do not know themselves at that level often have difficulty comprehending this truth. They may, if they have observed young children, still be able to consider my second point which is simply that little ones absolutely love to help out and be given responsibility. They delight in it and are so enthusiastic. We are born responsible. It is our nature. We do not need to "make" our children responsible. We do need to provide appropriate opportunities and guidance for how to express responsibility at different levels as they learn to master themselves and the outer world. For the interested reader, I discuss this issue at greater length in my book, 'The Wildest Colts Make The Best Horses.'

Psychiatry undermines responsibility by labeling those who embark on the hero's journey as "mentally ill" and then duping them into accepting, or forcing upon them soul-crunching, brain-damaging biological "treatments," such as psychiatric drugs and electroshock. The usual result of this approach is a demoralized individual whose capacity for self-awakening has been seriously impaired. Genuine support respects and encourages the truth that no psychiatric authority can do for others what they must do for themselves, that when it comes to transformation, everyone is her or his own authority. In the words of George Bernard Shaw, "Only those who have helped themselves know how to help others and to respect their right to help themselves."

> "The first stage in the process is the realization that 'there is something wrong about us as we naturally stand.' Without this realization, nothing happens." — William James (5)

Generally speaking, as long as we are comfortable and happy with where we "naturally stand," we will tend not to undergo the rigors of transformation. False pride and the need to avoid self-examination can be an obstacle; until we experience humility we will resist change. Simply put, the teaching is that we are motivated to change mostly through frustration and dissatisfaction. The thought or feeling that there is "something wrong about us" is a catalyst for growth. Psychiatry calls it a "symptom," and by "diagnosis" and "treatment" enforces an understanding of this as literal, concrete evidence of defective biology or genetics. Genuine support responds with appreciation and encouragement for the discontent which signals the beginning of the self-renewal process.

> "The first work of the hero is to retreat from the world scene of secondary effects to those causal zones of the psyche where the difficulties really reside." (6)

The conventional unwisdom being what it is, my perspective is that retreat from the world scene truly is a heroic act. Retreat is a betrayal of our society's prime value, namely productivity. For example, we still tend to follow the fast-food school of grief where one is encouraged to get over it in a weekend and get back to graduate school. The truth is more like in fairy tales where the widower covers himself in animal skins and ashes, and lives in a hollow tree for seven years. Psychiatry is more and more geared to support society's demand that people should and need to be always working. Not only do people on the "journey" not work, but they consume much less. None of this is good for the business of psychiatry or the economy. What would the effect of "withdrawal" on a large scale have on the stock market? A large part of the work life of corporate America is boring, repetitious, not at all inspiring and purposeful to those who do the work. The ubiquitous use of coffee to get going and the coffee breaks to keep going are essential to the enterprise. And now we give stimulant drugs to millions of our school children as well. It seems to me the rat race is getting rattier.

What would happen if America decided to face its addiction to stimulants, and the workers gave up coffee?

Slowing down means having space and time to think, ask questions, explore your life. This is dangerous and threatening to the demands of an economy based on incessant "growth" and productivity. And it feels very scary to those who keep their own inner demons and dragons at bay by constant activity. To quote Wes Nisker, a writer for the Buddhist journal 'Inquiring Mind', "Slowing down in this culture may be the most difficult tantric exercise ever conceived. Mindfulness may be the ultimate speed bump.

Kat Duff, in her moving and insightful chronicle of her own chronic health problems, 'The Alchemy of Illness' had significant wisdom to share about the necessity of retreat:

> "The alchemists insisted that two things must happen before the cure can be extracted from the disease: The problem must be kept in a closed container, and it must be reduced to its original state through a process of breakdown. The limitations and immobility of illness provide the closed container that enables this transformation, precisely because there is no way out. Early on in my illness my dreams offered the image of a snarl of snakes stuck in a bottle for my situation; alchemical texts are filled with images of dangerous animals — lions or wolves — trapped in the chemist's flask. Alice James called herself "bottled lightning ... a geyser of emotions, sensations, speculations, and reflections fermenting ... in my poor old carcass" when she was dying of cancer. The isolation and lack of sympathy or understanding that sick people often endure may even be necessary to secure the walls of the container, so that nothing is spilled or shared and the matter inside will reach the point of transmutation. The walled space of illness, like therapy, intensifies the brooding and incubates the egg." (7)

Psychiatry justifies its dehumanizing practices (forcibly ending the period of withdrawal) by defining retreat/ withdrawal as a cardinal symptom of "depression" or "schizophrenia" caused by a biochemical imbalance of one sort or another. Genuine support, based in the truth of human experience, allows ample space and time for retreat and honors the inner work that is integral to the transformation process.

> "There are those who go searching for an artesian well and come instead upon a volcano." (8)

Many of us are moved by inspirational writings or sermons that tell us of the beauty and glory of God's kingdom, of the joy of "walking in the Light." Perhaps we get an experience, a glimpse of greater love and joy, and we naturally want more. So we become seekers, and we tentatively follow the teachings to go within, that the kingdom is within. And we look for the light, and we fall into dark places inside of ourselves. One client of mine tells me that she lived for ten years in what she calls "the cleft in the rock," experiencing joyous connection with the spirit, through Jesus, in her prayers and meditations. Her life circumstances changed, and she fell into what she calls her "bloody pit." Suicide attempts, psychiatric hospitalizations, drugs galore, and electroshock followed in the next two years. She found me six years ago and has done enormous, intense personal work; it has been a profound ordeal. Her life remains challenging, but on a most definite upward trend. She is just beginning to feel that spiritual connection again. Cindy (of Chapter 1) was another client with deeply spiritual motivation. We met when she was feeling bright, pursuing her yoga practice, intending to enter a teacher training in Kundalini yoga. Searching for her artesian well, she most definitely hit a volcano. It remains to be seen how her story will unfold.

There are many others, of course, who come upon a volcano without any searching. The point is that great difficulties do, indeed, reside in the deep zones of the psyche. Psychiatry has abandoned these very zones from which comes its name (Psyche means soul; a psychiatrist is by root definition, if not in practice, a doctor of the soul) in favor of a belief that life experiences calling for a "time out, a period for reconsidering one's place in the world and the meaning of life, are the result of a biological defect. Genuine support for someone going through a transitional period can only come from those who know and respect the opportunities and risks inherent in this process, have confidence that positive growth can result, and stand ready to help if help is wanted.

> "The parent is in the role of Holdfast; the hero's artful solution of the task amounts to a slaying of the dragon. The tests imposed are difficult beyond measure. They seem to represent an absolute refusal, on the part of the parent ogre, to permit life to go its way; nevertheless when a fit candidate appears, no task in the world is beyond his skill." (9)

Holdfast is the archetype of the parent or any entity whose prime directive is to maintain the status quo. For my purposes here, I only remind the reader that maintenance of the status quo is the prime directive of biopsychiatry and our mental health system. Psychiatry interprets resistance to the status quo, and to itself as champion of the status quo, pathological, defining cooperation as insight. Genuine support validates the individual's struggle for self-realization always and in all ways, even when he or she challenges society's core beliefs and practices, so long as in doing so the rights of others are not violated.

> "The returning hero, to complete his adventure, must survive the impact of the world." (10)

Just as withdrawal and inner work are fraught with peril, so is the return. Newborn growth and awareness carries with it a great vulnerability, and our society can be harsh. Those who are satisfied with their place in the social order perceive the returning hero as a threat. If the hero is right, they must be wrong. And if they're wrong it follows they should change. And that is when the sparks begin to fly because people don't like change. It may be the product of eons of conditioning, just plain inertia, or a combination of both, but people will do just about anything rather than undergo a change, especially one that involves self-examination. To paraphrase the great philosopher and writer, Hermann Hesse, for most people, nothing is more distasteful than taking the path that leads to oneself. The presence in the community of a hero, a self-evolved individual, has that kind of effect on people. Psychiatry plays the role of keeping out or removing individuals who are shaking us up. If they are able to return to the community after being labeled and treated by psychiatrists, they return as damaged goods, unlikely to frighten or inspire others about the need to change. Genuine support entails easing the way of the hero upon his or her return. This might mean offering moral support, camaraderie, material assistance, or political protection (e.g., just be known as having some local friends can help prevent private or governmental sanctions). And if one is unable or unwilling to help, then the important thing is to stay out of the way.

"The deeds of the hero in the second part of his personal cycle will be proportionate to the depth of his descent during the first." (11)

This teaching echoes the theme of Chapter 8, that "madness" is necessary for the process of transformation, necessary in order to become spiritually mature. The quote further emphasizes that the "descent" is not only valuable to the individual, but also a treasure to the community. Psychiatrists believe that "dropping out" of external work is dangerous because they profoundly distrust human nature. Genuine support starts with an understanding that it is part of our nature to be responsible and to be of service to others. There are times, however, when because of unresolved problems or owing to the dictates of a higher imperative, inner work is the priority. Respectful, above all respectful, and compassionate attention and assistance can be crucial to the individual so engaged, and can lead ultimately to important benefits to the community once the phase of the renewal process has been completed.

Five Prerequisites of Change

Biopsychiatry is based on a profound ignorance of human nature. I am not suggesting alternatives to treating "mental illness." I am suggesting perspective and approaches that are helpful in supporting human growth and development. Psychiatry distorts reality by taking a specific manifestation, e.g., screaming in fear, and labeling it a condition of "mental illness." I view change not as a condition, but as an inevitable and necessary process. However much we can and do resist, the forces of change are constant. Knowing and acting on certain laws of transformation such as the principle of withdrawal and return can ease this process and increase the chances of a positive outcome. In a similar vein, the following five attitudes are conducive to positive change:

1/ Acceptance - One of my teachers, Jacquelyn Small, introduced me to a fundamental law of transformation called the Paradox of Change. The paradox is that in order for real change to occur, there must first be acceptance. Surface change is no problem, but genuine, profound and lasting change requires acceptance. As long as we resist, reject, judge, condemn or avoid some part of ourselves, we cannot really change that part. To heal our shame, we must embrace with compassion our inadequacies and defects, and share them with others we trust. To heal our guilt, we must acknowledge our action and forgive ourselves. Acceptance is the first and foremost law of the spirit.

A related need, addressed earlier in discussing Stan Grof's model of hylotropic and holotropic levels of consciousness, has to do with the importance of non-ordinary states of consciousness to the transformational process. While psychiatry's entire thrust is to suppress altered states of consciousness by any means, it is necessary to accept, allow and even safely amplify non-ordinary states to facilitate healing and growth.

2/ Humility - This point, discussed in reference to William James' assertion about the need to feel "something wrong about us as we naturally stand," bears repeating. In the beginning of our hero's journey or when we carry a heavy load of fear and shame, we have a hard time facing our situation. We either protect ourselves by an arrogant refusal to see our faults and limitations or we collapse in overwhelming helplessness and inferiority when we do see them. Psychiatry enforces both of these distorted perspectives. Humility means we see and accept the futility of continuing to live our lives according to the dictates of patterns we developed in order to survive our past. We recognize the need for change, and we humbly acknowledge the truth that we need help and support to recover and find our way.

As our understanding of human transformation and all its mysteries is so limited, humility is also a major prerequisite for those who purport to help others. An 1896 poem by Mary Elizabeth Coleridge lyrically speaks to this issue:

> Gifts
>
> I tossed my friend a wreath of roses, wet
> With early dew, the garland of the morn.
> He lifted it — and on his brow he set
> A crackling crown of thorn.
>
> Against my foe I hurled a murderous dart.
> He caught it in his hand — I heard him laugh —
> I saw the thing that should have pierced his heart
> Turn to a golden staff.

3/ Desire - Beyond recognition is desire. It's not enough to see it, we have to want it. Desire is one of the deepest parts of our inherent nature. We do not have to learn desire; we do, however, have to recover from the effects of having our desires shamed and suppressed in order to approach a level of spiritual maturity in this realm. There are countless faces of distorted desire; one of particular importance here is the face of immense discouragement (giving up that your desires will ever be met). The Buddha taught that desire is the cause of all suffering, liberation from desire the path to enlightenment. The Buddha's way beyond hope; it involves letting go of hope (desire). For o who is sunk in chronic hopelessness, however, as a memory feeling of having been hurt, let down, or abandoned as a child, a kindling of hope is necessary to move forward on the path of positive growth and transformation. My experience is that hope can be transmitted from one being to another, enough to at least facilitate a next step.

Remember that psychiatry is coercive; so long as this is the case, it can only do more harm than good. When an individual does not desire help, but is pressured or forced into "treatment," that is not compassionate care; it is punishment. It is a violation not only of human rights, but of the laws of transformation, particularly the aforementioned "Law of Acceptance." We need to give attention, to honor, even to love and embrace that which has been scorned and judged.

4/ Willingness - An individual, humbled and wanting change, generally doesn't know how to make fundamental change, or else she would have already done it. It's not about choosing from a rack of clothes in your closet; it's more like not even knowing what a closet is, and whether it's even a good thing to wear clothes. Transformation involves surrender to forces greater than one's ego, and a willingness to live in and with uncertainty. We have to be willing to try and do things differently than we have ever done before without any guarantee of results, and we have to be willing to feel and expose all the fears and embarrassments that we have striven all our lives to keep hidden. It takes courage to face and expose the inner demons. Even more difficult for many of us, at some point we have to be willing to face and accept the power and glory of who we really are. A quote from Nelson Mandela's inauguration speech as President of South Africa eloquently expresses this truth:

"Our deepest fear is not that we are inadequate. Our deepest fear is that we are powerful beyond measure. It is our light, not our darkness, that most frightens us. We ask ourselves, Who am I to be brilliant, gorgeous, talented, fabulous? Actually, who are you not to be? You are a child of God. Your playing small doesn't serve the world. There's nothing enlightened about shrinking so that other people won't feel insecure around you. You were born to make manifest the glory of God that is within you. It's not just in some of us; it's in everyone. And as we let our own light shine, we unconsciously give other people permission to do the same. As we're liberated from our own fear, our presence automatically liberates others."

5/ Commitment - Commitment is probably one of the most loaded words in popular use today. All of us seem to be struggling with commitment in most areas of life. And the rule seems to be that whatever we struggle with in life, we also struggle with in this process of transformation. We naively feel that inner work is about getting help from experts, that we can be non-expert victims, and that the experiences of our outer life do not apply. Psychiatry reinforces this as a "mentally healthy doctor/mentally ill patient" dichotomy, and distorts commitment to mean either incarceration in a "hospital," on the one hand, or faithfully taking prescribed drugs, on the other. The truth is that "life" and "transformation" cannot be separated; phases of withdrawal and return are just that, phases of a journey which is cyclical in process, but unified in nature. An individual who decides to undergo the hero's journey of personal transformation needs to know that a deep commitment is required, for as one hero said, "Straight is the way and narrow is the gate." Psychiatry is one especially treacherous obstacle to gaining spiritual maturity in today's world. As psychologist Ty Colbert has written, there are "two different paths a person may take in attempting to recover from an emotional disorder: the psychiatric medical path, which often leads to permanent disability, and the emotional recovery path." While I might choose a different word than disorder, I strongly agree with Dr Colbert's emphasis of "the need for absolute clarity about the choices involved." (12) Commitment is necessary to undergo the rigors of transformation; it is equally necessary to withstand the dual forces of persuasion and coercion that are wielded by psychiatry.

Help

In my comments on humility and desire, I addressed the importance of recognizing a need for help and of wanting to get help. Our society has severely distorted the reality of human existence in regards to giving and receiving help. This seems true for all of us, but men especially are heavily conditioned to believe in the value of rugged individualism, and that needing help is a disgraceful sign of weakness. Men tend to be extremely confused as well about responsibility, thinking that it means taking everything on our own shoulders, sacrificing our well-being, and doing it alone. Isolation is an accepted fact of life for so many of us. Given our conditioning and the resultant patterns just described, it is no wonder that we have such a hard time asking for and accepting help. We feel humiliated. Needing help means we are unworthy failures; better to suffer quietly and isolate, or turn to addiction or violence, or simply push on until we collapse, than to reach out and ask for help. Personal growth and spiritual maturity has to go through this place of feeling and working through any hurts we have about asking for and receiving help. Biopsychiatry validates the lie that needing help is proof of a defect; the truth is that we all need as much help as we can get. The polarity of dependence and independence can be resolved not by either end of this false dichotomy, but by an awareness of the truth of our complete interdependence at every level of our being. The air we breathe, the food we eat, the emotions we feel, the thoughts we have are all inextricably interrelated with our planet and our fellow humans; this is a core teaching of all spiritual traditions. We cannot help but be in this together; to think otherwise truly is to be "out of our right minds."

Four Foundations of Change

The above prerequisites are qualities which comprise a state of mind conducive to personal growth and development. Once a commitment is in place, an individual is ready and open to receive help and to accept active responsibility for his or her growth and development. The following four ingredients contribute to a solid foundation for growth.

1/ Individual Support - When we are hurting, especially when we are in crisis, we need the attention of another warm, caring human being. When we feel discouraged, we can draw from another's hope. When we are in crisis and feel desperate, we especially need support. Having one ally has made all the difference for countless souls in making their way back from overwhelm and the depths of despair. It is an illusion to think that such an ally must be a professional. It is not, however, an illusion to think that certain qualities and information are desirable and, at times, necessary for the helper. Most important is what we call love: caring and compassion for the one we seek to help. Other significant qualities include commitment, gentleness and patience. A helper with relaxed confidence that comes either from an abiding faith in human nature or a personal experience of having successfully gone through deep personal transformation makes it possible for an individual to really let go and express the deepest fears and hurts. Good information about the recovery process and the value of emotional release can help enormously. The bottom line is that we are relational beings. Just as our deepest hurts are suffered at the hands of individuals, so does our deepest healing occur in connection with one other caring person.

2/ Group Support - Martin calls it a "working group," (13) the 12-step programs call it a fellowship, some call it support, others group therapy. Judy Chamberlain, former "mental patient," current leader in the forefront of the movement to provide alternatives to established psychiatry, challenges the term "therapy" which separates people into "sick" and "well" and has as its goal the adjustment of an individual to the "reality" of her life. "Consciousness raising," on the other hand, is an ongoing process of challenging negative stereotypes and helping people see their so-called symptoms as real problems and real responses to real hurts and frustrations. (14) Whatever you call it, group support and involvement is a key foundation stone for positive change. Exposure and subsequent acceptance by a group of safe individuals is a particularly essential part of recovery from shame.

3/ Spiritual Development - The root problem of a profit-driven corporate society, and a reductionistic biopsychiatry, is that both are bereft of the Spirit. The human experience can ultimately be fulfilling only when we respect and honor the truth of our spiritual nature. On a practical level, this means that genuine support includes a place for our ongoing search for and development of meaning and purpose in our lives. And it means that this search and development must not be driven by the demand and constraints of the outer world. Authentic spirituality ha always meant a focus on the world behind the eyes. All pat include some form of prayer, meditation, or contemplation to develop and strengthen this inner connection. As discussed in Chapter 8, spiritual maturity requires a radical shift from being driven by the dictates of adopted beliefs and outer demands to a life guided by one's own inner truths. There are as many ways to seek spiritual development as there are people; nevertheless, prayer or meditation, study and service are common essentials. Positive group involvement is also most helpful as the "loy forces of the opposition" never seem to rest.

4/ Activism - Activism is a form of service, but with specific focus which flows from an individual's own person history. I included this fourth foundation stone because of my observation of myself and others that a certain level of recovery from the effects of past hurts seems to happen on by including this fourth ingredient. I am using the term activism here to refer specifically to active effort on the pa of individuals to challenge the oppression that is most central to their lives. Here is an inspiring example.

Judy Chamberlain, whom I mentioned just above, ha been a member of the President's Commission on Mental Health, and is now a leading figure at the National Empowerment Center (see Resources). Judy tells her stor in her book, 'On Our Own: Patient-Controlled Alternativ to the Mental Health System'. She describes herself as a bright New York Jewish girl who, though encouraged to c

so, did not want to go to college. Instead she got a
secretarial job, got married, and when she became pregnant
in 1965 at age 20, was excited about beginning a great
adventure. She reports that three months later, after a
miscarriage, the adventure was over. She did not just "get
over it." Amid mounting concerns of family and friends, and
increasing pressure, Judy finally, reluctantly, agreed to see a
psychiatrist. In her book, she describes in detail the making
of a mental patient, the stigmatization, the label of
"depression" which for so many years "thwarted my chances
to get my life moving in a positive direction," the threats,
the coercion, the drugging, the seclusions, etc. It is
especially valuable that Judy looks back and shares her
current understanding of what was really going on with her,
the truths so thoroughly ignored and obscured by
psychiatry. Unable at the time to articulate her need to
withdraw, she can now see that "My need was to return to
myself, to get in touch with my own feelings." No one
seemed to consider that her "depression" might be telling
her something about her life, or imply something about
others' lives; rather, it was a disease to be cured. In the
language of the heroine's journey, genuine withdrawal was
denied; the biopsychiatric alternative was coercive
incarceration.

   And what of the return? Without an authentic
withdrawal, there can be no heroic journey and return. The
six million plus Americans on Prozac are testimony to the
assertion that the pathetic caricature of Return offered by
psychiatry is a forced and broken return. In Judy
Chamberlain's case, upon her very first visit to a psychiatrist
he opened a desk drawer and selected orange and blue and
white ones from a brightly colored array. And he advised
her to go back to work and to take her pills. This was the

beginning of an all too common, horrific ordeal of hospitalizations, attempted suicide and misery. Judy was both strong-willed enough to keep fighting and fortunate enough to find a safe place in 1974 when she had "once again experienced the overwhelming sense of my life crashing down around me." This safe space was the Vancouver Emotional Emergency Center, an extremely rare non-psychiatric alternative started by a group of nonprofessionals. There Judy was safe, protected from psychiatry. She was able to work through a great deal of fear via emotional release, resulting in renewed energy for creative problem-solving in her life. Here is what she says about activism:

> "I used to feel that it was important to fight oppression but since I was one of the weak ones, I had to let others fight for me. I would always be one of the helpees, not a participant. Now I'm fighting — for myself and others. I found a place where I could plug in, where I could address myself to my most immediate oppression. It made me so happy." (15)

I am aware of and sensitive to the great terror often held by victims of psychiatry. I am also aware of the existence of real danger and the need for discernment in "coming out" as a psychiatric survivor. I have no desire to push anyone into this most challenging aspect of the return before they are ready. Nevertheless, there is a level of reclaiming power that seems to happen only when we walk through our deepest hurts and fears by speaking out and taking action against injustice, particularly the injustices perpetrated against us. There is also a level of self-love that may come forward as it did for Dianne Jennings Walker, another psychiatric survivor who found her voice:

> "My life story differs in only very particular details
> from the stories of so many other women who have been
> labeled schizophrenic. I could escape the label today; I
> could 'pass.' When I chose in 1975 not to pass it was the
> most nurturing thing I had ever done for myself. For once I
> feel that my mind, soul and body are mine. ...
> Psychotherapy oppresses us by teaching us that we are sick,
> crazy, maladjusted. We should forget grandiose and
> paranoid ideas (such as) that some societies just aren't
> worth adjusting to. My last psychiatrist couldn't understand
> why I wanted to work and be friends only with people who
> I knew was an ex-patient. He said, 'I don't understand your
> obsession with honesty.' He and another psychiatrist, who
> was allegedly radical, told me that I was not going to
> change the world by being militantly ex-crazy. Maybe not.
> Then again I hear there are more than twenty million of us
> in this country alone." (16)

My friend, Barb Lundgren, provided the following
editorial comment on the first draft of this section:

> "Activism does not need to take form against
> biopsychiatry, but is simply a way of taking a stand pro or
> con anything important in your life. The simple process of
> changing one's diet, choosing a religion, getting a divorce,
> homeschooling, etc., are all measures of activism."

I agree, and I also know that we often need to take this
stand against the specific oppression which has hurt us. For
psychiatric survivors like Judy Chamberlain and Dianne
Walker that is psychiatry. My argument in this book is that,
due to the ubiquitous influence of psychiatric oppression in

all our lives, we all need to, on some level, take a stand for liberation in this domain.

CHAPTER 15
A LEGEND IN THE MAKING

An enchantment has fallen over the land, the effect of a powerful spell successfully cast. So successfully, in fact, that the doer of this evil deed holds a place of great prestige, honor and fortune in the land. As with all successful enchantments, the enchanted are unaware of the spell's influence. Though bereft of the natural human powers of rational thought, free will, and conscious decision-making, they do not know it. Evidence of both the effectiveness and the cruelty of this enchantment is exceedingly clear. That we choose — rather obey like zombies the dictates of the evil one who holds us under the sway of his mighty spell — to give toxic drugs to millions of our children and brain-damaging electroshock to hundreds of thousands of our elders is alone enough to justify my assertion.

The effects of this enchantment are awesome. Perception, feeling, and thinking of persons under the effects of this enchanter's spell are altered so dramatically that they appear to have lost all hope of acting in a way consistent with what we call common sense, much less perceive anything at all approximating the true nature of reality. For those who operate outside the influence of this mighty wizard, watching the distortions of reality is so astounding as to be virtually unbelievable. Here are just a few examples of the black magic inversion of reality effected by this enchantment:

Terror is Delusion. Cruelty is Kindness. Coercion is Treatment. Force is Treatment. Toxic Drugs are Treatment. Brain-Damaging Electroshock is Treatment. Scapegoating is Helping. Name-calling is Diagnosis. Distress is Disease. Sadness is Disease. Fear is Disease. Inattention is Disease. Restlessness is Disease. Boredom is Disease. Violence is Disease. Irresponsibility is Disease. Unproductivity is Disease. Not sleeping is Disease. Sleeping too much is Disease. Not eating is Disease. Eating too much is Disease. Drinking is Disease. Drug Use is Disease. Nonconformity Disease. Resistance is Disease.

Under the effects of this spell, virtually any human behavior may be seen as evidence of Disease and need for Treatment.

Is it possible somehow to break the effects of such an awesome spell and restore the land and its people to a place of common sense, beneficence and kindness? First of all, never underestimate the importance of good information. With no reference point other than the defined contours, definitions and rules of the enchanter's spell, the situation appears bleak. Even the greatest s/heroes need good maps especially in treacherous, hostile or unknown territories. Good maps of the human unconscious seem hard to come by, experienced guides even harder. More amazing is that we have such lousy maps of the aboveground world of human living and relating in our homes, schools and places of work. Excuse me — they're actually extremely well-crafted wizard maps, highly effective in blinding us to the harm and ensuring our ongoing participation in the practices of psychiatric oppression. Think of this book as dual language dictionary or a decoding manual, translating psychiatry/sorcererspeak into plain speech. Perhaps even better, think of it as a pair of magic glasses that allows one to see more clearly even in the midst of an enchanter's fog. Or maybe, I hope it is, Shiva the destroyer, smashing to smithereens those eyeglasses of optical delusion. In any event, it is our good fortune that tradition, in the form of myths and fairy tales, tells us that the answer is yes to the possibility of breaking the spell, but that the task is daunting. These tales teach us that such an accomplishment is the feat of heroes and heroines, requiring tremendous qualities of courage, endurance, stamina, and the like.

How is it that men become heroes and women heroines? It appears that some manage not to fall under the black magic sway of powerful enchanters. We are told they are born into special circumstances or with unique characters, but in truth it is a mystery. Many of the stories involve s/heroes who come into the world with a handicap, or soon acquire one. It seems that such handicaps result in a tremendous vulnerability, precious in its demand to be open and sensitive to the inner life and to the harsh realities of oppression. Child abuse or other life shocks resulting in psychological trauma and unexpressed emotional pain constitute one such handicap with which most readers of this book are personally familiar. Anyone who has been harmed by psychiatry knows the added handicap of trauma upon trauma. Recovery from the bloody pits of grievous psychological (and physical) damage most definitely necessitates a growth and purification process equivalent to the greatest tales of heroic overcoming of adversity. The modern day drama of mental health liberation movement led by psychiatric survivors is an awesome and inspiring tale which will one day be the stuff of legends.

In one of the richest North American legends, a man known as Peacemaker, who spoke with a stutter, came forward over half a millennium ago to lead a group of warring, vengeful, and retaliative Native American tribes to reconciliation and union, resulting in the Iroquois Confederacy, a confederacy which played a major role in modeling for the founding fathers the constitution of the United States. This man is so revered by the Iroquois people that even today his birth name, Deganawidah, is used only in ritual storytelling. I ask that you honor the Iroquois tradition and refer to this man only as the Peacemaker in normal conversation. Now, I will share with you some of the teachings embodied in this legendary tale, described by psychologist and master storyteller Jean Houston, as guideposts toward breaking this enchanter's spell and liberating ourselves from the tyranny of psychiatric oppression. (1)

New Mind

Deganawidah was remarkable from earliest childhood — honest, good, highly intelligent, generous, and handsome. Born in a time of incessant violence among people living in constant fear, as a young man he is described as talking to the animals like Francis of Assisi. The warlike Huron peoples found him strange, and even foolish when he began to talk of peace. They mocked and laughed at him as he began to stutter out his message of peace and reconciliation. An early lesson learned is that to express the truth of who we are and what we really believe, we often, like the Peacemaker, have to go out into the world and leave those who watched us grow up and think they know us best. How many of you know the painful necessity of leaving friends and family behind in order to grow and change, and live closer to the truth of who you really are? We cannot allow the discouragement of our familiars to stop us.

This legendary man had a vision of peace in a warlike world, of reconciliation in a climate of revenge and retaliation. He had a "new mind," a way of seeing and experiencing life in a way radically opposed to a groupmind under the enchantment of Tadodaho, the wicked sorcerer. My view is that human nature is inherently wonderful, that we are all of us like the Peacemaker in our essence — honest, good, intelligent, loving, energetic, and thirsting after righteousness. The new mind is part of our inherent nature. In Chapters 5 and 6, I explained our susceptibility to evil enchantments and degenerate ways in a different parlance, that of psychological conditioning. Our essence is made to love and to serve, but we are born highly dependent, vulnerable to hurt and to conditioning which, like the warring people of Deganawidah's time, violates our nature. The effects of psychiatric oppression are awful and tragic, just like the effects of vengeance and retaliation among the Iroquois tribes. Passive fear and active bravado are equally hopeless and despairing responses, whether to the twisted minds of vengeful warriors or "benevolent," coercive psychiatrists.

Doing the Impossible

Deganawidah left his home tribe in a stone canoe. His mother and grandmother remarked that it would most certainly sink, and that he must be as crazy as everybody said. He replied, "No, it will float. You will see. And by this impossible action, you shall know that my words are true, and that I shall bring peace to the nations."

Attempting the impossible hones our skills, and calls forward courage, cunning and other resources we never imagined that we had. Taking a stand against the hopelessness and the coercive threat of psychiatry, and against the cultural norms of the "well-known, obvious, accepted, scientific truths of biopsychiatry," is a courageous and impossible task, especially for those of you who have directly felt its lash. I have tremendous respect, admiration and appreciation for all of you.

Nourishing a New Mind

As Deganawidah made his way out into the world, he was faced with the challenge of confronting a world of individuals living in constant dread and terror, who had acquiesced to doing whatever they could to exist in such a way as to avoid drawing attention, disapproval, and wrath down upon themselves. The story tells us that he came upc a woman living alone in the woods, whose lodge was a neutral resting place on the east-west path of the warriors. She welcomed him and offered to feed him, as she always fed groups of warring raiders who passed her way. She was surprised, however, when she learned that he was not a warrior. He shared with her his mission of peace and reconciliation, and asked her to stop feeding the raiders. S protested, "But that's what I do. That's my work. That's w I am. I am the woman who feeds the warriors." The Peacemaker admonished her to serve a higher cause and stop nourishing the raiders. He told her that by serving th cause of peace, she would discover who she really was. Th teaching promises us that by embracing an impossible task by standing for truth in the face of external or internalizec oppression, we will propel ourselves toward transformation; we will discover who we really are. But it will be difficult.

Jean Houston points out that this radical request presented the woman an extraordinary challenge on two levels. On a psychological level, the raiders may be seen as toxic thoughts, critical or negative self-judgments that we dwell upon, limiting conditions or shame-based identities that we have accepted and placed upon ourselves. She challenges all of us to stop feeding our toxic raiders, to stop investing our daily bread, the spiritual energy which sustains us, in negative self-talk. Even the "noblest born" must exert tremendous, ongoing discipline to maintain authentic freedom of thought and action; the price of freedom is eternal vigilance. Great discipline is required to change our ways and stand courageously as we shake with fear still held inside from times when external threats were originally made during our vulnerable, developmental years. Sometimes even greater discipline is needed to resist the times when the raiders reveal themselves in the guise of one whose stated intention is to take care of us, like a parent who says spanking hurts them more than it does us. Immense grief is usually associated with our refusal of these "benevolent" raiders.

Deganawidah's request to this woman is also extraordinary on the social level. He asked her to give up her livelihood, or at least to dramatically alter it. The teaching is that, in order to be peacemakers in society, or to live according to our inherent nature, we must be willing to look at all we do with radical honesty and open eyes, and be willing to make dramatic changes in our lives and our careers. We are required to develop a mindfulness by which we can see the unveiled truth of our condition. And, in Jean Houston's words, "We cannot embrace the New Mind by just sitting around and talking about it. It demands that we alter not just our thinking, but our way of living down to th smallest details." (2) The courage required of psychiatric survivors to reclaim their voice and speak about their experience is immense; there is understandably great fear held in the body as a result of past threats, coercions and assaults. I respect the need for long periods, perhaps even the rest of a lifetime, of safe asylum from possible confrontation and danger. Yet I have seen the healing that goes with reclaiming power. I think of an elder woman friend of mine who survived years of psychiatric coercion, including electroshock. As she began to talk, first to me, then on my radio show, she went through times of extremely intense terror and body pains related to remembering her tortures. It was only in reading the word of Holocaust survivors that she found a resonance that helped her accept the humanness of the terror, rage, and grief she felt as a result of her electroshock "treatments." The challenge for us professionals is also great. As I described in the chapters on conditioning, there are powerful, consistent, repetitious forces instilling fear and false information into our psyches. We are conditioned to be silent and go along. Making a noise in this world is difficult; risking our prestige, status, and especially incom is a daunting feat. No wonder so few professionals allow themselves to really see, much less speak out against psychiatric oppression. The challenge is terrifyingly awesome, thrilling, scary, and exciting. How can we possibl do it?

The Importance of Helpers

What makes the difference? Though much remains a mystery, one fact seems clear. Nobody makes it without a great deal of help. Some remarkable stories tell us about the helpers coming forward on the inner planes, as beings in the s/hero's psyche. More seemingly mundane, but profoundly true, is the need for helpers in human, physical bodies just like ours. Deganawidah shared his message first with the Haudenosaunee, People of the Longhouse, and the story goes that one woman responded in ceremonial language: "That is indeed a good message. I take hold of it. I embrace it." The agreement needs to be an active process. The Peacemaker's work began with one other person, and she was a woman. The woman, our feminine nature, receives and embraces. I myself, as I shared in the story behind the curse which begins this book, needed to gain rapport and involvement with my feminine nature to transform this manuscript from a long term paper into a more balanced and full-bodied work. Patriarchal psychiatry most assuredly needs a woman's touch and perspective, not merely a physical woman like Cindy's psychiatrist who is acting out of internalized oppression and is as dangerous as any one-sided man, but the essence of woman, a feminine consideration of nurturance, relatedness and depth of feeling. The Peacemaker named his first convert Jigonhsasee, which means New Face, because her face shone with the radiance of New Mind.

That she was of the people of the longhouse is also significant. As mentioned above, New Mind is vulnerable, and the habits of old mind are deeply rooted. A fresh seedling requires proper conditions and protection from harsh elements to take root and grow. Rather than a barrage

of criticism, doubt, discouragement, and expectation to bea
fruit (produce outer results) immediately, we need
nourishment, patience, encouragement and support,
especially in the beginning or after we've been hurt. The
longhouse is a living community of people; we humans nee
that in order to be all of who we really are. Your fledgling
efforts to find authentic, caring support of people expressin
and/or seeking New Mind are important. And we all need a
much help as we can get.

Seeing Our True Face

Deganawidah prepared to leave the Haudenosaunee people
and continue his journey, heading toward the sunrise,
toward the new. Jigonhsasee warned him that the path
toward the sunrise was dangerous because a cannibal lived
along that way. The direction of the sunset symbolizes the
old familiar ways; this man was committed to New Mind, l
was heading toward the sunrise, undaunted. I share with yc
here Jean Houston's recounting of this part of the story,
beginning with the Peacemaker's reply to Jigonhsasee:

> "That is what I am here to change; I am here to end
> such evils so that all paths become open and safe for
> everyone."

Deganawidah then traveled to the lodge where the
cannibal lived. Looking around, he saw that the man was
not there, so he climbed up onto the low roof of the
dwelling and lay down next to the opening in the roof use
for smoke to escape. Eventually, the eater of human flesh
returned, dragging a freshly killed human corpse. He fille
huge kettle with water and set it over the fire, adding his

gruesome dinner to the pot. Deganawidah shifted his body and deliberately looked down through the smoke hole into the water of the kettle.

When the cannibal approached to stir his pot, he looked into the water and saw a face reflected in the water looking back at him. He was stunned by the face. Not realizing he was seeing Deganawidah, the cannibal thought he was seeing himself. And what a face! Strength, forbearance, character, even wisdom, shone forth from the face he saw reflected.

He pulled back and sat down to think. His face, but also a True Face, the face of a noble and good being. "That's a great man looking out at me from that kettle," he said to himself. "I had not realized I looked like that. That is a face of goodness. That is not the face of a man who eats other people." He began to think about his situation, about who he really was and what he had become. This is the dawn of the New Mind: willingness to look fearlessly at what we have created of our lives.

After a while, doubts arose, and he began to wonder if he had really seen the face he thought he saw. Cautiously, he approached the kettle for a second look. The steadfast Deganawidah was still up on the roof, peering down the smoke hole into the kettle, and so the noble face was still looking up at the cannibal from the water.

"It is me!" cried the cannibal. "It is! That's really me! How about that? That is a tremendous person. That's a great man. That's not the face of a man who eats humans. What am I going to do with this soup? I'd better dump it."

Once he acknowledged the truth of his True Face, the cannibal realized that he could no longer act as he had acted, without conscience, mindfulness, or compassion. Struck with remorse, he took action immediately. He carried the kettle with its human stew out into the forest, burying it in the space left by the roots of an overturned tree.

Then he sat there, overcome with the grief and shock of self-awareness. "All right. I've changed my habits. I am no longer a cannibal. But now my conscience is torturing me because of all the evil I have done and the suffering I have caused." These reflections made him very morose, and he fell into an agony of guilt. In his shame, he said aloud, " wish someone would come along to tell me how to make amends to all the human beings that I wronged. I wish ther were someone who could show me a way of relieving my pain at having hurt others so badly. Is there any way I can take actions that will make up for the dreadful things I have done?"

These thoughts reflect the basic Native American ide of balancing evil deeds with right action. Evil cannot be erased, of course, but doing good can help redress inequiti in both the earth and ourselves. Thinking these thoughts, the man made his way back to his house. Standing there waiting for him was Deganawidah. Still puzzling over the day's events, the former cannibal invited his guest into the lodge and restored the fire; then the two sat facing each other across the flames.

Filled with wonder at what he had experienced, the man began to speak of the miracle of the face he had seen reflected in the water. He spoke eloquently, beautifully, sorrowfully: "Today something happened to change my lif I saw a face that I knew must be mine, and yet it seems impossible. It was not the face of the terrible man who has lived here. I know what I have been, and yet my face tells wondrous kindness. Now that I see what I really am, I am anguish over what I have become. What can I do?"

Deganawidah heard the passion and concern in the beautiful voice and invited the man to tell the story of how he had come to be a cannibal. (3)

Houston points out that this encounter between the Peacemaker and the cannibal takes us from the stuff of legends, where events, however remarkable, have a basis in historical fact, to the realm of myth, sending us into deeper, universal territory of the human psyche. This crucial encounter reveals an essential teaching: the need to see the True Face. I call it remembering our inherent nature. This man makes contact with his true nature, hidden beneath the horrible, cannibal patterns of distress, and he is transformed. The physical human, man or woman, often does not manifest the true nature of human being. Remembering this true nature, seeing our True Face, is absolutely necessary for healing and redemption. Yet it can be difficult, especially when the True Face is so distorted. The cannibal saw his True Face reflected in the water, through the smoky haze of his lodge. Realization depends on a kind of vision different than our normal physical sight. Houston shares the wisdom of a Navajo elder:

> "You must learn to look at the world twice. First, you must bring your eyes together in front so you can see each droplet of rain on the grass, so you can see the smoke rising from an anthill in the sunshine. Nothing should escape your notice. But you must learn to look again, with your eyes at the very edge of what is visible. Now you must see dimly if you wish to see things that are dim — visions, mist, and cloud people, animals which hurry past you in the dark. You must learn to look at the world twice if you wish to see all there is to see."

The True Face can only be seen with this second seeing, composed of water and smoke, of emotion and energy, as well as flesh and bone. We must remember our own True Face, and look and reach for the true nature hidden behind the distressed thinking and behavior of others. And we must realize that to really overcome the False Face we have assumed, we must do this in an active way as the cannibal is beginning to do, as Jigonhsasee modeled, "I take hold of it. I embrace it."

The anguish this man felt upon seeing his True Face another essential part of the story. Living out the horror o▶ his cannibalistic existence, he was unconscious, a victim of evil enchantment if ever there was one. Do you know this feeling? Do you know what it's like to wake up from years addiction, or thoughtlessness, or spanking your children because you thought it was right, or trusting the authority (doctor, teacher, parent, whomever) simply because it wou▶ never have occurred to you that they might not always be worthy of your trust? Or any kind of awakening to truth, especially to the truth of who you are at the deepest level? Do you know how wonderful it can be at first when you touch into your essential goodness, your loving, your carir▶ how it's usually because someone sees it inside of us when we couldn't, like the Peacemaker did for the cannibal? An◀ do you know the heart-rending experience that often follows, the guilt and the grief that comes like a flood as t▶ shock and numbness wear off? This is a profound teachin▶ revealing deep truth about human transformation.

This story speaks volumes about how to help people distress. Certainly this cannibal man was severely derange▶ as severely "mentally ill" as they come one would think. B▶ the Peacemaker's initial approach to him showed nothing the way of threat or coercion or force of any kind. And there was no gathering of mind and body-altering herbs from the forest to suppress or subdue his obvious "psychosis." He did not avoid the cannibal; he went right toward the sunrise. He did not use force; he simply found a way to remind the man of his True Face. And what was Deganawidah's response to the anguished plea of this man for help after he had awoken to the horror of his condition? He simply made himself available and invited him to tell the story of how he had become a cannibal. Do you wonder how such a beautiful, eloquent being could have so degenerated as to be eating the flesh of other humans? I have shared already my thoughts on how inherently good, intelligent, caring human beings can be conditioned to perpetrate and/or allow the harms of psychiatric oppression. The cannibal is a tremendous metaphor for psychiatry, which Thomas Szasz describes as "existential cannibalism." Szasz asserts that so-called therapeutic encounters "consist of the malefactor de-meaning his maleficiary — by destroying the meaning that he, the nominal beneficiary, has given his own existence. There are many ways of practicing existential cannibalism. In our society, the most popular form of it is to give one's 'beneficiary' a psychiatric diagnosis and impose on him a psychiatric treatment, neither of which he wants. This enables the 'benefactor' to claim he is helping and strengthening his 'beneficiary', while, in fact, he is harming him and is rendering him more powerless." (4) Let's continue now and hear the cannibal's story.

Telling Our Stories

The man who became the cannibal had been known as an orator, a man who spoke eloquently in the style and tradition of Native American peoples. He had lived among the Onondaga tribe, where there also lived a terrible sorcerer. The orator, a man of goodness and noble character, kept trying to persuade the sorcerer, whose name was Tadohado, to give up his evil ways. In addition to sorcery, Tadodaho was also a cannibal. As a result of his opposition to Tadodaho, the orator's family had sorcery inflicted on it, and his wife and four of his seven daughters had died. Whereupon the orator had become so filled with agony that he went mad and took on the very character of the sorcerer, saying, "I will outdo him in all his evil." So saying, the orator lost his true self and became a cannibal, living alone in the forest. But now this great persuader, this great orator, had looked into the kettle and had seen his Deep Face, his True Face. Because he had once been a great and good man himself and had committed such terrible wrong, his misery was enormous. He had been reminded by the face he saw of who and what he really was.

Deganawidah listened to the story and replied, "That is a wonderful story! You see what you have just done. You have shifted a basic pattern of vengeful response in your life and nothing is more difficult than breaking patterns set so deep within us. Congratulations! A new kind of awareness, New Mind, if you will, has been born in you today, a desire to see justice done, to restore health and sanity and, through this, a recognition of your path to spiritual power." (5)

In order to heal, in order to remember our True Face we must tell our stories, even, especially even, our most shameful and dangerous-seeming secrets. But not to just anyone. We need to tell them to someone who "carries the Mind of the Maker," who is able to rest in loving kindness and relaxed confidence in the goodness of our true nature, however awful our stories might seem to us. That's how we begin to unload the shame we carry and rediscover who we really are. Notice the Peacemaker's response: "That is a wonderful story! Congratulations!" Isn't this amazing? Deganawidah does not respond with "Oh my God!" or "How awful!" or "Let's change the subject because I can't stand to hear it." He does not try to distract by saying "It's over. Just forget about it and think positive. Don't upset yourself anymore." Deganawidah is so confident of his own and the cannibal's true nature, and of the restorative powers of the New Mind, that he knows the inevitability of positive transformation, given acceptance, encouragement and support. The cannibal is not so confident.

"But wait," the former cannibal wailed. "How can this be? All I feel is agony over my past."

Deganawidah answered him kindly. "Yes, agony, because the quality of your New Mind cannot bear to remember things done in blind ignorance. But do not shut down or cause those memories to go underground. Look at the truth about yourself, but know that there is a deeper truth and that it is possible for us to heal our past by working for peace and justice in the present. We can approach the people we have harmed and this time offer them solace and a healing."

"What can I do?"

"I have listened to you speak. You are a fine speaker, with a beautiful and persuasive power to your voice. My message requires just such a gift. As you hear, I cannot speak without stuttering. I ask you to work with me. Together we can carry the Good News of peace and power to all people who can hear us."

The former cannibal's reply followed the traditional

formula. "Your message is a good one. I take hold of it. I embrace it. How shall we begin?" (6)

Here again we see the anguish the cannibal feels as he awakens out of his frozen grief and numbness to realize the pain he has caused others in his unconscious lashing out. The Peacemaker gently acknowledges the pain. He offers no simple panacea, but gives accurate and hopeful information. He reminds the suffering man once again of his true nature, and that even the pain he now feels is a sign that he is awakening into his New Mind. And he emphasizes the crucial importance of staying open to the painful memories, saying he must not shut down or push the memories underground. This advice stands in stark contrast to the practices of biopsychiatry which main function is to shut people down, to suppress memory, feeling and emotional discharge. This is what psychiatric drugs are for. I am reminded of a woman friend of mine who finally quit her job as a psychiatric nurse at St. David's Hospital in Austin, Texas because she couldn't stand seeing patients come out of the room where they received their electroshock treatments. As an individual was taken into "treatment," she would ask herself the question, "What is it they do not want this patient to remember?"

The work of trauma recovery is painful and difficult, and usually takes a long time, all the claims of "brief therapy" to the contrary. We'll hear more about the cannibal's recovery as we go along. But we've also just been given another glimpse of the truth that authentic recovery much more than a counseling issue. The Peacemaker says we heal our own past by working for peace and justice for others. That is not about therapy; it is about the essential truth of our complete interrelatedness as human beings an the absolute need to be of service in order to be whole, to be residing in the Mind of the Maker. We see solid wisdom which is familiar to all who have walked the 12-step path — take an inventory of the damage you have done and make amends to those you have harmed. The cannibal's work, like all of us, is really cut out for him.

Finally, in this piece of the story, Deganawidah lets the cannibal know that this is about something way beyond his own personal recovery. He says, to paraphrase, "We need you, man. This is a big job, this business of changing the world, and I need your help." Deganawidah has observed and recognized this man's gifts. Don't we all need someone to see what we have to offer, and to encourage us, especially when we are down? Doesn't it help enormously to have opportunities to help, to be invited to be of service? Isn't that one of the most important tasks of parenting — to recognize and encourage and facilitate opportunities to develop and express the unique gifts of each of our children? The Peacemaker is performing the sacrament of ordination here, reminding and calling forth the vocation, that of an orator, with which this man was meant to serve his community. Finding and embracing our vocation, taking the sacrament of ordination, is an essential aspect of finding our True Face for all of us. Before he can embody his vocation, however, there is the huge ordeal of trauma recovery, and as I said above, it can take a very, very long time. But the cannibal is willing and ready, as expressed in his last question, "How shall we begin?"

Facing the Oppressor

Since his new friend was eager to begin his service,

Deganawidah gave him his first assignment. As might be expected, it was the most difficult task possible, physically and emotionally. With his New Mind, his new fearlessness, and so much pain to assuage, Deganawidah directed him to go first to the evil wizard of the Onondagas, Tadodaho, wh killed without mercy and devoured what he killed.

In dismay, the other replied, "But that's the man who caused me to go mad and become a cannibal!"

"Yes," Deganawidah replied, "and that is why he is th person you have to go to."

"Do you know what he's like?" Deganawidah's new friend asked. "He has a body with seven crooks in it. He h a club for his fist. He has a snake for a penis, which is wrapped around his body, and snakes for his matted hair. His evil power is enormous."

Deganawidah replied, "Yes, and that is why the cause of peace cannot go further without his becoming peaceful. Go to him again — again and again, if necessary. Go to hi with the message of peace. Of course, he will drive you away, over and over again. Expect that. But at last you will prevail. For this purpose, I will give you a new name. Fror this moment on you shall be Hiawatha, which means He Who Combs, for you shall comb the snakes out of Tadodaho's hair." (7)

"Whoa!" says this awakened cannibal/orator, and understandably so. Look again at the description of this sorcerer. He is a monstrous, twisted being, his evil power enormous, he kills without mercy and devours what he ki He is your worst nightmare, and many of you have been, like the cannibal, victims of such evil power, physically or sexually abused as children, raped as adults, ravaged by w degraded, humiliated, or beaten for the color of your skin

This sorcerer is a vivid archetype of the oppressor, an image of sexism, of racism, of adultism. For me just now, he represents the worst of psychiatry, the one who forces people into snakepit asylums against their will, and holds them down to inject them with drugs; that's what he did to Cindy. To the 33-year-old, self-acknowledged incest survivor who had a chronic pattern of self-injury, he lobotomized her in 1997 at Massachusetts General Hospital — twice — and made her into a human vegetable. (8)

And the Peacemaker tells this man to go first to Tadodaho! He can't mean it. In literal terms, I would never advise a client to go first to confront the man or woman who had perpetrated horrific abuse on him or her. I would advise them to counsel on this experience and relationship for a good while in a safe place with safe people. If they are strong and determined as is this reformed cannibal, they might indeed be ready to face the perpetrator, but to face him as he exists in the memories and functions of their body and psyche. In truth, we must face our most frightening demons to become whole. Nevertheless, it is almost always advisable to first work on the hurt and the internalized patterns associated with the traumatic experience. Then comes a confrontation in the flesh, if the individual still feels the need to do so in order to heal and reclaim their power. But that is a literal interpretation from the point-of-view of psychological healing and trauma recovery. A later installment of this story speaks, I think, to the truth of my advice to proceed gradually — the healing process is long and arduous.

At another level, the story speaks in mythological terms of the enormous truth that the cause of peace cannot go further without Tadodaho's becoming peaceful. As individuals, we must make peace with the twisted, perverted,

mean-spirited parts of ourselves. As a people, we must face
the evil in our society, in this case the institutionalized
oppression of psychiatry. This part of the story reveals
another psychological truth about facing evil, facing twisted
beings, facing what I call the acting out of chronic distress
recordings by deeply hurt human beings. Deganawidah
warns his new friend that Tadodaho will drive him away
again and again. This really is how it works. As a parent,
when your child is distressed, especially when he's hurt and
angry, he will reject your overtures to be with him and help
him, again and again. I have learned what a mistake it is to
take these rejections literally or personally. It seems that
young people, that all of us to some degree, work out
feelings of hurt and rejection by rejecting back. Our
willingness as parents to put our body on the line is the key
to helping our children restore balance. And I have seen it
work really well with "grownups" as parents re-create
closeness and affection with their horribly estranged adult
children. They do this by persistently making one-way
overtures, and being willing to keep going without
reciprocation or through the hard times of active rejection
as the adult child works out the hurts and gradually accepts
the possibility that things might be different now, and that
their parent might actually be trustworthy and sincere.

   Perhaps the biggest key to making possible a
seemingly impossible reconciliation is that, just as
Deganawidah saw the essence of New Mind in the canniba
even through the circumstances and appearances and
horrible actions of his degraded condition, these parents
hold the image of the True Face of themselves and their
children — that despite the alienation, rejection, hostility,
and/or apparent indifference, they and their children
naturally desire to be warm, close, and affectionate. So the

reached for the closeness, and, just as the Peacemaker
advised, they kept going back again and again and again.
They took on the energy of the ex-cannibal's new name,
Hiawatha, and combed snakes out of their children's hair,
just as someone must have done for them.

Fear, Rage, and the Tree of Falsehood

All of us, like Hiawatha, are haunted with the question of
how to break this cycle of oppression, of wounding and
devouring, of being so hurt and frightened by twisted, evil
beings and institutions that we lose heart and lose hope.
There is reaching for your angry child, and there is facing
Tadodaho, who will literally eat you if he gets the chance. I
assure you that I see the difference; there is more to come
about Hiawatha's awesome task. But first, be assured that
Deganawidah is not abandoning his friend and sending him
off to handle the dirty work. Like other authentic heroes,
the Peacemaker is eager and willing to confront evil. He
faces the sorcerer first, helping prepare the way for
Hiawatha.

   "You are invited to open your mind to new
possibilities of peace," Deganawidah told the snarling
sorcerer. "No more war. No more killing. No more
sorcery."
   The evil one, his head spiky with snakes, replied to
Deganawidah's quiet invitation with a great howling cry,
"WE-DO-NE-E-E-E-EH?" ("When will this be?")
According to one of my Iroquois friends, the sorcerer's cry
was the Onondaga equivalent of "over my dead body." (9)

Imagine yourself confronting one of the premier electroshock doctors or directors of in-patient psychiatric hospitals or any doctor who makes his living by prescribing psychiatric drugs. You say, "I invite you to open your mind to human kindness. No more shock. No more drugs. No more coercion." What might be his response? Perhaps, "You must be crazy," which might be translated as a threat to take away your liberty and torture you with drugs and/or electroshock; in other words, "over your dead body." This response is all too well-known by patients who challenge their psychiatrists; the challenge is labeled a symptom of disease, the consequences can be severe. Or the psychiatrist might try another tactic, attempting to avoid the issue and, in his mind, shame and discredit you. This was my own experience the first time I attended a lecture by Max Fink, one of the most zealous promoters of electroshock in the world today. I was with Doug Cameron and Diann'a Lope both of whom had been grievously hurt by electroshock, co founders of the World Association of Electroshock Survivors, an organization whose stated mission is to ban electroshock from the face of the earth. There was a protest outside St. David's Hospital where Dr Fink was speaking; the three of us went in to listen to his talk. When he invite questions, Diann'a asked him whether it was not true that the so-called therapeutic effect of ECT was due to a brain injury high, an example of temporary euphoria often show with closed head injuries. Fink immediately responded wit "I see we have three cult Scientologists here," and refused answer the question. I didn't even know what a Scientolog was at the time, but I had been around enough to know a shame-based, authoritarian defense when I saw one.

Deganawidah was not deterred by Tadodaho's rage. He continued his journey, presenting his message of peace to the desperate peoples along his way. He met with a few successes, but mostly encountered tremendous suspicion and incredulity. Nobody could imagine being the first to lay down arms in a world driven by fear, hatred, vengeance and retaliation. The Mohawk chiefs felt drawn to the Peacemaker's vision, but they felt responsible for their people and did not want them to be sacrificial lambs. Do any of us want to be the ones who feel the oppressor's blows when we take an opposing view? After you're hit on the head with a hammer enough, you will behave; the hammer is internalized, and as long as you obey its silent dictates, the outer blows are no longer necessary. The psychiatrist smiles kindly and holds your hand as you take your pills like a good patient, or willingly allow yourself to receive the electroshock he administers. Resist the "treatment," however, and it is likely that the demented face of Tadodaho will appear. Be a good professional, and honor the role of psychiatry as the proper head of the mental health hierarchy, and you'll get referrals or a job; talk the talk of psychiatric diagnoses and "medicine consults," and you'll receive those HMO clients and third-party payments. Refuse and you're out of that system. So finally the reluctant chiefs asked Deganawidah to perform some act that would assure them he was not an agent of another tribe, setting them up for a massacre.

Looking out over the landscape, one of the chiefs pointed to a tree nearby, a deformed and twisted oak, which grew over the edge of a waterfall. "If your words are true," they challenged, "climb into the tree that leans over the falls. We will cut the tree down, and you will fall with it a long, long, long way. If you are still alive in the morning, we will become part of the Great Peace."

And so Deganawidah climbed into the ancient oak, and the people began chopping at the tree with their hatchets. After a while, Deganawidah himself wrapped his legs around a branch, leaned down, and began to help hack down the tree with his own hatchet. As he did this, a strong rain began to fall. The Mohawks stood back amazed as Deganawidah attacked with a savage fury the tree which he himself named as the Tree of War. (10)

When reflecting on the meaning of great stories, it is always helpful to consider that, on one level, all of the players involved represent aspects of an individual psyche. There is the s/hero within, as well as their nemesis, the sorcerer, and many others. In this part of our story, the her is challenged by a group of good, but insecure and doubtir chiefs. Don't we all know the experience of having grand and spirit-filled ideas, made limp and impotent by our inn voices of fear and doubt. The Peacemaker is showing us here what is necessary to overcome and convince these hesitant doubters. He knows that words alone do not suffice; he must be willing to take heroic action, even to ri his life. This can be a physical risk; more often, it is a risk ego death, of exposing ourselves to shame and ridicule, to loss of status and prestige, to failure. To me, the most remarkable part of this passage is that Deganawidah attacked with a savage fury! The Peacemaker is showing savage fury, the stuff of which cannibals and sorcerers are made. Let us continue with the story, and see what we car make of this. Houston shares Ken Carey's version of Deganawidah's next words, from his book, 'The Return o the Bird Tribes.'

"It is I who have said that the twisted Tree of War m

be cut from your lives. It is I who will cut away this tree and fall with it into the gorge. My act will give you a teaching that my words have not. No man should ever be afraid to cut falsehood from his life, even if it is the very thing upon which he is standing. Once he recognizes it, he should not fear to let it fall away. For to remain standing upon a lie, once it is known to be false, is to destroy your own peace and joy. And there is no value to living if such as these are your roots."

The story continues with Deganawidah's dramatic fall, the ceasing of the rain, and the appearance of a magnificent rainbow. He has accomplished something that we all must do; he has hacked down the tree of falsehood. His savage fury was not directed at any human being; he unleashed it on the Tree of War, on fear, on desperation, on the vicious warrior patterns of revenge and retaliation, on the doubt and hesitation of well-intentioned but timid chiefs. If we are alive, we feel anger when insulted, frustrated, hurt or threatened. If we have been hurt in the past, and not been able to express ourselves and heal, we carry backlogs of anger, held as tension in our bodies. Without conscious intention and effort, our anger is unawarely expressed in hurtful ways, like Hiawatha's cannibalism, the ongoing tribal warmaking, or activities such as coercion and electroshock perpetrated by psychiatry. Or we just go passive, numb to the pain and unable to think rationally about any of it. It is vitally important to feel and express the power of our outrage, but to get it aimed in the right direction, at the oppressive beliefs and actions, not at the human beings who are still completely good beneath their distressed thinking and behavior, like Hiawatha in his cannibalism. When it comes to body memories of abuses suffered at the hands of abusive adults when we were children, the anger, usually rage, needs to be expressed, but we must find safe and appropriate ways to do it. It is very helpful to have the support of someone who holds the image of everyone's True Face, even as we release the awful memories of past traumas. The teaching is that, in order to come into New Mind, we must find a way to express our feelings of savage fury, aimed in the right direction, in ways that are safe and appropriate. And we must, like Deganawidah, be so completely wholehearted that even the most doubtful parts of ourselves are impressed with our commitment and sincerity. The Peacemaker survived his awesome fall. The Mohawks held a great feast, and these words were said.

In the tradition of the Iroquois, the Chief Warrior spoke for all when he said, "Yesterday, I was in great doubt, for words, however good, do not always betoken the thing that is. Now I am in doubt no longer. This is a great man, who reveals to us the Mind of the Maker of Life. Let us accept his message. Let us take hold of the Good News of peace and power."

Deganawidah responded, "The day is early and young and so is the New Mind young and tender. And as the new sun rises and proceeds surely on its course in the sky, so also shall the Young Mind prevail and prosper among humans. There shall be peace. Your children and your grandchildren and your descendants to the seventh generation — those whose faces are yet beneath the ground — shall live under the sky without fear." (11)

So the Mohawks became the first tribe to accept the Peacemaker's vision, and were the founders of the Iroquois Confederacy. Taking brave action, grounded in the reality our inherent nature, can really bring those doubting parts of ourselves around. And it can inspire a few others to be our allies as well.

An Archetype of Evil Power

Now let the story take us back to Hiawatha, whose assignment, you will recall, is to face Tadodaho, the man responsible for the death of his beloved wife and four of their seven daughters. Deganawidah has given him the task, but is this man ready to face his horrific perpetrator? Let me share Houston's description of this sorcerer.

Tadodaho was brilliant, with an evil intelligence that could always discern other people's weaknesses and play upon them. In some versions of the story, including the one told here, he had already done terrible damage to Hiawatha's life. He seemed to summon up the worst in people and then use this power for his own ends and to his victims' shame. Many young warriors were in his thrall, acting, it seemed, without conscience. His appearance was calculated to strike terror: matted and spiky hair, which is why people said he had snakes in his hair, and a twisted and contorted body. In the light of today's psychoanalytic knowings, we think of what must have happened to him as a child to deform his body, and why having a twisted body led to his having a monstrous, twisted mind — or the reverse. Tadodaho was said to be so powerful that he could kill opponents from a distance through sorcery and invade people's dreams at night with terrifying images of torture and murder. Cannibalism was but one atrocity in his catalogue of horrors. People who opposed him died in enigmatic ways. An archetype of evil power, like Hitler, Stalin, or certain Mafia chiefs, he assumed a command over people's psyches great enough to destroy any notions of peace. His terrorist warriors made life miserable not only for the Onondaga people but also for the nearby Cayuga and Seneca villagers farther west. (12)

An archetype of evil power — like Hitler or Stalin or Mafia chief. What about well-healed graduates of Western universities, civil and pleasant neighbors, members of our medical profession? What about the professional service people, the psychologists, counselors, social workers, and nurses, who fill out the ranks of our mental health system? Do these people deserve to be considered in the same light as the likes of Hitler and Stalin, men who presided over countless murders? In challenging psychiatric oppression, my primary focus is not on individuals, but on the institution of psychiatry. Most people who work in the Mental Health System are trying to do good. But the veil i thick, like an iron curtain. Let me quickly remind you of a few facts. There were 100,000 psychosurgeries in the 20 years following Egas Moniz' coining of the term in the mi 1930s. (13) Lest you immediately resort to dismissal of thi as times gone by, remember the woman I mentioned earlie receiving her "psycho-neuro-surgery" in 1997 at Massachusetts General Hospital. Insulin coma treatments were very popular for three decades from the late 1920s. Electroshock, often combined with insulin treatments in t 1940s and 1950s, eventually became the treatment of choice. Horror stories seem to have been the norm as mo than 100 children were electroshocked in a five year perio in the 1940s at Bellevue Hospital in New York, and patien even whole wards, were routinely lined up for indiscriminate use of electroshock as standard hospital management practice throughout the country. This practice slowed down during the 1960s as psychiatric drugs came to the fore and public protest grew, but electroshock has made a comeback, including a growing incidence of its use with children in recent years. How about Multiple Monitored ECT? Dr Goldfarb, in 1976, assures us that as many as 18 electroshocks can be given at the same session without deleterious effects. (14) Psychiatry considers the efficacy of intensive electroshock, referred to historically as "annihilation therapy" or "regressive therapy" or "blitz ," a matter of legitimate scientific debate on into the 1990s. (15)

Tadodaho may be seen as a mythological symbol of psychiatric oppression. As a human symbol, I nominate Max Fink as one archetype of evil; this is the man who declared in 1996 that "ECT is one of God's gifts to mankind." (16) Or how about Dr Ewen Cameron, 1953 President of the American Psychiatric Association? I'll share just one of the notorious experiments from his CIA-funded work on mind control theories. His "depatterning" techniques began with 15 to 30 days of drugged "sleep therapy." The patient was awakened two or three times a day for electroshock treatments 20 to 40 times more intense than ordinary. Bruce Wiseman, author of 'Psychiatry: The Ultimate Betrayal', shares the following:

John Marks, author of 'The Search for the Manchurian Candidate', tells us, "The frequent screams of patients (usually women) that echoed through the hospital did not deter Cameron or most of his associates in their attempts to 'depattern' their subjects completely. Other hospital patients report being petrified by the 'sleep rooms', where the treatment took place, and they would usually

creep down the opposite side of the hall." One doctor to
stories of stuporous patients, incapable of caring for
themselves, often groping their way around the hospital
urinating on the floor.

Patient L. McDonald, who was 23 when Cameron
"depatterned" him, had this to say — twenty-five years a
his treatment: "I have no memory of existing prior to 19
and the recollections I do have of events of the following
years until 1966 are fuzzy and few. ... My parents were
introduced to me ... I did not know them. (My five) child
came back from wherever they had been living. I had no
idea who they were." (17)

As Wiseman points out, none of this prevented
Cameron from sharing his research in prestigious medic
journals. He quotes Dr Donald Hebb, a psychology
department head at Montreal's McGill University when
Cameron was doing his work, in response to a query abo
how such hellish experiments could go on without censu
from the psychiatric community: "Look, Cameron was n
good as a researcher. ... He was eminent because of politi
Here was an archetype of evil who looked very good — a
eminent, well-endowed university professor, a president
his professional society. Wiseman reveals the final ironic
note which makes our circle of evil archetypes complete:
"Dr Ewen Cameron was a member of the Nuremberg
tribunal that judged Nazi war criminals who committed
inhuman crimes during the war." (18)

Tragedy, Desolation, Condolence, and Requickening

Returning to our story, there are two levels I want you to keep in mind as we go on. One is the personal healing of Hiawatha. The other is the incredible task involved in converting one so twisted, perverted and awesomely powerful as Tadodaho. Let us see what happens as Hiawatha attempts to fulfill his mission.

Remember that Hiawatha was from the same tribe as Tadodaho, the Onondagas. He invited all the Onondaga settlements to attend a council, where he, with his great oratorical skills, would present his proposals for the Great Peace. On the appointed day, there was a great attendance as the people yearned for a message that would end their sorrow and pain. But Tadodaho appeared just as the meeting was to begin. He said nothing, but his presence and negative charisma were so ferocious that he intimidated everyone. As his dark warriors moved silently through the crowd, looking from face to face, the people fearfully dispersed. Shortly thereafter, Hiawatha's oldest remaining daughter became sick and died. Any of you who have been trapped in psychiatric hospitals know what silent intimidation is like. And how easy it is to wither and die in such conditions. Hiawatha was grief stricken, yet he refused to give up. He called another council, and fewer people came.

Again Tadodaho appeared with his warriors, and again the people left without hearing the Good News. Following this second council, Hiawatha's second daughter became mysteriously ill and died. As is true in so many mythic stories of a confrontation between good and evil, the dark forces win in the early stages. Hiawatha had once taken up cannibalism, like his enemy, after he had lost four of his daughters. Now he felt his mind becoming more and more disturbed by the loss of two more daughters. Some of his courageous followers made an effort to talk to Tadodaho, but were drowned by the waves as they approached him in their canoes. Symbolically, these are the waves of negativity which drown our integrity and courage. Dissension and chaos were increasing. Day and night Hiawatha could hear Tadodaho's piercing shamanic chant, "HI-A-WA-THA-A-A-A-A!" Yet he still refused to surrender, and called a third council. He kept his daughter close to him, yet Tadodaho managed to incite a wild melee when he caused a great eagle to fall out of the sky, and the daughter was trampled and killed as greedy people rushed to tear out the prized feather of the eagle.

This time, Hiawatha's grief was all-consuming, and no one was capable of comforting him. No one lived in the New Mind in such a way as to be available for Hiawatha. Houston speculates that the Onondaga were so inured to tragedy that they were numb and out of touch with one another's grief. Certainly, we see vast numbness today as we are inundated with images of tragedy in the news, and it all seems surreal. We close our hearts so that we do not feel overwhelmed. Yet, in order to help ourselves, each other, and the world, our capacity for empathy must be reawakened. I share with you now Houston's telling of this next most significant part of our story.

This latest tragedy shattered Hiawatha. As the traditional storytellers describe it, he wept over his favorite daughter, saying, "I have now lost all my daughters. In the death of this, my last daughter, Tadodaho, you have killed two beings, my daughter and the child that was within her. Overcome with grief and despair, Hiawatha left the land of

the Onondaga and began a long and lonely journey away
into the forest, his mind becoming more and more
distorted. He felt that he was losing the essential noble
character which he had regained during his time with
Deganawidah. Once again the evil soul of Tadodaho seemed
to be filling him like an incubus, twisting his spirit, scarring
his mind, turning him away from his new work of bringing
in the Great Law, and making any form of peace seem
impossible.

Only nature offered Hiawatha any consolation, and it
was to nature that he turned for wisdom and comfort.
Because his deep face had been seen by Deganawidah, he
was not the same Hiawatha who had been so hideously
wounded the first time. So in this time of profound grief,
even though his pathology tried to assert itself, he did not
fall into the pattern of his previous criminal behavior.
Instead he fell into nature. As he wandered, Hiawatha came
to the beautiful area of the Tully Lakes, where the ducks
were thick on the water. Here he was able to witness —
some say to cause — a magical event. Like many of us
during soul-charged times, he was drawn to the water. "By
the waters of Babylon they sat down and wept," goes the old
song. But when Hiawatha carried his grief to the lakeside,
something utterly wondrous happened. As the ducks spread
their wings and lifted off, they carried all the lake's water
with them on their webbed feet. We can imagine Hiawatha's
feelings as he crossed the lake with dry moccasins. The
lifting up into the heavens of water perhaps put into his
mind the possibility of lifting the waters of grief and
offering them to the Spirit of the sky. As he crossed the
now-dry lake, he saw all that had been previously hidden.
Drawn by their brightness, he bent down to pick up some
shells from the lake bottom. These, some say, were the

shells he made into beads to use in the creation of wampum those strings of beads that the Iroquois use to commemorate their stories and to speak truth.

As the traditional story tells it, Hiawatha continued on his travels carrying his shells and came one morning upon a stand of elderberry rushes. He cut the rushes into three lengths and strung them with shell beads. Then he cut two forked sticks and planted them in the ground, placing a small pole across them. He lay the three strings over the pole, while saying to himself, "This would I do if I found anyone burdened with grief even as I am. I would console them, for they would be covered with night and wrapped in darkness. This would I lift with words of condolence; these strings of beads would become words with which I would address them." This, the Iroquois say, is the origin of their ritual of condolence, practiced as a way to mourn with and to comfort those in grief, even to the present day.

Then Hiawatha wandered, bereft, scarcely knowing where he traveled. Occasionally he camped outside a settlement, but no one came to comfort him — to lift the strings of condolence. So it is with ourselves. The grief-stricken seem to have an invisible barrier around them which we lack the courage to penetrate. We do what we can but aren't eager "to intrude," as we call it, on their grief.

When Hiawatha reached the edge of the forest near one of the Mohawk villages, he sat down upon the stump of a fallen tree — some say the tree from which Deganawidah had fallen. A woman passed by him and, seeing him sitting there, returned to her village and said, 'A man — or a figure like a man — is seated by the spring with his breast covered with strings of white shells.'

That night, Deganawidah, who was now living in the Mohawk village, went to the place where the smoke from

Hiawatha's fire was seen rising. As he approached, he saw Hiawatha meditating on the condolence strings which were hanging on the pole before him and heard Hiawatha saying again the words, "This would I do if I found anyone burdened with grief, even as I am. I would take these shell strings in my hand and condole with him. The strings would become words and lift away the darkness with which the person is covered. Holding these in my hand, my words would be true."

Then Deganawidah came forward and, lifting the strings from the horizontal pole, he held each strand, one after the other and spoke the words of what are called the Requickening Address. These words have been used ever since by people of the Iroquois nation in their ceremony of condolence. They comprise one of the most powerful psychological and spiritual remedies for grief that I have ever heard.

Presenting the first string, Deganawidah said, "When a person has suffered a great loss caused by death and is grieving, tears blind the eyes so he cannot see. With these words I wipe away the tears from your face, using the white fawn skin of compassion, so that now you may see clearly. I make it daylight for you. I beautify the sky. Now you shall do your thinking in peace when your eyes rest on the sky, which the Perfector of our Faculties, the Master of All Things, intended should be a source of happiness to humans."

Presenting the second string, Deganawidah said, 'When a person has suffered a great loss caused by death and is grieving, there is an obstruction in his ears, and he cannot hear. With these words I remove the obstruction from your ears so that you may once again have perfect hearing."

Presenting the third string, he said, "When a person has suffered a great loss caused by death and is grieving, his throat is stopped, and he cannot speak. With these words I remove the obstruction from your throat so that you may speak and breathe freely."

With these three basic statements of the condolence ceremony, Hiawatha's mind was freed from its sorrow, or rather, from its incessant dwelling on sorrow and grief. When the ceremony was completed, Hiawatha's mind was healed, and he and Deganawidah looked upon each other with wonder and astonishment. Hiawatha saw Deganawidah as the incarnation of goodness and fineness of spirit, and Deganawidah saw Hiawatha as the possible human, a strong and righteous man with many talents and extraordinary courage. Together they could advance the New Mind and spread the Good News to all the nations. (19)

Having seen his Deep Face, having a strong reference point to his true nature, Hiawatha maintained a dual awareness, even in the throes of his boundless grief. He still had enough attention available outside his distress to think and amazingly, to intuitively know what he needed to heal But he could not entirely bestow this gift of healing upon himself; he needed another human being, someone of the New Mind who rested in his own true nature, to help him. And so at last the Peacemaker came forward, through this ceremony of Condolence and Requickening, to free Hiawatha from his ceaseless dwelling on grief and sorrow.

I believe this story accurately reveals the process of recovery from grief, from traumatic injury and loss. Devastated by the loss of his first four daughters, Hiawatha had taken on the evil, twisted ways of Tadodaho. Isn't this how all oppression takes place? Remember the cycle of abuse — traumatic injury, internalization of both victim and perpetrator roles, repression and splitting off of the memories, unconscious identification with the perpetrator, and projection of the victimized self onto others out in the world who will now be the victims. Probably the most effective and powerful way of interrupting this cycle is to remind the injured one, now the abuser, of his true nature, not so much in words but by reflection, as Deganawidah did for Hiawatha. This process is not usually so instantaneous as in our story here, but it is deeply true. And, as with Hiawatha, this reflected glimpse of one's true face can be a tremendous catalyst for repentance and reformation.

A second step involves, as with Hiawatha, facing the truth of what has happened, facing the reality of Tadodaho, of whom or whatever has been the source of your great injury. Hiawatha was not a cannibal for no reason. His pain was enormous. Therefore, when he faced his tormentor without recourse to the pattern of unconscious revenge, he was forced also to face the intense emotional pain and grief which had driven his cannibalistic behavior. And his story reveals the lie in our American fast-food school of "take a weekend and then go back to graduate school" grief. The truth is more like Hiawatha's wanderings.

Finally, Hiawatha received again the complete attention, in the midst of his distress, of the Peacemaker. We all need the support of another caring human being who is whole and essentially healed to fully heal from our hurts. It is my belief that Deganawidah served Hiawatha not so much by magically lifting his grief, like the ducks on the Tully lakes, but by his warm presence and loving words that helped Hiawatha to shed his unshed tears, and express his withheld sobs. Emotional expression is vitally important for psychological healing.

We do not hurt others because we are born evil. Psychiatry does not coerce and confine people, and electroshock our elders, and drug our children because psychiatrists and all their assistants were born evil. To heal ourselves, or to support the healing of others, requires remembrance of the true nature of us all. Hiawatha was deeply hurt, perpetrators of psychiatric oppression were deeply hurt. Such hurt is always necessary to hold oppression in place. Hiawatha had enough character, perhaps because of his earlier years, that Deganawidah's reflection of his True Face was enough to interrupt the cannibalism. Sometimes it takes a more forceful interruption to shake someone out of their robotic perpetration of harm. Regardless, holding the focus of essential goodness is necessary for a truly positive outcome. Let us see what our heroes can bring to bear in their next efforts to rehabilitate the dreadful Tadodaho.

Building a Circle of Allies

The story continues with a brief rendition of how Deganawidah and Hiawatha brought peace and unity to the powerful Mohawk tribe, the people of the flint. This news traveled fast, so as they went forth now to other tribes, the were greeted with excitement and gained more and more allies as they went along. Still, the task was far from easy, continuing to require the utmost courage and persistence. Consider with me now, as Houston does in her book, the gifts these two men brought to their work.

First was the power of vision, a vision of New Mind, embodying a triple message of Righteousness, Health, and Power. Isn't this exactly what we are developing in our efforts toward mental health liberation — a message of truth and fairness, of accurate understanding and support for the natural process of psychological growth and healing, of reclaiming authentic personal power? Our Peacemakers asked the people to share in cocreation of this vision in thought and action. Isn't this what empowerment and destruction of traditional professional expert/unknowing lay person, doctor/patient, paternal authority/childlike victim roles of our mental health system is all about. Don't you love the name (National Empowerment Center) and telephone number (1-800-POWER-2-U) of one of our main advocacy organizations?

  Houston considers timing to be the second gift of the Peacemakers. The ability to "recognize and seize the open moment" is a crucial element of change. Deganawidah arrived at a time of profound need for his people, but he knew not only when to act, but when and how to wait. It is a tremendous challenge to manage our energies well in the face of a deeply felt need to change things, inwardly or out in the world. We can rush in too quickly without adequate preparation, out of desperation and urgency, and set ourselves up for failure. We can push ourselves into exhaustion trying to make untenable situations work, or by neglecting the rudiments of self-care. We can be harsh and demanding on ourselves when we most need gentleness and compassion. Patience and gradualness are so often the keywords as we challenge a pressured drivenness. The fact is that, in today's world, a "masculine" drive to control and dominate, though bringing us the fruits of technological progress, has gotten severely toxic (and can show up in our radical grassroots or reform organizations, mirroring that which we challenge, perpetrating the destruction internally which we outwardly challenge). This is clearly reflected in so many ways, in our cruel proliferation of military armaments, in our degradation of the environment, in our gross excess materialism, and most certainly in psychiatry's reliance on force, coercion, and technological assault. Our world is way out of balance; we desperately need to reawaken to the "feminine" energies of nurturance, gentleness, patience, and receptivity. Decisive action must be balanced with comfort and ease in resting, waiting, and nurturing ourselves and each other.

Creativity was another wonderful gift of the Peacemaker's troupe. They came singing songs, telling stories sharing symbols and ceremonies to inspire and upli the people. It reminds me of Creativity Night at Janet Foner's Mental Health System Survivor workshops, or of the poetry in 'Dendron' or so many of the other print resources in the psychiatric survivor movement. We need creative energy, brought forth in a spirit of joy, love, and glory to sustain us all.

Despite the constant hype in media advertising of all the myriad forms of instant pleasure and gratification, the truth remains that most things which truly nourish the bo and soul require sustained time and effort. Fast food promotes death; to nourish our bodies well, we are require to spend time in planning, growing or shopping for food, and preparing balanced meals. Our bodies are nourished n by time spent in front of the television eating TV dinners, but by the fruits of a hearth-centered home. Our minds ar nourished not by TV and print news, and other mainstrea media nonsense, but by thoughts and ideas possessing depth, and which take time and effort to assimilate. The Peacemakers' work was not about soundbites and spin control and Pollyanna magical instantaneous remaking of the world by switching the channel. Theirs was the enduring challenge of persistent, person-to-person, village-to-village, tribe-to-tribe work; garnering allies, one person at a time, one small group at a time, one village, one tribe; gradualness. Support Coalition International (SCI) is the mental health liberation movement's own version of the developing Iroquois Confederation. SCI was founded by David Oaks and Janet Foner, living examples of the type of persistent and inspiring leadership demonstrated by Deganawidah and Hiawatha.

    Jean Houston asserts, and I agree, that the most potent gifts of the Peacemaker were their everpresent sense of gratitude and reverence for life, and the ceremonies of condolence and quickening. This ceremony offered for the first time a way out of the vicious cycle of vengeance and retaliation in which these peoples were caught. Deganawidah entered a world where bloody raids and retribution were a way of life. To mourn the grievous loss of one's beloved in ceremony, and to be gently reminded that it is possible to bring one's mind back out of the pain and into the creativity of life, allowed for an incredible change. Rather than act out the unhealed pain by inflicting it on others, one could be supported to express the grief, to feel the loving concern of others, and to remember the inherent beauty of human nature. Today, we live in a world where forced incarceration and "treatment" by toxic drugs and brain-damaging electroshock are considered customary and usual standards of psychiatric medical care. Psychiatry's response to emotional pain is to subdue it, to punish those who somehow show their suffering or their dissatisfaction with the way things are. Isn't this what Tadodaho and those who embodied his ways did to Hiawatha and to everyone? The ceremony of condolence and quickening reflects profound understanding that vengeance and retaliation, like all harmful patterns of human behavior, are the result of psychological trauma. And that this distressed condition is not at all as hopeless as it feels. Not only is it not necessary to suppress the traumatic experience, it is harmful to do so for suppression unnecessarily perpetuates a dangerous and vicious cycle. This ceremony works because it facilitates th natural tendency of human beings to heal from trauma by expressing and releasing its hurtful effects with the supportive attention of a caring, aware and awake human being. This is what psychiatry should be offering to people who reach out for help. And this is what mental health professionals, like all human beings, need in order to remember and express their own True Faces.

Wholehearted Commitment

The Peacemakers were as determined and tenacious as the were creative and full of the spirit. This is how they managed to create a League including all the chiefs of five nations — the Mohawks, the Oneidas, the Onondagas, th Cayugas, and the Senecas — all but one, that is, the dread Onondaga wizard chief, Tadodaho.

Years of incredibly challenging, and at times tragical painful, work had brought them to a place where they we surrounded by a circle of allies, ready to face their major challenge. Without Tadodaho's compliance, the Iroquois could not have true peace.

"He stood for everything that obstructed the way of peace: tremendous negative charisma; static and unmovin power; autocracy, including the inner autocracy of the eg unwillingness to change; hunger for power and control; a the deep wounding that leads a person to wound the rest of the world. Tadodaho was so twisted he wanted the rest of the world to be twisted. Since time out of mind, humans have believed that it is possible to destroy an enemy to win our goals. Tadodaho, however, was indestructible; he could be neither killed nor nullified. This story teaches us, then, that so-called enemies need not be destroyed; they can be transformed.

Guided by the Mother of Nations (Jigonhsasee, the feminine principle), Deganawidah and Hiawatha prepared to use a combination of therapeutic methods on Tadodaho, including massage, singing and chanting, realigning his energies, a medicine ceremony, and political persuasion.

"Come," Deganawidah said to Hiawatha, "you and I alone shall go first to the great wizard. I shall sing the Peace Song; you will explain the words of the law holding the wampum in your hand. If we straighten his mind, the Longhouse will be completed and our work accomplished." We can imagine the careful preparations the two heroes made for this all-or-nothing encounter. The stakes had never been higher.

Entering their canoe, Deganawidah and Hiawatha began paddling across the lake. When they were about halfway across, they heard the voice of Tadodaho keening a fearsome chant, "ASONKE-NE-E-E-E-EH?" ("Is it not yet?")

"Ah,"joked Hiawatha, "he is impatient for our message."

Almost immediately, raging winds and waves, sent by Tadodaho as if in answer to his questioning cry, began to buffet the canoe. The wild elements were accompanied by the wizard's screaming declaration, "ASONKE-NE-E-E-E-EH!" ("It is not yet!") (20)

We can see what courage and determination it would take to keep canoeing in the face of raging winds and waves. Are you familiar with the psychologically equivalent storms of emotional resistance to change and progress, inside yourself or in those whom you encounter? Fortunately our heroes did not lose heart, but dug deep within and kept going. And notice that Tadodaho's first chant is a question, his second a scream of defiance. Do you recognize the tendency to desire change, and then to impatiently close your mind and heart to avoid the tension of possible failure or yet again another disappointment? In the face of such tense and fearful ambivalence, one must remain steadfast and persevere. For me, the lesson here is about the need for commitment, for whole-hearted decision to go for it, to take a risk, to stand by someone in trouble, to speak truth to power, to bear the fears and tensions of living in the unknown regions of unfamiliar thought, feeling and action. To what and to whom am I committed? And what is the level of that commitment? The pain, the recalcitrance, the doubt and uncertainty, the myriad faces of resistance to change are part and parcel of transformation of self and society. Deep commitment is absolutely necessary to withstand the pull of the old familiar, the seductive offering of the immediate pleasures of our materialistic culture, or the promised relief of mind and mood-altering pharmaceuticals. These promises of paradise serve the masters of the status quo, guaranteeing continuation of your private hell, under the illusion that settling for less is what will make you happy.

Creative Reconciliation

Besides commitment, great creativity is required to provide experiences which open new doors for people, which help us to see and understand the world in new and different ways. For one of my own nephews who had been abandoned by his father and sexually abused by a YMCA counselor, his mother and grandmother intervened upon his release from a weekend in jail where he almost killed a man in self-defense. They sent him to live for awhile in Southern Chile on his aunt's farm. While there, he went with his uncle into town and they stopped for awhile at a local cantina for a beer. He later told his aunt that, sitting at that bar, just hanging out with his uncle and a bunch of Chilean men, he suddenly experienced the world in a new and different way. He said that for the first time he could recall he felt safe with a group of men; he could let down his guard and relax. Our story continues.

In this spirit, Deganawidah and Hiawatha went to the wizard, and Deganawidah sang the Peace Hymn. As soon as he had finished the song, Deganawidah approached Tadodaho and began to soothe him by massaging his body with sacred herbs in a holy medicine ceremony designed to heal mind and body.

Then, holding the strands of wampum which were by this point richly beaded with the contributions of the allies, Hiawatha said, "These are the words of the Great Law. On these words we shall build the House of Peace, the Longhouse, with five fires, that is yet one household. These are the words of Righteousness and Health and Power. These are the words of the renewal of ourselves and our society."

For a moment Tadodaho was drawn to the vision, but then he said, "No! No! What is this nonsense about houses and righteousness and health and power?"

Deganawidah responded, "The words we bring constitute the New Mind which is the will of the Holder of the Heavens. There shall be Righteousness when people desire justice, Health when people obey cooperative reason and Power when people accept the Great Peace. These things shall be given form in the longhouse, where five nations shall live in harmony as one family."

Then he said a remarkable thing, "At this very place, Tadodaho, where the chiefs of five nations shall assemble, I shall plant the Great Tree of Peace, and its roots shall extend to far places of the earth so that all humankind may have the shelter of the Great Law, the Great Peace."

Again Tadodaho was drawn to the vision, but then he retreated to his usual state of self-aggrandizement, saying, "What is that to me?" — in other words, "What's in it for me?"

Then Deganawidah spoke words to the effect of "You shall be of higher usefulness in this world." He said, "You yourself shall tend the council fire of the Five Nations, the fire that never dies." To be the Fire Keeper was essentially to be the chief sachem.

"And the smoke of that fire that you are tending shall reach the sky and be seen of all people" — in other words, we are offering you the opportunity to use your tremendous talents for a higher good. (21)

It is important to take note here, as Houston does in her narrative, that the Peacemakers show no retribution or punishment toward Tadodaho; rather, they acted according to the deep truths of their guiding vision, a system of belief both practical and profound. It was practical in that the world needed this man's enormous power and skill, the ability to harness and direct energy in awesome ways. It was profound in being deeply rooted in the knowledge that every human being is inherently precious and valuable, no matter how crooked and twisted they may have become. Theirs was a practical spirituality which had the methods and resources necessary to facilitate redemption and transformation, determined that, ultimately, not one soul will be lost.

Utterly startled by these words, Tadodaho said, "Where's the power to bring it to pass? How could that happen?" Then he began to howl, "ASONKE-NE-E-E-E-EH!" ("It is not yet.")

Whereupon Hiawatha and Deganawidah turned around, jumped into the canoe, and paddled away like mad. Deganawidah said, 'Let's hurry, because this is the time. This is the open moment. We've got him now.'

When they neared the middle of the lake, they heard Tadodaho's voice rush out to meet them. "ASONKE-NE-E-E-E-EH!" ("It is not yet.") The winds lifted the waves against their canoe, but they persisted in their efforts and soon reached the other shore. They signaled the assembled people from the tribes that had agreed to the Peace. The wizard's cry still ringing in their ears, they launched a flotilla of canoes and hastened back across the lake to reach the wizard's camp. All these people gathered before Tadodaho, as if to say, "You asked about the power to bring this to pass. Here is Power."

Bringing him forward, Deganawidah introduced Tadodaho to the assembled people. Perhaps Tadodaho looked less ferocious because he was reeling from the effects of Deganawidah's proposal that he serve instead of terrify. Deganawidah told Tadodaho that the people in front of hi* represented the nations who had subscribed to the new League.

Tadodaho asked, "All these people?"

"All these people. And, Tadodaho, they are willing to acknowledge you as preserver of their council fire."

Another chief spoke, indicating with a sweep of the hand the assembly, the warriors, and especially Jigonhsase* the Peace Woman, the Mother of Nations, who also came forward: "These chiefs and this great woman, our mother, have all agreed to submit the Good News of Peace and Power to you. If you are able to approve and confirm this message, you will be the keeper of the fire of our confederate council. You will have a higher usefulness."

And then Deganawidah said to him, "Behold, my friend! Here is the power. These are the Five Nations. Their strength is greater than your strength, but their voi* can be your voice when you speak in council, and all peop* shall hear you. This shall be your strength in the future — not sorcery, but the will and creativity of a united people.*

Tadodaho finally broke his silence and said, "It is we* I now truly confirm and accept your message."

Thus the mind of Tadodaho was at last made straigh* Then Hiawatha, He Who Combs, combed the mattings, the twistings, the snakes out of the wizard's hair, and Deganawidah rubbed his body with wampum and herbs, with knowledge and with love. As Deganawidah massage* him, he straightened the seven crooks in Tadodaho's body the crooks that had filled him with such hatred.

Many mythic traditions tell the story of a monster v* is a powerful genius yet who hates and twists the world because he is so twisted. What is so deeply beautiful abou* this story is that, unlike many similar tales, here there is no battle done with the monster or dragon. Deganawidah and Hiawatha do not slay Tadodaho. Instead they heal him and enlist his help. The message seems to be that no face is so false that there is not truth within it, no life so twisted that it cannot be made straight.

Finally, Deganawidah addressed Tadodaho in his state of New Mind and openness, straightened, combed, massaged, healed, and made whole: "The work is finished; your mind is made straight; your head is now combed; the seven crooks have been taken from your body. Now you too have the New Mind. You shall from this time preside over the council, and you shall strive in all ways to make reason and the peaceful mind prevail. Your voice shall be the voice of the Great Law; all people shall hear you and find peace."

And with these final words the evil spirit left Tadodaho completely, and he bowed, "I accept your message, and I thank you."

Thus Deganawidah healed the wicked one, while Hiawatha combed the snakes from his hair. Together they invested the former monster with noble usefulness." (22)

There you have the culmination of a legendary story of peacemaking and reconciliation. The evil wizard is utterly transformed, and a group of vengeful, warring tribes has become the Iroquois Confederation. Houston has a final chapter to her book which shares a few of the principles which allow this Confederacy to democratically function in an ongoing way. There are ritual ceremonies such as "burying the hatchet" of grievance and retaliation. There are the wampum beads which carry the memory of agreed-upon traditions, laws, procedures, and other safeguards which ensure the rights and respect of individuals. The

Peacemaker also laid down teachings about leadership such as the notion that a leader's skin should be "seven thumbs thick," so as to be able to consider criticism without personal affront. You may not know that the "founding fathers" of the United States were influenced by the Iroquois Confederacy in forming our Constitution and government.

This story is a treasure of symbolic wisdom for challenging and transforming oppression, particularly the outer and internalized forms of psychiatric oppression. The Peacemaker reminds us that we must always remember our True Faces, our inherently good human nature, as a starting point. He reminds us that even the most atrocious evil does not contradict the truth of our loving essence; human harm doing is always the result of the unaware acting-out of distress resulting from past unhealed hurts. He teaches us the importance of allowing and encouraging emotional healing, and how this is what brings us to New Mind, to a clear mind and loving heart. As with Hiawatha, our first task is to take care of ourselves. The story also makes it clear, however, that ultimately it is not enough to merely focus on ourselves. Deeper healing requires acting on the truth of our complete connectedness. It means not only facing our individual pasts, particularly those who have harmed us, but also facing oppression wherever it hurts anyone.

My own thoughts at this moment are on the phenomenal people who are forming what we call the mental health liberation movement — psychiatric survivors and allies of various persuasions. It needs to be repeatedly acknowledged how remarkable it is that thousands of people have come together to take a stand against the very ones who purported to be their benevolent caregivers. In any legitimate branch of medicine, the profession would be expected to take notice and action. In psychiatry, such a movement stirs scapegoating, name-calling and resistance. Nevertheless, it is happening, it is growing, and it is having an effect. The Peacemaker story emphasizes that such an auspicious goal as this movement has, to transform society and the profession of psychiatry, is an awesome and heroic challenge. The story acknowledges that lives are lost and that the work is long and arduous.

The Peacemaker legend also clearly reveals, in the transformation of Tadodaho, that a very large circle of allies is absolutely necessary to really get to the heart of the beast. Creative, persistent, one person, one group, one coalition at a time, embracing the New Mind. We need to acknowledge and value each painstaking baby step of each individual, even as we hold the biggest picture in our minds. We must strongly resist the pressure to separate and divide within ourselves. This is what Deganawidah and Hiawatha faced as they tried to convince warring chiefs to unite around a common cause of Peace. It is what we face as we come together with unique histories and fears and doubts and suspicions. We need to continually clarify, take hold and embrace our common ground. At the very least, this common ground should include active resistance to all forms of coercion, active resistance to the belief system of biopsychiatry and its practices of electroshock and drugging of children, encouragement of genuine support and asylum for individuals to heal from the effects of hurt, and ongoing, creative remembrance of the truth of our inherent nature as human beings. This present-day story of transforming the degraded state of psychiatric oppression into a loving state of human relatedness is a legend in the making.

CHAPTER 16
THE REALITY OF
ALTERNATIVES

Service is a natural, even necessary expression to be fully alive and vital. When I think of service, I think of the River Jordan and how it flows into the Sea of Galilee teaming with life. The Sea of Galilee then flows into the Dead Sea, brackish and without life. What makes the Dead Sea dead? It is the fact that it has no outlet, no outpouring of the flow which fills it. We humans are like that. We are renewed daily with life energy; the sun shines and the rain pours down its waters on all of us, good or evil. But in order to thrive as individuals, we must extend the energy we receive to those around us. Without that expression, if we don't actually die, we lose something of our aliveness. And what good for us as individuals is also good for the whole. The simple truth is that we are all in this together, and we need each other to live well. So we must keep reaching for ways to help each other.

A discussion of alternatives can be tricky. Consider a experience that I have had since publication of my book, 'The Wildest Colts Make the Best Horses', which include strong critique of the widespread administration of stimulant drugs (e.g., Ritalin) to school-age children label as Attention Deficit Hyperactivity Disorder (ADHD). Sin publication, I have received many calls and letters, and several testimonial tapes offering products marketed as "alternatives to Ritalin for ADHD kids." While I encoura families to experiment with nutritional supplementation i world where it is difficult to get adequate, much less superior, nutrition from natural food alone, the thrust of these marketing efforts is not at all in line with the message of the book. In 'The Wildest Colts', I challenge the very existence of ADHD as a "mental disease." How can you "treat" a non-existent disease? The danger with the "alternatives to Ritalin" approach is that, while nutritional supplements are generally much more desirable than stimulants, the underlying assumption that the problem rests in the biology of the child easily remains intact; the idea of alternatives validates that ADHD is a real disease and Ritalin a real treatment.

Similarly, consideration of "alternatives to ECT" is an insult to all survivors of this barbaric practice as it legitimizes the notion that "mental illnesses" exist that warrant dramatic, even barbaric "treatments," and that ECT is a genuine medical alternative. It remains all too easy to avoid taking responsibility to inquire further into societal influences at every level. Labeling the individual acts to prevent examination and challenge of the status quo. So I offer my thoughts not as "alternatives to drugs and ECT," but with the hope of contributing to clearer thinking about how we can best support each other in growing, changing and making it through crises in living.

Types of Support

Judy Chamberlain considers that a true alternative must break through the need to distinguish between those who give and those who receive help; she points out that the vast majority of so-called alternatives continue to make this distinction, are in fact based on the idea that some of us who

don't need help can help those who do. Chamberlain's view
is that it is absolutely necessary to exclude professionals
because they use a model of helping which separates helper
and helped. She further observes that non-professionals
who believe in "mental illness" also tend to interfere with
consciousness raising because of their "mentalist" attitudes
Her experience is that people labeled as mental patients
need to form their own separate support alternatives to
create the necessary safety and space for consciousness
raising. (1) I agree that a helpful step in recovery for any
hurt and stigmatized group of people is to spend time in a
working group of others who share a common problem.
The enduring success of Alcoholics Anonymous is a prime
example. A safe place to work through fear and shame
associated with hurt and stigmatization is vital to recovery

Rigid separation of people into "sick helpees" and
"well helpers" is oppressive. For practical purposes and as
step toward recovery and empowerment, separation by life
roles and experiences is important. However, the real issu
involves abolition not only of these roles, but of three
fundamentally erroneous, related ideas:

1/ that some people need help and support and that
others don't;
2/ that those who need help are qualitatively differe
(i.e., mentally ill) than those who do not;
3/ that "mentally healthy" professionals know bette
than their "patients" what kind of help is needed.

Once these ideas are forsaken, the truth remains: th
we all need as much help as we can get, that we all have h
times and are vulnerable to hurts and hardships, and that
are all in this together. It is important for mental health

professionals to admit that we are all doing well to manage
our own lives, much less pretend to know what is best for
anyone else.

Our professionally-based mental health system needs
eventually to be abandoned in favor of an egalitarian system
of reciprocity and mutual support. This is, of course, the
ideal of a wise and compassionate community. In the highest
level of community, no need would exist for a mental health
system; creative and flexible response to individual needs
would flow naturally from strong bonds of support,
affection and interweaving of lives.

It is not remarkable that more and more people are
turning to the mental health system and its biopsychiatric
practices for help with life. Given today's fragmented urban-
industrial world, what is remarkable is that so many manage
to get by without it. Many even have enough extra energy to
be thinking about and building intentional communities
designed to meet human needs in a creative way.

Levels of Need

A useful discussion of alternatives for support of
psychological upheaval and personal transformation must
consider differing levels of need that individuals experience.
It must be guided by a clear understanding of the
psychological experience of human beings, and especially
the process of losing and regaining harmony, balance and
intelligence. Re-evaluation Counseling provides one such
theory. RC's understanding of and emphasis on the value
and necessity of emotional expression as a natural human
recovery mechanism is a direct contradiction to and a most
significant correction of the misguided, oppressive practices

of biopsychiatry.

In 'Broken Brains or Wounded Hearts', psychologist Ty Colbert presents an "emotional pain model" of psychological distress, and does a superb job of contrasting this with the views of biopsychiatry. He outlines a three-phase psychiatric model:

Phase I	Experiencing emotional pain
Phase II	Symptoms emerge
Phase III	Psychiatric intervention
Outcome	Possible life-long disability

Simply put, an individual experiences emotional pain from mild to major abuse. When these hurts are not resolved in a good way, a time comes when the individual begins to exhibit behaviors reflective of emotional overload. Psychiatry calls these "symptoms," and, according to Colbert, "Phase III is where biopsychiatry can become quite dangerous and seductive." (2) As I have chronicled throughout this book, the dangers come from psychiatry's coercion and harmful use of drugs and electroshock. The seduction, discussed most vividly in Chapter 11, "On the Taking of Psychiatric Drugs," lies in the desperate need for help and for relief from feelings of shame and guilt.

Now I will consider solutions to each of Colbert's three phases.

Phase I: Basic Life Support

It is important to take good care of ourselves and ou

children, and to learn to recognize and respond positively to the pain all children confront as they are growing up. This involves good information for parents and educators about the inherent nature of human beings, the effects of being hurt, and the process of healing from these hurts. Simple aware attention, allowing for our natural recovery process to work its "magic" via emotional expression, resolves most of the need for dealing with later interventions. It is the foundation of human relatedness, family life and education in a society. Thus, it is desirable for all of us to examine our lives and the lives we provide for our children in terms of what is provided to support and enhance development in each of these four basic domains: physical, emotional, mental and spiritual.

My view is that the center of human nature lies in our spiritual heart, that our challenge is always to discover and develop awareness of Spirit and to be guided by Spirit in daily life. For children and for all of us to some degree, physical , emotional and mental well-being, in about that order, needs to be established prior to a primary focus on spiritual development. Our emotions are not more important than our physical or mental needs; all three of these levels are vitally important. It's just that in our particular culture, we seem to give more credence to physical and mental development, and to neglect or deliberately suppress the emotions. So it makes sense to put some emphasis on this fundamental and misunderstood level of our being, especially in the context of a discussion of psychiatry, psychology, and response to human distress. The truth is that we need to routinely exercise and develop every level of our being.

Physical self-care: This means taking care of your body. Healthy nutrition, plenty of rest, and gentle exercise are key components. There is work to do, however, in challenging and overcoming distortions related to gender conditioning (e.g., male conditioning to push the body too hard and "play with pain"; female conditioning to deny and fail to develop physical power).

Emotional self-care: As mentioned above, this realm is sorely neglected and misunderstood. Particularly unfortunate is that mental health professionals are often ignorant of the impact of emotional hurts on psychological well-being, and of the importance of emotional expression in the recovery process. Fundamentally, emotional self-care means support for our feelings and opportunities to express them safely.

Mental self-care: This area is granted some credence in our culture; however, it also tends to be distorted. Self-directed intellectual development tends to be stifled by our compulsory age-graded educational system, and by overemphasis on marketplace considerations. Demands for production take precedence over time for personal study, reading and reflection not directly related to school/college education.

Spiritual exercise: Our culture pays homage to outer religious form, but tends to neglect the inner life. Some form of prayer, meditation, contemplation, or other inward devotional practice is most highly encouraged.

Here is a short list of possible self-care activities to stimulate your thinking. Be creative and do what works for you.

Call a friend
Take a walk
Go for a swim
Meditate
Read inspiring literature

Prepare a meal
Play with your child (or someone else's)
Take a bath
Take a nap
Plant a flower or tend your garden
Listen to your favorite music
Write in your journal
Get a massage
Ride your bike
Stretch or do yoga
Do an RC co-counseling session
Attend a support group or workshop

Phase II: Good Counseling

Even those critical of psychiatry present a range of opinion regarding the value of professional counseling, or psychotherapy. Leonard Frank's dictum is "Abolish involuntary psychiatry, abandon voluntary psychiatry." I agree with this slogan as it applies to biopsychiatry. Leonard includes in psychiatry the practice of psychotherapy, and agrees with Judy Chamberlain that the inherent separation between helper and helped outweighs the potential good in specific instances. In his view it is clear, to paraphrase the words of Thomas Szasz, that reforming psychiatric treatment of "mental illness" is like reforming slavery; it has to be abolished. I myself have made my living for many years as a "psychotherapist," and think of myself as one who has some understanding of emotional recovery and has helped a number of individuals along the way. Peter Breggin, in 'Toxic Psychiatry', presents a thoughtful exposition of these issues, concluding that "I am not yet ready to reject the concept of a profession of psychotherapy." (3) Professional psychotherapists such as Breggin, Ty Colbert and myself must continue to examine ourselves and challenge the notion that it is easier for a camel to go through the eye of a needle than for an individual to clearly examine the ethics of his livelihood. agree with Breggin that state licensure and control of the practice of counseling should be abolished. Licensing boards do not protect the people; they protect the interest of the state and of the professionals. After all, every biopsychiatrist is heavily credentialled and licensed by th state.

The desired goal is a society where attention is not commodity, and all of us are adept at counseling in the generic sense of supporting each others' well-being, emotional recoveries and personal transformation. Professional counseling may be thought of as a helpful transition step, the goal in mind always to assume an attitude and practice of mutual reciprocity when able. All services must always be voluntary.

We must de-mystify the major "symptoms" of emotional distress and the context in which they develop and understand how to deal with them when they begin t appear; for example, not panicking when someone begins hear voices. The level of need is greater, not because "symptoms of mental illness" have manifested, but becau of emotional overload. Response to an individual at this level of need (with the condition met that they want your help) tends to be most helpful when there is a clear understanding of the life of the emotions, and of principl and techniques for assisting people with emotional expression. More important than theory and method, however, is the presence of someone who is respectful, understanding and compassionate. Full, relaxed attention

90 percent of the work.

Re-evaluation Counseling

The best work I know of that teaches both an accurate theory of human nature and recovery from hurts, on the one hand, and a method of reciprocal support , on the other, is the Re-evaluation Counseling Community (RC). RC is a grassroots peer counseling program that not only operates completely outside the mental health system, but even teaches incisive theory on mental health system oppression. Here is a description of RC from the back of the RC journal, 'Present Time':

"Re-evaluation Counseling is a process whereby people of all ages and of all backgrounds can learn how to exchange effective help with each other in order to free themselves from the effects of past distress experiences.

Re-evaluation Counseling theory provides a model of what a human being can be like in the area of his/her interaction with other human beings and his/her environment. The theory assumes that everyone is born with tremendous intellectual potential, zest, and lovingness, but that these qualities have become blocked and obscured in adults as the result of accumulated distress experiences (fear, hurt, loss, pain, anger, embarrassment, etc.) which began early in our lives.

Any young person would recover from such distress spontaneously by use of the natural process of emotional discharge (crying, trembling, raging, laughing, etc.). However, this natural process is usually interfered with by well-meaning people ("Don't cry," "Be a big boy," etc.) who erroneously equate the emotional discharge (the healing of the hurt) with the hurt itself.

When adequate emotional discharge can take place, the person is freed from the rigid pattern of behavior and feeling left by the hurt. The basic loving, cooperative, intelligent, and zestful nature is then free to operate. Such a person will tend to be more effective in looking out for his or her own interests and the interests of others, and will be more capable of acting successfully against injustice.

In recovering and using the natural discharge process two people take turns counseling and being counseled. The one acting as the counselor listens, draws the other out, and permits, encourages, and assists emotional discharge. The one acting as client talks and discharges and re-evaluates. With experience and increased confidence and trust in each other, the process works better and better."

I have had good experience with RC and recommend it highly. At the same time, I must point out that the RC community has not come close to overcoming the need for separate places of recovery for psychiatric survivors. RC is made up of regular people who are as susceptible as any of us to "mentalist" attitudes; of greater importance, they have not yet developed the degree of resource that is sometimes necessary to deal with an individual in extreme crisis or who has been badly hurt by psychiatry, suffering from the effects of electroshock, caught in the throes of addictive and debilitating drugs, and/or trapped in the illusion that they are an inherently defective, "chronically mentally ill" person. Nevertheless, the RC community does great work and is continuing to move forward in this domain. A significant new piece of RC theory involves identification and reaching out to those "targeted for destruction by society;" these include the homeless, those condemned to prison, and, of course, those labeled as "mentally ill." Janet Foner is the International Reference Person for Mental Health Liberation in RC; she has written an excellent pamphlet on mental health system oppression, and also edited Recovery and Re-Emergence, an RC journal on mental health liberation. (4)

Trauma Recovery

There is one significant psychiatric contribution in the field of psychological healing that I want to share here. The theory and practice of trauma recovery work is an exceedingly useful window of rationality within psychiatry. It implies just what it says — recovery from the effects of trauma. Trauma recovery work is framed as a response to a problem called post-traumatic stress disorder or PTSD. I have repeatedly lamented the harm caused by stigmatizing individuals with labels of so-called mental illness, and I have decried the rapid increase in numbers of these "illnesses" with each addition of psychiatry's 'Diagnostic and Statistical Manual' (DSM). Aphrodite Matsakis, who authored one of the better books on trauma recovery, 'I Can't Get Over It', (5) points out something very interesting about the DSM. Of all the hundreds of listed psychiatric problems, PTSD is the only one that places the origin of symptoms on external events, in contrast to the overwhelming emphasis on individual personality defects. PTSD is the only diagnosis which acknowledges that its symptoms can happen to any human being, given sufficient trauma. So the theory is congruent with what I have presented in this book. Psychological distress is not about human defect, in biology or personality; it is the effect of being hurt, and it can happen to anyone. The "symptoms," mentally, emotionally and physically can be severe enough to qualify for virtually every other DSM diagnosis.

Trauma recovery is presented as a process, not of controlling an incurable "mental illness," but of healing from the effects of having been hurt. Various authors present slightly different stages of recovery work. I like Judith Herman's model presented in 'Trauma and Recovery', (6) which describes three basic stages — Safety, Remembrance, and Mourning, and Reconnection with ordinary life. A trauma victim must have safety to heal. And healing comes through the arduous work of remembering and mourning, telling one's story like Hiawatha did to the Peacemaker, and feeling the feelings. At some point, there comes a sense that, in Herman's words, "I know I have myself," and the task is to reconnect with others and the world — the Hero's Return after Withdrawal.

Saying Goodbye

Another counseling model which has proven most useful and effective to me was a gift from my friend and teacher, Dan Jones, outlined in his booklet, 'Saying Goodbye: Ten Steps for Closing A Relationship.' (7) The ten steps, designed for grieving a loss and completing relationships, are valuable guidelines for virtually all counseling. I share them here to amplify the central proce of Remembrance and Mourning in recovery from trauma:

1/ Moving out of Denial into Awareness. One must acknowledge a problem, "something wrong about us as w naturally stand," to make the all-important decision to he
2/ Moving out of Shock into Feeling. We must feel and express the feelings in order to heal. Dan's realization

was that when his clients told a shocking story without feeling, or were staying stuck in their recovery, it was often because they were still in shock and nobody realized it. He developed a beautiful process for gently coming out of shock and re-discovering the ability to feel.

3/ Moving out of Hopelessness into Confidence. After shock, chronic hopelessness is the most likely pattern to impede progress. This pattern pervades everything including, of course, counseling. Seeds of possibility that it truly can get better must be planted for the tree of recovery to grow.

4/ Moving out of Fear into Safety. Able to feel and armed with a ray of hope, numbing terror thaws into vividly experienced fear. Affirmation of the present-time reality that it is safe to heal, to remember, to feel, to let go, etc., can help to discharge fear.

5/ Moving out of Anger into Forgiveness. This step is not about pushing a victim into premature forgiveness. It's just that anger is virtually always a big part of griefwork and emotional healing, and anger may be the single most avoided feeling. Permission to feel, and encouragement to release anger is very important. Dan offers a statement of forgiveness as a surefire way to bring up anger, frustration, resentment, etc. When you say, in role play, to someone who has hurt you, "I forgive you completely for everything," you will discover the anger, and the discharge work can begin.

6/ Moving out of Guilt into Self-forgiveness. This is the flip-side of step five. The beginning direction is "I forgive myself completely for everything with whom or whatever."

7/ Moving out of Shame into Self-Appreciation. I discussed this, and fear and hopelessness, in some detail in

Chapter 11, in the section on emotional recovery work.

Dan's last three steps are what he calls the positive one they are:

8/ Gratitude and Appreciation.
9/ Love.
10/ Farewell and Release.

Steps 8 and 9 may not be relevant to healing from ve abusive relationships or certain kinds of traumas, but letti go and moving on always is. This means having your ener available again to reconnect with life, to make choices whi are supportive and empowering. I highly recommend Dan booklet, and I also recommend Bass and Davis' book, 'Th Courage To Heal'. (8) I like it that neither mentions the term PTSD or any psychiatric diagnosis for that matter. The issue is emotional healing or trauma recovery, plain a simple.

None of the books I have mentioned in this section trauma recovery has a word to say about psychiatric oppression and related trauma, except for caveats about sexual misconduct by a therapist. It is imperative to keep i mind the truth that our mental health system can pervert even the best theory and intentions, as the following stori illustrate.

Sally was a client who came to me for psychotherap with the primary problem identified as an unusual phenomenon in which she had "spells," lapses of consciousness averaging about fifteen minutes, almost ev hour. Sally had a series of electroshock "treatments" abou nine months previously in Ohio, after which the spells stopped for six months. Then they came back, worse tha ever, and this was so overwhelming and distressing that she was considering another round of shocks. Her concerned psychiatrist, from whom I was renting office space, referred her to me as a last-ditch alternative. She was also on five different psychiatric drugs at this time.

After working for a short while with Sally, it became obvious that her psychiatric crisis, precipitated by the breakup of a long-term marriage, involved emergence of long-repressed sexual trauma. She made a little progress, weaned off the drugs, and I supported her in a decision to enter a nationally renowned sexual trauma unit in a well-known freestanding addiction treatment facility in New Mexico. I had personally spoken with some of the program staff, including the psychologist, who assured me that they would view my client's "spells" as within the continuum of dissociation and that their philosophy was drug-free; they most certainly did not approve of electroshock for the healing of trauma victims.

Sally arrived at the treatment facility and continued to have some "spells." The facility's consultant psychiatrist counseled Sally to receive electroshock as an adjunct to her treatment. I found out and intervened. Sally was discharged, returned to Austin, and together we managed to undo the damage and continue her work. She worked with me for five years, unemployed and utterly "unproductive" economically. Fortunately, she had a divorce settlement which paid the bills during this intense period of withdrawal for her heroic recovery. After 25 years of being supported financially by her ex-husband's income (as a housewife, then during the five years after her divorce), she has now been stably employed for six years in the field of electronics. The story of my response to the New Mexico facility is told elsewhere. (9) One result was that the psychiatrist was replaced as

Sally's case forced the facility to deal with a situation so obviously incongruous with their stated policy.

Another woman, Linda, came to me having been on psychiatric drugs for nine years, on several at that time. In the six months before we met, she had lost her job, attempted suicide, been committed to a psychiatric hospital and "treated" with electroshock. She too was a trauma survivor, a victim of persistent physical and sexual abuse throughout her childhood. She was so terrified that just the thought of physical touch sent her into an experience of numb terror. Linda needed and wanted safe asylum; she felt desperate and self-destructive; abuse memories were beginning to surface. Within two weeks, she was admitted to a psychiatric hospital in San Antonio which purported to do trauma recovery work. Within two days of admission, she was caught in the proverbial catch-22; as she began to reveal the depth of her despair and suicidal feelings, which she had to do in order to heal, she began to lose her freedom. When she considered leaving, the responsible psychiatrist let her know that he would seek to change her status there from "voluntary" to involuntary. No doubt he was doing what he thought right and necessary; certainly, as he told me directly, he was liable in the eyes of the law. Regardless, Linda quickly discovered the truth that psychiatry is rooted in coercion. So long as the threat of involuntary commitment exists, there can be no truly voluntary commitment. The issue is the same whether the institution is public or private. Linda's saving grace was th even in her great despair, she had at least a modicum of awareness and common sense to respond in a way that promoted her survival. She was able to play the game well enough to gain release within three weeks, and even to lea a little more about herself in the meanwhile. In a similar situation, Cindy (Chapter 1) chose to fight and then succumbed, at least for this phase, to the identity her psychiatric perpetrators forced upon her. She could not get outside her pain enough to see the reality of psychiatric oppression, and play the game well enough to get out of harm's way. Linda did, and I continued to support her on the path of her painful recovery. I am happy to report that she completed a degree in journalism, is working as a writer, off all psychiatric drugs and loving herself more all the time.

Both Sally's and Linda's diagnoses were the key to third-party insurance reimbursement for "treatment." That sword cuts both ways. It helped pay me for counseling; it also got them into the hospitals whose very structure put them at risk. We know a lot now about the nature of human trauma and emotional healing, yet it seems more and more of us are believing the lies of biopsychiatric propaganda. Thomas Szasz, as he is wont to do, speaks to the heart of the lesson:

"Americans today are more misinformed and more gullible about the true nature of psychiatry than people anywhere have ever been. Accordingly, it is imperative that men, women, and children learn to protect themselves from the dangers of psychiatry. As adolescents must learn not to swim on beaches where the undertow is powerful, lest they be unable to make it back to the shore, and not to climb mountains during a thunderstorm, lest they be struck by lightning, they must also learn, when their lives are stormy, to avoid psychiatrists and stay away from mental hospitals, as the only buildings in America they can enter, but not leave, voluntarily." (10)

Phase III: Intensive Support

Phase III is what happens when there is a failure of helpful response to an individual's needs as emotional overload begins to take its toll. Phase III is about the need for intensive support; biopsychiatry calls it hospitalization and/or medicating an individual in order to control symptoms and progression of disease. As Ty Colbert emphasizes, we need non-drug therapeutic programs to help suffering individuals properly recognize and heal the pain inside of them. RC offers "intensives": large doses of one-way counseling for individuals in crisis or emotional overwhelm. A pool of individuals with available time and attention is a great resource. The vast majority of the time given sufficient support and counseling, individuals can work through even severe emotional overload without requiring a change in living situation.

The stories of Cindy, Sally, and Linda are examples ᴏ what can happen when the need for refuge and retreat get perverted by psychiatry. Nevertheless, there are times whe safe and supportive places are absolutely necessary to rest and recover from debilitating distress and emotional overload. Chamberlain's book , 'On Our Own', which I discussed above, is a good resource for consideration of hᴏ to set up such a program. She is especially sensitive to the needs of psychiatric survivors. Loren Mosher has written extensively on the Soteria House, a successful residential treatment center for young people labeled as schizophren᠁ in the early 1970s. (11) Soteria House was small (six beds᠁ home-like, had a non-professional staff, and used minima᠁ drugs. Interventions included "being with and doing with᠁ "extensive, intensive 1-1 contact as needed," living as a family, and house meetings: decidedly human, decidedly non-psychiatric. Soteria based itself on what Mosher calls the four threatening Ds; they Demedicalized, Dehospitalized, Deprofessionalized, and Dedrugged the treatment of psychiatry's sacred symbol, schizophrenia. And it worked; it was clinically effective and 50 percent cheaper than hospital treatment. And to quote Mosher from a 1996 speech he gave at the University of Maryland, "Like many dissident Argentines the Soteria Project became one of the 'disappeared'." Conservatism ruled, biopsychiatry ruled, Soteria was marginalized and forgotten.

Edward Podvoll, the Buddhist psychiatrist and author of 'The Seduction of Madness', has worked extensively with people in the most extreme states of mind and has some of the clearest ideas about what psychiatry calls "psychosis" of anyone I have read. I recommend his book to anyone who wants to learn and stimulate their thinking about work with people labeled "chronically mentally ill" and "psychotic." (12) Podvoll does use much of the psychiatric language I am challenging, and his Windhorse Project is a "false alternative" in Chamberlain's sense of the partnership model. Nevertheless, the Windhorse Project was quite successful, and his book provides detailed information about what they did and the sharing of lessons learned about such intensive work. An encouraging note is the founding of another organization, Windhorse Associates in Northampton, Massachusetts. This program is modeled after Podvoll's innovative program; its founders, Jeffrey and Molly Fortuna, were part of Podvoll's original group of Windhorse pioneers in Colorado. (13)

There is one other real, working alternative to traditional psychiatry that I know about. Founded by David Goldblatt and Catherine Burch Symmes in 1978, located in the White Mountains of New Hampshire, it is called Burch

House. This community has successfully helped to stabiliz
many people in what psychiatry calls "acute psychosis" for
twenty years, without recourse to neuroleptic drugs.
Modeled after R D Laing's communities in London, Burch
House shares many similarities with Soteria House. (14) W
have demonstrated that even intensely disturbed individua
labeled "psychotic," can be helped in gentle, humane ways
without drugs or electroshock. Loren Mosher's intention
was to reform the Mental Health System through his
Soteria research; Soteria depended on National Institute o
Mental Health funding and he was cut off. Perhaps its low
profile has allowed Burch House to endure. Reading
Podvoll's book, one gets a vivid image of the intense
dedication and zeal required of this one doctor to keep
Windhorse going. But it can be done.

Though Arnold Mindell, founder of process
psychology, has been a teacher of mine through his books
for years, I only discovered his work, 'City Shadows:
Psychological Interventions in Psychiatry', (15) as I was
completing this manuscript. I'm not able to elaborate
process theory here, but I strongly recommend this book
another resource for anyone who wants to see behind the
veil of psychiatric jargon and practice. Mindell shares mar
specific examples of his work with individuals labeled
"psychotic" or "schizophrenic," presenting as "chronically
mentally ill" patients at a public clinic in Switzerland. By
thinking about and engaging in these individuals' process
he was consistently able to relate and at least temporarily
expand their awareness in a positive way.

Remember also the field of transpersonal psycholog
As I described in Chapter 7, the Spiritual Emergence
Network was developed to help save people going throug
crises in spiritual transformation from being labeled as

"psychotic" and from the damages of biopsychiatric Phase III intervention. (16) Their work is useful in defending individuals against psychiatric interpretations, and subsequent harmful "treatments," in the face of arduous and, at times, agonizing pitfalls of spiritual transformation.

On Activism

Various schools of psychology have, over the years, offered useful perspectives on psychosocial causes and methods of recovery from psychological distress. It is encouraging to see these and other positive trends in the "mental health" field. It is not so encouraging, however, to see the reluctance of even the most inspired thinkers to take a strong, unequivocal stand against the ignorance and damage wrought through the theory and practice of biopsychiatry. It is the rare professional who has not bought in to the belief in biologically based "mental illness"; rarer still are those who take a public stand. The performance of professional organizations is especially pathetic. Associations of various groups (e.g., psychologists, social workers, professional counselors) are all extremely politically active in the areas of licensure and access to third party payment through our medical health care system, and extremely inactive when it comes to challenging the power and influence of biopsychiatry. In the peace movement, it is not unusual to have retired military officers working for the cause of disarmament and nuclear freeze; perhaps retired mental health professionals will feel free to challenge the system which formerly provided their livelihood.

Drop-in centers for psychiatric "patients," though by no means in abundance, are at least tolerated by the mental health profession. Overnight crisis centers where people ca get emotional and spiritual help without doctors, drugs, or shock machines are much more threatening to the vested interests of institutional psychiatry, and usually don't get of the ground because of funding or liability issues. The truth is that all of this is inseparable from the need for various levels of affordable housing. Psychological theorist Abraha Maslow became famous for articulating his well-known hierarchy of human needs; without basic physical care in place, personal growth and healing is mostly irrelevant. Freedom from psychiatric oppression necessitates much more than devising ways to meet the temporary needs of a individual's emotional recovery. A narrow-minded focus on the individual, even a sensible "alternative" approach, is sti oppressive if it acts to inhibit thinking and action on the broader issues of economic and social justice.

Please always keep in mind, however, even as we wor to challenge coercive biopsychiatry and create more helpful alternatives, that every individual and every situation is unique. Every gesture of help offers up a challenge and pu us on an edge of having to decide whether and to what extent we are willing to transform our lives. As a parent, I know that the choice again and again is to transform myse and my life or to suppress my children. The same is true o all of us and of our society. We do the work ourselves or w continue to use psychiatry as a means of suppressing our fellow human beings.

We are constantly faced with the practical question o how to help a friend or family member or anyone in need. Given the current state of available services for individual going through psychological crises, it is often extremely difficult, at times anguishing and tragic. The truth is there an array of biopsychiatric services and, at the level of intensive care, very few non-psychiatric alternatives. I myself cried recently when Cindy called from Colorado, slipping again into her extreme fear, lost on the road to Texas, no place to turn, knowing that she would likely end up again either in jail or the state hospital. I knew of only one place to recommend, Burch House in New Hampshire, that offers long-term, non-biopsychiatric care for individuals in crisis like Cindy. She did not go there, but she eventually made it back to Austin. She went briefly to jail, back to the state hospital, into a transitional living center, then a job as a live-in caregiver for an elderly woman, holding her fears at bay with neuroleptic drugs. The last time she called she had obtained a job as a file clerk with a state agency, and had been baptized in her brother's church. Right now, she is resigned to being a "mental patient." My hope is that one day she will be able to shed that identity and assume one more in keeping with the spirited woman I know she is.

We pay a high price to maintain any illusion that some of us can, in the long term, thrive at the expense of others. A shift in consciousness which honors and derives from our interconnectedness is the alternative, and our work is to learn and embrace this truth. Every single compassionate thought and act makes a difference, and is the antidote for psychiatric oppression, or any oppression.

Here ends this final chapter with a poetic offering which to me conveys the spirit of gentle asylum for which we all yearn, and at times so desperately need. I dedicate it to Cindy.

UPHILL

Does the road wind uphill all the way?
    Yes, to the very end.
Will the day's journey take the whole long day?
    From morn to night, my friend.

But is there for the night a resting place?
    A roof for when the slow dark hours begin.
May not the darkness hide it from my face?
    You cannot miss that inn.

Shall I meet other wayfarers at night?
    Those who have gone before.
Then must I knock, or call when just in sight?
    They will not keep you standing at the door.

Shall I find comfort, travel-sore and weak?
    Of labor you shall find the sum.
Will there be beds for me and all who seek?
    Yea, beds for all who come.

                      — Christina Rosetti, 18

APPENDIX A

Part I Electroshock References and Resources

References

Breggin, P. (1991) Shock Treatment is not Good for Your Brain, in 'Toxic Psychiatry.' New York: St. Martin's Press.

Breggin, P. (1997) Electroshock and Depression, in 'Brain Disabling Treatments in Psychiatry.' New York: Springer Publishing.

Frank, L., ed. (1978) 'The History of Shock Treatment.' Available from Leonard Frank, 2300 Webster St., San Francisco, CA 94115. ($12 postpaid)

Frank, L. (1990) Electroshock: Death, Brain Damage, Memory Loss, and Brainwashing. 'Journal of Mind and Behavior', 11, Nos. 3 and 4.

Friedberg, J. (1976) 'Shock Treatment Is Not Good For Your Brain.' San Francisco: Glide.

Friedberg, J. (1977) Shock Treatment, Brain Damage and Memory Loss: A Neurological Perspective. 'American Journal of Psychiatry', 134, 9, 1010-1013.

Additional Resources

'ShockWaves', Linda Andre editor, Committee for Truth in Psychiatry, PO Box 1214, New York, NY 10003. (212) 473-4786

This is an important newsletter for information related to ECT.

'Dendron', David Oaks publisher, PO Box 11284, Eugene OR 97440. (503) 341-0100.

The best newspaper available on mental health system oppression. David Oaks is also the contact point for Suppc Coalition International, an umbrella group of organizatior devoted to the work of mental health liberation. Their website is www.efn.org/~dendron.

'Psychiatry, Victimizing the Elderly', a booklet by the Citizens Commission on Human Rights (CCHR), 6362 Hollywood Blvd., Suite B, Los Angeles, CA 90028. In Texas, call 1-800-572-2905. For other states call 1-800-86 2247.

CCHR is a private, non-profit organization whose so purpose is to investigate and expose psychiatric violations human rights.

www.banshock.org, a website on the internet devoted making information available regarding electroshock treatment and attempts to ban or restrict its use. Many lin to other useful sites.

APPENDIX A

Part II Electroshock Annotated Bibliography by Moira Dolan, MD

EFFECTS OF ELECTROCONVULSIVE THERAPY: A review of the scientific literature

DEATH

In a large retrospective study of 3,288 patients getting ECT in Monroe County, NY, ECT recipients were found to have an increased death rate from all causes.

Babigian, H., et al. Epidemiologic Considerations in ECT. 'Arch Gen Psych' 1984;4:246-253.

Survival in 65 patients hospitalized and treated for depression was evaluated by researchers at Brown University. They reported that the 37 patients who received ECT had survival rates of 73.0 percent at one year, 54.1 percent at two years, and 51.4 percent at three years. In contrast, depressed patients who did not receive ECT had survival rates of 96.4 percent, 90.5 percent and 75.0 percent at one, two, and three years respectively.

Kroessler, D. and Fogel, B. Electroconvulsive Therapy for Major Depression in the Oldest Old. 'Am J Geriatr Psych' 1993;1:1:30-37.

The risk of death was doubled in depressed patients who got ECT in a seven year follow up study of 188 patients.

O'Leary, D. and Lee, A. Seven Year Prognosis in Depression — Mortality and Readmission Rates in the Nottingham ECT Cohort. 'British J of Psychiatry' 1996;169: 423-429.

The first three years of mandated recording of death within 14 days of ECT in the state of Texas yielded reports of 21 deaths. Eleven of these were cardiovascular, including massive heart attacks and strokes, three were respiratory, and six were suicides.

Don Gilbert, Commissioner, Texas Department of

Mental Health and Mental Retardation, 1996.

BRAIN DAMAGE

Over twenty years ago Cotman reported in Science that ECT disrupts (protective) protein production by brain cells. More recent studies show that electric shocks to the brain also causes an increase the production of inflammatory proteins inside brain cells.

Cotman, et al. Electroshock effects on brain protein synthesis. 'Science' 1971;178:454-456.

Marcheselli, et al. Sustained induction of prostaglandin endoperoxidase synthase-2 by seizures in hippocampus 'J Biol Chem' 1996; 271:24794-24799.

C. Edward Coffey, MD, a leading proponent of ECT, conducted a study at Duke University Medical Center and the Durham VA Hospital which looked at the brain scans (by MRI) of patients before and after ECT. Out of 35 patients studied, eight had changes on MRI after shock. That's 22 percent, or greater than one in five, with anatomy brain effects. Among those with the brain changes, one patient suffered a stroke and two had new abnormal neurologic signs on exam within six months of the ECT.

Coffey, et al. Brain Anatomic Effects of ECT 'Arch Gen Psych' 1991;48:1013-1021.

Weinberger looked at the effects of ECT on the brain of schizophrenics by comparing brain CT scans of those who had ECT with schizophrenics who never received shock. He documented that cerebral atrophy (brain shrinkage) was significantly more common in those who had been shocked.

Weinberger, et al. Structural abnormalities in the

cerebral cortex of chronic schizophrenic patients. 'Arch Gen Psych' 1979;36:935-939.

Another CT scan study done by Calloway looking at a similar group confirmed that frontal lobe atrophy (brain shrinking) was significantly more common in ECT recipients.

Calloway, et al. ECT and cerebral atrophy: a CT study. 'Acta Psych Scand' 1981;64:442-445.

Andreasen used MRI scans to demonstrate a strong correlation between the number of previous ECT treatments to enlarged ventricles (loss of brain tissue).

Andreasen, et al. MRI of the Brain in Schizophrenia 'Arch Gen Psych' 1990;47:35-41.

A study in England compared the brain CT scans of 101 depressed patients who had received ECT to 52 normal volunteers. They found a significant relationship between treatment with ECT and brain atrophy. In fact ECT recipients were twice as likely to have a measurable loss of brain tissue in the front area of the brain and a tripling of the incidence of a loss of brain tissue in the back of the brain. "Most significantly, the brain abnormalities correlated only with ECT, and not with age, alcohol use, gender, family history of mental illness, age at the time of psychiatric diagnosis, or severity of mental illness." (Quoted words are those of the study authors.)

Dolan, RJ, et al. The cerebral appearance in depressed subjects 'Psychol Med' 1986;16:775-779.

An animal study sought to discover whether giving supplementary oxygen during shock would prevent brain damage; they also gave vitamin E to lessen the effects of damaging "free radical" molecules that get released during shock seizure. They found no difference in the brain damaging effects of ECT-induced seizures by giving oxyge and vitamin E. These findings disprove the claim that modern ECT methods (complete with anesthesia and oxygen) are any less damaging to the brain than uncontrolled seizures.

Manoel, et al. Brain damage following repeated electroshock in cats and rats 'Rev Rom Neurol Psych' 1986;24:59-64.

CARDIOVASCULAR COMPLICATIONS
ECT-induced seizures cause a rapid rise in blood pressure; at the same time the brain experiences a significa reduction in blood flow.

Webb, et al. Cardiovascular response to unilateral ECT 'Biol Psych' 1990;28:758-766 .

Rosenberg, et al. Effects of ECT on cerebral blood flow 'Convulsive Therapy' 1988;4:62-73.

A Mayo clinic study of 34 elderly patients receiving shock found an 18 percent incidence of serious heart arrhythmias during treatment; four had ventricular tachycardia requiring IV lidocaine, two had supraventricu tachycardia requiring IV beta blockers. An additional two patients had other cardiogram changes.

Tomac, T. and Rummans, T. Safety and Efficacy of Electroconvulsive Therapy in Patients Over Age 85. 'Am Geriatr Psych' 1997;5:126-130.

After his eighth ECT, a 57-year-old man died of hear rupture.

Ali, P.B. and Tidmarsh, M.D. Cardiac Rupture During Electroconvulsive Therapy 'Anesthesia' 1997; 52: 884-895.

Physicians from Tulane University Medical School reported on a 69-year-old woman who developed brain hemorrhage during ECT. She was also left with epilepsy afterward. This was, as expected, associated with further deterioration in her mental status from her baseline depression. They conclude that the fragile vessels of the elderly may make some patients a particularly high risk for ECT.

Weisberg, et al. Intracerebral hemorrhage following ECT. 'Neurology' 1991; Nov: 1849.

EXTRA RISKS IN THE ELDERLY

In an analysis of 34 persons over the age of 85 who were subjected to ECT, researchers at the Mayo clinic documented that 79 percent suffered treatment complications, including a 32 percent incidence of confusion and delirium, 67 percent incidence of transient high blood pressure, 18 percent incidence of serious heart arrhythmias during treatment, two patients with other cardiogram changes, three with falls, one hip fracture due to fall.

Tomac, T. and Rummans, T. Safety and Efficacy of Electroconvulsive Therapy in Patients Over Age 85. 'Am J Geriatr Psych' 1997; 5:126-130.

ECT-enthusiast Dr Coffey and his associate Dr Figiel found that 10 out of 87 (that's 11 percent of) elderly patients getting ECT for depression remained delirious between ECT sessions for no discernible medical reason other than the ECT itself. (Italicized words are those of the study authors.) They documented by brain MRI scans that 90 percent of these unfortunate patients had lesions in the b ganglia areas of the brain, and 90 percent also had mode to severe white matter lesions.

> Figiel, Coffey, et al. Brain MRI findings in ECT-induced delirium 'J of Neuropsych and Clin Sci' 1990;2: 58.

Kroessler and Fogel's 1993 study on death rates reported above was done on the "oldest old," depressed patients at least 85 years of age. Mortality rates were significantly greater for those who received ECT, compa to those who did not.

> Kroessler, D. and and Fogel, B. Electroconvulsive Therapy for Major Depression in the Oldest Old. 'Am J Geriatr Psych' 1993;1:1:30-37.

EPILEPSY

In a review of the literature on the well-known ECT complication of epilepsy, researchers calculated 'that the age-adjusted incidence of new seizures after ECT was fivefold greater than the incidence found in the non-psychiatric population.' (Quoted words are those of the study authors.)

> Devinsky, O. and Duchowny, M.S. Seizures after convulsive therapy: A retrospective case survey. 'Neurolo 1983;33:921-5.

Persistent brain wave disruption to the point of statu epilepticus has been reported to occur following ECT. Individual reports by Drs. Weiner and Varma on differer patients both describe acute disorientation and deteriora of intellectual function immediately following ECT. Thi was found to be due to ongoing epileptic brain wave forms that was initiated by the ECT.

Weiner, R.D. Prolonged confusional states and EEG seizure activity following ECT and lithium use. 'Am Journal Psych' 1980;137:1452-1453.

Varma, N.K. et al. Nonconvulsive status epilepticus following ECT. 'Neurology' 1992;42:2263-264.

MEMORY LOSS

Publicly available data from the state of California's Department of Mental Health reveals that over 99 percent of ECT recipients complain of memory loss 3 months following treatment, with the average number of ECT sessions being five to six.

A. Lazarow, Chief, Office of Human Rights, California Department of Mental Health, 1996.

In a chapter on the cognitive effects of ECT in a psychiatry textbook, Sackheim indicates that cognitive effects (disordered thinking), particularly amnesia, can be long lasting after shock.

Sackeim, in 'Cognitive Disorders: Pathophysiology and Treatment', edited by Moos, et al 1992

The conclusion that amnesia can be a long lasting effect of shock is arrived at by both Squire and Weiner in separate studies.

Squire, et al. Retrograde amnesia and bilateral ECT: Long term follow-up. 'Arch Gen Psych' 1981;38:89-95.

Weiner, et al. Effects of stimulus parameters on cognitive side effects 'Ann NY Acad Sci' 1986;462:315-325.

LACK OF EFFICACY

In the large NY study cited earlier, the death rates from suicide among depressed patients given ECT were slightly higher at the one year mark. By five years the suicide rate was the same for depressed patients who got ECT as those who didn't.

> Babigian, H., et al. Epidemiologic considerations in ECT. 'Arch Gen Psych' 1984;41:246-253.

In a University of Iowa study of treatment effectiveness 1,076 depressed patients were categorized according to whether they received ECT, or high doses of anti-depressant medications, or low doses of anti-depressant medications, or neither (ECT nor meds). Long term follow up revealed that all groups had the same suicide rates, indicating that the incidence of suicide is not affected by treatment. The authors conclude: "Therefore, active biological treatments, such as ECT, may not be deemed as 'lifesaving' now as in the past."

> Black, et al. Does treatment influence mortality in depressives? 'Ann Clin Psych' 1989;1:165-173.

The same findings are documented in three other studies: ECT does not prevent suicide in depressed patient

> Eastwood, et al. Seasonal patterns of suicide, depression, and ECT. 'Br J Psych' 1976;129:472-475.

> Babigian, et al. Epidemiological considerations in ECT. 'Arch Gen Psych' 1984;41:216-253.

> Milstien, et al. Does ECT prevent suicide? 'Convulsive Therapy' 1986;2:3-6.

Dr Dolan periodically updates this research review. It may be obtained by sending $3.00 to Electroshock Review PO Box 4085, Austin, Texas 78765.

APPENDIX B

Working Axioms For Understanding Psychiatric
Oppression and Implementing A Program Of Personal and
Social Transformation

Understanding the Problem

1. Psychiatry, as represented by the institutionalized
mental health system, is our society's official response to
distress. It is also our society's primary enforcer of the
normative social order, when the enforcers cannot or do not
want to apply the statutes of criminal and civil law.
Psychiatric oppression is the systematic mistreatment of the
group of individuals selected and labeled as "mentally ill."

2. Psychiatry is coercive. Much coercion is overt;
people are incarcerated and given drugs or electroshock
against their will. Even more coercion is subtle, rooted in
the covert threat of involuntary "treatment." As long as such
involuntary treatment exists, there can be no truly voluntary
treatment in psychiatry. In fact, where there exists no
medical evidence of disease, as in psychiatry, there can be no
such thing as legitimate treatment.

3. The language of psychiatry is misleading and
confusing, based on false beliefs and concepts. It is
prescriptive rather than descriptive, statements of power
and control rather than of information and understanding.
Its purpose is to mystify and control.

4. Economics are the primary determining factor in
our country's health, including "mental" health, care system.
The medical industry (including doctors and their

professional associations, pharmaceutical companies,
hospitals, insurance companies, governmental regulatory
and research agencies and universities) is a very powerful
lobby, assuring state acceptance and support of psychiatric
authority. In return, Psychiatry is expected to fulfill its role
as a primary agent of social control.

5. In the second half of the twentieth century, and
especially in the last two decades, the pharmaceutical
business has become one of the most profitable
international industries. Governmental decisions,
psychiatric policy and practice, and public beliefs and
desires are increasingly shaped by the power of drug
company financial influence and propaganda. An
exponentially increasing amount of industry profits in the
last decade has come via psychiatric drug sales.

6. Psychiatry acts as a "stop sign" on liberation from
other forms of institutionalized oppression in our society.
This includes the root of economic oppression, classism,
and its attendant means of dividing people against each
other and themselves (eg., adultism, sexism, racism, ageisn▸
homophobia, etc.). By identifying troubled and troubling
individuals as biologically or genetically defective "mental
ill patients," we are effectively distracted from oppression
which is the real cause of our hurts and unmet needs. We
are also distracted from other ugly and very real
consequences of an irrational, oppressive society, includin▸
poverty, homelessness, legal and illegal drug use, crime,
violence and growing numbers of us in prison, pollution a▸
environmental degradation. A "benefit" we all receive is t▸
we are allowed to escape responsibility for each other, for
our community, and for our planet.

7. Psychiatry's guiding belief system is that of
biological psychiatry, or biopsychiatry for short. The

fundamental, erroneous assumptions of psychiatry are as follows:

a. Social adjustment is good.

b. Failure to adjust is the result of mental illness.

c. Mental illness is a medical disease.

d. Mental illness is the result of biological and/or genetic defects.

e. Mental illness is chronic, progressive, basically incurable.

f. Mental illness can be controlled primarily by drugs; secondarily, for serious mental illness, by electroshock.

g. People with mental illness are irrational, often unable to make responsible decisions for themselves; therefore, coercion is necessary and justified.

8. Psychiatry argues, the media propagandizes, and the public accepts that "mental illness" is a real medical disease. The truth is that no problem routinely seen by psychiatrists has been scientifically validated as a disease in the same way that legitimate medical illnesses are validated. Diagnosis of "mental illness" is based strictly on subjective reports of mood and behavior. The concept of "mental illness" was created as a metaphor for physical illness, and no matter how strong the rhetoric asserting otherwise, the truth is that it is still a metaphor.

9. There are a variety of organic illnesses, physical insults, and toxic invasions which can alter brain and central nervous system functioning severely enough to cause a wide range of troubled and troubling thoughts, feelings and conduct. Psychiatry calls these "symptoms" of "mental illness."

10. Nutrition is profoundly important for psychological well-being. We know so much now about the detelerious effect of junk foods, sugar, food additives,

pesticides, overconsumption of animal fats, etc., on mood and behavior. And we know the restorative value of optima nutrition. Failure to act on this common sense is a major flaw in Psychiatry.

11. Psychiatry's physical "treatments" are dangerous and harmful. Psychiatric drugs "work" by disabling the brain and central nervous system. One of the most commo causes of so-called psychiatric symptoms is the use of psychiatric drugs. Effects of withdrawal from psychiatric drugs are often misinterpreted as signs of "mental illness." Electroshock always causes brain damage. The damage is the "therapeutic" effect.

12. The core of psychiatric oppression is suppressio of the individual. Society defines certain thoughts, feeling and conduct as undesirable, and psychiatry enforces this normative opinion by suppressing the offending individua

13. We have a natural built-in mechanism for healin from the effects of distress. This mechanism involves specific forms of emotional expression or discharge, including animated talking, crying, laughing, shaking, trembling, sweating, and storming in anger. By defining these natural forms of expression as deranged medical conditions, and individuals as biologically defective "mentally ill patients," Psychiatry denies the possibility o positive growth and resolution.

14. We have an inborn urge to wholeness; unconsci aspects of ourselves relentlessly seek to be made consciou These include the effects of specific personal hurts, but a include transpersonal contents seemingly unrelated to ou personal biographical history. The challenge of facing an integrating these emergent experiences into consciousnes can be frightening and feel overwhelming. Psychiatry lab these and other non-ordinary states of consciousness,

necessary for psychological healing and for spiritual emergence, as pathological and suppresses them. Psychiatry disrupts and perverts the continuing process of individual and societal spiritual transformation, preventing movement to the next level of development.

15. We have a survival nature which comes from our evolutionary heritage and includes so-called negative emotions, including the fight or flight response and related emotions of fear and anger. Whereas fear and anger are necessary physical survival emotions, they are easily distorted and harmful to all forms of life.

16. Our nature also includes complex emotions peculiar to human brain development, mind and self-reflective awareness, including guilt, shame, envy and doubt. Whereas the initial twinges of these emotions are helpful self-correcting signals, they are also easily distorted, becoming toxic and harmful to both the individual organism and other life forms.

17. The effect of physical or psychological hurt on human beings is to cause distress, evidenced as alienation and impairment of function on all levels — physical, emotional, intellectual and spiritual. Thinking and relating are impaired by internal distress.

18. Non-organic hurts are sufficient in and of themselves to cause patterns of distress severe enough to meet the official psychiatric diagnostic criteria (all based on subjective reports of thoughts, feelings and conduct) for any of the so-called mental illnesses.

19. One of the core distresses resulting from hurt, occurring in utero or at birth for most of us, is the illusion of separateness, the false belief that we are isolated, separate beings, that we are not, in fact, completely connected to all of life. Psychiatry's oppressive practices add greater hurt and

distress, reinforcing isolation, hopelessness and despair.

20. Vast numbers of our citizens are spiritually bereft, spellbound by the incessant and eminently successful purveyors of the world view of consumerism. We are lost in the inherently unsatisfying demand for fulfillment through what we buy and have, pathetic victims of gross, materialistic excess. Psychiatry's reductionistic medical model, and reliance on external, physical "silver bullet" drugs and electroshock supports the materialistic worldview and the desperate search for outer solutions to the felt unsatisfactoriness of existence. An enormous challenge for all of us is to find a meaningful cosmology, and to deeply root ourselves there. This is an essential teaching of the perennial spiritual traditions throughout the ages

21. The effects of hurt, and the feeling of separateness tend to be cumulative and to become habitual over time. Habitual patterns of distress generally operate outside an individual's awareness such that the individual assumes that the pattern is actually his or her essential nature. An individual observing habitual patterns in others, when that individual lacks good information or when operating out of their own distresses, tends to make one of two false assumptions. If the observed pattern is similar to his or her own, the individual assumes that the other's behavior is human nature. If the observed pattern is different, it is assumed that the person suffers from an inherent defect (psychiatry calls this "mental illness"), rather than distress which can be overcome.

Implementing a Solution

22. The Universe consists of and is sustained by an invisible energy, sometimes called Spirit, which is inherent

benign and uplifting. We can call this energy loving because of its essential interconnectedness or relatedness, and its tendency to expand in communion or empathy.

23. We humans are essentially intelligent, creative, curious, zestful, adventurous, responsible, cooperative, loving, and gentle. We know this is our inherent nature by observing babies and children whose developmental needs are well met. We know this by observing how right, and how most alive we feel when we are expressing these qualities. We know how loving kindness enhances our physical and emotional well-being.

24. Each of us is doing the best we can with who we are and what we know, and to the extent that we have been hurt (or not) and emerged from the effects of hurt.

25. The energy of loving is abundantly available, waiting to be called upon. Loving is a natural contradiction to distress; when focused on another individual with delightful attention, the loving tends to trigger a natural healing expression of emotional discharge. We need each other, and we need to be safe in order to thrive.

26. Because of the powerful economic determinants of our "mental health" care system today, any lasting transformation of this system must also be a social revolution, affecting change in economic policy, and in any institutionalized systems of social injustice, including but not limited to oppression because of class, age, sex, race, creed, color, or circumstance.

27. Enduring transformation of the way we care for each other, in or out of crisis, must move decisively beyond theory which treats individuals as isolated entities whose well-being is purely a function of internal psychodynamics. Growing remembrance of human dependency on and utterly complete relatedness to the environment is offering

a ray of hope to the prospect of continuing this grand human evolution on planet Earth. Many of us are realizing that human well-being requires an awareness rooted in our natural selves in the natural world. All adults must reclaim their connectedness with nature, and extend this great gift to our children. Fortunately, it comes quite naturally to those who are not deprived of time and space to develop and enjoy themselves in the natural world.

28. Our society is undergoing a severe crisis of community. Many citizens are working, in the face of tremendous challenges, to create supportive community fo ourselves and others, but most of us still desperately need and desire a richer and more intimate experience of community. We need ongoing availability of support for individual development, and individual and community emotional healing. We learn by looking at certain traditional cultures, prior to industrialization, that the community has a solemn task of recognizing, embracing a supporting the unique gifts and talents of each individual member. In return for this great gift of recognition, suppc and valued inclusion, the community gains the lifelong benefit of that individual's contributions. We also learn th: another sacred task of the community is to provide uniqu tailored support for individuals in pain or transition, and f the entire community on important events such as births, funerals and a variety of significant times. These supporti events are called rituals, and bear little resemblance to the emotionally staid "ritualistic" ceremonies we typically see weddings and funerals in our society. Traditional rituals d have form, but, when properly done, participants are mov by the Spirit and abandon themselves to a cleansing outpouring of feeling. Rituals are a community experienc of emotional healing. Our Western society needs to learn

from these traditions, and remember and recreate the experience of community support and healing, both in times of crisis and in ongoing fashion for all of our sakes.

29. All decision-makers should bear in mind, learning from Native American tradition, the effects of any decision on children of seven generations yet to come.

30. Institutional actions are a summation of the consciousness of all the involved individuals. Psychiatric policy and practice is created, promoted and allowed by individuals. Therefore, in order to effect enduring social change, it is necessary that individuals change. The first step is to move from denial into awareness and recognition of the reality of psychiatric oppression. Next is to take responsibility for change.

31. Real change, authentic transformation, requires truth. Generally speaking, truth is best communicated and received on a 1-1 basis. However, societal change also requires that public channels of information become vehicles of truth. This means a reversal of the trend toward control of more and more media outlets by a very restricted number of corporate entities invested in perpetuating the status quo. We must restore a truly free press, open to all people and all points of view.

32. Openness to truth usually requires release of rigid or distressed patterns of thought, feeling and action in the receiving individual. When we are unaware of our distress-based rigidities, we inevitably project the patterns of hurt and distress, acting out our own abuse on others. Therefore, taking responsibility for and alleviating the effects of our own past hurts is necessary for transformation. In order to overcome the desire to dominate others and break this abusive cycle, it is necessary to do our own inner work.

33. Until supporters of psychiatry are able and/or

willing to honestly look at themselves, face their own emotional pain, and take full responsibility for harmful and coercive actions toward others, it is necessary that their actions be interrupted, to prevent harm and to allow them the possibility of change. This is why speaking out and challenging psychiatric oppression is important, valuable and necessary work.

34. Psychiatry and the law must be disentangled and separated. There must be immediate and complete cessati of the abrogation of civil liberties, with indeterminate psychiatric incarceration, of individuals who otherwise would have definite criminal sentences, or would, in fact, free as they were never actually convicted of any crime.

35. It is helpful to consider at least three levels in the continuum of care necessary to support individual psychological well-being:

Level One: Preventive/developmental. This involve good, accurate information and education, and support fo natural emotional expression. The uniqueness of individuals, the significance of emotional discharge for psychological well-being, and the value of non-ordinary states of consciousness must be understood. Conversely, harmfulness of enforced conformity, and suppression of thought and emotion should be understood and avoided much as possible. Natural, spontaneous expression flows, recognized, allowed, encouraged, and supported. As a giv a rational society provides excellent medical care, and bas human needs of food and shelter for all.

Level Two: Extra Support for Acute Distress. At thi level, the individual functions, but thinking and relatedne are impaired, and personal counseling is necessary to hea around patterns of emotional distress. With enough emergence as a society, this would be naturally available from family and friends in the community. Until this time, the society should provide training for a cadre of lay counselors, operating with excellent theory and having done significant personal work, to augment any gaps in an individual's personal network of support. Professional counselors may be necessary for crisis intervention, and through a period of transition, until more natural, less economically determined means of support are readily available. These counselors should be supported by the community as a whole, rather than a private pay situation which excludes those with less money. The critical work is for our society to support adults to take full responsibility for our own healing, and to challenge any and all excuses for adults to hurt children and justify it by blaming it on the children and the need to correct and shape them.

Level Three: Intensive Support for Severely Disabling Distress. Intensive support is necessary when an individual's functioning is severely impaired. This care is holistic in that physical, emotional, mental and spiritual needs are all considered. It must always be custom-tailored to the needs of each individual. It often happens that someone needs short-term intensive counseling to work through the emergence of pockets of deeply painful and overwhelming emotion; a few hours of counseling in one day, or over a few days can make all the difference. At other times, this level of support needs to be maintained for a few weeks. Rarer, but not uncommon, is the need for short- or long-term work in a place of great protection, safety and nurturance. It makes no sense whatsoever to put a bunch of people suffering severe, chronic distress all together, with professionals who see them as defective and primarily needing to be controlled. Healing and reemergence into inherent nature occurs most easily in the presence of people who are resting relaxed and confident in their own true nature and in the true nature of others expressing even the most troubling patterns of distress. Recovery is not so much a function of severity of distress as it is sufficiency of resource; it has been repeatedly demonstrated that even those individuals who carry the most severely stigmatizing, and supposedly incurable, label of "chronic schizophrenic" can and do recover with good care and enough time.

36. Countless numbers of us are entangled, lost, and often destroyed in the throes of substance addiction. Our continuum of care must include excellent understanding of the dynamics of addiction, and support at all levels for the process of recovery. Regarding psychiatric drugs, we have excellent, safe, and effective guidelines for the process of withdrawal. Until psychiatry as we know it is dismantled, support for psychiatric drug withdrawal must be readily available at all levels.

37. The process of spiritual transformation is an inner revolution, beyond the issue and scope of psychological theory. Our need and yearning for spiritual experience, wholeness, meaning, and connection is deep and everlasting. Furthermore, the movement of that invisible energy we sometimes call the Spirit is relentless and unceasing. Much of what we treat as psychiatric crisis can properly be understood as spiritual emergence. The efforts of those who are educating us in discernment and support of spiritual emergence deserve support. At the least, our care for each other must be gentle, non-judgmental, non-suppressive, tolerant, respectful, open to surprise, and rooted in a deep sense of reverence, mystery, and awe.

38. Fundamental to all of the above is a profound recognition and trust in the goodness and excellence of human nature. This should include a solid understanding

the mechanisms of psychological hurt, distress and recovery. We need to fully realize and continually affirm our complete interconnectedness, on all levels. A good-natured tolerance of our flaws and idiosyncrasies is essential. A basic attitude of loving kindness is the foundation which we should all keep reaching for, and from which we should move and act toward ourselves, each other, and the world.

ENDNOTES

Face Page

1. James Madison, quoted by Thomas Szasz in the Foreward to Seth Farber's 'Madness, Heresy and the Rume of Angels.' Open Court, 1993, p. XI.
2. Szasz, T. Ibid., p. xi.

Introduction

1. Breeding, J. 'The Wildest Colts Make The Best Horses.' Bright Books, 1996.
2. The Global Burden of Disease and Injury Series. Conducted by the Harvard School of Public Health and th World Health Organization. Reported by John Docherty, MD, in 'Spectrum', the quarterly newsletter of Merit Behavioral Care Corporation, Vol. III, Issue 1.
3. Glendinning, C. 'My Name is Chellis and I am in Recovery From Western Civilization.' Shambala, 1994.

Chapter 1

1. Szasz, T. From the Foreword to Seth Farber's bool 'Madness, Heresy, and the Rumor of Angels.' Open Cour 1993, p. xi.
2. Boswell, J. Involuntary Commitment A Threat to Personal Freedom. 'Austin Peace and Justice News', Jan/ Feb, 1995.

Chapter 2

1. Szasz, T.S. 'Cruel Compassion.' John Wiley and Sons, 1994.

2. Colbert, T. 'Broken Brains or Wounded Hearts: What Causes Mental Illness.' Kevco Publishing,1995.

3. Frank, L.R., ed. 'Influencing Minds: A Reader in Quotations.' Feral House, 1995.

4. Ibid., p. 165.

5. Podvoll, E. 'The Seduction of Madness'. Harper-Collins, 1990.

6. Alexander, J. Liberation from Mental Health Oppression. 'Recovery and Re-emergence No. 5', Rational Island Publishers, 1997.

7. Foner, J. The Adult Role and Feeling of Going Crazy. 'Recovery and Re-emergence No. 5', Rational Island Publishers, 1997.

8. Breggin, P. 'Brain-Disabling Treatments in Psychiatry.' Springer Publishing Co., 1997.

9. Thanks to Janet Foner, an international leader in the psychiatric survivor movement, for this metaphor.

10. Breggin, P. 'Talking Back to Prozac.' St. Martin's Press, 1994.

11. The Drug Enforcement Agency reports a six-fold increase of Ritalin use in the United States, just since 1990 International watchpeople, the Vienna-based International Narcotics Control Board, decries this distinctly North American aberration.

12. Reported by John Merrow in the New York Times, 10/21/95.

13. 'Harper's Magazine', June 1996.

14. I recommend Peter and Ginger Breggin's book, 'The War Against Children: How the Drugs, Programs, and Theories of the Psychiatric Establishment are Threatening America's Children with a Medical Cure for Nonviolence',

St. Martin's Press, 1994, for a detailed look at the so-called
Federal Violence Initiative.

15. Quoted from National Health Advisory Council
transcript by T. Roder, V. Kubillus and A. Burwell,
'Psychiatrists: The Men Behind Hitler.' Freedom
Publishing, 1994.

Chapter 3

1. In Szasz, T.S. 'Cruel Compassion.' John Wiley and
Sons, 1994, p. 101.

2. Roszak, T. 'The Voice of the Earth.' Simon and
Schuster, 1992, pp. 194-195.

3. Ibid., pp. 219-220.

4. Szasz, T.S. 'The Manufacture of Madness: A
Comparative Study of the Inquisition and the Mental
Health Movement'. Harper and Row, 1970.

5. Described in 'The Manufacture of Madness.'

6. Ibid.

7. Scheff, T. 'Being Mentally Ill: A Sociological
Theory.' Aldine, 1984.

8. Quoted in Szasz' 'Cruel Compassion.' (See above.'

9. Wertham, F. 'A Sign for Cain.' Paberback Library,
1969.

Lapon, L. 'Mass Murderers in White Coats' Psychia
Genocide Research Institute, 1986.

Muller-Hill, B. 'Murderous Science: Elimination by
Scientific Selection of Jews, Gypsies and Others in
Germany.' Oxford University Press, 1988.

10. In Roder, T., Kubillus, V. and Burwell, A.
'Psychiatrists: The Men Behind Hitler.' Freedom
Publishing, 1994.

11. Ibid., p. 43.

12. Ibid., p. 41.

13. Ibid., p. 44.

14. Wertham, F., 1969. (See above.)

15. Roder, T., Kubillus, V. and Burwell, A., 1994. (See above.)

16. Quoted in Roder, T., Kubillus, V. and Burwell, A., 1994. (See above.)

17. Muller-Hill, B., 1988, p. 87. (See above.)

18. Ibid.

19. Rothman, D. 'The Discovery of the Asylum.' Little, Brown, and Co., 1971.

20. Johnson, A. 'Out of Bedlam: The Truth About Deinstitutionalization.' Basic Books, 1990.

21. Frank, L.R. (ed.) 'The History of Shock Treatment'. San Francisco, 1975. Available from the author, 2300 Webster Street, San Francisco, CA 94115.

22. See the great social historian Michel Foucault's 'Madness and Civilization: A History of Insanity in the Age of Reason.' NY: Pantheon Books, 1965, for a comprehensive analysis of the so-called Age of Confinement.

23. Podvoll, E. 'The Seduction of Madness.' Harper-Collins, 1990, p. 62.

24. Ibid., pp. 63-66.

25. Albert Deutsch, quoted in Johnson, A. 'Out of Bedlam: The Truth About Deinstitutionalization.' Basic Books, 1990, p. 36.

26. Ibid., p. 40.

27. Breggin, P. 'Brain-Disabling Treatments in Psychiatry.' Springer Publishing Co., 1997, p. 52.

28. Johnson, A. 'Out of Bedlam: The Truth About Deinstitutionalization.' Basic Books, 1990, pp. 119-120.

Chapter 4

1. Lao Tsu, 'Tao Te Ching.' A New Translation by Gia Fu Feng and Jane English. Vintage Books, 1972.

2. Szasz, T.S. 'Cruel Compassion.' John Wiley and Sons, 1994, p. 4.

3. Colbert, T. 'Broken Brains or Wounded Hearts: What Causes Mental Illness.' Kevco Publishing, 1995, p. 2

4. Szasz, T.S. 'The Lexicon of Lunacy: Metaphoric Malady, Moral Responsibility and Psychiatry.' Transaction Publishers, 1993.

5. The work of Michel Foucault is seminal in understanding the dialectics of power relations concealed i language.

6. Mill, J. S. 'On Liberty', 1, 1859.

7. Frank, L. R., ed. 'The History of Shock Treatment. San Francisco, 1978.

8. The Global Burden of Disease and Injury Series. Conducted by the Harvard School of Public Health and th World Health Organization. Reported by John Docherty, MD, in 'Spectrum', the quarterly newsletter of Merit Behavioral Care Corporation, Vol. III, Issue 1.

9. Modrow, J. 'How to Become a Schizophrenic.' Appollyon Press, 1992

10. Mosher, L.R., Vallone, R. and Menn, A.Z. The Treatment of Acute Psychosis without Neuroleptics: Six-week Psychopathology Outcome Data from the Soteria Project. 'International Journal of Social Psychiatry', Vol. ‹ No. 3, pp. 157-173.

11. Khema, A. 'Being Nobody Going Nowhere.' Wisdom Publications, 1987.

12. Szasz, T.'Ideology and Insanity.' Doubleday and Co., Inc., 1970.

Chapter 5

1. Roy, A. 'The God of Small Things.' Random House, 1997, pp. 52-53.

2. Grof, S. 'Beyond The Brain.' State University of New York Press, 1985.

Leonard, J. and Laut, P. 'Rebirthing: The Science of Enjoying All of Your Life.' Trinity Publications, 1983.

3. Liedloff, J. 'The Continuum Concept'. Addison-Wesley, 1985.

4. This is a popular quotation of Albert Einstein, which I regrettably cannot just now find its original source.

5. Sogyal Rinpoche. 'The Tibetan Book of Living and Dying.' HarperSanFrancisco, 1992.

6. In Szasz, T.S. 'Cruel Compassion.' John Wiley and Sons, 1994, p. 201.

7. Miller, A. 'Banished Knowledge'. Doubleday, 1990.

8. Roszak, T. 'The Voice of the Earth.' Simon and Schuster, 1992, p. 230.

9. Bradshaw, J. 'Healing the Shame That Binds You.' Health Communications, Inc., 1988.

10. In Roder, T., Kubillus, V. and Burwell, A. 'Psychiatrists: The Men Behind Hitler.' Freedom Publishing, 1994.

11. Siebert, A. Unpublished letter to Newsweek, 6/5/96.

Chapter 6

1. Gatto, J. Lecture in Austin, Texas, 1994.

2. Gatto, J.'Dumbing Us Down: The Hidden Curriculum of Compulsory Schooling.' New Society Publishers, 1992.

3. Wiseman, B. 'Psychiatry: The Ultimate Betrayal.' Freedom Publishing, 1995.

4. Breeding, J. 'The Wildest Colts Make The Best Horses.' Bright Books, 1996.

5. Wiseman, B., pp. 282-285. (See above.)

6. Breggin, P. 'Brain-Disabling Treatments in Psychiatry.' Springer Publishing Co., 1997, p. 157.

7. Mosher, L.R., Vallone, R. and Menn, A.Z. The Treatment of Acute Psychosis without Neuroleptics: Six-week Psychopathology Outcome Data from the Soteria Project. 'International Journal of Social Psychiatry', Vol. 4 No. 3, pp. 157-173.

8. Sarason, S. 'Caring and Compassion in Clinical Practice.' Jossey-Bass, 1985.

9. Weil, A. 'Spontaneous Healing.' 1995.

10. Dostoevsky, F. 'The Possessed', 1871, quoted by Franz Neumann, 'Anxiety and Politics', 1957. In Eric and Mary Josephson, eds., 'Man Alone: Alienation in Modern Society', 1962. Found in Frank, L. R., ed., 'Random Hous Webster's Quotationary.' NY, 1998.

11. Benedict, A. and Saks, M. The Regulation of Professional Behavior: Electroconvulsive Therapy in Massachusetts 'The Journal of Psychiatry and Law', Summer 1987

12. Sarason, S., 1985, p. 163. (See above.)

13. Glendinning, C. 'My Name is Chellis and I am ir Recovery From Western Civilization.' Shambala, 1994.

14. Dass, R. and Gorman, P. 'How Can I Help?' Alfr A. Knopf, 1985.

15. Hubbard, L.R. 'The Scientology Handbook.' Bridge Publications, 1994.

16. Janet Foner's workshop, 'Take Charge of Your Mind', is offered through Support Coalition Internationa

They can be reached at (541)345-9106.

17. Walker, A. 'Possessing The Secret of Joy'. Pocket Star Books, 1994.

Chapter 7

1. Bragdon, E. 'A Sourcebook for Helping People in Spiritual Emergency.' Lightening Up Press, 1988, p. 10.

2. Szasz, T. 'Ideology and Insanity.' Doubleday and Co., Inc., 1970, p. 11.

3. Ibid.

4. Sealey, R. 'Unipolar Depression Survival Kit.' Available from the author, 291 Princess Ave., North York, Ontario M2N 3S3. Another resource is B.J. Sahley, who has done much work on nutritional supplemental approaches to mental and emotional symptoms at the Pain, Stress and Therapy Center in San Antonio, TX (Telephone 800-669-CALM or 210-614-PAIN)

5. Podvoll, E. 'The Seduction of Madness.' Harper-Collins, 1990.

Chapter 8

1. Critzer, G. Oh, How Happy We Will Be: Pills, Paradise and the Profits of Drug Companies. 'Harper's Magazine', June 1996.

2. Frank, L. R. Electroshock: Death, Brain Damage, Memory Loss, and Brainwashing. 'Journal of Mind and Behavior', Vol. II, Nos. 3 and 4, pp. 489-512.

3. Szasz, T.S. 'The Manufacture of Madness: A Comparative Study of the Inquisition and the Mental Health Movement.' Harper and Row, 1970.

4. Szasz, T.S. 'Cruel Compassion.' John Wiley and

Sons, 1994.

5. Alexander, J. Function and Dysfunction in a Drug-Dependent Society. 'Recovery and Re-Emergence No. 5', Rational Island Publishers, 1997.

6. Ibid.

7. Levey, J., and Levey, M. 'Living in Balance.' Conar Press, 1998.

8. See Peter Breggin's book, 'Talking Back to Ritalin.' Common Courage Press, 1998.

9. Carolyn Myss' best-selling book, 'Anatomy of the Spirit', covers the same ground as this dynamic tape series

Chapter 9

1. Quoted in Frank, L.R., ed., 'Influencing Minds: A Reader in Quotations.' Feral House, 1995.

2. Gotkin, J. 'Too Much Anger, Too Many Tears'. Quadrangle Press: NY, 1975.

3. Publicly available statistics from the Texas Department of Mental Health and Mental Retardation, 1994.

4. Cameron, D. ECT: Sham Statistics, the Myth of Convulsive Therapy, and the Case for Consumer Misinformation. 'Journal of Mind and Behavior', 1994, 1 pp. 177-198.

5. Texas Department of Mental Health and Mental Retardation Report, 1996.

6. American Psychiatric Association task force report 'The Practice of Electroconvulsive Therapy', 1990.

7. Ibid.

8. Wisconsin Coalition for Advocacy (WCA) 'Inform Consent for Electroconvulsive Therapy: A Report on Violations of Patients' Rights by St. Mary's Hospital,

Madison, WI 1/17/95. WCA, 16 N. Carroll St., Madison, WI 53703.

9. Benedict, A. and Saks, M. The Regulation of Professional Behavior: Electroconvulsive Therapy in Massachusetts. 'The Journal of Psychiatry and Law', 1987,15, 2, 247-275.

10. Baughman, F. E-mail correspondence, September 10, 1998.

11. Sackeim, H., et al. Stimulus Intensity, Seizure Threshold and Seizure Duration. 'Psychiatric Clinics of North America', 1991,14, 4, 803-843.

12. American Psychiatric Association, 1990. (See above.)

13. 'Physician's Desk Reference: 53rd Edition.' Montvale, NJ: Medical Economics Co., 1999.

14. Rifkin, A. ECT versus tricyclic antidepressants in depression: A review of evidence. ' Journal of Clinical Psychiatry', 1988,49,1, pp. 3-7.

Consensus Conference on ECT, 1985. Reported by Peter Breggin in 'Brain-Disabling Treatments in Psychiatry', 1997, p. 135.

15. Crow, T. and Johnstone, E. Controlled trials of electroconvulsive therapy. 'Annals of NY Academy of Sciences', 1986,462, pp. 12-29.

Chapter 10

1. Benedict, A. and Saks, M. The Regulation of Professional Behavior: Electroconvulsive Therapy in Massachusetts. 'The Journal of Psychiatry and Law', Summer 1987.

2. 'Psychiatric News', 6/20/89.

3. Wisconsin Coalition for Advocacy Report, 1995.

(See above.)

4. Szasz, T.S. ' Cruel Compassion.' John Wiley and Sons, 1994, p. 4.

5. Fanon, F. 'A Dying Colonialism', 1965, p. 138 quoted in Frank, L.R., ed., 'Influencing Minds: A Reader in Quotations'. Feral House, 1995.

6. Kesey, K. 'One Flew Over the Cuckoo's Nest.' 1962. p. 64.

7. Kalinowsky, L. and Hoch, P. 'Shock Treatments, Psychosurgery and other Somatic Treatments in Psychiatry', 1952, 3.B.13.

8. Frank, L.R., ed., 'Influencing Minds: A Reader in Quotations'. Feral House, 1995, p. 149.

9. Leddy, M. 'Different Voices', 1992.

10. Lewis, C.S. The Humanitarian Theory of Punishment. 'God in the Dock', 1970. Quoted in Frank, L.R., ed. 'Influencing Minds: A Reader in Quotations.' Feral House, 1995.

11. 'Amarillo Daily News'. 5/18/97.

12. 'Dallas Morning News'. 5/24/97.

Chapter 11

1. Breggin, P. 'Brain-Disabling Treatments in Psychiatry.' Springer Publishing Co., 1997.

2. Ibid.

3. Modrow, J. 'How to Become a Schizophrenic'. Appollyon Press, 1992.

4. Critzer, G. Oh, How Happy We Will Be: Pills, Paradise and the Profits of Drug Companies. 'Harper's Magazine', June 1996.

5. Karp, D. 'Speaking of Sadness'. Oxford University Press, 1996.

6. Berger, P. and Luckman, T. 'The Social Construction of Reality.' Doubleday, 1967.

7. Podvoll, E. 'The Seduction of Madness.' Harper-Collins, 1990, p. 146

8. Cohen, D. 'Rational withdrawal from Psychiatric Drugs.' Audiotape of talk given at National Association for Rights Protection and Advocacy, 1997 Conference. Available from Merchants of Vision, (800) 595-2763.

9. Richman, D. 'Dr Caligari's Psychiatric Drugs.' Available from L.R. Frank, 2300 Webster St., San Francisco, CA 94115.

10. Ibid.

Chapter 12

1. The Re-evaluation Counseling Communities may be contacted at PO Box 2081, Main Office Station, Seattle WA 98111.

2. For more information about this cycle of abuse, see the books of Alice Miller, including Banished Knowledge, Doubleday, 1990.

3. John Bradshaw's book, 'Healing the Shame That Binds You' (Health Communications, Inc., 1988), is one of the better resources for those interested in detailed guidance about the work of shame reduction.

4. Blanton, B. 'Radical Honesty: How to Transform Your Life By Telling The Truth.' Dell, 1996.

5. Prescott, L. 'The Truth About Women, Sexual Abuse and Revictimization.' Audiotape of talk given at National Association for Rights Protection and Advocacy, 1997 Conference. Available from Merchants of Vision, (800) 595-2763.

6. Mindell, A. 'Sitting In The Fire' Lao Tse Press,

1995.

7. Lee, J. 'Facing the Fire.' Bantam, 1993.

8. My teacher and friend Dan Jones' wonderful poem, 'Shameless', is included in my book, 'The Wildest Colts Make The Best Horses', pp. 98-102.

9. Alexander, J. Discharging the Effects of Drugs.' Recovery and Re-emergence No. 5', Rational Island Publishers, 1997.

10. Podvoll, E. 'The Seduction of Madness.' Harper-Collins, 1990, p. 25.

11. Rinpoche, S. 'The Tibetan Book of Living and Dying.' HarperSanFrancisco, 1992.

12. See Resources for addresses and phone numbers o▮ these and other key organizations.

Chapter 13

1. 'Boston Globe', 11/25/88.

2. Betty Ford and Joseph Califano, 'Under The Rug: Substance Abuse and the Mature Woman.' Press Release ▮ The National Center on Addiction and Substance Abuse ▮ Columbia University, June 4, 1998.

3. Breggin, P. 'Psychiatric Drugs: Hazards to the Brai▮ Springer, 1983.

4. 'New York Times', 10/21/97.

5. Webster, J. 'The Duchess of Malfi', 5.2, 1623.

Chapter 14

1. Mead, G.H. 'Mind, Self and Society.' University o▮ Chicago Press, 1934.

2. Grof, S. Beyond The Brain.' State University of N▮ York Press, 1985.

Grof, S. 'The Adventure of Self-Discovery.' State University of New York Press, 1988.

3. Mindell, A. 'Dreambody: The Body's Role in Revealing the Self.' Sigo Press, 1982.

4. Campbell, J. 'The Hero With A Thousand Faces.' Princeton University Press, 1949, p. 260.

5. Martin, P.W. 'Experiment in Depth: A Study of the Work of Jung, Eliot and Toynbee.' Routledge and Paul, 1955. p. 11.

6. J. Campbell, 1949, p. 17. (See above.)

7. Duff, K. 'The Alchemy of Illness.'

8. P.W. Martin, 1955, p. 207. (See above.)

9. J. Campbell, 1949, p. 344. (See above.)

10. Ibid., p. 226.

11. Ibid., p. 321.

12. Colbert, T. 'Broken Brains or Wounded Hearts: What Causes Mental Illness.' Kevco Publishing, 1995, pp. 280-281.

13. P.W. Martin, 1955, p. 11. (See above.)

14. Chamberlain, J. 'On Our Own: Patient-Controlled Alternatives to the Mental Health System.' McGraw-Hill, 1978.

15. Ibid., p. 71.

16. Quoted in Chamberlain, p. 113.

Chapter 15

1. Houston, J., with Rubin, M. 'Manual For The Peacemaker.' The Theosophical Publishing House, 1995.

2. Ibid., pp. 26-27.

3. Ibid., pp. 58-60.

4. Szasz, T. From the foreword to Seth Farber's book 'Madness, Heresy, and the Rumor of Angels.' Open Court,

1993.

    5. J. Houston, pp. 67-68. (See above.)

    6. Ibid., pp. 68-69.

    7. Ibid., pp. 70-71.

    8. Reported by Laurie Ahern of the National Empowerment Center in 'Coercion and Force: How Not Treat People', an audiotape from the 1997 NARPA Conference, available from Merchants of Vision, (800) 59: 2763.

    9. J. Houston, p. 81. (See above.)

    10. Ibid., p. 86.

    11. Ibid., p. 88.

    12. Ibid., pp. 97-98.

    13. Wiseman, B., 'Psychiatry: The Ultimate Betrayal. Freedom Publishing, 1995.

    14. Frank, L.R. (ed.), 'The History of Shock Treatment.' San Francisco, 1978. Available from the auth 2300 Webster St., San Francisco, CA 94115.

    15. Breggin, P. 'Brain-Disabling Treatments in Psychiatry.' Springer, 1997.

    16. Boodman, S. 'Shock Therapy: It's Back', Washington Post, 9/24/96.

    17. Wiseman, B., p. 101. (See above.)

    18. Wiseman, B., p. 102. (See above.)

    19. Houston, J. (see above), pp. 100-103. (See above.

    20. Ibid., pp. 120-121.

    21. Ibid., pp. 122-123.

    22. Ibid., pp. 124-126.

Chapter 16

    1. Chamberlain, J. 'On Our Own: Patient-Controlle Alternatives to the Mental Health System.' McGraw-Hil

1978.

2. Colbert, T. 'Broken Brains or Wounded Hearts: What Causes Mental Illness.' Kevco Publishing,1995, p. 214.

3. Breggin, P. 'Toxic Psychiatry: Why Therapy, Empathy, and Love Must Replace the Drugs, Electroshock, and Biochemical Theories of "The New Psychiatry.' St. Martin's Press, 1991.

4. See Resources for information on Re-evaluation Counseling and Janet Foner.

5. Matsakis, A. 'I Can't Get Over It.' New Harbinger Publications, 1996.

6. Herman, J. 'Trauma and Recovery'. Basic Books, 1992.

7. Jones, D. 'Saying Goodbye: Ten Steps For Closing A Relationship.' To order copies, send $7.00 to Saying Goodbye, 102 S. Laurelwood, Austin, TX 78733.

8. Bass, E. and Davis, L. 'The Courage To Heal.' Harper and Row, 1988.

9. Breeding, J. Mental Health Care and Addiction Treatment: Empowering Counselors Against Oppression. 'Professional Counselor', February 1992.

10. Szasz, T. From the foreword to Seth Farber's book, 'Madness, Heresy, and the Rumor of Angels.' Open Court, 1993, p. xii.

11. Mosher, L.R., Vallone, R. and Menn, A.Z. The Treatment of Acute Psychosis without Neuroleptics: Six-week Psychopathology Outcome Data from the Soteria Project. 'International Journal of Social Psychiatry', Vol. 41, No. 3, pp. 157-173.

12. Podvoll, E. The Seduction of Madness.' Harper-Collins, 1990.

13. Contact Jeffrey Fortuna, M.A., at (413) 586-0207

for further information about Windhorse Associates, Inc.

14. Burch House, Inc., 249 Main St., Bethlehem, NH 03574.

15. Mindell, A. 'City Shadows: Psychological Interventions in Psychiatry.' Arkana, 1991.

16. Bragdon, E. 'A Sourcebook for Helping People in Spiritual Emergency.' Lightening Up Press, 1988.

Lightning Source UK Ltd.
Milton Keynes UK
UKOW03f0611240517
301900UK00001B/94/P